A REINTERPRETATION OF ROUSSEAU

LIST OF PREVIOUS PUBLICATIONS

2005

"The Overcoming of Violence in Christianity and Buddhism." In *Menschenrechte, Kulturen und Gewalt: Ansätze einer interkulturellen Ethic* [Human Rights, Cultures, and Violence: Contributions to an Intercultural Ethics], ed. Ludger Kuehnhardt and Mamoru Takayama, 437–48. Baden-Baden, Germany: Nomos Verlagsgesellschaft.

"Commentary." In *Menschenrechte, Kulturen und Gewalt: Ansätze einer interkulturellen Ethic* [Human Rights, Cultures, and Violence: Contributions to an Intercultural Ethics], ed. Ludger Kuehnhardt and Mamoru Takayama, 467–69. Baden-Baden, Germany: Nomos Verlagsgesellschaft.

"The Place of the Victim." *Victims and Victimization in French and Francophone Literature, French Literature Series*, ed. Norman Buford 32:111–18.

"Religiöses Leben in der Gegenwart" [Spiritual Life in the Present]. In *Zusammenleben der Religionen: Eine interreligiös-interkulturelle Aufgabe der globalisierten Welt* [Religions Living Together: An Interreligious and Intercultural Task for a Globalized World]. A Symposium from the Series "The East—The West." Berlin: Japanese-German Center Zentrum.

2004

"The Scandal of Origins in Rousseau." *Contagion: Journal of Violence, Mimesis, and Culture* 11 (Spring): 1–14.

2003

"Openness to Mystery: Nakae Chomin's *A Year and a Half—Continued.*" In *Wandel zwischen den Welten: Festschrift für Johannes Laube* [Passage between the Worlds: Festschrift for Johannes Laube], ed. Hannelore Eisenhofer-Halim, 17–32. Frankfurt: Peter Lang.

"A Scandal to the West, a Folly to the East." In *Zukünftiges Menschsein: Ethik zwischen Ost und West*, ed. Ralf Elm and Mamoru Takayama, 399–422. Baden-Baden, Germany: Nomos Verlagsgesellschaft.

2002

"Rousseau and Original Sin." *Revista Portuguesa de Filosofia* 57 (4): 773–90.

2001

"Listening to Nietzsche." *Revista Portuguesa de Filosofia* 57 (1): 61–71.

"Rousseau's *First Discourse* and Scandal." *International Philosophical Quarterly* 41, no. 161 (March): 49–62.

2000

Robert Spaemann. *Happiness and Benevolence.* Translation. South Bend: University of Notre Dame Press.

1999

"Sheringu *Tetsugaku to Shukyou* ni Okeru Zettaisha ni Tsuite [*The Absolute in Schelling's Philosophy and Religion*]." *Fihite Kenkyuu* 7 (November): 37–50.

1998

Benshouhouteki 'Isuto' [The Dialectical 'Is']. *Sheringu Nempou* 6 (July): 65–74.

1997

"Mieno Nakani Yo-in wo Nokoshiteiru Shisou: Uitogenshutain no *Tetsugaku Tankyuu* wo Megutte [The Echo of a Thought in Sound]." *Tetsugakka Kiyou* (21): 57–71.

"Shizensei kara Hanarete: Dazai no Tachiba kara *Seishinngenshougaku* wo Yomu [Separating from Nature: Reading Hegel's *Phenomenology of Spirit* from the Viewpoint of Original Sin]." *Hegeru Tetsugaku Kenkyuu* (3): 39–50.

"Tanpen to Chikara: Ruso no *Shakai Keiyakuron* wo Megutte [Fragments and Strength: Considering Rousseau's *Social Contract*]." *Tetsugakka Kiyou* (23): 37–52.

"Gouri Shingaku Kyougi [The Lectures on Rational Theology]." In *Kanto Jiten* [A Kant Dictionary], ed. Kougaku Arifuku and Megumi Sakabe, 574–76. Tokyo: Kobunsho.

"Shizen Shingaku [Natural Theology]." In *Kanto Jiten* [A Kant Dictionary], ed. Kougaku Arifuku and Megumi Sakabe, 206–7. Tokyo: Kobunsho.

Recent Japanese Philosophical Thought 1862–1996: A Survey, with a New Survey (1963–1996), by Naoshi Yamawaki and Gino Piovesana. Translation. Richmond, UK: Japan Library.

1996

Die verlorene Einheit: Die Suche nach einer philosophischen Alternative zu der Erbsündenlehre von Rousseau bis Schelling. Frankfurt: Peter Lang.

"Akashi Suru Chinmoku [In Silence Witness]." In *Tsumi to Megumi: Kami no Maeni Tatsu Ningen* [Sin and Grace: Humans Standing before God], *ed.* Takeo Iwashima and Eiji Inou, 268–92. Tokyo: San Paulo.

"Ruso-no Genzaikan [Rousseau's View on Original Sin]." *Katorikku Kenkyuu* (64): 35–60.

1995

"The Self-Overcoming of Nihilism According to Nishitani." *Journal of Sophia Asian Studies*, no. 12 (March): 11–21.

1991

"Alfred Delp: Jesuit." *The Month* 252, no. 1483 (July): 289–306.

1989

"On the Concept of Life," by Robert Spaemann. Translation. *Zen Buddhism Today*, no. 7 (October): 77–83.

1988

"Kiso Shinkgaku—'Choetsuronteki-Suikoronteki' Teigi. [Fundamental Theology—A Transcendental Pragmatic Approach]." *Kattoriku Kenkyu*, no. 53 (July): 133–53.

"Seeking the Word." *Religion and Intellectual Life* 6, no. 1 (Fall): 25–29.

1987

"Simon, I Have Something to Say to You." *Review for Religious* 46, no. 5 (Fall): 759–70.

A REINTERPRETATION OF ROUSSEAU

A RELIGIOUS SYSTEM

JEREMIAH ALBERG

First published in 2007 by
PALGRAVE MACMILLAN™
175 Fifth Avenue, New York, N.Y. 10010 and
Houndmills, Basingstoke, Hampshire, England RG21 6XS.
Companies and representatives throughout the world.

PALGRAVE MACMILLAN is the global academic imprint of the Palgrave Macmillan
division of St. Martin's Press, LLC and of Palgrave Macmillan Ltd. Macmillan® is a
registered trademark in the United States, United Kingdom and other countries.
Palgrave is a registered trademark in the European Union and other countries.

ISBN-13: 978-0-2306-0055-3
ISBN-10: 0-2306-0055-7

Library of Congress Cataloging-in-Publication Data
  Alberg, Jeremiah, 1957–
  A reinterpretation of Rousseau : a religious system / Jeremiah Alberg.
       p. cm.
  Includes bibliographical references (p.).
  ISBN 0-230-60055-7 (alk. paper)
  1. Rousseau, Jean-Jacques, 1712–1778—Religion. 2. Sin, Original. 3. Forgiveness of
sin. 4. Catholic Church and philosophy. I. Title.
  B2138.R4A43 2007
  194—dc22
                                    2007003379
                                    2007003434

A catalogue record of the book is available from the British Library.

Design by Scribe Inc.

First edition: September 2007
First Palgrave MacMillan paperback edition: September 2007

10 9 8 7 6 5 4 3 2 1

Printed in the United States of America.

This book is dedicated to Yumi, my wife.

CONTENTS

FOREWORD

by René Girard

Until about a century ago, Rousseau was admired not only as a great artist but also as a great thinker, a prophet not merely of a bygone revolution but, quite possibly, of revolutions still to come, in some still–politically backward countries. In the last century, this contemporariness of Rousseau has declined. His political relevance has become chiefly historical. The change seems to be due not merely to the historical circumstances that have become less favorable but also to Rousseau himself, whose psychic peculiarities seem more disturbing to us than they once did.

Admirers of Rousseau have always been aware of his constantly disturbed relations with other people. Until recently these difficulties were not regarded as serious enough to affect his relevance as a political thinker, or as a theoretician of education. Now they are. If you mention Rousseau in learned company these days, something like a cloud will pass over the eyes of some of your listeners. They will make it clear that, in their eyes, such questions as the feasibility of his *Social Contract* are preempted by the question of how seriously his personal problems affected his lucidity as a thinker. But the relevance that Rousseau has lost as a creator of ideas, he retrieves as a psychological riddle that everybody is eager to solve. "Give me one minute," these people all say, "and I will show you what the problem with Rousseau really is." These people have an insight, no doubt, and they urgently want to share it with us, but the more they try, the less they succeed. After the requested minute has elapsed, the would-be explicators become so irritated with their own ineptitude that, quite frequently, they cannot refrain from invoking once again the story of the foundling institution to which Jean-Jacques entrusted his five children from his legitimate wife, Thérèse Levasseur.

This story is the weapon of mass destruction in discussions about Rousseau. It has been recycled so many times already that the latest recyclers feel ashamed of themselves. They resent their own cheapness, but they resent Rousseau even more because—not without reason perhaps—they feel that he, himself, set the trap in which they were stupid enough to fall. One of Rousseau's main motivations when writing was to involve all his readers in the inextricable conflicts between himself and everyone else.

If the relevance that Rousseau once had as a philosopher has diminished, some of it, at least, he is retrieving as a beautiful case of psychic entrapment for both writer and reader. What makes a writer great is the quality of his language, and Rousseau's French is incomparable. His prose is simple without being simplistic, elegant without being mannered, didactic without being dull. In the whole eighteenth century—with the possible exception of Voltaire—no one could write a more limpid and delectable French than Rousseau, in spite of his *déclassé* status or his lack of formal education.

Not only did Rousseau have this magnificent linguistic tool at his disposal, but he also had more to say than anybody else. In the second half of the eighteenth century, there was a whole new range of emotions and passions in Western Europe that no writer had yet fully expressed. They were the emotions and passions of the rising middle class, and, by turning them into sentimental literature, Rousseau made them even more fashionable than they already were. All over France and Europe, countless readers felt that Rousseau alone understood their *sensibilité*, and they idolized him. All by himself, Rousseau represented a whole new literary era, the last before the French revolution, and it was soon named the era of *sensibilité*. Two centuries later, we can see that it hardly exists as a separate era. It makes more sense to regard it as the first flowering of *romanticism*. Rousseau is the first romantic writer in the French language and, probably, the greatest.

Far from being the outcast that he claimed he was—a victim of diabolical plots hatched by his implacable rivals, the Parisian intellectuals—Rousseau was praised, feted, and lionized more than any other writer of the period. Even Voltaire, it seems, was a little jealous of Rousseau, although never seriously enough to plot in earnest against his confrere's reputation. The two of them, Voltaire and Rousseau, were the first writers in France to achieve the celebrity status previously reserved for royalty and some members of the higher aristocracy.

This did not prevent Rousseau's relations with most people, even his most devoted admirers and protectors, from ending in spectacular disasters. This explains why, almost from the beginning, critics of Rousseau have felt compelled to provide some explanation for his perpetual unhappiness. Instead of writing books about Rousseau's ideas, in the last century, more and more explicators wrote about his psychic difficulties. For a long time, most of these books betrayed the direct or indirect influence of Freud.

The problem with literary psychoanalysis is that, in most instances, for its source material, it must rely primarily or exclusively on the literary works of the psychoanalyzed writer. Can this material replace the confidential interviews that patients are supposed to have with their psychoanalysts? Freud's answer to this question was no, but he violated his own rule so often that his advice was disregarded.

To make their investigations fruitful, the literary analysts must attribute a symptomatic value to whatever irregularities they discover in the style of the analyzed writers. They must assume that the literary texts do not hide the personal secrets of their authors more efficiently than their unguarded speech. Rousseau is too sure-footed a writer not to outsmart the simplistic illusions of psychoanalysts. He portrays his own *angoisse* in the most serene French imaginable; he expresses his existential disharmony in perfectly harmonious sentences. That may be the reason why attempts to analyze him have proved even more unrewarding than they normally do.

And now here comes Jeremiah Alberg, who approaches Rousseau from an entirely different perspective. He does not see Rousseau as the enemy whose secrets must be conquered by ruse and violence. He does not seek a weapon of even more massive destruction than the available ones. Rather, he seeks the unity of Rousseau's work in an ancient idea that no avant-garde *littérateurs* would even regard as possibly pertinent:

the idea of original sin and its stubborn rejection by Rousseau. The book you are about to read renounces all psychological and psychoanalytical recipes of the last century and relies entirely on the theological theme of Rousseau's stubborn rebellion against certain objects or people that embody, in his eyes, the scandalous notion of original sin.

Behind *scandalum* in the Latin vulgate and *skandalon* in the original Greek, there is a still older word in the Jewish Bible, a Hebrew word that means the same thing, *obstacle*, as the other two words, but with more of an emphasis on the physicality of that obstacle. *Skandalon* is not the inert and always predictable obstacle from which we can easily protect ourselves by keeping clear of it. It is a truly diabolical obstacle against which we repeatedly stumble because it attracts at the very moment that it repels, and it repels at the very moment that it attracts. The reason for this is that my *skandalon* and yours may well turn out to be one and the same. The man whose desire I resent because I imitate it may well be the man who resents my desire because he imitates it. The two of us, in the end, cannot fail to stumble together.

In order to convince his readers as well as himself that he is not enslaved to mimetic desire, Rousseau assures us, and himself, that he loves himself single-handedly, if I may say, in a solitary fashion, without the help of anyone. Like a god, in other words, he calls his self-love *amour de soi* and opposes it to amour-propre, which seems to be the same thing but in reality is totally different, because amour-propre relies on admirers and imitators.

The more we try to get away from our *skandalon*, the more inextricably entangled in it we become, and the same is true of our secret rival, our perfect counterpart.

With his topology of the *skandalon*, Jeremiah Alberg explicates the writing of Rousseau more smoothly, efficiently, and elegantly than, in my estimate, has ever been done before. What Jeremiah Alberg shows us is extremely simple, ultimately, but easy to misunderstand. The fancy new knowledge invented by our modern world—the new philosophical and psychological tricks of which, until recently, we were so proud—must be rearranged and reorganized along the paradoxical lines of the *skandalon*.

What makes *scandal* superior to all our psychological and psychoanalytical notions is that instead of reflecting the false mastery of the doctor-patient relationship—in which the doctor gives all the answers because he also asks all the questions—the scandalous relationship is a reciprocal one—in which the two scandalized human beings imitate each other's desires and become implacable rivals for the same objects.

This beautiful book suggests that our psychological era has now exhausted its possibilities. What the author shows is that in order to defeat the sterility that threatens our culture, we must go back to the real spiritual substance of our world, to the notions we inherited from the Judaic and Christian Revelation.

ACKNOWLEDGMENTS

I first conceived some of the ideas for this book many years ago and I wrote it in a number of different settings, thus allowing me to benefit from the kindness of a lot of people along the way. I would like to begin by acknowledging my indebtedness to three of my "teachers." The late Prof. James Collins of St. Louis University taught me how to read a text. Prof. Robert Spaemann of the University of Munich, the Director of my doctoral studies, first introduced me to Rousseau's thought and showed me that he was worth the effort of serious study. Finally, although I only met him after completing my PhD, I still consider Prof. René Girard to be one of my teachers. His kind counsel has been very important. I am very grateful to him for writing the Foreword.

When I began this research I was a member of the Philosophy Department of Sophia University in Tokyo. I am grateful to my colleagues there, especially to Prof. Yoichiro Ohashi. Some of the research that led to this book was supported by a joint research project titled, "Philosophy and Religion," funded by Japan's Ministry of Education (*Monbusho*). The bulk of the research was carried out at Santa Clara University with the support of a fellowship from the Bannan Institute. I am grateful to the institute, the university, and its philosophy department for their hospitality. I was very much saddened when I learned of the death of its director, Prof. William Spohn, who had been very solicitous during my stay. In this context I also wish to thank Prof. Michael Meyer, who served as chair at the time and was the source of much sound advice. I thank Rev. Gerald McKevitt, S. J., for his friendship and the reading of some chapters. The Jesuit Community, especially Rev. Michael Zampelli, S. J., made life enjoyable. I hope that Rev. Sonny Manuel, Dr. Lori Goldfarb-Plante, and Dr. Elizabeth Mahler can find in these pages some of the life they gave me.

I was able to do some writing during the pleasant year I spent at Gonzaga University and I am grateful to the philosophy department there. For the past several years, the University of West Georgia has been my home. I appreciate the interest of my colleagues and students in this work. I was a recipient of a Faculty Research Grant in 2004–05 that greatly facilitated my research.

Several chapters have appeared in journals and I thank their editors and publishers for permission to use them. Different sections from Part Two on the novel *Emile* appeared as "The Place of the Victim," *Victims and Victimization in French and Francophone Literature, French Literature Series*, 32 (2005): 111–18. An earlier version of Chapter 7 was published as "The Scandal of Origins in Rousseau," *Contagion: Journal of Violence, Mimesis, and Culture*, 11 (Spring 2004): 1–14. A version of Chapter 9 was published as "Rousseau's *First Discourse* and Scandal," *International Philosophical Quarterly* 41, no. 1 (March 2001): 49–62.

My heartfelt gratitude goes to Prof. Christopher Kelly for his careful reading of the manuscript. The few times I did not follow his advice were done with fear and trembling. At a time when pressed with many other occupations Rev. Kevin Burke, S. J., made time to read and comment on the manuscript. For his friendship and support throughout the writing I am deeply grateful. At a number of points, Prof. William Rehg, S. J., generously read and commented on different sections. Rev. Richard Schenk, O. P., has kept me intellectually honest over the years. Prof. Robert Snyder brought his editor's pen to many of the chapters, thus raising the quality of the manuscript as a whole. I feel it is important to mention that although several scholars will find themselves criticized in this book, it is those of whom I am most critical that I learned the most.

I have to express simple wonder at the graciousness and generosity of Prof. Jean Starobinski for his support and encouragement in this project. I am grateful to the members of both the Rousseau Association and the Colloquium on Violence & Religion who listened to and commented on papers I presented at their meetings. I am also grateful to the group of people who meet regularly at Stanford University with Prof. Girard. The great grace there, beyond all I learned, was the friendship of Robert Hammerton-Kelly and Gil Bailie that resulted from those meetings. I have already mentioned the debt I owe to Prof. Girard, but I would be remiss if I did not explicitly thank his wife, Martha, for her hospitality and goodness.

I thank Amanda Moon and her assistant, Brigitte Shull, for making this into a book. Candace Barrett did an excellent job helping me construct the index.

Those who have written a book while starting a family know the importance of both a spouse who, through his or her love, creates the quiet, creative space that allows the reflection and writing to happen, and of the children who interrupt that space. Yumi, my wife, and Hannah and Yuriko, my daughters, fulfilled these respective tasks for me and I love them for that.

LIST OF ABBREVIATIONS

Beaumont   Jean-Jacques Rousseau, *Letter to Beaumont*, in *Collected Writings of Rousseau*, vol. 9, ed. Roger D. Masters and Christopher Kelly (Hanover, NH: University Press of New England, 2001).

Confessions   Rousseau, *The Confessions*, in *Collected Writings of Rousseau*, vol. 5, ed. Roger D. Masters and Christopher Kelly (Hanover, NH: University Press of New England, 1995).

CW   Rousseau, *The Collected Writings of Rousseau*, 12 vols., ed. Roger D. Masters and Christopher Kelly (Hanover, NH: University Press of New England, 1990).

d'Alembert   Rousseau, *Letter to d'Alembert*, in *Collected Writings of Rousseau*, vol. 10, ed. Roger D. Masters and Christopher Kelly (Hanover, NH: University Press of New England, 2004).

Dialogues   Rousseau, *Rousseau, Judge of Jean-Jacques: Dialogues*, in *The Collected Writings of Rousseau*, vol. 1, ed. Roger D. Masters and Christopher Kelly (Hanover, NH: University Press of New England, 1990).

Emile   Rousseau, *Emile, or On Education*, ed. Allan Bloom (New York: Basic Books, 1979).

First Discourse   Rousseau, *Discourse on the Sciences and Arts*, in *The Collected Writings of Rousseau*, vol. 2, ed. Roger D. Masters and Christopher Kelly (Hanover, NH: University Press of New England, 1992).

Launay   Rousseau, *Oeurvres complètes*, ed. Michel Launay (Paris: Seuil-l'Intégrale, 1971).

Pl.   Rousseau, *Oeurvres complètes*, ed. Bernard Gagnebin, and Marcel Raymond (Paris: NRF-Editions de la Pléiade, 1959–95).

Reveries   Rousseau, *Reveries of a Solitary Walker*, in *Collected Writings of Rousseau*, vol. 8, ed. Roger D. Masters and Christopher Kelly (Hanover, NH: University Press of New England, 2000).

Second Discourse   Rousseau, *Discourse on the Origin of Inequality*, in *The Collected Writings of Rousseau*, vol. 3, ed. Roger D. Masters and Christopher Kelly (Hanover, NH: University Press of New England, 1992).

PART I

INTRODUCTION

Jean-Jacques Rousseau and Scandal

Jean-Jacques Rousseau began his career as a writer prophesying, "I foresee that I will not easily be forgiven for the side I have dared to take" (*First Discourse, CW* 2:3; *Pl.* 3:3).[1] Somehow he understood that his position or "side" both required yet made forgiveness "difficult." This book is an exploration of that requirement and its difficulty.

That forgiveness is necessary implies an offence. One does not have to look hard to find offence in Rousseau's writings. They have been labeled "scandalous" from the beginning. He gained fame by proclaiming to a French academy that the arts and sciences had a pernicious effect on society's morals. His later works were burned by governments, condemned by the churches, and repudiated by his erstwhile friends. The offense has been real—or so it seems.

This book is premised on the fact that, contrary to expectations, humans cannot truly know the offense or sin until one has forgiven it. Without forgiveness, there is no epistemological access to the sin and so sin is only seen in its passing out of existence, in its being forgiven. Accordingly, insofar as politicians, churchmen, and scholars have found fit to condemn Rousseau, there is a real possibility that they have not understood him.

Paradoxically, I am not necessarily arguing that those who have found offense in Rousseau's writings were wrong to have found it. Rather, it is their response, their way of interpreting, that I am implicitly challenging. I propose a reading that forgives Rousseau and thus allows us to truly understand his offense as well as his genius.

Let us take the most obvious problem head on: concretely what could it mean— either in Rousseau's day or in our own—for the reader to forgive him? How does one forgive an absent author, or, for that matter, a text? Specifically, how does one forgive Rousseau? At the very beginning of his writing, the prosopopoeia of Fabricius in the *Discourse on the Sciences and Arts*, Rousseau confronts us with an indirect condemnation of the reader. At the very end, the *Reveries of a Solitary Walker*, he explicitly banishes the reader. Between these two, Rousseau's isolation from his reader grows ever greater. For there to be forgiveness, there would have to be a healing of this fractured relationship between the author and the reader.

Forgiveness in this context means that this reading will not turn around and banish Rousseau. Healing the relationship between Rousseau and his reader means allowing a new interpretation to emerge from the very texts that generated the alienation. Reading Rousseau in a theological key brings forth the new interpretation by allowing the theological dimension of his thought to bestow a profound unity on everything he wrote.

One forgives Rousseau when one realizes that his writings evince a deeper grasp of the terrible truth of the Christian Gospel than the writings of any of his contemporaries. If, instead of forgiving, one were to condemn him for flinching in the face of that truth, how could anyone hope to obtain mercy?

This book offers a comprehensive interpretation of Jean-Jacques Rousseau's system. Its starting point is the problem of natural goodness. In Rousseau's position natural goodness appears as an independent principle, but it is derivative in the sense that it is the consequence of Rousseau's (ultimately unsuccessful) rejection of a specific point of revelation.

Other critics have well understood that the doctrine of natural goodness entails the rejection of original sin. Some have even seen how natural goodness is dependent in a negative way on Christianity—in the sense that this principle could not have been arrived at by a pagan Greek. I argue that even these interpreters have not penetrated Rousseau's thought deeply enough because they have failed to see that the Christian account of original sin is itself derived from something more fundamental, namely, the revelation of God's forgiveness in Christ. Rousseau's rejection of original sin is, in fact, a reaction against this more fundamental revelation. Moreover, because Rousseau misunderstood original sin, he is not entirely conscious of what he is rejecting.

Thus, Rousseau's system cannot be interpreted as the straightforward development of his principle of natural goodness. Since Rousseau's reaction against proffered forgiveness is the abiding source of natural goodness, his system finds its ultimate ground in this reaction. The theological term for this is "scandal." Hence, my thesis is that *Rousseau's system is rooted in scandal.* It comes out of his scandal at Christ, and it leads to his giving scandal to others. These two senses of the term "scandal"— refusing forgiveness and leading others into sin—are two sides of one coin: inhabiting a universe in which there is no forgiveness.

This proposal may appear dubious. For one thing, an examination of the indices of the secondary literature on Rousseau rarely turns up an entry for "scandal." This lack is somewhat surprising. Beginning with the Controversy[2] following the *First Discourse*, and then in such writings as the *Letter to d'Alembert* and *Rousseau, Judge of Jean-Jacques: Dialogues*, scandal explicitly plays what can only be called a substantial role. In other works, as I hope to show, it is operative, even when not explicitly present.

I cannot go further without giving some preliminary indication of what the term "scandal" meant in the eighteenth century. At the time that Rousseau was writing, "scandal" underwent a profound secularization. Instead of hiding scandals, they were publicized. This secularization is with us still and its results are visible in the media. What is less understood today are the theological roots of the notion of "scandal."

After examining these roots, this chapter explicates some of the implications of reading Rousseau from the viewpoint of biblical scandal. Rousseau's scandal underlies both his theory of natural goodness and his rejection of original sin, and so it is the fundamental reality or principle of his system.

The thesis that Rousseau's system is rooted in scandal helps bring to light the unity of Rousseau's thought, thus answering the questions of whether or not he had a system and in what that system consisted. The thesis also gives us a new understanding of Rousseau's relationship vis-à-vis Christianity. Because the reader needs to know a little of the history of the controversy that has surrounded these two questions of Rousseau's system and its relationship to Christianity, a few representative positions are given. But the hope of this research is to move beyond these positions. At the same time it will become clear where some of my own intellectual debts lie. The chapter ends with a summary of the way forward.

THE MEANING OF SCANDAL

Let us turn for a moment to what "scandal" meant in Rousseau's time. D'Alembert's *Encyclopedia*, the vehicle of the French Enlightenment, contains an entry for "Scandale" and for "Scandaleux." A **scandal** is "an action or omission that leads those who witness or have knowledge of it to sin"; in particular, the article points out, "Jesus Christ was, from the standpoint of the Jews, a stumbling block and a **scandal** against which they were broken, through their own fault, unwilling to recognize him as Messiah, despite the proofs that demonstrated it to them." The **scandalous** is "that which causes a scandal" and "is said of both things and of people." There are two kinds of scandal, active and passive. Active scandal is the "induction to evil on the part of the one who scandalizes," and passive scandal "is the disadvantageous impression made by a **scandal** on those in whom it leads to or incites evil." The examples that the entry gives illustrating the meaning of "scandalous," may give the impression that only priests are scandalous; all the examples of scandalous actions are taken from the acts of Jesuits or other priests. In this way, the *Encyclopedia* turns the concept against the institution that most employed it for its own benefit. (One was not to publicly criticize the Church, even when the criticism was true, to avoid giving scandal.) More important is the fact that the entry breaks off, saying, "One could find all kinds of examples of scandal without going much further, but there are those things which it is difficult to speak of without outrageously scandalizing women, men, and little children."[3] It is difficult to speak of scandal in a way that does not give scandal.

The presence of these entries gives a hint of the importance this concept held for eighteenth-century European society. Canon law (and often civil law) forbade the giving of scandal, understood as a flagrant example of sin that might cause others to sin. The *Encyclopedia* also mentions "**Scandal** *of the great, scandalum magnatum*," as a term of law that refers to "offense done to a considerable individual."[4] Clearly the legal concern here is the kind of scandal that could undermine proper authority in a community.

The *Dictionnaire de L'Académie française* (first edition, 1694), tells us that the noun "scandal" can refer to both the bad example as well as the indignation caused by that bad example. The relationship between the bad example and the indignation caused by it is such that someone who is scandalized almost automatically also gives scandal by expressing the indignation. Thus, scandal is highly contagious. But the *Dictionnaire* makes clear that this more ordinary meaning rests upon a basic religious meaning. In this sense, scandal comes from the Scriptures and refers to the "predication that the Cross was a scandal for the Jews."[5]

There were, then, in the eighteenth century, two poles of meaning for scandal, both of which can be traced back to the New Testament. On the one hand, the term refers to the crucified Christ, especially in relation to the Jews, and on the other, it also, and most often, means the giving of a bad moral example or the taking offense at such a bad example. As regards the former, I do not want to "descandalize" the biblical concept of scandal. However, racist thinking is not the primary reason it was so closely associated with the Jewish people, although that certainly played a role. Rather, it is because the concept itself has Jewish roots. There is no record of the use of the Greek word *skandalon* in pagan sources. When Paul wrote that Christ crucified was a "stumbling block to the Jews and foolishness to the Gentiles" (1 Cor. 1:23), he is not granting any superiority to the Gentiles. Rather, he is using the trope of an exhaustive dilemma: there are no more groups beyond Jews and Gentiles, and so everyone is in some way offended by the Cross.

IMPLICATIONS OF ROUSSEAU'S THOUGHT IN THE LIGHT OF BIBLICAL SCANDAL

One way of introducing the implications of reading Rousseau in light of scandal is to look again at a familiar problem—Rousseau's rejection of original sin and his theory of natural goodness.[6] The primary reason for the condemnation of *Emile* was the judgment that in it, Rousseau had denied the dogma of original sin. The clearest statement of this denial does not occur, as might be expected, in the "Profession of Faith of the Savoyard Vicar" or in the context of a discussion of infancy, but in Book II, when the child is already at least two years old. Rousseau writes, "let us set down as an incontestable maxim that the first movements of nature are always right. There is no original perversity in the human heart. There is not a single vice to be found in it of which it cannot be said how and whence it entered" (*Emile*, 92; *Pl.* 4:322).[7] The archbishop of Paris, Christophe de Beaumont, in his *Mandement*, or pastoral letter, issued against Rousseau and the book, viewed this as an "abominable doctrine" that led to "overturning natural law and to destroying the foundations of the Christian Religion" (*CW* 9:16).[8]

In more recent times, Ernst Cassirer points to Rousseau's denial as one of the epoch-making traits of his thought. In his text, *The Question of Jean-Jacques Rousseau*, Cassirer makes plain that not just an arcane theological debate but, "in fact, an inescapable decision, vital to the history of the world and to cultural history, was involved. What irrevocably separated Rousseau, despite all his genuine and deep religious emotion, from all traditional forms of faith was the decisiveness with which he rejected every thought of the *original* sin of man."[9] Much of Rousseau's significance as a thinker is connected with this denial.

Rousseau himself responded to the archbishop's condemnation in a work titled, *Letter to Beaumont*.[10] The archbishop's sole proof for his claim that "the author of

Emile [proposed] a plan of education that, far from agreeing with Christianity, [was] not even suited to making Citizens or Men" (*CW* 9:4) is the denial of original sin. In the archbishop's words, this dogma is the "ray of light that lets us know the mystery of the human heart." It explains the "striking mixture of greatness and baseness, of zeal for truth and taste for error, of inclination to virtue and penchant to vice, . . . a contrast whose source revelation uncovers for us in the deplorable fall of our first parents" (*CW* 9:5).

In his response, Rousseau reaffirms his own doctrine of the natural goodness of man and sets it out once more. Then he gives arguments against the doctrine of original sin. I will not explicate all of his arguments, but his conclusion is clear: "Original sin explains everything except its own principle, and it is this principle that has to be explained" (*CW* 9:31; *Pl.* 4:939). After Rousseau has summarized the positions of both the archbishop and himself, he says, "Man was created good. We both agree on that, I believe. But you say he is wicked because he was wicked. And I show how he was wicked. Which of us, in your opinion, better ascends to the principle?" (*CW* 9:31; *Pl.* 4:940). Rousseau is correct in maintaining that original sin cannot explain its own principle, but both he and the Archbishop have a misconception of the function of the dogma of original sin.[11] Both see original sin as purporting to explain something. That is, they see it as some sort of foundational reality that helps, more or less adequately, to assign blame for the predicament in which humans find themselves.[12] The archbishop finds in human existence "a contrast whose source revelation uncovers for us in the deplorable fall of our first parents" (*CW* 9:5).

Understood correctly, this is true. Revelation—the revelation of God's forgiveness in Christ—does reveal sin, as that sin is passing out of existence.[13] But there is no access to this reality of sin independent of its forgiveness. Original sin cannot, and should not be expected to, explain its own principle. In one sense its principle is its forgiveness, in another sense it is the nothingness and vanity that are being forgiven and not simply controlled. Rousseau is right when he complains that original sin does not explain; he is incorrect to presume that it should. One cannot fault Rousseau or the archbishop in that this view of original sin was prevalent in the eighteenth century. The question of epistemological priority is crucial: does one understand salvation through original sin, or original sin through salvation? To claim that only one direction is possible would be incorrect. Obviously, once the doctrine of original sin has come to light through soteriological reflection and has been formulated, it can be, and has been, used to deepen Christians' understanding of that salvation. Still, Rousseau and Beaumont share in some misuses of the doctrine.

Rousseau and the archbishop share an understanding of the dogma that relies on accusation;[14] this shared understanding leads them in diametrically opposed directions: one denies and the other affirms original sin. Still, they resemble each other in the accusations that they aim at one another. To appreciate this, one can look at the following questions with which Rousseau begins the *Letter to Beaumont*: "Why must I have something to say to you, your Grace? What common language can we speak, how can we understand one another, and what is there between you and me?" (*CW* 9:21; *Pl.* 4:927).[15] Their shared understanding of original sin as an accusation is the ground of their unity about which Rousseau has so insistently asked. It helps to explain why the archbishop had to condemn Rousseau, and why the latter had to respond to this condemnation.

This is the common language that the two share, and that not only allows them to speak to one another, but also demands that they condemn one another. Both the archbishop and Rousseau interpret the dogma as an accusation against Adam and Eve—the former as a justified accusation, the latter as an unjustified accusation. Further, Rousseau's interpretation is at least an implicit accusation against Christianity, and the archbishop responds with his own accusation against Rousseau. In his response, Rousseau explicitly accuses the dogma of failing to do what it was never meant to do. Finally, Rousseau accuses the archbishop of accusing him: "Your Grace, you accuse me of iniquity without cause" (CW 9:74; Pl. 4:995). This accusation and counteraccusation make this much of the archbishop's *Mandement* and Rousseau's response sterile stuff indeed.

How, then, is one to read Rousseau's system if one wishes to avoid the mistake of the archbishop and not get bogged down in arguments and accusations that lead nowhere? Most readings begin with the assumption that Rousseau's system is based on the principle of natural goodness. As Rousseau himself says in the *Letter to Beaumont,*

> the fundamental principle of all morality about which I have reasoned in all my Writings and developed in this last one [*Emile*] with all the clarity of which I was capable, is that man is a naturally good being, loving justice and order; that there is no original perversity in the human heart, and that the first movements of nature are always right. (CW 9:28; Pl. 4:935–36)

Given the clarity of Rousseau's assertion, most commentators simply follow Rousseau. Thus, they hold that Rousseau can articulate an alternative view of humanity because he has proven the natural goodness of man and, concomitantly, has rejected the doctrine of original sin.

I am arguing that this common conception is false in the sense of being incomplete. To interpret Rousseau's system as based on the principle of natural goodness, with the rejection of original sin as its corollary, is to accept both the state of nature and original sin as fundamental realities. It is to accept that original sin is an accusation against humanity and that the state of nature will deliver us from that accusation. In the context of the *Discourse on Inequality*, we shall have the opportunity to discuss in detail the way in which Rousseau reaches the state of nature. The state of nature is not simply an origin; it is also, as the "Preface" to the *Discourse on Inequality* makes clear, a conclusion. In this, it holds the same status as the dogma of original sin holds for Christianity—it is a teaching that one reaches as a conclusion, not as a principle. For now one must hold to the insight that original sin, as seen earlier, is only grasped as it is passing out of existence. Thus, we will not interpret Rousseau's system from either the perspective of natural goodness or the rejection of original sin. But does that mean that scandal is a better perspective?

It was the understanding that neither natural goodness nor the rejection of original sin could serve as the foundation of Rousseau's system that led me to look for another.[16] To put my thesis in its baldest form, it is Rousseau's refusal of forgiveness in Christ, which is the most fundamental definition of scandal, that renders sin epistemologically inaccessible and thus leaves him with "natural goodness."[17] For Christianity, it is only in the light of that salvation, in the light of forgiveness, that reality of sin, especially original sin, becomes epistemologically accessible.[18] To refuse that salvation would involve a loss of that light and thus of the epistemological access it provides.

By way of comparison, in *Rousseau's Exemplary Life*, Christopher Kelly reads the *Confessions* as "the epistemological foundation of [his] system."[19] According to Kelly, Rousseau's system is "based on the assertion that man is naturally good and has been corrupted by society."[20] The epistemological status of this assertion is rendered problematic by the very corruption that society has wrought—how could anyone know they were corrupted? Kelly detects an "ambiguity" in Rousseau's discovery of nature. The ambiguity exists because the discovery of nature is true but not a "necessary outcome of every course of reflection."[21] It has an "arbitrary, fortunate origin" in the life of Rousseau.[22]

What Kelly terms the "arbitrary, fortunate origin" of this discovery consists in "decisive moments."[23] The moments he designates are the encounter with the Venetian courtesan Zulietta, recounted in Book VII of the *Confessions*, and the famous illumination on the road to Vincennes that took place a few years later. Each of these incidents will be carefully examined in later chapters to show that in each, Rousseau experienced theological scandal. In the illumination, he also chose to give scandal in return. Rather than being an ambiguous combination of the necessary and the arbitrary, the origin of Rousseau's system is a choice about scandal, and its epistemological foundation is the refusal to acknowledge forgiveness.

The rejection of forgiveness of sin has a theological dimension. Rejecting forgiveness is to remove the central scandal of the Cross from the Gospel, because the scandal of the Gospel is Christ crucified—that is, the forgiveness of sin made manifest through the death and resurrection of the Son. Removing that scandal and removing forgiveness are the same thing. Removing the forgiveness of sin entails removing the light by which one sees what sin is. And so one can say that the deepest truth and unity of Rousseau's thought are not the natural goodness of man, nor conversely the rejection of the dogma of original sin. Neither of these cuts deep enough. Rather, Rousseau's scandal at the forgiveness offered by God in Christ grounds the unity of his system.[24] Where there is no forgiveness, there is no sin, and then one is left with the theory of natural goodness, which is taken to imply that there is no need for forgiveness, and so there can be no original sin.

OTHER ATTEMPTS

Another way to shed some light on what I am trying to accomplish is to compare my project with some previous efforts. My thesis concerns two very large debates in the history of Rousseauian scholarship. First, there is the longstanding question of the unity of Rousseau's thought or system, and second, the question of Rousseau's relation to Christianity. As regards the former, Arthur Melzer's *The Natural Goodness of Man* is probably the best attempt at developing a truly systematic understanding of Rousseau in the English world.[25] While his study is valuable, his analysis leaves something to be desired. For the latter, I would like to compare and contrast my approach with two very different views, that of Pierre-Maurice Masson and that of Jacques Maritain.

Following Melzer, the biggest difficulty in understanding Rousseau's writings has been the consistent inability of readers to grasp it "comprehensively, as a single, systematic whole."[26] This is due to the perceived inconsistencies in Rousseau's writings. According to Melzer, two explanations have been given to account for Rousseau's inconsistencies. The first is that the contradictions result from changes in his opinion over time, and the second is that Rousseau simply did not notice the contradictions. With regard to the first explanation, Rousseau claims a consistency in his writings, and this claim is credible given the relatively advanced age at which he started writing (at the age of thirty-eight) and the short period of time (twelve years) within which his major works were produced. The second view tends to base itself on some statements that Rousseau himself made regarding the difficulty he had with sustained thinking. This view becomes problematic, however, if one reads his writings. The apparent contradictions, of which Rousseau shows complete awareness, pale in comparison with the dense unity of thought. Hippolyte Taine was very aware of the apparent contradictions as follows:

> But on the other hand, in this burning furnace, under the pressure of this prolonged and intense meditation, his style, incessantly forged and reforged, acquires a density and a hardness that one does not find elsewhere. . . . Moreover, the pieces of his writing are linked together; he writes not just pages but books; there is no logician more strict. His demonstration is woven stitch by stitch over one, two, three volumes, like an enormous web without exit where, willingly or unwillingly, one remains held. He is a systematist who, turned in on himself, with his eyes obstinately fixed on his dream or on his principle, penetrates into it a little more each day, unravels its consequences one by one, and always keeps the webbing as a whole in his grasp.[27]

I think that careful readers of Rousseau would agree that his writings are much more systematic and unified than they appear on a first reading. This is not to claim that his system or its unity is easy to articulate.

According to Melzer, Rousseau blamed the continued inability of readers to grasp his thought on the readers themselves: "Turning around the accusation just directed at him, he claims that they are unaccustomed to truly systematic thinking such as he alone practices, for 'nothing is so contrary to the philosophic spirit of this century.'"[28] Melzer chooses not to explore this logic of accusation and counteraccusation, turning instead to his own accusation against Rousseau.

For Melzer, the reason that readers fail to grasp Rousseau's thought is due to the way Rousseau wrote his books. There is no systematic statement of Rousseau's system, for, according to Melzer, "he allowed his system to dribble out in disconnected parts."[29] Melzer's position is that "Rousseau's *thought* is indeed exceptionally systematic—but his *writings* are exceptionally unsystematic."[30] Thus, there is a "radical incongruity" between Rousseau's thought and his presentation.[31] This is the source of the difficulties.

Melzer develops this position by pointing out the accidental and external occasions of many of Rousseau's writings. They are responses to prize questions posed by various academies (the *First* and *Second Discourses*), or part of a larger project (*Discourse on Political Economy* is an entry for the *Encyclopedia*), or responses to various requests. Thus, Melzer feels that one can claim, with some exaggeration, he admits, that "Rousseau took the various pieces of his unified system of *thought* . . . and scattered them unsystematically throughout his *writings*."[32]

Finally, Melzer accuses Rousseau of doing the very thing against which he so violently reacted in the *First Discourse*. His writings "appear to be the very opposite of what they are."[33] They appear to stand alone, when, in fact, they are exceedingly interdependent. Such is Melzer's criticism of Rousseau. He holds that in order to put the system back together, all the works have to be read in a sense simultaneously, because they are all so interdependent. The works are "ultimately incoherent unless cross-referenced at every point."[34]

Melzer's conclusion is that "we must find the system, then, that Rousseau has dismantled and scattered among his desultory writings."[35] Now, whether Melzer means, by the use of the term "desultory," "marked by lack of definite plan, regularity, or purpose," or "not connected with the main subject," or "disappointing in progress, performance, or quality," this interpretation is surely not adequate.[36] This kind of radical distinction between Rousseau's thought and writings is certainly suspect. There is no preexisting whole system that Rousseau "dismantled" and that now has to be "put back together again."[37] Not to deny the value of building up an account of Rousseau's thought by taking various parts of the arguments from different works, one must still insist that Rousseau's works are also artistic wholes. To be understood, each must be interpreted in a way that respects that fact. Further, one cannot simply present Rousseau's "system" apart from his mode of presentation. Accordingly, each work needs to be read as an autonomous whole. This helps to keep the drama that is in most of his writings alive, rather than reducing Rousseau's thought to a conceptual system abstracted from the works in which it finds expression. The unity of the system can be comprehended adequately only by understanding it in its mode of presentation.

More to the point, Rousseau himself indicates that there is an order to his texts and that reading them in a certain way does enable one to grasp his system. Melzer backs up much of his own argument with quotations from the *Dialogues*, but he underplays the importance of some quotations. The following description of how Rousseau's writings are to be read undermines much of Melzer's approach:

The Frenchman:
I resolved to reread his writing with more consistency and attention . . . I hadn't grasped the whole sufficiently to make a sound judgment about a system that was so new to me. Those books are not . . . collections of detached thoughts on each of which the reader's mind can rest.

From my first reading, I had felt that these writings proceeded in a certain order which it was necessary to find in order to follow the chain of their contents. I believed

I saw that this was the reverse of their order of publication, and that going backward from one principle to the next, the Author reached the first ones only in his last writings. To proceed by synthesis, then, it was necessary to begin with these, which is what I did, by focusing first on *Emile*, with which he finished. (*CW* 1:211; *Pl.* 3:933)

Rousseau himself has indicated the order of reading. After looking in more detail at the *Dialogues* in which this claim is made, this order will be followed by examining *Emile* and seeking to "proceed by synthesis." Proceeding by synthesis means, according to Rousseau, that the reader proceeds by means of "combination rather than resolution or starting at the elemental and building up" (*Emile*, 171; *Pl.* 4:434). This implies that the reader should read each work separately and yet combine them with what has gone before.

The principle uncovered in *Emile* will call forth the *Discourse on Inequality* as its "sequel." The two parts of the system that the works represent—namely the former, an answer to the question, "who are we now?" and the latter, an answer to the question, "where did we come from?"—will then be completed by the *Discourse on the Sciences and Arts* that provides an answer to the question, "what are we to do?"

Let us turn now to the second interpretative problem upon which my thesis directly touches—the relationship of Rousseau's thought with Christianity.[38] Masson published his massive three-volume work, *La Religion de Jean-Jacques Rousseau*, in the early part of the last century. John McManners says of these volumes, "As a chronological study of Rousseau's spiritual development, and as an exhaustive account of his reading and intellectual borrowings, they could hardly be bettered."[39] However, Masson's conclusion that Rousseau was more or less a Catholic has gone, as McManners also notes, largely unaccepted. Maritain, on the other hand, condemns Rousseau with the following words: "By nature he himself tends directly to an abominable sentimentality, to a devilish parody of Christianity, the decomposition of Christianity and all the sicknesses and apostasies which follow; and to them he leads modern thought."[40] By placing the idea of scandal in the center of this interpretation, the reader can grasp what would lead to two such disparate understandings of Rousseau's relation to Christianity, and see a further alternative.[41]

Rousseau is scandalized by the Gospels and so he excises the scandalous parts from them. Whatever offends his reason is no longer included therein. Masson, for his part, excises this part of Rousseau. In a sense, he preempts his own scandal at Rousseau. He is not, and he refuses to be, scandalized by Rousseau. One could say that he tries to "save" Rousseau for the Church.

Maritain gives in to the scandal. His condemnation of Rousseau is thorough, precise, and penetrating. He titles the final section of his interpretation of Rousseau, "Debased Christianity." Maritain grants that "without this transit [of twenty-six years] through Catholicism, without the misuse of holy things and divine truths of which his Catholic culture made him capable, Rousseau would not have been complete, there would have been no Jean-Jacques."[42] On the one hand, Rousseau "perceived great Christian truths which his age had forgotten," and on the other, "he perverted them."[43]

Further, Maritain interprets the theory of natural goodness as signifying that man originally lived in a "*purely natural* paradise of happiness and goodness, and that

Nature herself will in future perform the function which grace fulfilled in the Catholic conception."[44] He sees this dogma as "only a cutting down of the Christian dogma of adamic Innocence to fit the scheme of romantic naturalism."[45]

Thus, Maritain recognizes the essential role that Christianity plays in Rousseau's thought, but he misrecognizes the nature of that role. Rousseau scandalizes Maritain, and so Maritain cannot see Rousseau's scandal. Maritain does not explain and cannot explain the depth of Rousseau's insight into Christianity beyond the meager generalization that he had a religious disposition and that he had "great religious needs."[46] Maritain does not see that to be scandalized by Christ means to fall victim to a certain fascination and repulsion with Christ. Christ becomes a rival for Rousseau.

As we saw above, the inadequacy of Melzer's approach to Rousseau's system helped bring into relief the reason why I approach Rousseau's texts as artistic wholes, and the importance of following a certain order in reading them. In an analogous way, the inadequacy of Masson's and Maritain's accounts of the relationship between Rousseau's system and Christianity means that a way must be sought that neither ignores the scandal nor gives in to it.

In a very generous reading, André Ravier finds a kind of parallel structure between Rousseau's religious system and Christianity: the origin of humanity is in a state of innocence, and a historical "fall" results in an interior struggle between "good" and "evil" without the possibility of a return to innocence.[47] He locates the origin of the difference between Rousseau and Catholicism in Rousseau's conception of *amour de soi* (love of self) as being always correct. Catholicism sees this as fundamentally good, but "wounded" by the sin of Adam. While I do not disagree with him, again I think this analysis does not get to the heart of the matter. Ravier takes Rousseau's religiosity, his claim to Christianity, with great seriousness, but he cannot put his finger on what simultaneously makes Rousseau Christian and separates him from the disciples of Christ.

There are several scholars who have already opened up the path that I follow. Chief among these is Jean Starobinski. As the subtitle of his justly famous work, *Jean-Jacques Rousseau: Transparency and Obstruction* (*La transparence et l'obstacle*) suggests, he has been very sensitive to the notion of scandal in the sense of it being an "obstacle" in Rousseau's thought. I consider this book to be an amplification and explication of Starobinski's statement that "by Rousseau's own admission, the scandal of deceit was the driving force behind all his theorizing."[48] The difference in our approaches lies in the fact that, although *l'obstacle* is the *skandalon*, Starobinski's focus is primarily on the psychoanalytic dimension of this phenomenon. Ultimately, I am more concerned with the properly theological dimension.

In his reading of Rousseau, Jacques Derrida shows that his writings, and especially his *Essay on the Origin of Language*, as exemplary of those writings, are inscribed within the logic of scandal. Indeed, according to Derrida, "the dangerous supplement . . . is a sort . . . of scandal (*scandalon*)."[49] By linking the concept of "supplement" to "scandal" in this way, Derrida shows that scandal is the deeper reality and the one more in need of explanation.

This work also has a deep debt to a variety of scholars, such as Pierre Burgelin, Albert Schinz, Robert Derathé, and Charly Guyot, who see Rousseau's religious thought at the very center of his work. Burgelin sums it up in small book titled,

Jean-Jacques Rousseau et la religion de Genève, by saying, "telle nous apparaîte, dans sa complexité et sa diversité, la religion de Rousseau, au coeur de sa vie, de sa pensée, de sa système même."[50] By finding the key to his system in scandal, both its systematic and its religious dimensions can be brought together.

Although he has never written directly on Rousseau, René Girard's theory of scandal has been of enormous value for this work.[51] Girard says the following about scandal: "Even in its accepted modern meaning, which converts scandal into a mere matter of representation, the notion of the scandalous cannot be defined univocally."[52] This lack of univocity will upset some readers. Every effort has been made to clarify the particular meaning of each use of the word "scandal." Scandal is a biblical concept, but its various usages in the New Testament meant that trying to develop a coherent "theory of scandal" turned out to be very difficult.[53] As was pointed out above, Christ crucified is proclaimed as a scandal (1 Cor. 1:23), yet Christians are forbidden to cause scandal to others (1 Cor. 8:9), especially to the younger and weaker.

It might seem that use of the same word to describe the experience of offense at salvation coming through the Cross, and the everyday experience of setting a bad example for others, could be simply a case of the way words develop in meaning, leaving their original context and picking up new denotations that can be quite unrelated to their origin. The fact of the matter is that, as the quotations above indicate, each of these meanings can be traced back not only to the New Testament, but also to the same author, Paul, in the same text, the First Letter to the Corinthians.

Girard unites these usages by seeing in biblical scandal an inchoate theory of human desire. Girard calls this desire "mimetic," or desire that one receives from another and then imitates. With the onset of mimetic desire, two people desire the same thing, and this easily results in conflict. Furthermore, this type of desire leads to the "mutual reinforcement between desire and indignation through a process of *feedback*."[54] The more one desires something, the more defensive one is when someone else challenges the attempted possession, and the more defensive one becomes, the more that can call forth the challenge of the other.

It is on this mundane level that the connection with Rousseau first becomes evident. Rousseau is well-known for his concept of amour-propre. Rousseau's definition of amour-propre makes its connection with offense (another translation of the biblical word for "scandal") quite clear. Speaking of man in the primitive state, he remarks, "for the same reason [that he is not capable of making comparisons] this man could have neither hate nor desire for revenge, passions that can only arise from the opinion that some offense has been received; and as it is scorn or intention to hurt and not the harm that constitutes this offense, men who know neither how to evaluate themselves nor compare themselves can do each other a great deal of mutual violence, . . . without ever offending one another" (*CW* 3:91; *Pl.* 3:219). In other words, there is no scandal in the state of nature. The quotation is taken from the famous note in the *Discourse on Inequality* explaining the distinction between self-love (*amour de soi*) and amour-propre.

In a literally parenthetical remark, the famous literary theorist Tzvetan Todorov states, "The 'mimetic desire' of Girard is only another name for the amour-propre of Rousseau."[55] The constellation of comparison, passion, offense, and growing conflict is the same in each. For his part, Girard defines the *scandalon* (that which causes the scandal) in the following way: "It is not an obstacle that just happens to be there and merely has to be got out of the way; it is the model exerting its special form of temptation, causing attraction to the extent that it is an obstacle and forming an obstacle to the extent that it can attract."[56]

Rousseau's analysis of amour-propre as that which excites without satisfying, seduces without delivering, and promises without fulfilling parallels Girard's analysis of mimetic desire as the doomed-to-be-frustrated reaching for the *scandalon*. In the coming pages, the scandalous phenomenon in which each step toward the desired object also becomes a step away will often make its appearance.

Mimetic desires, amour-propre, lead to mundane bickering, empty contests over prestige, and other conflicts. These conflicts always have the potential to lead to victimization—a releasing of pent-up aggression and violence on a person or persons who cannot retaliate. The Crucifixion is one example of this process. It causes particular attraction and repulsion because it reveals the truth of human involvement in this kind of victimization. The very feelings that lead to low-level scandals are connected with the overt violence that is normally shunned. The problem of violence is never far from the surface in Rousseau's writings, and neither will it be in my interpretation.

THE WAY OF PROCEEDING

I begin with a reading of *Rousseau, Judge of Jean-Jacques: Dialogues*. I do this for several reasons. First, although it is often ignored, the *Dialogues* hold an important place in Rousseau's *oeuvre*. Roger Masters and Christopher Kelly see it as a kind of culmination: "That the *Dialogues* is meant to bring Rousseau's literary enterprise to a sort of completion by stressing the connection of his first and last works is also indicated by Rousseau's choice of epigraph, *Barbarus hic ego sum quia non intelligor illis* (Here I am the barbarian because no one understands me)" (*CW* 1:xv). Further, as I alluded to earlier, it contains Rousseau's teachings on how to read his work.

This culminating text also establishes two facts that are critical to my investigation. More than any of his other writings, the *Dialogues* makes clear that Rousseau denies the possibility of forgiveness. Second, the *Dialogues* also brings out the importance of scandal as an element in his thought. While scandal can be shown to be important from the texts of the Controversy, forgiveness is a different matter. Rousseau rarely speaks of it. Only in the *Dialogues* does he make clear his position on forgiveness; otherwise it is present mainly through its conspicuous absence. Since the lack of forgiveness plays such a large role in my analysis, it is important that I establish that it is textually based.

As we saw above, the Frenchman in the *Dialogues* learns to read Rousseau's work in the reverse order of their publication. Thus, he begins his reading with *Emile* and tries to "follow the chain of their contents."

The Frenchman:
   In this second reading, better organized and more reflective than the first, following the thread of the meditations as best I could, I saw throughout the development of his

great principle that nature made man happy and good, but that society depraves him and makes him miserable. The *Emile*, in particular—that book which is much read, little understood, and ill-appreciated—is nothing but a treatise on the original goodness of man, destined to show how vice and error, foreign to his constitution, enter it from outside and insensibly change him. In his first writings, he tries even more to destroy that magical illusion which gives us a stupid admiration for the instruments of our misfortunes and to correct that deceptive assessment that makes us honor pernicious talents and scorn useful virtues. Throughout he makes us see the human race as better, wiser, and happier in its primitive constitution. . . . His goal is to rectify the error of your judgments in order to delay the progress of our vices. (*CW* 1:212–13; *Pl.* 334–35)

Thus, I will follow my interpretation of the *Dialogues* with four chapters on *Emile*. In *Emile*, Rousseau establishes the place of the natural man in society, and that place is that of the victim. The proof that the interpretation offered here, that Rousseau's system is grounded in scandal, will be long and somewhat indirect, as befits a text structured by an absence, structured by the rejection of forgiveness.

In Chapter 3, "The Forming of *Emile*," I begin by analyzing some examples used in Book II of the novel to show that they involve scandal in a double sense. Emile is scandalized in being led into sin, and he is further scandalized by the indignation caused when he is sinned against. This double scandal forms little Emile's consciousness. In the following chapter, I will show that in "Profession of Faith of the Savoyard Vicar," Rousseau's exclusion of testimony in the second part has another goal beyond that of avoiding the fanaticism and dogmatism that lead to violence.[57] The expulsion of testimony in the second half of the "Profession" has a deeper significance than being the form of rationalism that many interpreters take it to be. It has its own specific aim.[58] The expulsion of testimony in general is the expulsion of the testimony of expulsion in particular. The thing that can only be witnessed and cannot be "proven" is the expulsion of the victim. The scandal of Jesus' death is then converted by Rousseau into an accusation against the perennial victims of Europe—the Jews. Chapter 5 explores how Rousseau offers the world in the character of Emile a new Christ: a Christ not crucified, a Christ who is not the occasion of scandal. Finally, Chapter 6 explores the political implications of rejecting forgiveness. Through all of this, it will become clear how this novel about education is, in fact, an education of the reader.

The search for origins, which is taken up in Chapter 7, is always determined by where one thinks one is now. If one is going to replace the "image of man as a born sinner with that of born victim,"[59] then one needs also to replace the biblical account of origins that supports the image of man as sinner. This leads us to examine the *Discourse on Inequality*. The discovery that God reigned both in and through sinful history led Israel to develop its peculiar creation myth with the story of the Fall. The discovery that sin has been forgiven led the Church to develop its interpretation of that myth as containing the doctrine of original sin. Rousseau's discovery that he must reject the forgiveness of sin led him to develop the myth of the state of nature and the doctrine of natural goodness.[60]

Rousseau's scandal, his rejection of forgiveness, was not an act done once and then forgotten. It is the continual source of his system. He takes the moment of rejection and draws it out, structures it, and develops its conceptual possibilities. Chapter 8, on the body of the *Discourse on Inequality*, shows what kind of a universe one inhabits when forgiveness is turned away.

Having answered the question of who we are and where we came from, Rousseau turns finally to the question of what to do. If scandal is the source of the system, then one needs a continual source of scandal to keep the system going. Rousseau provides his readers with such a source in the *Discourse on the Sciences and Arts*. As demonstrated in Chapter 9, Rousseau sets up a logic of scandal that virtually assures the reader's getting caught up in scandal regardless of whether he or she agrees or disagrees with him. More importantly, each successive step back in the order of his writings reveals another dimension of the scandal. It is in the Controversy surrounding the *First Discourse* that Rousseau's Christological scandal finally becomes clear.

By making the *Confessions* the subject of Chapter 10, the book takes a step forward in terms of the chronology of publication and step backward in terms of the ground of the system. The *Confessions* are chronologically later than the *Discourses* and *Emile*. But the episode from the *Confessions* that will be examined with great care here occurred before Rousseau had published *Discourse on the Sciences and Arts*. The interpretation moves closer to the source of the system through a more intimate look at Rousseau's experience of scandal. The notion of scandal contains within itself a drive toward confession and autobiography. Girard describes scandalized consciousness in the following way:

> The person who is scandalized wants to bring the affair out into the open; he has a burning desire to see the scandal in the clear light of day and pillory the guilty party. . . . Scandal always calls for demystification, and demystification—far from putting an end to scandal, [it] propagates and universalizes it.[61]

The rejection of forgiveness does not do away with the accusation. One is no longer free simply to confess forgiven sins, the way Augustine did. Rather, one has to prove one's innocence. For Rousseau, innocence always means innocence of that of which one is being accused. Thus, confession becomes a form of self-justification. We see in the autobiographical writings the claim not only of his own innocence, but also of the evil of the other. The other is always present to Rousseau, even, as will be seen in the *Reveries*, where he seems most alone.

My examination in Chapter 11 of the *Reveries of a Solitary Walker* finds that this text answers the question, to where does scandal lead? If one follows the logic of scandal with consistency, what is the result? The result is consciousness structured by its expulsion from society and its own expulsion of society.

The work concludes with a backward look at the journey that has just been summarized. The reader returns at the end to the beginning, and grasps more clearly the hermeneutical principle that has been animating and guiding this work.

CONCLUSION

Rousseau's claim, made to the archbishop of Paris, that "[he was] Christian, and sincerely Christian, according to the doctrine of the Gospel" (*CW* 9:47; *Pl.* 4:960) is true, and it is true because the doctrine of the Gospel is scandal. Rousseau also exclaimed in the same letter, "[I will speak of my religion] because I have one, and I shall speak of it loudly because I have the courage to do so and because it would be desirable for the good of men if it were that of the human race" (*CW* 9:47; *Pl.* 4:960). We cannot yet speak of it being the religion of the human race, but Rousseau's religion of scandal has become more and more widespread.[62]

To be scandalized at the Gospels is to be in a different category not only from one who believes, but also from one who simply rejects Christianity without scandal, and again from someone who has never heard of it. To be scandalized in a theological sense is to take Christ or the Gospel as one's model at the same time that one makes Him or it into one's rival. It is to both embrace and reject Christianity. One tries to emulate Christ, one accepts the Gospel, and one sees the beauty of the Beatitudes at the same time as one does away with Christ, tries to replace him, and sees that "this same Gospel is full of unbelievable things, of things repugnant to reason and impossible for any sensible man to conceive or to accept" (*Emile*, 308; *Pl.* 4:627). To be scandalized is to become the Savoyard Vicar; it is to become Rousseau.

The scandal does not have to be particularly religious. Scandal is a theological reality with a political dimension. But its political dimension will not be fully understood—in the life of the reader or in Rousseau's thought—unless the theological reality is grasped. What makes Rousseau Christian is not his rejection of a misunderstood dogma, like original sin, but his uncanny grasp of the centrality of the victim.[63] By a careful study of his thought, this understanding may become more widespread.

Is it possible to take into account Rousseau's scandal without participating in the scandal? As we saw above in the *Encyclopedia* entry for **scandaleux**, it is difficult to speak of scandal without causing it. It is difficult to read about it without being scandalized. If the roots of scandal were the rejection of forgiveness in Jesus Christ, then the only reading that could take Rousseau's scandal seriously without participating in it would be a reading that is adequate to the text.

In the course of this study, I hope to make clear in what precisely Rousseau's offence consists. That is, I hope to clarify both how Rousseau is offended and how he offends. There is a forgiveness that corresponds to the offense. In fact, the depth of the offense cannot be made clear, unless the offer of forgiveness is also made manifest.

Rousseau requires, in effect he asks for, a forgiving reader. I have tried to be that reader. I leave the judgment of my success or failure to the reader. This is not an uncritical reading. Rather, it is a reading that takes precisely those parts of Rousseau's text that have most often been ignored, discounted, mutilated, or expelled, and lets those texts speak. Precisely these texts open up this new possibility of interpretation.

CHAPTER 2

"Everything Relates to That First Accusation"

Introduction

Beginning with a character named Rousseau expressing his scandal at Jean-Jacques, and ending with this same character and his dialogue partner promising their devoted presence at Jean-Jacques' death, *Rousseau Juge de Jean-Jacques: Dialogues* encompasses and exemplifies the whole of Rousseau's system.[1] Composed of three dialogues, the drama, and not just the exposition, make this achievement possible.[2] The *Dialogues* is a story of conversion.[3] Put in the baldest terms, the interlocutors "Rousseau" and the "Frenchman" change from being with the "Gentlemen" and against Jean-Jacques in the "First Dialogue," to being against the "Gentlemen" and for Jean-Jacques at the end of the "Third Dialogue." In the course of this transformation, the author reveals his system. The *Dialogues* shows that, far from being an abstract starting point, the principle of natural goodness is the positive expression of an absence of forgiveness that constitutes the true heart of Rousseau's system. The Frenchman claims that throughout the works of Jean-Jacques, one sees the "development of his great principle that nature made man happy and good, but that society depraves him and makes him miserable" (*CW* 1:213; *Pl.* 1:934).[4]

But the story of the *Dialogues* reveals that this development takes place in a space in which all forgiveness is lacking. Jean-Jacques does not forgive, he is not forgiven, and forgiveness is to him a cause of scandal. More profoundly, the logical space of the *Dialogues* is created through the portrayal of Jean-Jacques as the one who is not forgiven by others for the injustices that *they* have committed *against him*.[5] This portrait of a figure to whom forgiveness is positively denied, on the one hand, and who therefore does not require it and indeed scorns it as an outrage, on the other, gives this work its complexity as well as its unity. The refusal of forgiveness and Jean-Jacques' rejection of needing it are mirror images of each other. The Gentlemen's refusal to extend forgiveness creates the "underground" of the conspiracy that so dominates the *Dialogues*, while Jean-Jacques' rejection of forgiveness creates the opposing "ethereal realms." Rousseau never conceived of Jean-Jacques' innocence as simply being a lack of wrongdoing; rather his innocence is formed as the positive aspect of the others' refusal to forgive him for their crimes. Jean-Jacques does not forgive others because that would require a degree of virtue that he admits he has not attained.

What results, then, is a system that has scandal as its starting point, moves through the successive ways in which forgiveness can be denied, and uses these to reach its denouement in a society without love based on a reconciliation without forgiveness.

The scandal, the denial of forgiveness, and the reconciliation are dramatized in the relationship between Rousseau, the character, and the Frenchman, as well as in their assessment of the credibility of the Gentlemen. Still, the decisive figure for displaying the system is the author's portrayal of the paradoxical figure of Jean-Jacques as both innocent and unforgiven. It seems obvious that if one is innocent, one does not need forgiveness, but Rousseau reverses these categories, so that being refused forgiveness becomes a necessary condition for innocence or natural goodness.

Forgiveness is surely a Christian theme.[6] In the New Testament, forgiveness is offered in Jesus Christ, and one can be offended by that or accept it. When Jesus tells the paralytic who has been lowered through the roof by his friends, "Son, your sins are forgiven," (Mk. 2:5) the teachers of the law think that he has committed blasphemy. In the *Dialogues*, Jean-Jacques is the figure who can neither forgive nor be forgiven. He is the one who is both offended and offends, who is scandalized and scandalizes.

At its deepest level, theological or Christological scandal is the offense taken by someone at the free offer of forgiveness by the one whom he has crucified. Rousseau grasps this and puts Jean-Jacques in a similar but reversed position. Whereas Christ is the one who forgives and enables others to forgive, Jean-Jacques cannot forgive and makes it impossible for others to forgive. Both are the victims of the crowd. With Christ, the crucifixion means the end of the separation between God and humans, as is symbolized by the rending of the veil in the Temple at the moment of Jesus' death. With Jean-Jacques, the absence of forgiveness creates the difference between the underground and the ethereal realms. The underground belongs to those who will not forgive him for their faults, and the ethereal realms are populated by the unforgiven who do not need forgiveness. Jean-Jacques now occupies the position of the persecuted innocent one. Not persecuted because he is innocent, but rather innocent precisely because he is persecuted, Jean-Jacques is the new *skandalon*, or "the rock that makes them [in this case the "Gentlemen"] fall [*petra skandalou*]" (1 Pet. 2:8).[7]

THE DIALOGUES AS A SELF-PORTRAIT

Before looking in more detail at the content of the *Dialogues*, it is necessary, as always with Rousseau, to reflect upon the genre of the work. *Rousseau, Judge of Jean-Jacques* is, as the subtitle indicates, a dialogue, but it is a kind of interior dialogue that functions as a self-portrait. In a more explicit way than in many of his writings, the *Dialogues* is an instantiation of what it is about. It is about Rousseau's judgment of Jean-Jacques. As such, it is also Rousseau's self-portrait.

Rousseau begins the *Dialogues* with a prayer addressed to the reader. The prayer implores the reader to read "all of it (*tout entier*)" (*CW* 1:2; *Pl.* 1:659). Even with this simple petition, Rousseau is "very certain" that this "favor (*grace*)" will not be granted to him, so he retreats into silence and surrenders to providence (*CW* 1:2; *Pl.* 1:659). Why is this considered a grace, and why is he so certain that it will not be bestowed? It does not seem like such a difficult request, and certainly many readers have fulfilled it. So again, why the explicit request and the certainty of refusal?

Rousseau is not asking the reader simply to let his eyes fall on each page or to sound out every word. His request is that one read—that is, that one interpret and understand "all of it." Rousseau is certain that this will not be granted to him, because he is certain that the reader will understand the part belonging to the character Rousseau as expressing the author's thought, while the part belonging to the Frenchman will be viewed as the thought of another, or as part of the drama that does not add anything substantial to Rousseau's position.[8] Rousseau is certain that people will not make the effort to read this work as a whole and will instead use the *Dialogues* as the source of proof texts to buttress their own interpretations of his thought. He was prophetic.[9] What Rousseau is petitioning for in the prayer is a reader who can read the *whole* text as one large self-portrait that contains other perspectives, and even other self-portraits, yet still forms a coherent whole.

Rousseau, the author, gives us clues for a comprehensive interpretation of the *Dialogues*. In the preface, which is titled, "On the Subject and Form of This Writing," and which follows the prayer, he deepens the demand that the work be read as a whole. He makes explicit in the preface that he has constructed the thoughts of his accusers. The text consists of a dialogue of his thoughts, his interpretations, and his way of making sense of the situation. He is in isolation, and all that he can rely on is his own conjectures. He describes his situation thus: "The profound, universal silence is no less conceivable than the mystery it veils, a mystery that has been hidden from me for fifteen years with a care that I refrain from characterizing and with a success that appears extraordinary. This terrifying and terrible silence has kept me from grasping the least idea that could clarify these strange attitudes [of Parisians, of the French, of Europeans] for me" (*CW* 1:4; *Pl.* 1:662). This statement by Rousseau needs to be taken literally. Rousseau has no way of understanding the behavior of others toward him. He has to construct an interpretation.

The "Second Dialogue" also contains a similar indication of how to interpret the text. The author constructs the *Dialogues* so that Rousseau, the character, meets Jean-Jacques at the time that the latter is writing "a kind of judgment of them [the Gentlemen] and of himself in the form of a Dialogue" (*CW* 1:136; *Pl.* 1:836). Rousseau even tells the Frenchman that the writing is "rather like the one that may result from our conversations" (*CW* 1:136; *Pl.* 1:836). In having the character Rousseau tell the Frenchman this, the author is reminding the reader that he or she is reading fiction.[10] All of it comes from the mind of Rousseau. It is not intended to be a transcript of what someone might say. Rather, the whole of it is a judgment: Rousseau, the character, judges the Gentlemen and Jean-Jacques in a way that reveals the judgment of the author, Jean-Jacques Rousseau.

The whole of the *Dialogues* is about portraits—self-portraits, literal portraits, literary portraits, depictions, sketches, disfigurations, and blackenings.[11] Hardly a page goes by without some mention of portraits or portrayal. Indeed, at the beginning of the "Second Dialogue," Rousseau writes what he calls the "history" of some actual portraits of Jean-Jacques. He explains to the Frenchman the curious goings-on surrounding the portraits and engravings. The "exposé," as the Frenchman terms it, is occasioned by Rousseau's following recollection of his first meeting with Jean-Jacques, a meeting that is supposed to have occurred in the interval between the "First" and the "Second Dialogue": "Based on the much praised portraits of him that are displayed everywhere and extolled as masterpieces of likeness before he returned to Paris, I expected to see the face of an awful Cyclops like the English portrait or of a grimacing little valet like that of Fiquet" (*CW* 1:89; *Pl.* 1:777). But this is not what he sees. Rousseau finds that, to his surprise and delight, Jean-Jacques has an "open simple physiognomy, which suggested and inspired confidence and sympathy" (*CW* 1:90; *Pl.* 1:777). Thus, Rousseau finds it odd that these unflattering pictures and engravings have been so highly praised, so widely distributed. In Rousseau's judgment, "[if these portraits do not do a better job of] depicting the original's moral character than they do his physical appearance, he [Jean-Jacques] will surely be badly known through them" (*CW* 1:90; *Pl.* 1:778). The unflattering, physical portraits are spread in much the same way that the unflattering rumors about Jean-Jacques are spread.

Rousseau learns that Jean-Jacques' "protectors," the Gentlemen, are the ones who have had these engravings made from the portraits at a great expense and have had them circulated. Rousseau relates what he has been able to learn about the history of one particular portrait, the English one. There are some "very extraordinary circumstances" concerning that portrait (*CW* 1:91; *Pl.* 1:779). David Hume arranged to have it done by Allan Ramsay. The following is Rousseau's description of it: "J.J. is made to wear a very black hat, a very brown coat, and he is positioned in a very somber place; and there, in order to paint him seated, he is kept standing, bent over, leaning with one hand on a very low table, in a position where his tightly tensed muscles modify his facial features" (*CW* 1:91; *Pl.* 1:779). Thus, even if the portrait is faithful, it cannot help but be unflattering. It is this portrait that serves as the model for an engraving. The engraving has been reproduced and sold throughout Europe, but Jean-Jacques was not allowed to see it. Finally, he succeeds in getting a look at it and expresses his displeasure with it. The result is: "Everyone ridicules him" (*CW* 1:91; *Pl.* 1:779). In the end, Hume appears to the public as a generous benefactor for having a portrait made by such a famous painter, but he appears to Jean-Jacques as the one who gave him "the face of a fearsome Cyclops" (*CW* 1:91; *Pl.* 1:780).

The Frenchman thinks that this exposé of the portraits will reveal many things about the conspiracy, but "who will assure [him] it [the story] is true?" (*CW* 1:91–92; *Pl.* 1:780). Rousseau responds that "the face in the portrait" would assure him of the truth of the story: "On the question at hand, this face will not lie" (*CW* 1:92; *Pl.* 1:780). The question at hand is whether the portrait accentuates Jean-Jacques' best features or shows him in an unflattering light. In order to judge this, it is not necessary for the Frenchman to be able to compare the portrait with the original. The copy itself will testify against itself, if its features do not coalesce. Without being able to compare the copy with the original, the only thing that can be done is to compare various portraits.

This is the problem of the *Dialogues* as a whole. The readers are in the position of the Frenchman, unable to compare the portrait with the original. We are confronted with many copies and no original. In spite of that, the reader should be able to make a judgment about the person of Jean-Jacques based on the Gentlemen's depiction of Jean-Jacques and Rousseau's sketch of him in the "Second Dialogue." This sketch of Jean-Jacques is to be compared not only with the portrait that the Gentlemen paint, but also, and more importantly, with the self-portrait contained in Jean-Jacques' writings.

This "exposé" of the portraits, which the character Rousseau attributes to Jean-Jacques' imagination, contains even deeper implications for our interpretation of the *Dialogues* (*CW* 1:91; *Pl.* 1:780). At the end of this discussion, Rousseau comments that the history of the portraits looks like "the rather natural fruits of an imagination beset by so many mysteries and misfortunes. So without either adopting or rejecting these ideas at this point, let's leave all these strange portraits and return to the original" (*CW* 1:94; *Pl.* 1:782). Rousseau, the character and, *a fortiori*, Rousseau, the author, are aware of Jean-Jacques' tendency to paranoia. The *Dialogues* is not a result of this tendency; rather, it is one of the ways that Rousseau masters this tendency. Rousseau tells the Frenchman, "I don't mean to give you as realities all the troubling ideas suggested to J.J. by the profound obscurity in which they persist in surrounding him. The mysteries made for him about everything are so black it is not surprising that they affect his frightened imagination with the same coloration. But among the exaggerated and fantastic ideas he can get from that, there are some that deserve serious examination before being rejected, given the extraordinary way he is treated" (*CW* 1:92; *Pl.* 1:780–81). These kinds of reflections on the thoughts that trouble him demonstrate that Rousseau, the author, is not controlled by them. They are a part of the self-portrait presented in the *Dialogues*, but they should not be allowed to dominate or negate it.

Rousseau suggested to the Frenchman that they "leave all these strange portraits" and "return to the original." The character no longer speaks about other portraits; rather, he sketches one of his own. His return to the original is, then, a turn for the reader to his portrait, to his version of the original, but it also means a turn to the text as both an original and a portrait. Rousseau, the author, is playing with the idea of original and portrait here. In his history of the portraits, there is an original subject and his portrait. But there is also the original portrait and its copies. What status does the long sketch in the "Second Dialogue" occupy?

The character reflects on precisely this problem. He feels that even the "peaceful but certain observations of an impartial man" would be useless for disproving the "noisy assertions of passionate people" (*CW* 1:107; *Pl.* 1:799). Even though he would be telling the Frenchman facts that had been witnessed by his own consciousness, and that should carry more weight than those simply asserted by others, he is aware that this would "produce no effect." Furthermore, Rousseau is convinced from his experience that "in certain respects J.J.'s situation is even too incredible for it to be capable of being well unveiled. . . . It has to be seen to be believed" (*CW* 1:107; *Pl.* 1:799).

Rousseau is looking for "some other route" besides arguing Jean-Jacques' case. He tells the Frenchman, "[I wish to make you] feel all at once, through a simple and immediate impression, what I cannot persuade you of, given the opinions you hold, by proceeding gradually." (*CW* 1:107; *Pl.* 1:799). Rousseau says to the Frenchman, "I would like to sketch for you here the portrait of my J.J. as its idea has become imprinted in my mind after a long examination of the original" (*CW* 1:107; *Pl.* 1:799). The Frenchman can then compare this portrait with the Gentlemen's and judge "which of the two is better unified in its parts, and seems to better form a single whole" (*CW* 1:107; *Pl.* 1:799). Rousseau is looking for a criterion of adequacy that will allow him to say that his description is superior to that of the others. He finds that criterion in the internal coherence of the portrait.

There is another meaning here for the prayer to the reader that Rousseau placed at the beginning of the text. He wants this "sketch," which stretches over approximately sixty pages of text, to be read as if it were a picture. It is to be taken in whole, as one takes in a portrait. This is what Rousseau means when he prays that he finds someone "to read all of it" (*CW* 1:2; *Pl.* 1:659). Only then shall the Frenchman, as well as the reader, "know [J.J.'s] situation to the bottom" (*CW* 1:107; *Pl.* 1:799).

The figural portrait of Jean-Jacques by Rousseau will be the polar opposite of the one that has been presented by the Gentlemen. Even before giving his "sketch," Rousseau gives a "concise idea" of his observations as follows: "Take the opposite of everything, the good as well as the bad, of your gentlemen's J.J. and you will have very precisely the person I found. Theirs is cruel, fierce, and harsh to the point of depravity. Mine is gentle and compassionate to the point of weakness. Theirs is intractable, inflexible, and always rejecting. Mine is easygoing and soft, unable to resist endearments he believes to be sincere, and letting himself be subjugated, when the right approach is used, by the very people he does not respect" (*CW* 1:106; *Pl.* 1:797–98). The text goes on, drawing out the oppositions. The complete opposition between these two portraits underlines their inner unity. Given that everything in the one has its counterpart in the other, they are related as mirror images, or as a negative is related to a photograph. Ultimately, this connection is based on the fact that both portraits are portraits of the same subject. Here, as in the case of the actual portraits, it does not seem to be so much a question of accuracy as of whether they portray Jean-Jacques favorably or not. Thus, Rousseau repeatedly asserts that the Gentlemen's portrait consists in their taking innocent acts of Jean-Jacques, isolating them, and making them appear evil.

The portrait of Jean-Jacques by the Gentlemen and the one by Rousseau do not exhaust the portraits that are mentioned in the *Dialogues*. There is also the self-portrait that the Frenchman finds contained in Jean-Jacques' writings—that is, in *Emile*, the *Discourse on Inequality*, and the *Discourse on the Sciences and Arts*. While reading these works, the Frenchman focuses his attention not on the doctrine *per se*, but rather on the relationship of that doctrine to the "character of the person whose name it bore" (*CW* 1:214; *Pl.* 1:935–36). A necessary condition for the possibility of these writings was a model. Without that, Jean-Jacques could not have depicted the natural man. Yet where was this model to be found?

> Where could the painter and apologist of nature, so disfigured and calumnied now, have found his model if not in his own heart? He described it as he himself felt. These

traits so novel for us and so true once they are traced could still find, deep in people's hearts, the attestation of their correctness, but they would never have sought them out themselves if the historian of nature hadn't started by removing the rust that hid them. . . . In short, a man had to portray himself to show us primitive man like this, and if the Author hadn't been as unique as his books, he never would have written them. (*CW* 1:214; *Pl.* 1:936)

As is evident from the quotation, the Frenchman is now able to recognize the model because he has judged that the Gentlemen have "disfigured" him. The portrait in the writings is accepted, because of the striking relationship it has with the person depicted by Rousseau, the character, in his sketch. This relationship is "decisive" for the Frenchman. Nevertheless, he draws attention to the opposition of this portrait with that of the "J.J. of our Gentlemen." The latter is the depiction of a monster. Thus, the self-portrait in the writings not only matches the sketch made by Rousseau in the "Second Dialogue," but it also brings more clearly to light the parallel oppositions with the Gentlemen's portrait.

The Gentlemen's portrait of the monster and the self-portrait in the writings further parallel each other in that each constitutes a system. The Frenchman declares that, in reading Jean-Jacques' works, he found "things that were profoundly thought out, forming a coherent system" (*CW* 1:209; *Pl.* 1:930). Rousseau often refers to the plot or the conspiracy of the Gentlemen as a "system." In his system, Jean-Jacques "portrayed himself truthfully" (*CW* 1:212; *Pl.* 1:934). The Gentlemen's system is also a system of portrayal of Jean-Jacques; they portrayed him "as he was" (*CW* 1:38; *Pl.* 1:708). Jean-Jacques gave expression to his system by telling his story. For the Gentlemen to express their system, they too did it "by telling his story" (*CW* 1:38–39; *Pl.* 1:709). Jean-Jacques' system is the work of "the effervescence of a genius." The enterprise of the Gentlemen was also conceived by a "genius" (*CW* 1:37; *Pl.* 1:706). The system of Jean-Jacques is the system of one man, isolated, meditating in solitude. At several points in the *Dialogues*, Rousseau indicates that even though he sees it as a conspiracy, the plot has a single author (*CW* 1:54, 230; *Pl.* 1:729, 956) who has not only constructed a system from the conspiracy, but has also "meditated [on it] for a long time" (*CW* 1:206; *Pl.* 1:927).

Both systems demand that ordinary forms of judgment be suspended. The Frenchman defends the suspension of the normal rules of justice with regard to Jean-Jacques, because the "ordinary forms" are not necessary when the offense has been well proven (*CW* 1:38; *Pl.* 1:708). Rousseau does not accept this, but he does argue that since Jean-Jacques is in such a singular position, "the ordinary forms on which human judgments are established can no longer be adequate for making sound judgments concerning the person in this position and every that relates to him" (*CW* 1:81; *Pl.* 1:765). Given that there is a conspiracy, it is not enough to be sure that the ordinary forms are followed: "it is not enough to follow the ordinary rules in judging the proofs [the conspiracy] advances" (*CW* 1:83; *Pl.* 1:767).

I have highlighted these points of commonality between the system of Jean-Jacques and the system of the Gentlemen because they are not fortuitous. Rather, they are related as "doubles." I will now show that the common root of these opposed yet united systems is scandal.

Scandal

The "First Dialogue" opens *in medias res*. Rousseau has just learned from the Frenchman some "incredible things" concerning Jean-Jacques (*CW* 1:8; *Pl.* 1:667). He is shocked to learn that Jean-Jacques is wicked. It could even be said that he is scandalized. The Frenchman has "portrayed" as a "soul of mire" an author whose writings "portray" virtue in all its beauty and charms (*CW* 1:8; *Pl.* 1:667). It is this juxtaposition that so confounds Rousseau. In fact, the question becomes metaphysical: can such a being—"one who can coldly contemplate virtue . . . [and] . . . its most touching charms without being moved by them" (*CW* 1:8; *Pl.* 1:668)—exist? For Rousseau, it is simply impossible. Very quickly, he reaches the position that there are two different persons being spoken about—the author of the works and the author of the crimes. For the Frenchman, fact proves possibility. The scoundrel does exist and is the object of the Gentlemen's attention—and indeed, surprisingly, of their solicitude.

At the beginning of the *Dialogues*, the Frenchman, while not being one of the Gentlemen, is certainly sympathetic to them and convinced that they are doing the right thing. According to the Frenchman, the Gentlemen are friends of Jean-Jacques who have been seduced "by a decent and simple exterior, by a temperament thought then to be easygoing and sweet" (*CW* 1:32; *Pl.* 1:701). From the start, he admits that what drives the Gentlemen is rivalry. It is only when they see Jean-Jacques "rising to a reputation that they could not reach" that they become suspicious of his "apparent simplicity" and see instead a "veil hiding some dangerous project" (*CW* 1:33; *Pl.* 1:701). What they find is that "this great preacher of virtue was only a monster laden with hidden crimes, who for forty years masked the soul of a scoundrel beneath the exterior of a decent man" (*CW* 1:33; *Pl.* 1:701–2). In short, they are scandalized at his hypocrisy. This is "classic" scandal in the sense that someone who is expected to be, and who claims to be, virtuous is found instead to be debauched.

Following this discovery, the Gentlemen enter an unusual path. They do not want to let evil continue, but they do not want to have Jean-Jacques publicly tried and punished. "After having had the misfortune to live intimately with this scoundrel, they could not deliver him over to public prosecution without exposing themselves to some blame" (*CW* 1:34; *Pl.* 1:702). But most of all, the Gentlemen want "to avoid scandal" (*CW* 1:34; *Pl.* 1:702). This is their primary justification for acting the way they do. In fact, the Frenchman describes the scandal as the cause of the way their system operates as follows: "I see that the basis of the system they follow with regard to him is the duty they assumed to unmask him thoroughly, to make him well known to all and yet never make any explanation to him, to deprive him of any knowledge of his accusers, and of any clear enlightenment about the things of which he is accused. This double necessity is based on the nature of the crimes, whose public declaration would be too scandalous, and which does not allow that he be convicted without being punished" (*CW* 1:50; *Pl.* 1:724). Thus, he is able to see this all as a "system of beneficence toward a scoundrel" (*CW* 1:92; *Pl.* 1:781).

FORGIVENESS

In order to avoid scandal, the Gentlemen "pardon" Jean-Jacques. That is, they do not prosecute him publicly for his crimes. At first, Rousseau can accept that in "wishing to spare a scoundrel the treatment he deserved," the Gentlemen find it necessary to "take extraordinary precautions to prevent a scandal about this indulgence and place it at such a high price that others would not be tempted to desire such indulgence nor would they be tempted to take advantage of it" (CW 1:54; Pl. 1:730). But in the end, Rousseau himself uses the avoidance of scandal as one of the main reasons for demanding that the Gentlemen abandon their way of proceeding and directly confront Jean-Jacques. This confrontation would be the best way to punish him and would prevent "two big scandals"—namely, "that of the publication of the crimes and that of their impunity" (CW 1:71; Pl. 1:751). He continues, "However, your Gentlemen allege as the reason for their fraudulent procedures the concern to avoid scandal. But if scandal consists essentially in publicity, I don't see what scandal is avoided by hiding the crime from the guilty person who cannot be ignorant of it and by divulging it to all other men, who know nothing of it. The aura of mystery and reserve given to this publicity only serves to accelerate it" (CW 1:71; Pl. 1:751–52). Rousseau's proposal for avoiding the "double scandal of the crimes and their impunity" is a confrontation between the accused and the accusers.[12] Indeed, this would prevent an even greater scandal: "This would have prevented the scandal of a maxim as deadly as it is foolish, that your Gentlemen seem to want to establish through his example, namely that provided one has wit and writes fine books, one can commit all sorts of crimes with impunity" (CW 1:72; Pl. 1:753).

The talk of pardon and clemency, allegedly meant to prevent scandal, ends up scandalizing the character Rousseau. Once he has grasped it in all its implications, the Gentlemen's system "shocks" Rousseau (CW 1:61; Pl. 1:739). He sees that in their system, the "first and holiest of the social laws"—the right of the accused to face his accusers—has been openly violated (CW 1:58; Pl. 1:735). This form is sacred, and the sacred is being profaned by this system for "the first time since the world began" (CW 1:58; Pl. 1:735). It inspires horror in Rousseau because its principles "reverse all principles of justice and morality" (CW 1:75; Pl. 1:756). The right to pardon, according to Rousseau, is based on the right to punish, and that, in turn, is based on the prior conviction of the criminal. Absent the conviction, all this talk of pardon is "deceptive and false" (CW 1:65; Pl. 1:743). Indeed, "an innocent person who deserves no punishment needs no pardon" (CW 1:65; Pl. 1:743). Further, and in this case, just as important, is the actual nature of the pardon: "It consists of dragging the one who receives it from disgrace to disgrace and from misery to misery without leaving him any possible means to protect himself" (CW 1:65; Pl. 1:743). This is "torture," according to Rousseau (CW 1:65; Pl. 1:743).

What I wish to emphasize here is neither the objective historical behavior of those who opposed Rousseau nor his psychological state, but rather the logic of his position as he struggles to interpret the way that others are treating him. The others, he says, are claiming to be kind, to be beneficent, in pardoning Jean-Jacques for his crimes—"crimes," we find out in the "Third Dialogue," that Rousseau acknowledges and admits that Jean-Jacques knew others would find unpardonable.[13] In fact,

Jean-Jacques is the new stumbling block, the new scandal. The author interprets their reaction to the "unpardonable crimes" of this scandalous man precisely as a pardon, a pardon that is itself a crime and a form of torture—pardon as persecution.

This pardon is not a side issue. It is at the heart of the Gentlemen's system. For Rousseau, this system is "nothing but a refinement of cruelty to crush an unfortunate with miseries worse than death, to give the blackest treachery a look of generosity, and to charge with ingratitude the person they defame because he is not imbued with gratitude for the troubles they take to overwhelm him and deliver him defenseless into the hands of the cowardly murderers who stab him without risk while hiding from his view" (*CW* 1:66; *Pl.* 1:745). This characterization of the Gentlemen's behavior is an expression of Rousseau's scandal. He can interpret their behavior as a pardon only when the pardon is interpreted as a theft. There must be a cause for this behavior. Here emerges the deepest secret that Jean-Jacques has been able to uncover. The ultimate cause of the pardon is the Gentlemen's refusal to forgive Jean-Jacques: "I discern in all this the secret cause that unleashed the fury of the authors of the plot. The route J.J. had taken was too contrary to their own for them to forgive him for providing an example they didn't wish to follow and for generating comparisons that were uncomfortable for them to endure" (*CW* 1:173; *Pl.* 1:883). While the fundamental cause of the conspiracy is their inability to forgive, it is not as if Jean-Jacques did anything that needed forgiving. Rather, the plotters hate him because he has gone down a road they do not wish to tread, and in so doing, he has taken some of their glory away from them. In a word, they are jealous of their rival.

The Gentlemen hate Jean-Jacques for a reason—his adoption of principles opposite to their own. These principles confer a sense of superiority on him over them: "They could not forgive him for not twisting his morality to his own benefit as they do" (*CW* 1:175; *Pl.* 1:886). The Gentlemen hate him because otherwise they would have to admit that they are wrong.

The inability to forgive Jean-Jacques is the secret principle of the Gentlemen's system. Rousseau spends a fair deal of time developing the argument that their hatred is not directed at any perceived evil, but rather at his person. The hatred results in this inability to forgive. Clearly, it is not a refusal to forgive any sin of Jean-Jacques; rather, the Gentlemen will not forgive him for his being—for being who he is insofar as that being reminds them of their own wrongdoing. Even if it is true that this particular clique of people hate Jean-Jacques, this does not explain the hatred of the general public toward him. This too has to be explained.

THE TWO WORLDS

With Jean-Jacques on one side and "everyone" else on the other side, it is no surprise that the world of the *Dialogues* is divided. At the very beginning of the "First Dialogue," Rousseau asks the Frenchman to "picture (*Figurez-vous*) an ideal world" (*CW* 1:9; *Pl.* 1:668). The main difference of this world, which is "similar to ours, yet altogether different," is that its inhabitants "have the good fortune to be maintained by nature, to which they are more attached, in that happy perspective in which nature placed us all, and because of this alone their soul forever maintains its original character" (*CW* 1:9; *Pl.* 1:669).[14] These "superlunary beings" aspire to a heavenly state(*CW* 1:22; *Pl.* 1:686). The obstacles they encounter can never become their obsession. Since these "great and strong souls" are able to better preserve the "gentle, primitive passions born directly from love of self," they do not become entangled in those passions that "tear apart unhappy human beings" (*CW* 1:10; *Pl.* 1:670). The denizens of this other world are "bounded on all sides by nature and reason" (*CW* 1:11; *Pl.* 1:672).

This world serves as a background to the portrait that Rousseau sketches of Jean-Jacques, for Jean-Jacques is an inhabitant of this ideal world, as is Rousseau. Inhabitants of the ideal world express themselves differently from ordinary people. Rousseau explains:

> It is impossible that with souls so differently modified, they should not carry over into the expression of their feelings and ideas the stamp of those modifications. If this stamp is not noticed by those who have no notion of that manner of being, it cannot escape the notice of those who know it and are themselves affected by it. It is a characteristic sign, . . . and what gives great value to a sign so little known and even less used is that it cannot be counterfeit, it can never act except at the level of its source. (*CW* 1:12; *Pl.* 1:672)

This sort of communication serves to stress the divide between those who are members of this world and those who are not. A sign, which cannot be counterfeited, is a sort of shibboleth by which one knows one's own. As Rousseau explains it, "this distinction makes itself felt equally in writings" (*CW* 1:12; *Pl.* 1:672). It is only much later in the "Second Dialogue" that Rousseau speaks explicitly about Jean-Jacques' writings, such that "those who occupy our ethereal regions joyfully recognized one of their own" (*CW* 1:131; *Pl.* 1:829).

Set over against the ethereal regions is the underground. Note that Rousseau begins his following description of the underground with the same verb that he used in his description of the ethereal region quoted above:

> Picture (*Figurez-vous*) people who start by each putting on a well-attached mask, who arm themselves to the teeth with swords, who then take their enemy by surprise, grab him from behind, strip him naked, tie up his body, his arms, his hands, his feet, his head so he cannot move, put a gag in his mouth; poke out his eyes, stretch him on the ground, and finally spend their noble lives massacring him slowly for fear that if he dies of his wounds, he will stop feeling pain too soon. (*CW* 1:75; *Pl.* 1:756)

The underground is the Gentlemen's "system." It is described as having "triple walls of darkness" (*CW* 1:196; *Pl.* 1:913). Their ways are "obscure" and impossible to follow. Rousseau believes that he has perceived "an occasional air vent in one spot or another above these tunnels which may indicate their windings" (*CW* 1:173; *Pl.* 1:884). These "caverns of misfortune" into which Jean-Jacques has been thrown have existed for many years.

The distinction between the ethereal realms and the underground seems complete, yet Jean-Jacques inhabits both. His state is to be "in the midst of his afflictions and his fictions" (*CW* 1:119; *Pl.* 1:815). Jean-Jacques' underground existence is such that he lives "surrounded by lies and darkness, waiting without murmur for light and truth; buried alive in a coffin, [he] remain[s] rather still without even invoking death" (*CW* 1:129; *Pl.* 1:827). Clearly, this is a fictional description, as is the depiction of the underground. The underground is as much a product of Rousseau's imagination as is the ideal world that he paints for the reader.

In fact, it is only when he is in the underground that he "soars to the highest heaven, surrounded by charming and almost angelic objects (*CW* 1:153–54; *Pl.* 1:858). He does this through his "reveries," and of these, Rousseau tells the Frenchman, "of all the keys to his character, this is the one that best reveals its mechanical parts" (*CW* 1:152–53; *Pl.* 1:857). For in his reveries, Jean-Jacques' "beneficent imagination" is able to reach its goal, to reach the objects that he covets, "by leaping over obstacles that stop or frighten him" (*CW* 1:153; *Pl.* 1:857). Even more than that, his imagination removes everything in the object that might make it less desirable for him, and it presents it to him "as suited to his desire in all respects" (*CW* 1:153; *Pl.* 1:857). In this way, desiring and enjoying become one. At the same time, in a completely opposite way, his desire is enough to make the desired object disappear in his underground existence.

The imaginary goods of the reveries are worth more than those that "really exist." Rousseau will admit that the latter are "more real," but they are also "less desirable" (*CW* 1:153; *Pl.* 1:858). This is Jean-Jacques' defense against the plot of the Gentlemen. They may succeed in taking away the goods of this life, but imagination returns them to him. Indeed, "only he is securely happy, because . . . nothing can take those of the imagination away from whoever knows how to enjoy them. He possesses them without risk and without fear" (*CW* 1:119; *Pl.* 1:814).

The difference between the ethereal realms and the underground is clear. In the ethereal realms, there are no obstacles. There is nothing to trip Jean-Jacques. He follows his desires, and they lead instantaneously to their objects, which he enjoys without regret. In the underground, everything is an obstacle. His desire is the assurance that he will not be satisfied. But the place where these two different realms meet is Jean-Jacques himself. On the one hand, he is "the human being least destined for hatred, who never had either the interest or desire to harm another, who never either did, wished, or rendered harm to anyone; who, without jealousy, without competitiveness, without aspiration, and always keeping to himself, was not an obstacle to anyone else" (*CW* 1:173; *Pl.* 1:883). On the other hand, he is the one whom the Gentlemen cannot forgive, and from that comes the whole of the underground.

THE OPPOSITION BETWEEN EVERYONE AND JEAN-JACQUES

Although the Gentlemen's inability to forgive is the manifestation of their hatred, Jean-Jacques' inability to forgive is not to be interpreted in this way. Jean-Jacques is, according to Rousseau, "unacquainted with hatred" (*CW* 1:148; *Pl.* 1:851). Rousseau acknowledges that the "most sublime of virtues, that which requires the most greatness, courage, and strength of soul is the pardon of wrongs and the love of one's enemies" (*CW* 1:154; *Pl.* 1:859). He also acknowledges that Jean-Jacques, who has only "mediocre virtue," does not attain that level(*CW* 1:154; *Pl.* 1:859). But then again, he is certain that Jean-Jacques does not need this virtue: "He does not have the merit of forgiving offenses, because he forgets them. He doesn't love his enemies, but he doesn't think about them" (*CW* 1:154; *Pl.* 1:859).

In spite of this lack of love, Jean-Jacques is a sort of mirror image of Christ. He, too, is the innocent victim of persecution, but the persecution is the cause of his innocence. It is the offer of happiness, of a better life, and of salvation that Jean-Jacques makes, not just through his teachings, but also through his person that causes the jealousy and hatred of his rivals. His teaching is based on his person, and this is why the notion of self-portrayal is so important. In fact, the person of Jean-Jacques serves a kind of decisive, apocalyptic function as follows: "He is everything to himself; he is also everything to them. For as for them, they are nothing either to him or to themselves; and as long as J.J. is miserable, they need no other happiness. Thus, he and they, each from his own vantage point, have two great experiments to make; they, to heap all the hardship conceivable to man on the soul of an innocent man, and he, to use all the resources that innocence can draw from itself alone to endure them" (*CW* 1:155; *Pl.* 1:860).

According to Jean-Jacques himself, in one of the few places that Rousseau, the character, quotes him directly, it would be "too great a misfortune for the human race," if the way that he has been treated were allowed to become a "model and an example" (*CW* 1:228; *Pl.* 1:953). Were this to happen, he foresees the following result: "Good people, thrown entirely to the wicked, would at first become their prey and finally their disciples. Innocence would no longer have a refuge, and the earth, having become a hell, would be covered only with Demons busy tormenting each other. No, Heaven will not allow such a fatal example to open a new path, unknown until now, to crime" (*CW* 1:228; *Pl.* 1:953–54). Jean-Jacques is the figure that has determined his generation's destiny: "Take away this one object of passion that carries them away, in all other respects they are decent people like everyone else" (*CW* 1:171; *Pl.* 1:881).

In the end, Rousseau's vision is apocalyptic. The Gentlemen have spread their "doctrine of materialism and Atheism" in conjunction with their plot against Jean-Jacques (*CW* 1:239; *Pl.* 1:968). The purpose of this doctrine is to ensure no late repentance when faced with death. The lack of a "Poul-Serrho of the Persians," that is, of a "dogma of the reestablishment of the moral order in the next life used to redress many wrongs in this one," means an increase in fanaticism pushed on by "fearless and shameless libertinage" (*CW* 1:239; *Pl.* 1:968). As discipline, morals, faith, law, and duties of conscience get destroyed, the results are not difficult to foresee: "Europe prey to masters taught by their own teachers to have no other guide than their interest nor any God besides their passions, at times secretly starved, at times openly devastated, inundated everywhere with soldiers, Actors, prostitutes, corrupting books and destructive vices, seeing races unworthy to live be born and perish in its bosom, will sooner or later feel that these calamities are the fruit of the new teachings" (*CW* 1:242; *Pl.* 1:971–72). The fate of Jean-Jacques Rousseau occupies a central place in the history of Europe. What makes this claim credible and gives it power is the analogous claim that Christianity makes for the person of Christ.

At several points in the course of the give-and-take between Rousseau and the Frenchman, the discussion reaches the dilemma that either everyone is right and Rousseau is wrong, or Rousseau is right and everyone else is wrong. Rousseau's first attempt at answering this dilemma is to point to the power of a conspiracy. It seems that everyone assumes that Jean-Jacques is a criminal, but there never has been a trial. This is the result of the conspiracy. Here is how the conspirators might operate:

> Who has determined the extent to which powerful, numerous conspirators, unified as they always are for crime, can fascinate the eyes, when people who are not believed to know one another are planning well together; when at opposite ends of Europe, intelligent imposters led by some clever and powerful plotter, will behave according to the same plan, speak the same language, present an identical picture of a man who has been deprived of his voice, his eyes, his hands and who is delivered bound hand and foot to the mercy of this enemies. (*CW* 1:83; *Pl.* 1:767)

The public is easy to fool and falls into error when the singularity of a man "shocks its amour-propre" (*CW* 1:84; *Pl.* 1:768). Still, Rousseau is sensitive to the Frenchman's criticism that his position seems absurd. The Frenchman objects: "You justify a single man whose condemnation displeases you at the expense of a whole Nation, or, what am I saying, of a whole generation which you make into a generation of scoundrels," a generation without a single "friend of truth" (*CW* 1:77; *Pl.* 1:759).[15]

On the other hand, from Rousseau's viewpoint, the Frenchman's explanation seems to presume that an entire generation is angelic, cooperating in a great venture out of virtue, beneficence, and charity for an evil Jean-Jacques. As we shall see, Rousseau believes that the solution has to be found in "some middle ground," in "some disposition natural to the human heart" (*CW* 1:78; *Pl.* 1:760).

According to Rousseau, the Jean-Jacques that the Gentlemen have "fabricated" is "a being such as never existed, a monster beyond nature, beyond probability, beyond possibility and made up of dissociated, incompatible parts that are mutually exclusive" (*CW* 1:74; *Pl.* 1:755). For Rousseau, it is the Gentlemen, who make "this unfortunate man the plaything of the public, the laughingstock of the rabble, the horror of the universe," and who are the monsters (*CW* 1:65; *Pl.* 1:743).

According to the Frenchman, it would be extraordinary for so many people to be so mistaken, especially when, if one listens to Rousseau, one need only open one's eyes and have a bit of decency to see Jean-Jacques' innocence. The opposition between Jean-Jacques and the public, which the story is about, gets replicated in the story itself as the opposition between Rousseau and everyone else. This is how the Frenchman presents it:

> What? An entire generation agrees to calumny an innocent man, heap mud on him, to suffocate him, so to speak, in a quagmire of defamation? Whereas all that is necessary, according to you, is to open one's eyes and look at him to be convinced of his innocence and of the blackness of his enemies? . . . If J.-J. were as you saw him, would it be possible for you to be the first and only person to have seen him in that light? Are you really the only just and sensible man left on earth? If there is another one left who doesn't think as you do about this, all your observations are annihilated, and you stand alone charged with the accusation you bring against everyone: that you saw only what you

desired to see and not what was really there. Answer this one objection, but respond correctly [*juste*] and I will yield on everything else. (*CW* 1:169; *Pl.* 1:878)

Before we look at Rousseau's response, which is a most uncharacteristic response, it is necessary to reflect on the logic of what the Frenchman has said. Either Rousseau is right and Jean-Jacques is innocent, thus convicting a whole generation, or Rousseau is wrong, thus convicting Jean-Jacques and vindicating his contemporaries. The rightness of one side implies the condemnation of the other. Further, all that is needed is to find "*une autre*," just one other, to declare with the same justice and sincerity as Rousseau that Jean-Jacques is evil. Rousseau would then stand condemned by his own accusations.

Rousseau's response as follows is remarkable: "I begin by declaring that this one objection to which you summon me to respond is, in my view, an abyss of darkness in which my understanding loses itself. Jean-Jacques himself understands no more than I do" (*CW* 1:169; *Pl.* 1:878). Up until this point, it was the conspiracy itself that was characterized as an abyss in which Jean-Jacques was kept imprisoned in darkness. Rousseau does not intend this simply to mean that part of the conspiracy is to hide that there is a conspiracy. More profoundly, Rousseau, the author, is confessing here to his loss of the "good of intellect."[16] He no longer knows if there is one other person besides himself who is just. The abyss is the abyss of understanding "*une autre*." Jean-Jacques' attempt to interpret the behavior of others ends in an abyss of darkness. He is lost.

This abyss of darkness has metaphysical implications for the others. Jean-Jacques is no longer capable of seeing his contemporaries as human beings: "He sees in it [the entire generation] neither good people, nor bad people, nor humans. He sees beings about whom he has no ideas. He doesn't honor them, nor does he despise them or have a conception of them. He doesn't know what it is" (*CW* 1:169; *Pl.* 1:878).

Rousseau then concedes that if the Frenchman's assent to the results of his research depends on the solution of his single objection, no agreement is possible. Since the solution to the problem the Frenchman posed is impossible, Rousseau adopts an epistemological stance concerning matters of faith that will come to the fore again in the "Profession of Faith of the Savoyard Vicar." Rousseau says, "I yield to direct conviction without stopping at the objections I cannot resolve" (*CW* 1:170; *Pl.* 1:879).

Having made these concessions, Rousseau does make an attempt not to resolve the difficulties but to explain their possibility. The principal difficulty is "the unanimous collaboration of the entire current generation in a plot of imposture and iniquity against which it would be either too harmful to the human race to assume that not one human being would protest against it if he saw its injustice, or—given how obvious this injustice seems to me—too proud of me and too humiliating for common sense to believe that this is not perceived by anyone else" (*CW* 1:170; *Pl.* 1:880). Rousseau's answer is that there are "epidemics of the mind," a kind of contagion, whereby people simply think the way others do. The source of the contagion is the hatred of the Gentlemen and their inability to forgive Jean-Jacques for being better than they are.

THE FRENCHMAN'S CONVERSION

Jean-Jacques is the victim of others' hatred and jealousy. He becomes the scapegoat of this group. At its root, the hatred of the Gentlemen is mirrored in the abhorrence that the Frenchman has for Jean-Jacques. He, too, cannot forgive Jean-Jacques for his own sin. But with the Frenchman, the outcome is different. The Gentlemen proclaim virtue and cannot forgive Jean-Jacques for actually living it without any self-interest. The Frenchman's sin is an injustice against Jean-Jacques in that he has defamed Jean-Jacques. The text explicitly raises the question of whether the Frenchman and Jean-Jacques will ever be reconciled. This is the question that Rousseau proposed to the Frenchman toward the end of the "First Dialogue":

> Rousseau
> Assuming for a moment that after attentive and impartial research, rather than the infernal monster you now see in J.J., he turned out on the contrary to be a simple, sensitive, and good man, whose innocence—universally recognized by the very people who treat him with such indignity—forced you to give him back your esteem and to reproach yourself for the harsh judgments you made of him. Look deep in your heart and tell me how you would be affected by this change.

> The Frenchman
> Cruelly, you can be sure. I feel that while respecting him and doing him justice, I would then hate him more, perhaps, for my errors than I hate him now for his crimes. I will never forgive him for my injustice toward him. (*CW* 1:78–79; *Pl.* 1:761)

In the phrase, *"I will never forgive him for my injustice toward him,"* Rousseau, the author, expresses not only an incisive psychological fact, but also a profound theological mystery. In the presence of someone who has wronged a person, that person's heart can harden. This is yet another manifestation of scandal.

How did this feeling arise in the heart of the Frenchman? According to Rousseau, it came about when the hatred the Frenchman rightly felt toward the depiction of Jean-Jacques and his vices got transferred to the person of Jean-Jacques himself. In other words, it is one thing for the Frenchman to hate the vices of the scoundrel, whose portrait was presented to him, but to let it be carried further, not through any judgment but rather through an impetuous passion that dominated him without his knowing it, is something else (*CW* 1:171; *Pl.* 1:881).

Rousseau explains that the "active, ardent, tireless" hatred of Jean-Jacques is "not the hatred of vice and wickedness, but hatred of the individual himself" (*CW* 1:175; *Pl.* 1:885). He sees that it does not matter if Jean-Jacques is good or evil, because his acts will always be interpreted to reflect badly on him. These ways of the conspiracy are "underground."

Rousseau knows that this hatred, this animosity, is the disposition of this generation toward Jean-Jacques by the "look that is given him when he walks through the streets" (*CW* 1:171; *Pl.* 1:881). "All the signs of hatred, of scorn, even of rage that can tacitly be shown to a man without accompanying them with an open and direct insult are showered on him from all quarters" (*CW* 1:172; *Pl.* 1:882). The signs of hatred are tacit; they need to be interpreted. Rousseau and Jean-Jacques can understand what they signify, but not why they signify it. The interpretation is constitutive of the experience, and it is the experience of being in the abyss. There is no "open and direct insult" that might somehow have escaped the need to be interpreted.

The only possible explanation for this behavior on the part of the public is provided by the Frenchman's honest response that Jean-Jacques is not forgiven for the sin that the other has committed against him. Rousseau sees that the "recognition of his innocence would serve only to make him more odious, and to transform the animosity of which he is the object into rage" (*CW* 1:175; *Pl.* 1:885). He goes on to say, "he is not forgiven now for shaking off the heavy yoke everyone wants to place on him; he would be forgiven even less for wrongs about which they would reproach themselves, and since you yourself have briefly experienced such an unjust feeling, would these people, so imbued with amour-propre endure without bitterness their own baseness compared to his patience and gentleness?" (*CW* 1:175; *Pl.* 1:885–86). Jean Jacques' patience, his gentleness, makes him the victim of the public's hatred.

The Frenchman is scandalized at Jean-Jacques' crimes at the beginning of the work, but this scandal takes on different meaning as he goes through the process of conversion. At the beginning of the "Third Dialogue," he is scandalized by the attacks that Jean-Jacques has made on all the stations of society. The Frenchman calls them, with irony, of course, but also with recognition of the truth, "unpardonable crimes" (*CW* 1:205; *Pl.* 1:925). They are unpardonable not so much because of the gravity of the charges, but more so because the Frenchman knows that the parties offended will not pardon Jean-Jacques.

This leads to more scandal. The Frenchman is scandalized now by the falseness and duplicity of the Gentlemen. In all of his dealings with them concerning Jean-Jacques, they never reveal to him that they are the object of some of Jean-Jacques' criticism. They never reveal that they would have a motive for persecuting him. But since he accepts Rousseau's thesis from the "First Dialogue" that the author of these books is not Jean-Jacques, this only means that the fate of Jean-Jacques is that "one wicked man [is] prey to other wicked men" (*CW* 1:209; *Pl.* 1:929).

So the Frenchman begins to read more and finds "things that were profoundly thought out, forming a coherent system, which might not be true but which offered nothing contradictory" (*CW* 1:209; *Pl.* 1:930). His method for judging the "true good" of the writings is to consult the "dispositions of soul into which they placed and left" him (*CW* 1:209; *Pl.* 1:930). In this way he believes he can penetrate the disposition of the author when he wrote them. He finds "only a doctrine that was as healthy as it was simple . . . directed only to the happiness of the human race" (*CW* 1:209; *Pl.* 1:930).

The Frenchman has esteem now for the author, but he still has aversion for Jean-Jacques, the supposed author of the crimes. The author of these works seems to have a totally different character from the one he believed Jean-Jacques to have. This leads the Frenchman into a crisis. Given that he can no longer esteem the Gentlemen, does this mean that he is to esteem no one in the world? He feels the "wish" (*désir*) grow in him that Jean-Jacques not be wicked (*CW* 1:210; *Pl.* 1:931). This desire is mediated to him by Rousseau. It is the seed from which all else grows. Having lost faith in the Gentlemen, he is open to the story that Rousseau tells him. He begins to acquaint himself with the idea that seemed so "ridiculous: that J.J. was innocent and perse-cuted" (*CW* 1:210; *Pl.* 1:932).

The Frenchman reaches this stage of reflection after listening to Rousseau's "sketch" of Jean-Jacques in the "Second Dialogue." Between the "Second Dialogue" and the "Third Dialogue," the Frenchman goes to the countryside in order to reread Jean-Jacques' writings "with more consistency and attention that [he] had to that point" (*CW* 1:211; *Pl.* 1:932). He meditates on his words and "carefully compare[s] the Author with the man whom you [Rousseau] had portrayed" (*CW* 1:211; *Pl.* 1:932). He believes that each of the two objects can shed light on the other, and in this way, he will be able to tell if they fit together in such a way that everything belongs to one individual. The Frenchman's reflections follow a specific order here that mirrors Rousseau's order in the story, and follows the order that the author set for himself. First, one has to judge Jean-Jacques' accusers to be false. Only then is one ready to judge Jean-Jacques himself. When Rousseau reports that Jean-Jacques is "attending once again to his destiny and to his persecutors," he says that he "wrote a kind of judgment of them and of himself in the form of a Dialogue" (*CW* 1:136; *Pl.* 1:836). Accordingly, the Frenchman feels that by combining his own reading with the enlightenment he has gotten from Rousseau, he will be able to "judge the accused man for [him]self after having judged his accusers" (*CW* 1:211; *Pl.* 1:932).

The Frenchman has been unjust to Jean-Jacques. He has believed that Jean-Jacques is a base scoundrel and he has helped spread this belief, particularly to Rousseau. According to the Frenchman, the way things have developed is an advan-tage, perhaps a "happy fault." Jean-Jacques now has the "additional honor" of having wrested his esteem "without benefit of any help from [the Frenchman's] inclinations" (*CW* 1:214; *Pl.* 1:937). The Frenchman may never love Jean-Jacques, because love is something a person can neither control nor predict. He honors Jean-Jacques on account of justice. But what about the evil he has done to Jean-Jacques? "The wrong I did him by thinking so ill of him was the effect of an almost invincible error for which I cannot in any way reproach my will. Even if my aversion had remained in full strength, I would be no less disposed to esteem and pity him" (*CW* 1:214–15; *Pl.* 1:937). "Invincible error" is a theological term for an error that is not the fault of the person in error and that that person could not reasonably be expected to correct. Evil done out of invincible error is not imputed to the person as a sin.

The Frenchman needs no forgiveness, either from God or from Jean-Jacques. He can now be reconciled with Jean-Jacques. And true to his statement in the "First Dialogue," he does not forgive Jean-Jacques for his own injustices, either. Rather, they increase the value of the esteem that he is now to bestow. The logic in the text is foundational. It is only in judging Rousseau's enemies to be evil and in understanding that one does not need forgiveness that one can grasp the principle of natural good-ness. The principle of natural goodness is not a starting point; it is something one reaches at the end of a very long dialogue with Rousseau. It is dependent on the fact that Rousseau cannot forgive others and that he himself is not forgiven. Within the space opened up by this reality, the space that is at one and the same time the ethereal regions and the underground, the principle of natural goodness reigns supreme.

This study will now follow the route laid out by Rousseau through the character of the Frenchman. First, *Emile* will be analyzed in order to let the first principles of Rousseau's system emerge. After this, the two *Discourses* are examined in order to grasp the "system in all its ramifications," and then compare this system to the portrait of Rousseau in the autobiographical writings—the *Confessions* and the *Reveries of a Solitary Walker* (*CW* 1:213; *Pl.* 1:935).

PART II

EMILE

CHAPTER 3

THE FORMING OF EMILE

THE HUMAN AS VICTIM

The late Judith Shklar ends her outstanding study of Jean-Jacques Rousseau's political thought with this reflection upon the ending of *Emile*: "The happy ending of *Emile* is false, especially to the tone of its opening pages, so full of dark foreboding. It is man, not the situation, that is being remade, and Emile's character cannot reveal itself until he really becomes a man, that is, a suffering victim."[1] According to Shklar, the book's true conclusion is contained in its unfinished sequel, *Les Solitaires*,[2] which tells the tale of Sophie's unfaithfulness and Emile's resulting exile, capture, and slavery. I take up Shklar's suggestive comment to show that this vision of the human as suffering victim shapes the novel *Emile* and not simply its sequel.

In *Emile*, Rousseau establishes the place of the natural man in society and shows that this place is the place of the victim. Jean-Jacques, Emile's tutor, reveals this to him in the story, and Rousseau reveals it to the reader throughout the story. But this revelation is accomplished only at a price. Emile is not allowed to see himself as a victim without also seeing himself as a victimizer, and the same holds true that the reader will not be allowed to see him- or herself as a victim without first seeing him- or herself as a victimizer. Rousseau intended the book to be "the history of [his] species," but it becomes "a romance" because of the reader "who depraves it" (*Emile*, 416; *Pl.* 4:777).[3] Thus, it is not only the character Emile who gets victimized; the text that bears his name is not spared his fate, nor, for that matter, is the reader.

The next four chapters will examine how the tutor forms Emile into a victim. This chapter concentrates on the role that scandal plays in the examples that Rousseau uses to illustrate his educational theory. The next chapter looks at the way the scandal of the Gospel gets neutralized in the "Profession of Faith." Desire, its mediation, and the tragedy that results without that mediation will occupy Chapter 4. Finally, the summary of Rousseau's political philosophy, which Book V of *Emile* contains, will be examined in the light of everything that has come before it.

SENTIMENTS OF NATURE IN THE CIVIL ORDER

One of the great Rousseauian scholars, P. Burgelin, wrote the following in his study, "L'idée de place dans l'*Emile*": "Un homme est perdue, quand il n'a plus de place [A man is lost, when he no longer has a place."[4] The notion of place—of being in one's place, finding one's place, staying in one's place, and losing one's place—looms large in all of Rousseau's writings, but most especially in *Emile*. In fact, the whole goal of what Rousseau calls his "negative pedagogy" is precisely to keep the person in his original place and to never let him leave it. Negative education does not mean simply being passive. It is exactly the opposite of being "swept along in contrary routes by nature and by man" (*Emile*, 41; *Pl.* 4:251). Rather, it means to keep in one's place, not to move, and to resist the different forces that would attempt to dislodge one. The task of negative education seems simple—maintain the pupil in his pristine condition—and Rousseau often speaks this way. He urges caution for the young tutor, lest "your vessel drift without you knowing" (*Emile*, 41; *Pl.* 4:251).

However, the problem is deeper than that of simply maintaining a status quo. The human condition and the modern age have combined to make this holding still very difficult. To be born into the human condition means that a person's personal fortune or that of his family or nation may change, and this could have the effect of making the person change his place. But if his "place" is first, and foremost, being human rather than being a magistrate, soldier, or priest, then "he will always be in his own place," no matter what fortune might do (*Emile*, 42; *Pl.* 4:252).

The "mobility of human things" is not the only challenge that this education has to meet. There is also the "restless spirit of the age which upsets everything in each generation" (*Emile*, 42; *Pl.* 4:252). Even when everything around the pupil changes, he must always be able to orient himself. The problem with the usual form of education is that if the "pupil makes a single step on the earth, if he goes down a single degree, he is lost (*perdu*)" (*Emile*, 42; *Pl.* 4:253).

Two different but related sides of the problem emerge here. On the one hand, the pupil can lose his place in the civil order. But Rousseau uses the metaphor of place not only to indicate a stable location, but also to point to a person's place on the road of the march of nature. Thus, Rousseau is intent on helping the student find and stay in the place that nature has assigned him, but just as often, Rousseau uses the image, not of keeping in a place, but of keeping on a path or a way. In this metaphor, he sees himself as following the "movement natural to the human heart" (*Emile*, 51; *Pl.* 4:265). Since the movement along this path is natural, the education is still negative. One needs only to remove obstacles or prevent pernicious influences for the movement to take place.

This problem of place in *Emile* is not limited to the pupil. It is a problem for the author as well. Rousseau states that whoever "in the civil order wants to preserve the primacy of the sentiments of nature does not know what he wants" (*Emile*, 40; *Pl.* 4:249). Rousseau is the one who wants to preserve this primacy. The double object of being a man and being a citizen is the great tension that Rousseau has set out to resolve, yet the shape of that resolution is not clear to Rousseau. Insofar as we, the readers, want this, too, we share his ignorance. If one does not know what one wants, if one is not certain where one is going, then one is in great danger of getting lost. Rousseau is in this position, and he is worried about "getting lost."

That is why Rousseau makes the decision very early in the book to give himself an imaginary pupil. The first purpose of this methodological move is "to prevent an author who distrusts himself from getting lost in visions" (*Emile*, 51; *Pl.* 4:264). This should help to ensure the success of the project. He is concerned about making sure that the book is useful rather than it just being a "visionary's dreams about education" (*Emile*, 34; *Pl.* 4:242). Closely related to this, the figure of the pupil will help prevent not only the author but also the reader from getting lost, because the imaginary pupil is designed to serve as a sort of test case for the new practices in education that Rousseau will introduce. Thus, the reader will be able to sense whether or not the author follows the "movement natural to the human heart" (*Emile*, 51; *Pl.* 4:265). The very wealth of detail about how the tutor applies the practice to the pupil should ensure that the proposals can be put into practice. Such is the plan as Rousseau conceives it; it is up to the reader to judge if he has succeeded.

Of course, if an education whereby the sentiments of nature are conserved will issue a result that is, as yet, unknown, then the problem of judging this result becomes acute. If one does not know what one wants, how does one judge whether one has achieved it or missed the mark? Rousseau tells us that to be able to make this judgment, "the natural man would have to be known" (*Emile*, 41; *Pl.* 4:251). One will have to read the book *Emile*, a book comprised of "researches" into the inclinations, progress, and development of this natural man, in order to make him known (*Emile*, 41; *Pl.* 4:251). By following these various observations concerning the natural man, the reader will be able to get a view of the man "raised uniquely for himself" (*Emile*, 41; *Pl.* 4:251). The reader will at last be able to see the natural man "fully formed," then be able to judge whether in fact Rousseau has been able to remove the great obstacle to happiness: the double object of being both man and citizen that sets man in contradiction with himself. According to Rousseau, if this double object could be joined into a single one, then humans would, first of all, really *be*, and thus be able to be happy. At the very point that the project is completed, the reader will become able to judge that the project has been accomplished and no judgment is possible until then.

For the purposes of this interpretation, one aspect of this plan needs to be emphasized. By electing to give himself an imaginary pupil, Rousseau has given this book the character of a story rather than that of simply an "educational treatise." He knows of such treatises that are filled with "many fine precepts which are impossible to follow" (*Emile*, 50; *Pl.* 4:264). Thus, the examples that he uses are not merely peripheral. As Rousseau remarks, "Reader, spare me words. If you are made for understanding me, you will be quite able to follow my rules in my detailed examples" (*Emile*, 433; *Pl.* 4:802).

I understand this to mean that the production of a story by an author and its being read by a reader acts as a control on these researches and serves to verify their truthfulness. Although at the beginning of the writing and the reading, neither the author nor the reader knows what they want, they will come to know it in the course of the writing and reading. In this way, *Emile* is, then, not only a book on education, but also itself an education.[5] It educates the author and the reader by demanding certain acts of understanding in order to reach its goal. Just as the pupil, Emile, is the character of Jean-Jacques' pupil in the book, so, too, is the text, which bears the child's name, the author's progeny, and the reading of the text, like its writing, engenders a new consciousness in the reader.

EXAMPLES

What role do the examples in the book play? The answer to this question emerges in my examination of two of the examples in detail—the story of Emile and Robert, the gardener, and the story of Emile and the magician.

After looking briefly at how Rousseau gets started in this novel, I concentrate on these two key episodes because they help to demonstrate that *Emile* articulates its system by providing an account of the role of both the victim and the victimizer in scandalous situations. These stories represent the tutor, Jean-Jacques, as being both the victimizer of and the covictim with Emile. He both scandalizes and is scandalized. The tutor is not scandalized in the usual sense of the word, though, so that his perception of something scandalous induces him to give scandal to others. Rather, Jean-Jacques appears to be scandalized by his own scandal. This is possible because he operates in the story through a third party in order to occlude his involvement in the scandal from Emile and to be able to credibly pose as his fellow victim. This triangular relationship between tutor, pupil, and third party is designed to evoke a similar relationship between the author, Rousseau, and the text, *Emile*, with the third party now being the reader. Rousseau, the author, is, like Jean-Jacques in the novel, both victimizer and victim, using the reader to victimize his own text so that he may appear as its fellow victim.

There will be questions about my choice of episodes. Why do I privilege these episodes and leave out other important stories, like the one of the young Rousseau going in the dark to the temple to fetch the Bible? There are five reasons for this. First, Rousseau himself tells us that these two particular examples or models are important.[6] In each case, Rousseau alerts the reader to pay special attention. Second, in contrast to this, in those cases in which the examples concern the historical Jean-Jacques, such as the incident with the Bible and, perhaps, the "Profession of Faith," Rousseau specifically tells the reader that these are not being proposed as models.[7] Third, while it is not clear whether both of these examples concern Emile, the pupil of Jean-Jacques, Rousseau does refer to the character in the story as "Emile."[8] Thus, there is greater cause for drawing a connection between what forms the child Emile and what forms the text that bears his name. Fourth, these two examples are referred to again in other parts of the book, thus underlining their importance.[9] These references show these episodes to be foundational in forming Emile, and so, I wish to argue, they are foundational in the way the book forms the reader. Finally, both stories have exactly the same structure. I believe this structure is fundamental to an understanding of Rousseau's purpose in *Emile*.

AN ANALYSIS OF THE MODELS

In order to understand how the two episodes function in an exemplary manner in the book, some background is needed. The moral world for Rousseau is the world of human relations, the world in which the will of one person becomes pitted against another.[10] Rousseau will delay this point as much as possible by making sure that the child feels only dependence upon things. Dependence itself is not bad; in fact, it is necessary that the child be dependent in the right way: "There are two sorts of dependence: dependence on things, which is from nature; dependence on men, which is from society. Dependence on things, since it has no morality, is in no way detrimental to freedom and engenders no vices. Dependence on men, since it is without order, engenders all the vices, and by it, master and slave are mutually corrupted" (*Emile*, 85; *Pl.* 4:311). Dependence upon men is without order; being without order is to be lost. Rousseau gives very precise descriptions of how this comes about. Human relations make us practice foresight in an attempt to overcome the lack of order in human affairs rather than practicing the resignation that the natural order instills. This foresight takes us "ceaselessly beyond ourselves and often places us where we shall never arrive" (*Emile*, 82; *Pl.* 4:307). With human attachments, we become attached to everything—"everything which is, everything which will be" (*Emile*, 83; *Pl.* 4:307). In this way, each person extends himself over the earth, thus increasing the possibility that a catastrophe anywhere will become a catastrophe affecting him.

This self-alienation is not the work of nature. Rousseau's complaint that "we no longer exist where we are, we only exist where we are not" is another example of how the notion of place operates in his thought. Thus, he addresses humankind as follows: "Oh man, draw your existence up within yourself, and you will no longer be miserable. Remain in the place which nature assigns to you in the chain of being. Nothing will be able to make you leave it" (*Emile*, 83; *Pl.* 4:308). How can a child be raised so that he will remain in the place that nature assigns? One begins by realizing that nature "enchains" the child in that place through weakness (*Emile*, 88; *Pl.* 4:316). One must keep the child in it by force, but not by the personal force of one's will, which Rousseau would call domination. Dominating the child opens the door for the child to experience his own power of domination, and once that has happened, it "awakens and flatters amour-propre, and habit strengthens it. Thus, whim succeeds need; thus, prejudices and opinion take their first roots" (*Emile*, 68; *Pl.* 4:289–90). According to Rousseau, this is the "principle," and knowing this principle, one also sees the "point where one leaves the path of nature" (*Emile*, 68; *Pl.* 4:290). To leave the path of nature is to lose one's place; it is to be lost in the double sense of the word: confused and abandoned.

The child must instead be kept in his place through the impersonal force of nature. Rousseau is not afraid of saying that the child must bear the yoke of the human condition, the "heavy yoke of necessity" (*Emile*, 91; *Pl.* 4:320). Again, this necessity is to be seen only in things and not in the "caprice of men" (*Emile*, 91; *Pl.* 4:320). For a child, the will of any person will be seen as caprice because the child is not yet in a position to understand the reason for things that clash with his whims.

The child is born weak and needy; thus he has to demand help, and help should be given. The tears that demand this help can, and often do, come from a legitimate need. Rousseau calls these tears the "first link in that long chain of which the social order is formed" (*Emile*, 65; *Pl.* 4:286). But it is only a slight movement from crying out of true need to crying for the pleasure of having someone do one's will. The weakness of children is the source of both their factual dependence and their feeling that dependence. But it is the feeling of dependence that is dangerous because it can give birth to the idea of domination. "But since this idea is excited less by their needs than by our services, at this point moral effects whose immediate cause is not in nature begin to make their appearance" (*Emile*, 66; *Pl.* 4:286). And the point at which moral effects appear is the point that one can leave or be drawn off the path of nature. Thus, there is no "natural spirit of domination" in children, but they are quick studies (*Emile*, 68; *Pl.* 4:289). Only a little experience of making the universe move with one's tongue is enough to develop a liking for it. Rousseau gives an example early in the book of what is to be avoided.

The Angry Nurse

A child cries to show his discomfort, having no other way of communicating. Because this form of communication is not articulate, one cannot always discover the problem. One seeks to comfort the child in order to quiet him. But if the tears persist and the cause is not found, the caretaker can grow impatient and sometimes strike the child. Rousseau notes, "[these sorts of] behavior [are] strange lessons for [the child's] entrance in life" (*Emile*, 65; *Pl.* 4:286). He then gives one of his examples. He tells of seeing "one of these difficult criers thus struck by his nurse" (*Emile*, 65; *Pl.* 4:286). The child did indeed become immediately quiet. Rousseau took this to be a sign of a servile spirit, but then he looked more closely. "The unfortunate was suffocating with anger; he had lost his breath; I saw him become violet. A moment after came sharp screams; all the signs of the resentment, fury, and despair of this age were in his accents" (*Emile*, 66; *Pl.* 4:286). In reality, the blow had been rather light, but the fury of the child was provoked by the fact that it was "given in the manifest intention of offending him" (*Emile*, 66; *Pl.* 4:287).[11]

For Rousseau, this is the critical point that needs examination. Is this disposition to fury, spite, and anger from nature? Absolutely not. "As long as children find resistance only in things and never in wills, they will become neither rebellious nor irascible," he states (*Emile*, 66; *Pl.* 4:287). But to find resistance in the will of another is not only to open the door to anger and other passions, but also to draw the child out of his place. This will, which is an obstacle to the child and thus offends him, leading to anger, can be called a form of scandal. Put more briefly, to strike a child with the intention of offense is scandalous behavior. We see here one way that scandal can occur: when one human will is seen to oppose another. Significantly, the tutor is never to appear to oppose the child's will.

The Gardener

Rousseau admits the impossibility of raising a child to the age of twelve "without giving him some idea of the relations of man to man and of the morality of human actions" (*Emile*, 97; *Pl.* 4:329). For Rousseau, it is enough to make sure that these notions come as late as possible and are limited to "immediate utility" (*Emile*, 97; *Pl.* 4:429). Making these ideas known to the pupil prevents him from believing that he is "the master of everything and from doing harm to others without scruple and without knowing it" (*Emile*, 97; *Pl.* 4:329). But the child can come to this understanding only by being scandalized, or by being offended by the will of another. Accordingly, Rousseau develops a strategy of using scandal to counteract the bad effects of scandal. It is, as we shall see, an explicit strategy of enchainment, of forcing the child to learn first what the concept of place is and then to learn to stay in it.

Rousseau also admits that there are children of violent natures who need to be made to enter into moral relations long before their twelfth year, "so as not to be obliged to put them in chains" (*Emile*, 97; *Pl.* 4:329). This image of chains and enchaining indicates the threat of chaos and disorder that only a very strong force will be able to control. This image occurs often in *Emile* and frames the story.

Entry into the moral world requires a sense of justice, and the first sentiment of justice that a person develops is a feeling of what is owed to him or his rights. In order to feel that one is owed something, and in order even to have something, one must understand, on however a rudimentary level, the concept of property. Rousseau will return to the origin of this concept in order to inculcate it in the child.

The governor, Jean-Jacques, gives the child an understanding of the concept of property by giving the child a "place." Rousseau emphasizes throughout *Emile* that one always has to consider what the child can understand, and that nothing should be taught him that he is incapable of grasping, lest error enter his mind. Therefore, Jean-Jacques will not attempt in any way to explain the notion of property. He will bring the child to experience it, to possess it in a concrete manner.

Rousseau shows how he implants and cultivates the idea of property in the child by using an agricultural example. That which is being written about, cultivating the idea, is being performed in the story by cultivating the land. While Emile re-enacts the way property first came into being, the reader understands how the concept comes into being. What is happening in the story to Emile is being re-enacted in the reader.

Rousseau, following John Locke, sees the origin of property in the labor invested in the land. The governor and pupil live in the countryside. Given his age, the child will "want to create, imitate, produce, give signs of power and activity" (*Emile*, 98; *Pl.* 4:330). The child has seen labor in the fields, and, having seen gardening and its produce, Emile will want to imitate this endeavor. Jean-Jacques does more than encourage him. He shares the child's desire and works with Emile, "not for his pleasure but for mine; at least he believes it to be so" (*Emile*, 98; *Pl.* 4:330). If Emile is too weak to do the actual plowing, Jean-Jacques does it for him. The moment of taking possession comes when Emile plants a bean.[12]

Each day, the two go to the garden to care for it and watch its growth. One can well imagine the child's joy at seeing the first emergence of the delicate sprouts from the beans he himself has planted. Rousseau tells that Jean-Jacques increases the child's joy by telling him, "This belongs to you" (*Emile*, 98; *Pl.* 4:331), and explaining what the word "belong" means. He does this by making the child feel that his person has been extended to the field upon which he has labored: "There is in this earth something of himself that he can claim against anyone whomever" (*Emile*, 98; *Pl.* 4:331). Rousseau, by extending the child beyond his physical body, is using one of the sources of human misery to help the child.[13]

Something quite unexpected, both for the child and for the reader, occurs: "All the beans are rooted out, the plot is torn up, the spot (*la place meme*) is not to be recognized" (*Emile*, 98; *Pl.* 4:331). Before any accusations or any victims, we have sudden violence. This kind of violence creates problems in a community. Given the way that the child has been led to identify himself with the place, the consequences of this unforeseen event are quite understandable. The child is angry. Normally this would be a sign of his leaving the path of nature. But observe what actually happens. His heart has been aroused. "The first sentiment of injustice comes to shed its sad bitterness in it. Tears flow in streams. The grieving child fills the air with moans and cries. I [Jean-Jacques] partake in his pain, his indignation" (*Emile*, 99; *Pl.* 4:331). This indignation is a sign that the child has been scandalized, and, so it appears, has Jean-Jacques along with him.

Now with the idea of property comes the idea of justice and due process. Thus, Jean-Jacques and Emile behave like policemen. They "investigate" a crime and find that "the gardener did the deed." They have him "summoned" (*Emile*, 99; *Pl.* 4:331). It is necessary to understand this as the first accusation in the story. Emile and Jean-Jacques are accusing the gardener of doing them harm.

Here again something quite unexpected happens. It is now the gardener's turn to accuse them. This second accusation in the story concerns a crime that preceded the crime of the first accusation. It turns out that it is the gardener who is harmed. The child, with Jean-Jacques, is, in fact, the guilty party. The child and Jean-Jacques inflict more harm on the gardener than they suspect the gardener of inflicting on them. The gardener, Robert, planted expensive, rare seeds to cultivate Maltese melons. These melons, the gardener tells them, were to have been shared with the child. Instead the child rooted up these seeds to plant "miserable beans" (*Emile*, 99; *Pl.* 4:331). The damage done to the gardener is "irreparable" (*Emile*, 99; *Pl.* 4:331). The child learns that he is guilty of the very crime of which he accused Robert, and, on top of that, he has harmed himself by depriving himself of melons. Before ever being made angry and indignant, the child had already been scandalized in another, more profound sense of the word: he had been led into wrongdoing by his tutor.

A scene is then recorded like a small morality play within the novel. The conversation between Jean-Jacques, Robert, and Emile is set off typographically, and we are allowed to overhear it. The first speaker is Jean-Jacques. He admits their offense. Robert already put his labor and effort into that particular piece of land, and they have ruined his work. Now they will make reparations, as is just, and they promise never to touch a piece of land without first learning whether or not someone else has already labored on it. The crime here strikes at the foundations of civil society.

Robert is mollified but informs them that, if that is the case, they will not be working any land because all of it has already been taken. He got his piece of property from his father, and so it goes. "All the lands you see have been occupied for a long time," he says. (*Emile*, 99; *Pl.* 4:332). It is now Emile's turn to speak. He asks whether melon seeds are often lost. Robert explains that no one touches his neighbor's garden: "Each respects the labor of others so that his own will be secure" (*Emile*, 99; *Pl.* 4:332). Emile complains that he has no garden. That is, Emile as yet has no place and no prospect of getting one. Robert responds coldly that that is none of his concern. His preoccupation is to make sure that Emile does not ruin his work. Finally, Jean-Jacques proposes an arrangement. Robert could grant them a small corner of his garden to cultivate on the condition that they give Robert half the produce. Robert grants the request without the condition, but ends with another warning that he will plow up their beans if they touch his melons. Thus, the story ends with Emile learning about injustice by both experiencing violation and then realizing that he is already guilty of the same violation. In order to understand the violation, it is necessary not only that Emile offend someone, but also that he be offended. For this to happen he has to "have" something—something has to belong to him. Only when his bit of land is violated can he grasp that he has, in fact, already violated Robert's land. With the injury received comes knowledge of the injury given.

Rousseau "begs" the young masters reading the book to think about this example (*Emile*, 99; *Pl.* 4:333). One of the lessons to be learned is a pedagogical one. The lessons given to children ought to be more in actions than in words. The child will retain more easily what he has done or what has been done to him rather than what he has said or what has been said to him. But the lesson goes deeper. This is Emile's first encounter with a will that has the manifest intention of offending him. The tutor has arranged this encounter in such a way that Emile experiences it as a response to an evil that he, Emile, committed. Emile can then understand that Robert, the gardener, would feel the very indignation that Emile himself feels when he sees his beans uprooted. The possession of the land becomes something "sacred and respectable" by means of the labor Emile invests in it. As has already been pointed out, the land is an extension of Emile. All this is violated, but it is violated because Emile is already guilty of a violation. Emile is not "punished" in an arbitrary way, but the effect of his own wrongdoing comes back upon him. Such is the world that Emile is being raised to inhabit.

The story is not yet over. Rousseau follows this episode with yet another example underlining the importance of how one gives discipline. In brief, the angry child of the example continually breaks windows. Rousseau would have the child locked up in darkness in a place without windows. Once the child sees the advantage of promising not to break the windows in exchange for his freedom, he is released. From this, the child learns about the "faith of commitments and their utility" (*Emile*, 100; *Pl.* 4:334).

As mentioned earlier, Rousseau enters into these two examples by saying that children of a violent nature have to be brought more quickly into the human world, the world of property and promises, lest they have to be "enchained." He ends with the following admonition: "Follow all the links of this chain. The naughty child hardly dreamed, while making a hole for planting his bean, that he was digging for himself a dungeon where his science would not be long in shutting him up" (*Emile*, 100–101; *Pl.* 4:334). The literal chain that threatens a violent child is replaced with the metaphorical links of an example that tells the story of a chain of forces and violent encounters. The child is enchained not with irons, but rather with science, for he ends by shutting himself in a dungeon. Once he has planted a bean and made the claim, "this is mine," he finds that he has opened himself to a world in which others can make the same claim. Thus, he realizes, too late, that in making the claim, he has always already offended another, and he is able to understand why that other would protect his own labor, even to the point of depriving him of his freedom. The exchange of freedom for respect of another's goods has meaning for him.

In order for the child to learn what justice is, he has to learn what injustice is, and in order to learn that, he has to have an injustice committed against him. But simply experiencing an injustice would lead to outrage. Rousseau has to arrange it so that the child will find that he is already guilty of the crime he wishes to charge to another. The child awakes to the moral world as a guilty person.[14]

The Magician

At the very end of the episode with the gardener, Rousseau writes that in it, Emile unknowingly digs himself "a dungeon where his science would not be long in shutting him up" (*Emile*, 101; *Pl.* 4:334). In the following story, Emile is again in danger due to science or knowledge, but this time the danger is in his becoming lost, rather than being imprisoned. As Book III opens, the pupil is entering the "time of labors, of instruction, of study" (*Emile*, 166; *Pl.* 4:428), because he can do, for a short period of time, more than he desires. The choice of what things he will study is important. These should be things that "really contribute to our [the tutor and Emile's] well-being" (*Emile*, 166; *Pl.* 4:428). But even with the right choice, the dangers are great. The following excerpt reveals the impending chaos and challenge: "Darkness of human understanding, what reckless hand dared to touch your veil? What abysses I see opened up around this young unfortunate by our vain sciences! O tremble, you, who are going to lead him in these perilous paths and raise nature's sacred curtain before his eyes. Be sure, in the first place, of his balance and yours; fear lest one or the other, and perhaps both of you, get dizzy. Fear the specious attraction of lies and the intoxicating vapors of pride" (*Emile*, 167; *Pl.* 4:428).

Emile learns the meaning of the concept of place in the first story through a concrete piece of earth that becomes a part of him. The second story tells of "place" in the more abstract sense of answering the question: Where am I? To answer this question, the pupil has to make a double abstraction, first from concrete place to maps. But much more difficult is the second abstraction, from the concrete way of constructing meridians for the purpose of making the maps to the use of a compass for the same purpose.

Just as Jean-Jacques enchained the young pupil in the first story by having him desire to imitate a farmer, so now he will use Emile's curiosity as a chain to bind him more firmly in his place. Rousseau distinguishes between the "chain of general truths by which all the sciences are connected with common principles out of which they develop successively" and the "entirely different chain by which each particular object attracts another and always shows the one that follows" (*Emile*, 172; *Pl.* 4:436). Rousseau, the author, is using the first chain on the reader, and Jean-Jacques, the tutor, is using the second chain on Emile. Immediately after commenting on the two kinds of chains, Rousseau writes, "In orienting ourselves to draw our maps, we had to draw meridians" (*Emile*, 172; *Pl.* 4:436). It is necessary to read this both on the literal level of finding different methods by which the pupil can draw accurate north-south lines for a map, and, on the figural level, of teaching the reader to orient him- or herself in the world.

The first maps will be very simple ones: "His [Emile's] first two points of geography will be the city in which he dwells and his father's country house; then will come the intermediate places, then the neighboring rivers, and finally the sun's position and the way of orienting oneself by it" (*Emile*, 171; *Pl.* 4:434). Rousseau, the author, addresses the reader to say that he or she is already sensing the advantage of "putting a compass in his eyes" (*Emile*, 171; *Pl.* 4:435).

But this will not be enough. The pupil will be learning how to make more exact maps, and in order to do this, one must have meridians. It is not that meridians in and of themselves are so difficult; rather, the problem here is one of concentration. The pupil must have a strong enough interest in constructing them to concentrate his mind so that he can pay attention continually to the same object. If his mind loses its concentration, if it gets lost, the pupil will never be able to find his place in the world. Only pleasure or desire produces this kind of continual attention, and only they will be acceptable motives for Emile; he is never to do anything "in spite of himself" (*Emile*, 172; *Pl.* 4:436).

Drawing meridians by using "the two points of intersection between the equal shadows of morning and evening" is, in itself, an excellent method, but it suffers from the following disadvantages: first, these meridians disappear; second, practically a whole day is needed to draw them; and third, one must always work in the same place (*Emile*, 172; *Pl.* 4:436). Boredom surely follows, but Jean-Jacques has already foreseen this development and has found a way to get around it.

Only now, with all this background, is the reader adequately prepared for the example itself. Rousseau has prepared him or her for it with the discussion of getting lost and the efforts needed in order to be able to orient oneself. At this point, the author interrupts his story to address the reader about his or her supposed impatience at his "lengthy and minute details" (*Emile*, 172; *Pl.* 4:437). This example will indeed be lengthy, but that is because it is "the most useful part of the book" (*Emile*, 172; *Pl.* 4:437). Rousseau intends the example to be a map for the reader. If Emile needs to learn how to read a map, so the reader needs to learn how to read this example.

The governor and pupil go to a fair where they witness something they do not understand. The fair's magician is able to attract a wax duck floating in a tub of water with a piece of bread. Neither the governor nor the child is tempted to accuse the magician of being a "sorcerer" (*Emile*, 173; *Pl.* 4:437). Rather, after talking about it, they decide that they want to imitate what he has done. The child already has experience with magnetism, so it does not take long for them to figure out that if they were to implant a "good, well magnetized needle" in a piece of wax shaped like a duck, and then place some iron in a hole cut into a piece of bread, they could produce results similar to the magician's trick (*Emile*, 173; *Pl.* 4:437).

At this point, so that the readers do not forget the ultimate goal of the lesson, Rousseau explicitly mentions that "to observe the direction the duck faces when left at rest in the water is something we can do another time" (*Emile*, 173; *Pl.* 4:437). Right now, the child and governor occupy themselves fully with their "plan," and this concern causes the pupil to begin to wander from the path, while Jean-Jacques lets him lose his way. The child does not know his place well enough to stay in it and observe the position of the duck. He is already someplace else and, without being aware of it, in grave danger of losing his way. The internal compass will, however, eventually be found.

The two return to the fair, where Emile, with a great deal of excitement, performs the trick he has learned to imitate before the magician and the crowd. Rousseau calls

Emile "my little doctor," no sobriquet of approval, but a sign that he is in danger (*Emile*, 173; *Pl.* 4:437). Further, he apparently has trouble "containing himself" from excitement. Before performing the trick itself, Emile tells the magician that it is not difficult. This attitude is yet another sign of danger, because this is not the attitude that Jean-Jacques has been striving to inculcate. The child performs the trick with his heart thumping and his hands quaking. The crowd applauds. The child is a great success. The mountebank has the graciousness to ask Emile to return the next day to perform before an even larger crowd.

Rousseau now calls Emile, "[his] proud little naturalist" who wants to chatter (*Emile*, 173; *Pl.* 4:438). Clearly, Emile is heading toward all the things from which Jean-Jacques has tried to protect him. A little knowledge is a dangerous thing. Jean-Jacques leads the child, who is "covered with praise," away (*Emile*, 173; *Pl.* 4:438). The child is, of course, excited about the next day in the way that only a child can be. He "counts the minutes; . . . he invites everyone he meets; he would want the whole of humankind to be witness to his glory" (*Emile*, 173; *Pl.* 4:438). The next day, Emile's heart swells as he enters the hall where he is to perform. This is the swelling of pride fed by vanity. It is, without Emile and perhaps without the reader being aware of it, a most dangerous moment. Emile is in danger of getting lost and being condemned forever to wandering the byways of human opinion.

The child is announced to the public. He takes out the piece of bread he has especially prepared to offer it to the duck, "and . . . new vicissitude of things human!" (*Emile*, 173; *Pl.* 4:438). The duck is no longer attracted by the piece of bread; instead it turns and swims away. It positively avoids the hand that feeds it. Emile is jeered; he complains to the magician and feels deceived. This is the first accusation of the story. Emile accuses the magician of having substituted the wax duck for a different one, and he defies the magician to attract the duck.

Of course, the magician rises to the challenge. He leads the duck with a bit of bread, and then gives the bread to Emile and asks him to do the same. Emile cannot. Emile is mocked even by the duck as it turns pirouettes rather than follow the bread. Now Emile is confused and does not want to hear the jeers of the crowd. The magician goes so far as to take the bit of bread that Emile brought and remove the hidden piece of iron from of it. "Another laugh at our expense," writes Rousseau. The magician goes on leading the duck by his finger and even by the mere command of his voice. The crowd responds warmly, and this "redoubled applause is that much more of an affront to us" (*Emile*, 174; *Pl.* 4:439). Emile and Jean-Jacques escape unnoticed, their plan of recounting their success being ruined.

This story is important in allowing the reader to understand the whole of *Emile*. It is only here, in the most significant part of the book, that the role of the crowd is made clear. The collective element of violence that is so central to Girard's analysis is, for the most part, absent from *Emile*. Only in this story does it play a central role, both in puffing up Emile's vanity and in deflating him. Emile is to be raised free from the noxious influence of the crowds that so easily builds him up and tears him down, but in this example, Rousseau shows how necessary and powerful that influence is.

The following morning, Jean-Jacques and Emile hear a knock at the door. It is the magician. He makes the second accusation of the story, directed toward Emile and

Jean-Jacques. He complains in a manner very similar to Robert, the gardener, that these two have behaved in such a way that could discredit his games and thereby ruin his livelihood. "What is so wonderful about the art of attracting a wax duck to make it worth purchasing this honor at the expense of an honest man's subsistence?" he asks (*Emile*, 174; *Pl.* 4:439). Again, the crime violates the social order. Emile is in a hurry "to show off giddily" what he knows (*Emile*, 174; *Pl.* 4:439). Thus, he errs, and so comes the lesson he needs to learn. Like the experience with the gardener, the learning of this lesson has to be set up in a particular way. Emile has to be induced to unknowingly harm the magician in the way that the magician later harms him. He has to see that what actually brings on his humiliation is his own thoughtless humiliation of the magician, which is goaded by his vanity. Only then does the lesson have its desired effect.

The magician has another reason for coming to visit them. He has come, he says, "out of the goodness of my heart to teach you the secret that has perplexed you so" (*Emile*, 174; *Pl.* 4:439). He pulls back the veil of the trick that he performed the day before that not only humiliates Emile but also leaves him in confusion. He shows the two a machine or device consisting of a lodestone encased in soft iron that a child hidden under the table manipulates. Somehow, being a victim of humiliation renders Emile safe to imbibe a more deeply hidden knowledge. His experience forecloses the possibility of his misusing it. The magician humiliates him in self-defense, and this even the young Emile can grasp.

As in the story with the gardener, Jean-Jacques and Emile apologize. This time, they also give thanks for what the magician has taught them. They offer him a present, but the magician refuses. He wishes to leave the two obliged to him. He says, "It is my only vengeance. Learn that there is generosity in every station" (*Emile*, 174; *Pl.* 4:440).

Before leaving, the magician directs his words to Jean-Jacques, but so that Emile can also hear. For the author, Rousseau, the words are most unusual. The magician says, "I willing excuse . . . this child. He has *sinned* only from ignorance. But you, *monsieur*, who ought to know his mistake, why did you let him make it?" (*Emile*, 174–75; *Pl.* 4:440; emphasis added). There is sin, then, in Emile's universe, but it is sin of a particular type: it is the sin of ignorance. Not only does this kind of sin have a long philosophical tradition that goes back to Socrates (and so Rousseau refers to the magician in the next paragraph as "our magician-Socrates"; *Emile*, 175; *Pl.* 4:440), but it also has a long theological tradition. It is the one sin that does not need forgiveness. Indeed, the magician does not forgive Emile, but instead he excuses him. To "sin from ignorance" is not really to sin at all, unless the ignorance is culpable.

The magician both reinforces the idea that Emile does not need forgiveness and shows that his formation depends upon scandal. In saying that Emile sinned innocently, he accuses Jean-Jacques of scandal in the classic sense of letting Emile sin. The tutor knew the mistake and should have warned his charge against it. Both the tutor and the pupil feel a healthy embarrassment upon the departure of this unexpected guest. The tutor now says to Emile that he is willing to warn the child of his mistakes before he makes them, something the child will now be eager to receive.

The pair make a final pilgrimage to the fair to see the magician. Jean-Jacques and Emile have moved, in the two days that the incident covers, from being struck by effects whose causes they do not know, to seeing again the trick of whose secret they are aware. More important, though, is the knowledge they gain of their fellow man. They look at the magician in a different way. Jean-Jacques says: "We approach our magician-Socrates with profound respect. We hardly dare to raise our eyes to him" (*Emile*, 175; *Pl.* 4:440). They are humiliated by the very kindnesses the magician shows to them. Emile now "knows everything," but this time he does "not breathe a word" to anyone (*Emile*, 175; *Pl.* 4:440). The knowledge will not be shown off. Rousseau ends by making the underlying threat explicit as follows: "If my pupil dared so much as to open his mouth, he would deserve to be annihilated" (*Emile*, 175; *Pl.* 4:440).

Whether Emile knows it or not, the threat of annihilation hangs over his head. Rousseau makes the reason for this threat clear only much later in the book. In Book IV, Rousseau tells the reader that "the sole folly of which one cannot disabuse a man who is not mad is vanity. For this there is no cure other than experience—if, indeed, any can cure it" (*Emile*, 245; *Pl.* 4:537). Vanity is an infectious, fatal disease—fatal in the one sense that matters to Rousseau: it is capable of leading his pupil astray, of making him lose his way. The pupil has to be exposed to all the vicissitudes that can show him that he is like other humans. In order to counteract vanity, "the adventure with the magician would be repeated in countless ways" (*Emile*, 245; *Pl.* 4:537). This story, like the episode with the gardener, begins with imitation and ends with, if not outright violence, real harm. The pain and humiliation that Emile feels are precisely what he inflicts on the magician.

With one part of the story complete, Rousseau addresses the reader. He emphasizes how much more important each detail of the example is than it may seem. Its importance lies in teaching how to combat vanity: "How many mortifying consequences are attracted by the first movement of vanity!" (*Emile*, 175; *Pl.* 4:440). Rousseau is clear in stating that if the master can identify the first movement and make "humiliation and disgrace" arise out of it, the second movement will not come for a long time.

Rousseau then returns to the outer frame of the story. Some readers will complain that to implement this kind of example will take too much preparation. Rousseau agrees: there is so much preparation "and all for the sake of making ourselves a compass to take the place of a meridian" (*Emile*, 175; *Pl.* 4:440). In fact, the compass has not yet been found, but now that is easy. Again, they imitate the magician in recreating his elaborate trick. Playing with this magnetized duck often, Jean-Jacques and Emile "finally notice that the duck at rest always points in pretty nearly the same direction" (*Emile*, 175; *Pl.* 4:441). By further investigation, they find that this direction is north. "Our compass is found, or as good as found. Now we are into physics" (*Emile*, 175; *Pl.* 4:441). The last sentence reveals the point as it concludes the story. The overarching problem of this stage in the pupil's life is that of entering into science without getting lost. They have found the compass, which is humiliation and disgrace in the place of vanity. They can enter the world of physics without the danger of getting lost.

The need for the compass springs from the short attention span of the pupil that renders the making of meridians tedious and confining. The need for meridians is for learning how to orient oneself in the physical world. In the midst of teaching the child how to find his way, no matter where he is, Rousseau teaches him another, deeper lesson about his place in the world.

As in the earlier episode, the means for teaching this is to scandalize the child, both in the sense of leading him into sin, and in the sense of humiliating and disgracing him publicly. The child finds himself in a situation in which he has sinned more than he was sinned against, for he has already done wrong to the magician, though without knowing it. The governor shares in his humiliation and even suffers a further one in the presence of the pupil when the magician tells him that he must use his authority to control the boy. The pupil is again being enchained here by the events that Jean-Jacques instigates and controls.[15]

So ends the two main episodes that shed light on our interpretation. The rest of Book III continues to be concerned with this theme of teaching Emile to know his place and to stay in it. The episode in which Jean-Jacques and Emile get lost in the woods north of Montmorency has obvious connections with the search for the compass. But, as Rousseau himself reminds the reader, one should not look so much at the skills that Emile is acquiring as at the "direction" that Jean-Jacques is giving him (*Emile*, 188; *Pl.* 4:460). The "place" that Emile knows at this point in the book is limited in many ways to his physical place. He does not yet know other humans as humans: "He does not yet have a sufficient sense of his relations with his species to be able to judge of others by himself. He knows no human being other than himself alone, and he is far from knowing himself. . . . He does not know the place of others, but he feels his own and stays in it. In place of the social laws which he cannot know, we have bound him with the chains of necessity" (*Emile*, 187; *Pl.* 4:458). Once again, the image of enchainment is linked with the image of place to emphasize how Emile is being controlled by his tutor. Rousseau closes Book III by telling the reader that Emile, at this point in his life, can think of himself without regard to others. He makes no demands and does not believe that anyone has a claim on him. "He is alone in human society" (*Emile*, 208; *Pl.* 4:488).

CONCLUSION

Even in the parts of the book dealing with Emile as a young child, Rousseau is concerned with the problem of violence. Rousseau ends the violence by revealing the guilt of the victim, so that the violence Emile suffers turns out to be the violence that he has already inflicted. The reconciliation is based upon the collusion of the tutor and the third party, the victimizers, in agreeing to give different forms of scandal. The tutor scandalizes Emile by leading him into sin, the third party by inflicting harm on this innocent victim. The system is precarious and depends upon the total control that the tutor exercises.

This analysis of *Emile* thus far supports another of the major claims made in the Introduction and in Chapter 1: there is reconciliation without forgiveness. Emile unknowingly offends Robert and the magician, and is in turn offended by them. Each scene ends in a form of reconciliation, but forgiveness is neither requested nor proffered. Emile continues his education without any sense of being a new creation; rather, he is kept in his place.

CHAPTER 4

PROFESSING FAITH

INTRODUCTION

Rousseau's *Profession de foi du vicaire savoyard* is, not coincidentally, both the most scandalous of his writings and the "*clef de voûte*" of his thought (Schinz, *La Pensée*, 451).[1] It was, to his contemporaries, certainly the most provocative and controversial. More than anything else in *Emile*, it caused the book's condemnation. In asking why the Church and the government found the work so worthy of condemnation, Rousseau tells that it was because he denied the doctrine of original sin. I will continue to argue in this chapter that this is no longer an adequate understanding of what is at stake. It would be much more adequate, if a bit more obscure, to say that the scandal of the "Profession of Faith" was precisely *its* scandal at the scandal of the Gospel. It is his scandal at the Gospel that impels Rousseau to rewrite them in a nonscandalous way, and it is precisely this that Christians find scandalous. The "Profession of Faith" was the most scandalous aspect of *Emile*, and it achieved this scandal by rejecting the scandalous aspects of Christianity. Rousseau was able to use scandal in the very act of rejecting it.

I will detail the ways in which the "Profession of Faith" can appear to be a self-contained unit, only to argue that, in fact, it is not. Rather, the "Profession of Faith" will show itself to be deeply embedded in the novel through its textual connections with the gardener and the magician episodes that were explained in the previous chapter. These episodes will now reveal themselves to be necessary conditions for the "Profession of Faith." They prepare the reader both to grasp and to be grasped by its message.

The standard interpretation of the "Profession of Faith," goes back to Rousseau himself. According to this interpretation, the "Profession of Faith" consists of two parts.[2] The first part establishes the reasonableness of the existence of God as well as that of the human conscience. That being established, the second part is a rather skeptical critique of revelation. The function of the first part is to help prevent the rampant injustice that Rousseau firmly believes will result from the loss of a belief in God. Rousseau is arguing against the *philosophes* here.[3] The second part is to protect against the intolerance that occurs when the adherents of one religion believe that some sort of special revelation elevates their belief to a status such that one must believe in it or be condemned.

In spite of its illustrious pedigree, I wish to challenge this standard interpretation as being incomplete and therefore misleading. It is true that the first part argues for the existence of God, but the kind of God it argues for has to be taken into consideration. It is not the "God of the philosophers." Rousseau needs a violent God, a God who punishes evildoers, if not in this life then in the next. Or, at the very least, he needs a God that allows His followers to wreak vengeance on their oppressors after death.[4] If this is true, then the second part cannot be read as simply combating fanaticism, for this danger seems, for the audience Rousseau is addressing, remote. Rather, this part is designed to disallow human testimony from having any weight in establishing the truth. Again, it is the kind of testimony or witness being expelled that needs to be taken into consideration. Rousseau expels the crucial testimony of the expulsion of Christ precisely because this testimony would show that the economy of divine violence, upon which the first part relies, has been fatally compromised.

I will begin by presenting the reasons why the "Profession of Faith" can and does appear to be so independent from the rest of *Emile*, only to argue that this is deceptive and has to be understood within the larger purpose of *Emile*—securing the place of the victim. The "Profession of Faith" deepens the rejection of the possibility of forgiveness by protecting the place of the victim, which has been established in the first three Books of *Emile*. Then I will present Rousseau's own interpretation in the context in which it occurred, his debate with Christophe de Beaumont, the archbishop of Paris. This interpretation is misleading. The first part does not establish merely the existence of God, but rather that of a certain kind of God, and the second part is not really about fanaticism at all, but rather much more about protecting the result of the first part—that God punishes the wicked and rewards the virtuous.

THE PLACE OF THE "PROFESSION OF FAITH" WITHIN EMILE

The "Profession of Faith" is clearly set off from the rest of the text in a number of ways. First, it has its own subtitle (similar to the sections titled "Sophie or the Woman" and "On Travel" of Book V), and Rousseau signals to the reader when the "Profession" ends. But it is set off in other ways, as well. Rousseau presents it as the one and only transcription in the novel.[5] He draws attention to this fact not only at the beginning of the text but also at the end, thus never fully resolving the question of who the "I" is in the "Profession of Faith."

While most readers simply assume, with ample reason, that the youth in the "Profession of Faith" is Jean-Jacques, the author of *Emile* never verifies that. The text of the "Profession of Faith" itself is presented as the words of someone else, "a man more worthy than I [the young man in the story]" (*Emile*, 260; *Pl.* 4:558). Rousseau, in transcribing the "Profession of Faith," departs from Emile, considered an example, and switches to a different, more useful, example. This gives us grounds for thinking that it is Rousseau.[6] While there are several other stories in *Emile* that concern the young Rousseau, the "Profession of Faith" is unusual in that the main character is not Jean-Jacques. Rather, Rousseau allows the character of the vicar to speak at length.

Emile will never hear the "Profession of Faith," which reveals that not only is it not about him, but also that it is not for him. Rousseau transcribes the "Profession of

Faith" for the reader. Jean-Jacques will educate Emile about natural religion. Further than natural religion, Emile cannot be taken and remain within the confines of a natural education. Specifically, Emile has no need for the second part, the critique of revelation. No errors have been allowed to contaminate his thinking, and so no corrective is needed.

A final feature that sets the "Profession of Faith" apart is the striking difference in the tone of the author toward the reader. Both leading up to and following the "Profession of Faith," the alienation or distance between Rousseau and his reader grows. The story of the "Profession of Faith" is inserted between two assertions of this distance. Rousseau adverts to this growing distance before he enters into his discussion on teaching the pupil about God. "The force of things" pulls him forward, but this force does not attract the reader (*Emile*, 253; *Pl.* 4:548). The reader sees Rousseau's ideas as fantastic, while Rousseau sees the reader as bound by his or her prejudices as follows:

> I know that they [the readers] will persist in imagining only what they see; and therefore they will take the young man whom I evoke to be an imaginary and fantastic being because he differs from those with whom they compare him. They do not stop to think that he must certainly differ from these young men, since he is raised quite differently, affected by quite contrary sentiments, and instructed quite otherwise from them; indeed it would be much more surprising if he were to resemble them than to be such as I suppose him. This is not the man of man; it is the man of nature. (*Emile*, 253; *Pl.* 4:549)

Again, almost immediately after ending the "Profession of Faith," Rousseau addresses the reader in order to assert this distance: "Reader, I am well aware that no matter what I do, you and I will never see my Emile with the same features" (*Emile*, 315; *Pl.* 4:637).

According to Rousseau, the reader will accuse him of not forming Emile, but rather of creating him or pulling "him out of his brain" (*Emile*, 315; *Pl.* 4:637). For Rousseau, the two pupils, his pupil and that of the readers, do not resemble each other, but that is because his is in conformity with nature. The two pupils differ in that the readers' pupil both knows about and forsakes God long before Emile has even heard of Him. But once Emile has heard of God, Rousseau will make a "veritable theologian out of an ardent, lively, intense, and impulsive young man at the most ebullient age of life" (*Emile*, 315; *Pl.* 4:637). In all this, the relationship between the author and the reader is deteriorating from one of cooperation to one of antagonism.

Contrast this with the highly unusual form of address from within the "Profession of Faith." Rousseau transcribes a story written in the third person about a "young expatriate" who is destitute. This young man changes his faith and goes through several harsh experiences before meeting up with the vicar. Once the sins of this youth are confessed, and as the attention of the narrative turns from the youth to the vicar himself, the author of the text Rousseau is transcribing makes the following declaration: "I am tired of speaking in the third person. And the effort is quite superfluous, for you are well aware, *dear fellow citizen*, that this unhappy fugitive is myself. I believe myself far enough from the disorders of my youth to dare to admit them, and the hand which drew me away from these disorders merits that, at the expense of a bit of shame, I render at least some honor to his benefactions" (*Emile*, 264; *Pl.* 4:563; emphasis added). It is a form of address that harks back to the "Dedication" of the *Second Discourse* and tells the reader that Rousseau did intend this piece of writing to be useful to his fellow Genevans.

Given all of the above, the "Profession of Faith" appears to be kind of foreign body within the novel. Without denying all of the ways in which it is set off from the rest of the narrative, a closer examination of the text shows how deep the unity of this novel goes. There is textual support for holding that the story of Emile and the Gardener, as well as that of Emile and the magician, is connected to the "Profession of Faith." Since these episodes do not serve to prepare Emile himself for the "Profession of Faith," it is safe to assume that they are there to prepare the reader. The way Rousseau has written the "Profession of Faith" shows that the reader needs a scandalized consciousness to hear it. This fact roots the "Profession of Faith" in the whole of the novel and marks it not only as an integral part, but also even as its climax.

Rousseau begins his transcription of the "Profession of Faith" by relating the sad story of a "young expatriate." This young man is a Calvinist but finds himself destitute in Italy. In order to eat, he changes his religion and thus finds admittance into an almshouse for proselytes. The religious instruction undermines rather than strengthens his faith, and the morals he encounters there are worse than the religious instruction. Rousseau relates the story as follows: "He saw morals that were still newer to him. He saw them and almost became their victim. He wanted to flee; they locked him up. He complained; he was punished for his complaints. At the mercy of his tyrants, he saw himself treated as a criminal for not wanting to give way to crime. Those who know how much the first taste of violence and injustice arouses a young heart without experience will be able to picture the condition of his own heart. Tears of rage flowed from his eyes; indignation choked him" (*Emile*, 261–62; *Pl.* 4:559). The vocabulary here calls to mind the story of little Emile and his garden, which was examined in the previous chapter. Concerning Emile and his destroyed bean patch, Rousseau wrote, "This young heart is aroused. The first sentiment of injustice comes to shed its sad bitterness in it. Tears flow. . .I partake of his pain, his indignation" (*Emile*, 98–99; *Pl.* 4:331).

Thus, the readers "know how much the first taste of violence and injustice arouses a young heart" because Rousseau has already evoked this experience once before. Rousseau never makes absolutely clear that the young man in the story is himself, in the same way that he never makes clear exactly which Emile he is speaking of in the episodes. This lack of exactitude helps prevent the reader from simply seeing the character in the story as "someone else." Rousseau wants to ratify the possibility that the person in the story could be the reader. Hearing the "Profession of Faith" requires that the reader be scandalized in the way that both Emile in the story and the young man of the "Profession" are. One needs to have experienced, at least vicariously, being victimized by injustice.

Looking at the figure of the vicar confirms that scandal is the narrow gate into the "Profession of Faith." He has a sexual fault. The text does not say in what precisely it consists, but it becomes known. Thus, "the scandal had to be expiated" (*Emile*, 267;

Pl. 4:567). Thus far, it would seem that the vicar is the cause of the scandal and not its victim. But in fact, the vicar is "arrested, interdicted, driven out" (*Emile*, 267; *Pl.* 4:567). He, too, becomes a victim.

In the earlier episodes Emile moved from being a victim of injustice with Robert, to being lost and without a compass in the story of the magician. For a while, Emile has no way of orienting himself. Uncertainty and doubt are the narrative expressions of being lost. Emile and his tutor first reach this state in their perplexity at the magician. Belief in magic would have been the easy way out of the doubt and uncertainty, but Rousseau equates belief in magic with dogmatism and fanaticism.[7] The experience of doubt in the narrative concerning Emile finds its echo in the narrative concerning the young man and the vicar that precedes the actual "Profession of Faith." The young man describes himself in the following terms: "Without knowing anything of what is, without imagining anything about the generation of things, he wallowed in his stupid ignorance with a profound contempt for all those who thought they knew more about these things than he did" (*Emile*, 263; *Pl.* 4:560–61). Recall that Emile is on the verge of contempt toward the magician before his experience of humiliation.

The vicar, for his part, not only describes his own condition as one of being lost, but he also draws a parallel with the young man in the following words: "Seeing the ideas that I had of the just, the decent, and all the duties of man overturned by gloomy observations, I lost each day one of the opinions I had received. Since those opinions that remained were no longer sufficient to constitute together a self-sustaining body, I felt the obviousness of the principles gradually becoming dimmer in my mind. And finally reduced to no longer knowing what to think, I reached *the same point where you* [the destitute young man] *are*" (*Emile*, 267; *Pl.* 4:567; emphasis added). Both the vicar and his charge reach, at different times, the point of not knowing what to think. They are "lost" in a way analogous to the condition of Emile before the magician reveals his secret, before Emile himself discovers his compass.

Rousseau makes the connection textually explicit by repeating here the image of the compass. The vicar, in a state of uncertainty and doubt, meditates on the "sad fate of mortals, floating on this sea of human opinions without rudder or compass" (*Emile*, 267, *Pl.* 4:567). Entering into the "Profession of Faith" requires, then, this experience of being lost. Rousseau makes this point again at the beginning of the second part. There, the vicar says that he would have hesitated to tell the young man everything if the young man's beliefs were settled, but his present condition of instability is a sign that he will profit from thinking as the vicar does (*Emile*, 295; *Pl.* 4:607).

If belief in magic is associated with fanaticism, then exposing the magician's secret is associated with a vanity that upsets the public order. The knowledge must be kept secret from those with steady beliefs (i.e., those who believe in the magic), and given to those whose beliefs are unsteady or are beginning to be enlightened. This has to be done in an indirect manner. To the public, Rousseau is saying, "Believe in God and follow the local religion." To his real audience, he is saying, "These beliefs are necessary for the weak."

Finally, one can go further and say that Rousseau has prepared the reader for the "Profession of Faith" not simply by writing *about* the scandal and the lostness of

Emile, but also by giving the readers an experience with scandal and lostness in and through the text. The reader experiences indignation at the injustice of what the tutor does to Emile through Robert in connection with the garden. The reader does not know what to think in regard to the tutor's treatment of the child in the case of the magician. The vicar, the young man, and the reader are all to be in a position similar to Emile at this point in the book.

The "Profession of Faith" is regarded as one of the greatest of Rousseau's writings, but it is often detached from its narrative context and thereby deprived of much of its power. The preparation for the presentation of the "Profession of Faith" in the novel, both immediate and remote, is extensive and well thought-out. The "Profession of Faith" has scandalized consciousness as the necessary condition for its possibility.

ROUSSEAU'S INTERPRETATION OF THE "PROFESSION OF FAITH" IN HIS LETTER TO BEAUMONT

Chapter 1 discussed the *Mandement* of Christophe Beaumont, the archbishop of Paris. In this official letter, he attacks *Emile* primarily for denying the original sin, but he does not stop there. He accuses Rousseau of rejecting revelation, a charge that Rousseau denies, and further charges him with rejecting natural religion. Beaumont claims that Rousseau has opened the door "to all superstitions, to all fanatical systems, to all the deliriums of the human mind" (*CW* 9:12; *CW* 9:75; *Pl.* 4:996).

In responding to these accusations, Rousseau gives us his own understanding of the structure of the "Profession of Faith." Specifically, Rousseau shows the bad faith of his accuser by explicating the respective aims of the two parts that compose the "Profession of Faith" as follows:

> The first part, which is the longer, the more important, the more filled with striking new truths, is intended to combat modern materialism, to establish the existence of God and natural Religion with all the force of which the Author is capable.
>
> The second part, very much shorter, less regular, and less thorough, raises doubts and difficulties about revelations in general, ascribing to ours, however, its true certitude in the purity and sanctity of its doctrine, and in the wholly divine sublimity of the person who was its Author. The object of this second part is to make each more circumspect from within his own Religion about accusing others of bad faith within theirs, and to show that the proofs of each one are not so conclusive to all eyes that those who do not see them with the same clarity as we do must be treated as guilty people. (*CW* 9:75; *Pl.* 4:996–97)

Such are the basic positions of the first and the second part of the "Profession of Faith." According to Rousseau's own testimony, the first part is "decisive and dogmatic" (*CW* 9:75; *Pl.* 4:997). The vicar "believes, he affirms, he is powerfully persuaded" throughout the first part. The second part is of a different nature. In it, the vicar "proposes his objections, his difficulties, his doubts" (*CW* 9:76; *Pl.* 4:997). The vicar has proven the "essential dogmas" and remains in "respectful skepticism" about the rest (*CW* 9:76; *Pl.* 4:997).

These positions each have a negative purpose. They are meant to prevent the dele-terious effects of the vices they oppose. The function of the first part is not merely to prove the existence of God; it has, rather, the practical aim of helping to prevent injustice and immorality, which would result from the loss of a faith.[8] In a similar way, the second part is meant to protect against the socially disruptive phenomenon of intolerance or fanaticism. Intolerance occurs when believers in one religion or sect hold that their version of divine revelation carries with it the obligation to be believed by all or to suffer condemnation. The following closing words of the "Profession of Faith" express most succinctly these extremes and their effects: "Proud philosophy leads to freethinking as blind devoutness leads to fanaticism. Avoid these extremes. Always remain firm in the path of truth (or what in the simplicity of your heart appears to be the truth), without ever turning away from it out of vanity or weakness. Dare to acknowledge God among the philosophers; dare to preach humanity to the intolerant. You will perhaps be the only member of your party, but you will have within yourself a witness which will enable you to do without the witness of men" (*Emile*, 313; *Pl.* 4:633–35). Rousseau wants the reader to see the first part as his acknowledgment of God before the *philosophes*, and the second part as his own ser-mon to the intolerant.

More importantly, this quotation from the "Profession of Faith" can be viewed as a kind of prophecy. Rousseau, as a result of publishing this text under his editorship, finds himself, as the vicar suggests, alone, "the only member of his party." This gives him what the "Profession of Faith" ultimately demands: a witness that enables him to do without the "witness of men" (*Emile*, 313; *Pl.* 4:635).

To summarize, according to Rousseau, the purpose of the "Profession of Faith" is combating the two extremes of atheism and intolerance. Rousseau seeks to combat them not because either atheism or fanaticism is in and of itself evil, but rather due to their harmful effects on the common good. The good of society is the controlling factor in all his considerations about religious belief.

THE INADEQUACIES OF THIS INTERPRETATION

It is clear that the "Profession of Faith" is divided into two parts, that the first part argues for the existence of God, and that the second part offers a critique of revela-tion. Why should this be called into question? I do so because this characterization is incomplete. To view the primary aim of the second part as the combating of fanati-cism will not stand up to scrutiny. Once this is called into question, the aim of the first part also needs to be re-examined.

The dramatic context that structures the "Profession of Faith" calls Rousseau's interpretation into question. The story in which Rousseau presents the teaching makes it hard to accept that the second part could be intended as a defense against the fanaticism that results from dogmatism. The vicar is addressing the young man who may or may not be Rousseau. As the vicar begins the second part, he confesses his reluctance to share his uncertainty and doubts. He then says, "If your sentiments were more stable, I would hesitate to expound mine to you. But in your present con-dition you will profit from thinking as I do" (*Emile*, 295; *Pl.* 4:607). Rousseau, as editor, attaches a footnote to this sentence that reads, "This is, I believe, what the good Vicar could say to the public at present" (*Emile*, 295n; *Pl.* 4:607n). This provides the reader with an important hermeneutic key to the "Profession of Faith." Rousseau is publishing it because he believes that the spiritual state of Europe is now similar to the state that he was in as a young man. What is that state?

After he finishes reciting his actual "Profession of Faith," the vicar tells the young man what he sees in the youth's soul that leads him to make this confession. He contextualizes this by saying that, as long as there is "some sound belief" in people, one should not disturb or alarm the "faith of simple people"—that is, one should not cause scandal (*Emile*, 310; *Pl.* 4:630). The vicar continues as follows: "But once everything is shaken, one ought to preserve the trunk at the expense of the branches. Consciences which are agitated, uncertain, almost extinguished, and *in the condition in which I have seen yours*, need to be reinforced and awakened; and in order to put them back on the foundation of eternal truths, it is necessary to complete the job of ripping out the shaky pillars to which they are still attached" (*Emile*, 310; *Pl.* 4:630; emphasis added). According to the vicar, then, the young man is in danger of losing his faith, not of becoming a fanatic. We can extrapolate that Europe's faith has been shaken, that the consciences of even the "simple people" are becoming uncertain.[9] This can and does lead to violence and unrest, but not to the unrest of religious fanaticism. Rousseau is clearly concerned with a weakening of religion's role in society that will lead, in turn, to a deterioration in the maintenance of public order. The only way to fight this apparent danger is through another form of violence: sacrificing the branches and ripping out the pillars.

Given the putative purpose of fighting dogmatism, the first part would presume the second part.[10] In other words, normally, one would first rip out the shaky pillars (the second part) and then put the conscience of the young man on the more secure foundations of the first part. But if the purpose of the second part is to protect the ideology of the first part, then the order in which they are presented makes sense. As has already been said, the vicar establishes the existence of a violent God and then protects that existence from anything that might call it into question.

LOOKING AGAIN AT THE FIRST PART

If the second part is not a defense against fanaticism, then what is its aim? To answer this, one needs to look more closely at the first part and what is being accomplished there. Instead of simply being an establishment of the existence of God, it has to be seen more specifically as establishing God as the sanction of moral law.

According to Rousseau, violence results when belief in God is absent. In the buildup to the "Profession of Faith" itself, Rousseau couches the point in the following maxim: "The forgetting of all religion leads to a forgetting of the duties of man" (*Emile*, 263; *Pl.* 4:561). This maxim gets repeated with slight variations in the middle of the "Profession of Faith" by the vicar when he states, "If the divinity does not exist, it is only the wicked man who reasons, and the good man is nothing but a fool" (*Emile*, 292; *Pl.* 4:603). At the end, Rousseau inserts a footnote that spells out the problems of violence and injustice that occur when religious belief is weakened. This will be discussed more later, but here, one must recall Rousseau's own words that follow almost immediately after the "Profession of Faith":

> Abandon this [the promise of durable happiness in the afterlife], and I no longer see anything but injustice, hypocrisy, and lying among men. Private interest, which in case of conflict necessarily prevails over everything, teaches everyone to adorn vice with the mask of virtue. Let all other men do what is good for me at their expense; let everything be related to me alone; let all mankind, if need be, die in suffering and poverty to spare me a moment of pain or hunger. This is the inner language of every unbeliever who reasons. Yes, I shall maintain it all my life. Whoever speaks otherwise although he has said in his heart, "There is not God," is nothing but a liar or a fool. (*Emile*, 314–15; *Pl.* 4:636–37)

What then leads to this loss of faith, and how can it be prevented? It is this question that the first part addresses.

In the first part, the vicar claims that he has an idea of happiness as a reward for being good, and that he experiences a need for this to be true. This idea and need represent a promissory note from God. And yet he experiences that "the wicked man prospers, and the just man remains oppressed. Also, see what indignation is kindled in us when this expectation is frustrated! Conscience is aroused and complains about its Author. It cries out to Him in moaning, 'Thou has deceived me!'" (*Emile*, 282; *Pl.* 4:589) Against his own experience, the vicar gives God's answer as follows: "Why do you say, 'Virtue is nothing,' when you are going to enjoy the reward for yours? You are going to die, you think. No, you are going to live, and it is then that I shall keep all the promises I have made you" (*Emile*, 282; *Pl.* 4:589). On the one hand are humans scandalized by the historical vision of evil triumphing over good; on the other is a God who enables humans to overcome their scandal with the assurance that appearances are deceiving and that all will work out in the end.

The Vicar is no longer scandalized. In his past, the triumph of the wicked and the oppression of the just are "so shocking a dissonance in the universal harmony" (*Emile*, 283; *Pl.* 4:589–90) that he has to seek to resolve it. He tells the young Rousseau that his metaphysical dualism—his belief in an immaterial soul that survives the physical death of the body—is the key to the resolution. Things are restored to order after death, when the soul is rewarded or punished according to the life that it has lived. "The life of the soul begins only with the death of the body" (*Emile*, 283; *Pl.* 4:590).

The primary purpose of the first part of the "Profession of Faith" is the neutralizing of the scandal of evil through the establishment of a God who rewards the virtuous, even if they suffer injustice in this life, and punishes the wicked, even if they seem to triumph. One can now explore the purpose of the second part beyond its stated purpose of preventing fanaticism.

THE SECOND PART AS THE OBFUSCATION OF EXPULSION

The primary purpose of the second part of the "Profession of Faith" is to disqualify or expel human testimony in matters of divine revelation. According to the vicar, reason gives humanity its "greatest ideas" of the divinity (*Emile*, 295; *Pl.* 4:607). He argues in the first part that the order of nature and conscience tell humans that God exists. In the second part, he poses the following truly critical question: "What more will men tell us [other men seeking to know religious truths]?" (*Emile*, 295; *Pl.* 4:607).

Human revelations do not elevate mortal conceptions of God; instead, they degrade it. The vicar says that these dogmas, "far from clarifying the notions of the great Being, confuse them; that far from ennobling them, they debase them; that to the inconceivable mysteries surrounding the great Being they add absurd contradictions; that they make man proud, intolerant, cruel; that instead of establishing peace on earth, they bring sword and fire to it" (*Emile*, 295; *Pl.* 4:607). Rousseau, through the vicar, is alluding to the scriptural passages in which Jesus says, "Do not think that I have come to bring peace on earth; I have not come to bring peace, but a sword" (Matt. 10:34).[11] Luke, in his parallel to this passage, begins by having Christ say, "I came to cast fire upon the earth; and would that it were already kindled!" (Luke 12:49).

These sayings are not incidental to the New Testament. The vicar has uncovered an important truth about Christianity: it does not simply bring peace but also disturbs it and disrupts the human community. Here is a paradox worthy of Rousseau: Christianity brings fire and the sword to the earth precisely to the degree that it undoes the social order held together by the threat of divine violence. The question then becomes: does Christianity cause conflict because it supports humans in their illusions of having supernatural knowledge, or does this happen because it reveals the violent foundations of conventional peace, and in so doing provides a new foundation?

The vicar holds that for a revealed religion to be able to claim that humans must believe in it or be damned to hell, its revelation would have to be available at all times and in all places, and it would have to be intelligible to people of every station. In effect, it would have to be a natural religion. What the vicar seeks is a divine guarantee of the veracity of the revelation that does not depend upon human mediation. Thus, when other humans claim that God has spoken to them, that is well and good, but why should He not also speak directly to the vicar? When humans claim that miracles are not to be directly experienced, but rather are to be believed based on human records, then this is too far removed from the vicar to be compelling. There is too much chance of error or misunderstanding entering into the transmission of these events.

The vicar has set aside human authority, leaving everyone on the common ground of human reason. By definition, then, any unreasonable doctrine will never convince, and so much of the discussion about revealed religion becomes a waste of time. As the vicar summarizes it, "See, then, what your alleged supernatural proofs, your miracles and prophecies come down to: a belief in all this on the faith of others, and a subjection of the authority of God, speaking to my reason, to the authority of men" (*Emile*, 301; *Pl.* 4:617). To require humans to believe, under pain of damnation, in one religion rather than in another is to damn them to a life of study and research so that they can verify this requirement. And if one takes the more moderate position that it is not absolutely necessary to engage in this research, that one can give some weight to human authority and so follow the religion of one's own people, then everyone—Muslims, Buddhists, Hindus, as well as Christians—can do the same and should not be proselytized. For this reason, the vicar keeps his faith restricted to primary notions. Realizing that he will never be so learned, the vicar "closed all books," but as later becomes evident, one remained opened to him (*Emile*, 306; *Pl.* 4:624).

Rousseau adds to the vicar's position in a footnote that he attaches to the vicar's warning against those atheistic philosophers who "deprive the afflicted of their last consolation of their misery, and the powerful and rich of the only brake on their passions" (*Emile*, 312; *Pl.* 4:632). The *philosophes* see themselves as engaged in a struggle against violent fanaticism. Rousseau can agree that Pierre Bayle, author of the famous *Dictionary*, has proven that atheism is less harmful than fanaticism, but he points out what is lost by simply replacing the latter with the former. Fanaticism is "a grave and strong passion which elevates the heart of man, makes him despise death, and gives him sublime virtue" (*Emile*, 312n; *Pl.* 4:633n). Against this is "irreligion," or what he equates with it, "the reasoning and philosophic spirit in general" (*Emile*, 312n; *Pl.* 4:633n). Rousseau repeats here in the footnote what the vicar has affirmed at least three times—this spirit saps the foundations of every society. In the final analysis, the tranquility produced by philosophic indifference is the "tranquility of death," which is "more destructive than war itself" (*Emile*, 312n; *Pl.* 4:633n).

It is not just religion in general that Rousseau credits with giving governments a more solid foundation. He also points to the pivotal role of Christianity and the Gospels as follows: "Our modern governments incontestably owe their more solid authority and less frequent revolutions to Christianity" (*Emile*, 313n; *Pl.* 4:634n). The institutions of the Christian religion help undo injustice by the reparations they require.

Rousseau ends the footnote with an example taken not from the Christian tradition, but rather from the Muslim tradition. He quotes Sir John Chardin, who describes the Persian Muslims' belief in the bridge called Poul-Serrho. This is the bridge that all will have to pass over after death. The belief is that one will not pass over this bridge until one has "rendered the last penny to those one has oppressed" (*Emile*, 314n; *Pl.* 4:634–35n). If this doctrine is removed, that is, if the belief that there is a place "where the oppressed wreak vengeance on their tyrants after death," is removed, then, says Rousseau, the final barrier preventing oppression will fall away. Because the loss of this belief would result in real harm to society, Rousseau is confident that the taking away of this salutary belief—a professed goal of the Enlightenment—could not be the truth. Rousseau concludes, "Philosopher, your moral laws are very fine, but I beg you to show me their sanction. Stop beating around the bush for a moment, and tell me plainly what you put in the place of Poul-Serrho" (*Emile*, 314n; *Pl.* 4:635n). Rousseau's religious system works politically to counter the violence of oppression and tyranny. This comes in the form of either a violent God, or a place where God allows the weak to avenge themselves on the strong. Without this sanction, Rousseau cannot see what role religion might have.

HUMAN TESTIMONY

At this point, I would like to return to Rousseau's controversy with the archbishop of Paris because the acceptance or rejection of human testimony becomes one of the main points of contention. The argument becomes rather nuanced in its development in three different texts, namely, the "Profession of Faith," the archbishop's condemnation of that text, and Rousseau's response to the condemnation. Still, it is worth following.

To begin, the vicar and, as the controversy will confirm, through him, Rousseau, clearly affirm the "majesty of the Scriptures" and the "holiness of the Gospel" (*Emile*, 307; *Pl.* 4:625). The vicar confirms the goodness of the Bible against the books of the philosophers. In this book, particularly in the Gospels, the vicar finds "gentleness," "purity," "grace," "wisdom," "presence of mind," and "finesse" (*Emile*, 307; *Pl.* 4:625). Thus, he does not close all books.

He immediately calls into question the traditional comparison between Socrates and Jesus, only to make that comparison himself. According to him, Jesus Christ in death far outshines Socrates. Socrates's death was as easy as his life. He had many outstanding examples of virtue, and all he needed to do was to reflect intelligently on them. For the vicar, the death of the philosopher was "the sweetest one could desire" (*Emile*, 308; *Pl.* 4:626). There is no hint that Socrates was persecuted or unjustly convicted. Athens suffers no reproof from the vicar.

Jesus' death, in contrast, is, according to the vicar, the "most horrible one could imagine" (*Emile*, 308; *Pl.* 4:626). This is due to the fact that he lived among the most furious fanaticism and "the vilest of all people"—the Jews (*Emile*, 308; *Pl.* 4:626). For the vicar, the Gospels have characteristics of truth at which no Jew could have arrived. The Gospels tell the story of the crisis caused by the introduction of Jesus' purity, wisdom, grace, and finesse into the worst fanaticism and the vilest of people. This just man is covered with opprobrium by these particular people and is killed. As Jesus' executioners, they are relentless. Jesus' death was one of torment and reprobation by "a whole people" (*Emile*, 308; *Pl.* 4:626). When the vicar says, "yes, if the life and death of Socrates are those of a wise man, the life and death of Jesus are those of a God," it is clear that it is his manner of death that makes him a God.

The archbishop, for his part, quotes, almost in full, Rousseau's praise of the Gospel and his comparison of Socrates's and Jesus' death. He does so in order to "edify" his flock. He edits out most of the anti-Semitic elements and concludes the quotation with the comment, "It would be difficult, My Very Dear Brethren, to pay a more beautiful homage to the authenticity of the Gospel" (*CW* 9:11).

Rousseau, for his part, thanks the archbishop for admitting that he respects the Gospels, and then he proceeds to restate this part of the "Profession of Faith" with the anti-Semitic elements restored, thus claiming this part of the "Profession of Faith" most strongly as his own. He restores the text to its original form, saying the following about the archbishop's omissions: "not that those he left here are absolutely insidious, as they are in other places, but because the lack of continuity and sequence weakens the passage when it is truncated. And also given that my persecutors carefully suppress everything I said so wholeheartedly in favor of Religion, it is good to restore it whenever the opportunity arises" (*CW* 9:72n; *Pl.* 4:992n). Significantly, it is precisely this passage that appears in all three of the texts that I am analyzing. According to this passage, beyond the wisdom of Jesus, the Gospels tell the story, on the one hand, of the innocence of Jesus and the arbitrariness of his victimization, and on the other hand, of the violence and fanaticism of the Jews. They reveal persecution, yet they become the pretext for further persecution.

The Archbishop accepts, as much as the vicar or Rousseau, that Jesus' death is the death of a God, rather than seeing it for what it truly was—another human victim arbitrarily sacrificed by a crowd, composed in the main of those who had the highest religion and the most preparation to know better than to victimize. It is this religion that did, in fact, help some of them to see the significance of this death. It is not the absolute uniqueness of Jesus of Nazareth's death that is central to Christianity (many others died on the Cross).

To return to the "Profession of Faith" after having praised the Gospels, the vicar goes on to argue against them, exclaiming that they are full "of unbelievable things, of things repugnant to reason and impossible for any sensible man to conceive or to accept" (*Emile*, 308; *Pl.* 4:627). He does not get more specific. This is not simply the standard Enlightenment move against the miracles reported in the Bible. Rather than their impossibility, the problem with miracles for the vicar is that they are not unambiguous proof of God's intervention; the devil can also perform miracles. The implication is that the elements of the Gospels that are "unbelievable" and "repugnant" to reason are precisely those parts that stand in need of human testimony in order to be accepted.

Thus, what the vicar most objects to is having to accept the testimony of other humans. The archbishop accuses him of an inconsistency and says that one cannot claim to love the Scriptures and not accept human testimony. Rousseau, in his response to the archbishop, counters by saying that the acceptance of human facts, such as the existence of Sparta, on the basis of human testimony is appropriate and, further, that no one will be eternally damned for not believing in the existence of Sparta. On the other hand, if God wants to talk to Jean-Jacques about his own eternal salvation, then why did he go through Moses, as the archbishop would claim? Rousseau's conclusion is that "the moral proofs sufficient to establish facts which are in the order of moral possibilities, no longer suffice to verify facts of another order, purely supernatural" (*CW* 9:69; *Pl.* 4:989).

The singularity of Rousseau's position here needs to be appreciated from a historical viewpoint. He has managed to combine an Enlightenment distrust of authority with a Calvinistic distrust of human mediation. Naturally, the Roman Catholic archbishop sees here the great contradiction of the "Profession of Faith." On the one hand, Rousseau, through "the assumed character that serves him as a mouthpiece" (*CW* 9:8), gives this "beautiful homage to the authenticity of the Gospel" (*CW* 9:11), and on the other, he expends "the greatest efforts to discredit the human testimony attesting to Christian Revelation" (*CW* 9:11). But Rousseau's position is not inconsistent. He is quite consistently working out a certain type of human reason, a reason that does not accept human testimony in supernatural matters.

The exact charge of the archbishop is that Rousseau is "manifestly contradicting himself" when, "after the greatest efforts to discredit the human testimony attesting to Christian Revelation, the same Author nonetheless defers to *it* in the most positive, most solemn manner" (*CW* 9:11; emphasis added). In his response, Rousseau points to an ambiguity in the construction of the archbishop's sentence. The "it" to which the archbishop claims Rousseau defers could be either Christian revelation or human testimony. "But if it refers to human testimony, you [the archbishop] are wrong" (*CW* 9:71; *Pl.* 4:991). Rousseau argues that he himself reads the Gospels, and that he himself sees and judges the sublimity in it "without any attesting to it" (*CW* 9:71; *Pl.* 4:991). He holds that no one else repeats to him that the Gospels exist. One cannot conclude that there are men between him and God. In the Gospels, Rousseau recognizes the divine Spirit: "That is as unmediated as it can be. There are no men between that proof and me" (*CW* 9:73; *Pl.* 4:994). Rousseau is enough a part of the Enlightenment to try to free supernatural truth from vagaries of history, and still enough of a Calvinist to eliminate human mediation between the individual believer and God.

Rousseau explicitly states that he does not reject revelation (cf. *CW* 9.74; *Pl.* 4:996). This claim is critical to my argument. It implies that seeing the second part as a rejection of revealed truth that leads to fanaticism is inadequate. Rousseau is rejecting not revelation but the mediation of humans: the vicar states, "We have set aside all human authority" (*Emile* 300; *Pl.* 4:614). Once anything is given to human authority, all is lost. This is the constant theme of the "Profession of Faith," especially in the second half. Rousseau rejects testimony, and thus the "Profession of Faith" itself becomes a text of expulsion, expelling human witness from the Gospels. But with the human witness gone, the text itself is transformed into a text that accuses the Jewish people. The author designs the "Profession of Faith" to restrain violence by means of the economy of violence. That is, it establishes God as a sanction of the moral law and the Jewish people as the object of contempt.[12] For all their differences, these are points upon which the archbishop of the Church, the Savoyard vicar, and Rousseau agree.

The vicar claims that if he were a better reasoner, perhaps he could accept this claim of Scripture or "sense the truth of revelation" (*Emile*, 307; *Pl.* 4:625), but what if the truth being witnessed to is precisely that truth that one cannot reach with reason alone? What if the expulsion to which the Gospels witness is precisely unreasonable and "repugnant to reason"?[13] What if this testimony concerns the irrational truth of violence that makes our present form of reason possible? Then reason on its own power will never be able to reach the expulsion upon which it is based, but will be condemned instead to endless repetition of this act of expulsion. Condemned, that is, until a testimony reveals to it the arbitrariness of the expulsion, the innocence of the victim, and the guilt of reason's involvement in this expulsion. And if this is true, then the essence of the Gospel is witness.

If this is true, then the vicar would have expelled the one element that would have prevented the Gospels from being used as a text to accuse the Jews. Indeed, this is what has happened. The great irony is that in the attempt to arrive at a reasonable, nonviolent God, Rousseau has created a God that sanctions human vengeance. The very thing that the Gospels are meant to destroy, Rousseau ends up perpetuating.

The question becomes whether the vicar is proposing a program that will lead to peace or simply another version of the same story of violence, even if that is not what he intends. Is this peace built on exclusion and violence? It would seem not. The vicar is called by Rousseau the "man of peace." Although this is a story, we do not need to doubt the sincerity of Rousseau in transcribing the figure of a cleric who hopes to serve, in love, the people of his village regardless of their religious affiliation, and who hopes with all his heart to reconcile neighbors and to establish a community. It would be difficult to find fault with a man who affirms the following sentiments: "I would bring them all [Protestants as well as Catholics in his area] to love one another without distinction and to regard one another as brothers, to respect all religions, and to live in peace, with each observing his own" (*Emile*, 310; *Pl.* 4:629). Still, one can ask if the vicar's "Profession of Faith" provides the resources necessary to sustain this sentiment.

It is the nature of the violence that humans commit that they think that it is justified. It is not as though either the vicar or Rousseau wants to cut out all testimony to violence. Both of them have been victims of violence and even of persecution, and they do not repress or deny that. But that kind of accusatory testimony is only one kind of testimony, and it does not, as the vicar rightly sees, convince anyone. One can always make a counteraccusation. Reasons are needed to justify and judge the accusations. But there is another form of testimony that in many ways is peculiar to the Hebrew and Christian Scriptures. It is the voice of the innocent victim who does not accuse, but instead forgives. It is the voice that reveals the arbitrariness (the nonrational nature) of the expulsion. The vicar does not expel anyone directly, but he expels the one voice that robs the mob of its unanimity and thus robs the mob's reason of its rationality. Reason will never be able to know if it was formed by an expulsion.

Reason on its own, in the way it is constituted, cannot reach this position. Here is a certain impasse. If one will accept only reasoned argument, which seems like a perfectly rational position, then there is no way to get beyond rational argument or to see the possibility of another form of reason.

To put it another way, Rousseau rules out the possibility that a true religion can contain elements scandalous to reason. And further, if Rousseau is arguing against intolerance, he is making an implicit claim that none of the beliefs he champions is capable of offending anyone else. Thus, all attacks on him are not only evil but also inexplicable. He becomes the innocent victim. If one accepts Rousseau's arguments, the most scandalous of his works, the "Profession of Faith," judged by the reaction it provoked, is rendered nonscandalous. If one believes in God and is tolerant, then one should not be scandalized by this text, and the fact that Christians were scandalized (meaning in this case, shocked) by Rousseau's scandal (meaning in this case, leading people away from the scandalous faith) was considered by Rousseau to be a scandalous reaction.

The whole of the "Profession of Faith" helps to ensure belief in the existence of God, for "without faith no true virtue exists" (*Emile*, 312; *Pl.* 4:632). Without faith, without belief in the existence of God, the good man is nothing but a fool. What the "Profession of Faith" removes is precisely the possibility, attested to in the Gospels, that the good man is indeed a fool. There is no room for this thought in the system of the vicar as it is taken up by Rousseau. In effect, there is no room for the Gospels. The vicar, in his search for truth, has turned away from books. These books would only lead him astray, but as Henri Gouhier points out, the one book of the Scriptures remains open to him while the message of that one book has been ruled out.[14]

CONCLUSION

Finally, there remains the question of why Rousseau did not simply reject Christianity and the Gospels *in toto*. Why the "beautiful homage" yet the rejection? There are two reasons. On the one hand, the Scriptures are the metanarrative that gives structure and meaning to the parts forming the context of the "Profession of Faith" as well as the *Letter to Beaumont*. Both the young man and the vicar are victims. The vicar, who is "so poor, exiled, persecuted," is the one who holds the key to happiness (*Emile*, 266; *Pl.* 4:564). The young man, as the victim who has been snatched from infamy and who can now be rendered to virtue, is the one who can receive it. In the footnote quoted from the *Letter to Beaumont*, Rousseau refers to his "persecutors" (*CW* 9:72n; *Pl.* 4:992n). The structure of the Gospels, the one righteous man against all others, gives the *story* its moral weight.

There is a deeper, more hidden, reason for Rousseau's attachment to the Scriptures. The "Profession of Faith" is a text of expulsion. In order for it to be a text of expulsion, there must be something to expel. The object of the expulsion is not witness or testimony in general. The "Profession of Faith" is too dependent on the Gospels not to be a form of testimony itself. The vicar is testifying in good faith, and so is Rousseau. But the "Profession of Faith" is structured around the expulsion of the testimony of expulsion. It testifies indirectly to that which it rejects. Rousseau cannot completely separate himself from the Gospels without the "Profession of Faith" collapsing upon itself, and he cannot accept them without having to reject the main premise of the "Profession of Faith."

This interpretation allows for a new assessment of Rousseau's achievement in the "Profession of Faith." In particular, it allows its true originality to emerge. The violence from the religious wars of the sixteenth and seventeenth centuries produced a body of proposals for religious toleration. One could view the "Profession of Faith" as belonging to the tradition, beginning with at least Michel de Montaigne's *Essays*, of arguing for toleration based upon a moderate skepticism. And certainly this understanding of the "Profession of Faith" is not incorrect. The need for toleration has not lessened in the 230 years since *Emile* was published. Acts of violence supported, if not caused, by religious fanaticism are familiar to everyone.

However, this interpretation clarifies the way in which the "Profession of Faith" moves beyond this tradition and opens up another world that is also familiar. This is not the world of religious fanaticism, but rather the world of religious indifference. Rousseau is doing more than arguing against fanaticism and for toleration.

Rousseau is writing for those whose traditional beliefs have been shaken, for those who are unsure what to believe. He writes to remove the very thing that is causing this uncertainty and lack of surety—the Scriptures. The Scriptures undermine every attempt to found a social order on a violent God, and therefore they must not be allowed to speak. The Bible calls into question every form of community based on violence, not excluding the Church. In this sense, rather than seeing Rousseau as the last effect of the Thirty Years' War, one can see him as the first cause of a post-Christian age.[15] The vicar has thrown out not only the subtleties of doctrine that could cause dissension and unrest, but also all of the "unbelievable things" that are "repugnant to reason and impossible for any sensible man to conceive or to accept"

(*Emile*, 308; *Pl.* 4:627). He has removed the scandal from the Gospels, and in so doing has transformed the death of Christ from something that reveals human sin and universal complicity in violence into something that reveals the special fault of one group, the Jews. These two movements are not unrelated; they imply each other. If one is not implicated in the Cross, it is because one can blame someone else.

I began by showing how the "Profession of Faith" is embedded in the novel through the allusions and echoes of earlier events. It is time to comment on how it helps set the stage for what is to follow. Emile is at the age at which "the heart is still free, but ardent, restless, avid for a happiness it does not know" (*Emile*, 293; *Pl.* 4:604). His heart seeks this happiness. Such is the age of Emile as we enter this transcription, and such also is the age of the young Rousseau as he listens to the "Profession of Faith." Neither has yet been deceived by the senses. If that happens, then one settles on a "vain image of happiness" (*Emile*, 293; *Pl.* 4:604). The vain image of happiness is sexual intercourse. The purpose of the "Profession of Faith" is to give the true image of happiness.

The tutor wants some transcendent restraint in place before he relinquishes his hold on the child through deceitfulness. Once the pupil knows that God is always watching, then the tutor can treat him as a friend and reveal not only the secrets of generation, but also all the ways he has dealt with him.

The interpretation offered here brings out the relation between the "Profession of Faith" and Emile's romance with Sophie as well as Rousseau's political philosophy. If the Scriptures are gone, a new Christ, a new Church, and, in fact, a new Trinity become necessary. In the romance and political philosophy that make up Book V, Emile becomes the new Christ, society the new Church, and with Rousseau as the Father, Emile as the Son, and Sophia or wisdom as the Spirit; a new creation.

CHAPTER 5

THE SCANDAL OF DESIRE

INTRODUCTION

This chapter takes up the text beginning at the end of the "Profession of Faith" in Book IV and follows it to the summary of the *Social Contract* contained in the sub-section, "On Travel" in Book V.[1] A variety of writing confronts the reader. The tutor describes Emile's future mate, whom he names "Sophie." Then the author steps forward and in his own name gives an essay on taste; this concludes Book IV. Book V opens with Rousseau's essay, "On Woman," in which he opines on the female's character, strengths, weaknesses, as well as on her upbringing. Rousseau then tells the tragic tale of an alternative "Sophie," before he finally turns to the story of the courtship of Emile and Sophie.

The problem of human desire and the link that the text asserts between this desire and death unify these seemingly disparate elements. Human desire is mimetic or imitative, and, according to Girard, mimetic desire is deeply connected with scandal. "The *skandalon* is the obstacle/model of mimetic rivalry; it is the model in so far as he works to counter the undertakings of the disciple and so becomes an inexhaustible source of morbid fascination."[2] As will become clear, the tutor, even more than the woman, becomes the obstacle and model of Emile's desire in this part of the book.

This discussion of idyllic romance cannot be divorced from the context of violence in which it appears. Before it lies the "Profession of Faith," which suppresses the scandalous elements of the Gospels in order to argue for a violent God who acts as the ultimate sanction of moral behavior. After it comes Rousseau's political philosophy, which keeps in check the violence that is constantly threatening to engulf the political community.[3]

Until this point in the story, Emile has not suffered what would be termed today, alienation. He has done what he has wanted. The tutor has protected him thus far from mimetic rivalry. Emile has not had to come into conflict with another over an object of desire. As long as Emile remains unified in this way, he cannot enter into the social contract, because the social contract demands that a citizen subordinate his desires or his particular will to the commands of the general will. Thus, the tutor has to introduce a split in Emile's makeup and help him reach the point at which he is able to follow his duty rather than his inclinations.[4] Romance is the means to accomplish all this. The depth of this split should not be underestimated. In fact, the text will justify saying that Emile becomes another—he becomes his tutor.

If the problem is human desire, so then is the solution. Throughout this section, one will see how both the tutor and the author become the mediator of desire—the former for Emile and Sophie, the latter for the reader. This mediation of desire prevents death in the sense of sacrifice, as demonstrated in the story of the "other" Sophie, and so leads to the social contract.

Rousseau's aim in writing about this romance is ultimately religious in the sense that he is presenting Emile as the new man, the new Christ, and the goal of the history of the human species. Emile becomes the new man by having another experience of scandal and by having that experience directed by the tutor. The reader becomes capable of understanding Emile as the new man through the experience of scandal involved in reading a romance and being guided in that experience by the author. The novel *Emile* begins to resemble the Gospels more clearly in that both are an occasion of scandal, and that scandal can be either given into or overcome.

Rousseau reflects explicitly in the latter part of *Emile* on the role of the mediator and the possibility of reaching the truth through fiction. That is, he reflects upon his novel as a possible mediator of the truth. In the story, Jean-Jacques mediates Emile's desire through a fictional Sophie, so that Emile comes to desire the real Sophie, and then Jean-Jacques serves as the mediator of their mutual desire.[5] From the reader's standpoint, Jean-Jacques guides Emile to Sophie through a fiction. Rousseau, in turn, wants to mediate the reader's desires so that he or she will come to love the real natural man through a fictional portrait. First, Jean-Jacques must direct Emile to Sophie through the fiction of "Sophie," and then he must direct Sophie to Emile through Francois de Fénelon's novel, *Telemachus*, to reach the goal of their desire, true love. In the same way, Rousseau hopes to lead the reader to the truth through his fiction.

Further, through his story of the "other Sophie," Rousseau shows that there are in the end only two choices, death or desire, and that the difference between them is the presence of a mediator. In this tale, "Sophie" dies due to reading fiction. This is the result that Rousseau would like to avoid, but also the risk that he must run in order to achieve his goal.

THE CHANGE IN THE RELATIONSHIP
BETWEEN JEAN-JACQUES AND EMILE

Before the "Profession of Faith," Jean-Jacques prepares to teach Emile how to think about God. He prepares him for the day when the meaning of his sexuality will be revealed to him. That day has come. Jean-Jacques has aimed all of these preparations at one thing—"not to remove him from his place but to keep him in it" (*Emile*, 316; *Pl.* 4:639).

Following the "Profession of Faith" and preparing for the entrance of Sophie, three important concepts are introduced: moral relationships, sexuality, and imitation. With the coming together of these three, the relationship between the tutor and the student undergoes a radical change. As Emile becomes a physical man, so he becomes a moral friend of the teacher, and his teacher passes from being a kind of playmate to being both a model for and obstacle to Emile. Emile imitates the tutor's desires.

The change in the relationship between Jean-Jacques and Emile can be summarized by saying that they become friends.[6] Rousseau addresses the reader as if he were the tutor and says, "he [Emile] is your friend, he is a man. From now on treat him as such" (*Emile*, 316; *Pl.* 4:639). The friendship does not yet mean full equality, but the inequality that exists depends upon Emile's knowledge and consent. According to Rousseau, now one begins to use one's authority with the pupil.

At the same time that Jean-Jacques becomes more forthright and transparent with Emile, Rousseau becomes more forthright and transparent with his reader as follows: "Up until now you got nothing from him [Emile] except by force or ruse. Authority and the law of duty were unknown to him. He had to be constrained or deceived to make him obey you. But see how many new chains you put around his heart. Reason, friendship, gratitude, countless affections speak to him in a tone he cannot fail to recognize" (*Emile*, 316; *Pl.* 4:639). Before, Jean-Jacques has secretly mediated desires for Emile (e.g., his desire for a garden or his desire to perform the magic act), but he has never been the obstacle, never the will that Emile might have to cross. He emphasizes that he has never had to command Emile to get him to do anything. Until this point, Jean-Jacques has always hidden behind the other, be it Robert or the magician, to accomplish his will. He has appeared as Emile's accomplice, not only in striving after the thing desired, but also in suffering the punishment that follows as a result of this desire.

At the moment that Emile becomes aware of his capability to be sexually generative, Jean-Jacques reveals to him how he has been generated through the efforts of his tutor. Jean-Jacques reveals to the young Emile all that he has done for him. Further, he reveals that he has, in fact, done all this for himself and not for Emile. For the first time, Jean-Jacques speaks to Emile of his own interests. The sentiments of friendship, generosity, and gratitude are inflamed. Rousseau refers to precisely these sentiments as the "chains" that the governor has put around the heart of his pupil to take the place of ruse or force. They will take the place of the physical constraint or deception that has kept Emile in his place up until now.

From the viewpoint of his own interests, Jean-Jacques makes clear to Emile who he is. He calls him "[his] property, [his] child, [his] work" (*Emile*, 323; *Pl.* 4:649). He continues, "It is from your happiness that I expect my own. If you frustrate my hopes, you are robbing me of twenty years of my life, and you are causing the unhappiness of my old age" (*Emile*, 323; *Pl.* 4:649). This is the first indication of a fusion between Emile and the tutor. This will only strengthen from here.

Rousseau makes it clear to the reader in the following quote that Jean-Jacques is the one who indicates to Emile what is desirable, and at the same moment denies it: "If I have been able, in accordance with these maxims, to take all the necessary precautions and to make speeches to my Emile suitable for the juncture of life that he has reached, I do not doubt for an instant that *he will come by himself to the point where I want to lead him*" (*Emile*, 325; *Pl.* 4:651; emphasis added). The language itself reveals the tension. Does Emile actually move on his own accord, or is he led by

Jean-Jacques? The fascinating aspect of desire at this point is that one can lead and the other can be led, and still one feels as if he is following his own desires. This is the basic, hidden illusion of spontaneous, autonomous desire. This illusion, always presumed but never revealed by Rousseau, is the ground upon which the illusion of love, which he does reveal, is based. It is also the fundamental misapprehension upon which the book is based.

Jean-Jacques incites Emile's desire through the obstacles he places in its path. This strategy derives from Rousseau's theory of the human passions: "One has a hold on the passions only by means of the passions. It is by their empire that their tyranny must be combated; and it is always from nature itself that the proper instruments to repulse nature must be drawn" (*Emile*, 327; *Pl.* 4:654). Emile sees the dangers with which his sexuality threatens him, and so comes to put himself back under the authority of the tutor. He seeks from the master defense against his enemies, both internal and external. Emile begs him, "Make me free by protecting me against those of my passions which do violence to me. Prevent me from being their slave; force me to be my own master and to obey not my senses but my reason" (*Emile*, 325; *Pl.* 4:652).

LEADING EMILE TO SOPHIE

Jean-Jacques uses Emile's imagination as the chief instrument to guide his desires toward Sophie. Jean-Jacques paints a portrait of his future beloved and wife. Through this, Emile arrives at the proper disposition of his sentiments "with respect to what they ought to seek or flee" (*Emile*, 329; *Pl.* 4:656). At the same time that Jean-Jacques is telling the readers about his method for leading Emile, Rousseau is informing the readers about his method in *Emile*. It does not matter that the object he depicts (Sophie for Emile, Emile for us) is imaginary. What matters is that Emile and the readers prefer the chimera to the real objects that strike their eyes. This has to do with Rousseau's conception of love: "And what is true love itself if it is not a chimera, lie and illusion? We love the image we make for ourselves far more than we love the object to which we apply it. If we saw what we love exactly as it is, there would be no more love on earth" According to Rousseau, love is the magic veil without which love disappears. Jean-Jacques is in charge of the imaginary object, and thus he is the "master of comparisons" (*Emile*, 329; *Pl.* 4:656). Through the illusion of love, Jean-Jacques can prevent Emile "from having illusions about real objects" (*Emile*, 329; *Pl.* 4:656).

What makes an object desirable for Emile? In what does its desirability consist? It consists in *the tutor's desire*. He communicates to Emile that he too desires this object, that he finds it desirable. According to Rousseau, neither the imagination nor the senses cause something to be desired. The model causes this, and thus he is the key. The models that a young person sees indicate what is desirable and what is not. Thus, the identity of the model is crucial. As Rousseau remarks, a "young man entering society . . . yields more to the inclinations *of others than to his own*, and amour-propre produces more libertines than love does" (*Emile*, 331; *Pl.* 4:659; emphasis added).

It is imitation, then, that is the ultimate source of the trouble. Imitation corrupts. "But who in the world is less an imitator than Emile?" asks Rousseau (*Emile*, 331; *Pl.* 4:659) Rousseau wishes for this rhetorical question to be answered with a resounding "no one." Rousseau is aware that no one is more of an imitator than Emile. Emile is a model for the reader to imitate. He is the model of one who imitates without appearing to, and in this generations of Rousseau's readers have imitated him very well.

Emile's docility to Jean-Jacques proves that Jean-Jacques' years of effort to create this kind of hold on Emile have paid off. He remarks, "he is now sufficiently prepared to be docile. He recognizes the voice of true friendship, and he knows how to obey reason. It is true that I leave him the appearance of independence, but he was never better subjected to me; for now he is subjected because he wants to be. As long as I was unable to make myself master of his will, I remained master of his person" (*Emile*, 332; *Pl.* 4:661). To be "master of his will" is to control what Emile desires, and this is done through the imagination.

Building upon his own analysis of imitation in *Principles of Melody*, Rousseau holds that "it is important to observe that something moral enters into everything connected with imitation" (*Emile*, 340; *Pl.* 4:672). Imitation in art inspires the same passion or desire in the beholder as in the source through a medium that does not resemble the passion. The source of an artistic activity is a passion and is, therefore, moral. The medium becomes moral, insofar as through it, one imitates something moral and incites a passion in the observer. Imitation as a fundamental condition of art lies at the root of Rousseau's discussion of taste.

Taste leads to the union of the sexes, but taste also receives its form, good or bad, in these relations. Hence, not only can art have an effect on morality, but morality itself forms taste. At least a part, and a very important part, of the role that good morals play in society is to make the satisfaction of citizens' desires more difficult, to make the attainment of the desired object require more cultivation. Without this, the satisfaction becomes easy, the desire cools, and taste degenerates.

Jean-Jacques is forming Emile's taste so that it will lead to a moral union with Sophie. Emile wants to know what is pleasing to others, so that he can be pleasing to Sophie when he meets her. Although this taste in and of itself is not directly connected with what is useful, it is indirectly connected insofar as "knowledge of what can be agreeable or disagreeable to men is necessary . . . to someone who wishes to be useful to them [men]" (*Emile*, 341; *Pl.* 4:673). Both Emile and Rousseau wish to be useful to humans. To be useful is Rousseau's ultimate goal, and in order to achieve this, he recognizes that one must please others, and then adds that "the art of writing is far from an idle study when one uses it to make the truth heard" (*Emile*, 341; *Pl.* 4:673). Rousseau's use of the word "art" here indicates that his writing is intended to raise in the reader passions that Rousseau himself feels—passions that may not resemble those in the text through which they are communicated. Rousseau is signaling here, as clearly as he can, that he is using fiction or a lie to make a moral truth heard.

THE ESSAY ON TRUE TASTE

At this point there is a break in the narrative. Rousseau claims that the example of Emile will no longer suffice. His heart is too pure to be used as a rule for anyone. Rousseau himself must step forward and give himself as an example of true taste.

This intermezzo on taste accomplishes two things. First, it makes explicit that *Emile* is not simply about Emile's education, but is itself an education, because when Emile cannot serve as an appropriate model, he is put aside. Second, Rousseau is establishing his credentials to serve as a model for the reader in matters of taste. Rousseau is about to begin to write about the romance of Emile and Sophie, a subject that many would consider unsuitable and lacking in taste for an educational treatise.

In the essay on taste, Rousseau begins by admitting that in becoming rich (in order to freely indulge his taste), he would also become like the rich. As he succinctly puts it, "due to my situation I would be an enemy of all humanity, of all equity, of every sort of virtue" (*Emile*, 345; *Pl.* 4:678). But in other ways, he would not be at all like other rich men. Rousseau sees himself as being more "sensual and voluptuous rather than proud and vain" (*Emile*, 345; *Pl.* 4:678). His luxury would not be ostentatious. And so it appears that the author, were he a rich man, would be less drawn than other rich men to display his wealth. This suggests, along with the whole of the discourse on taste, that Rousseau would not be concerned with what others think and would enjoy simply what he himself truly enjoys.

Thus, the discussion on taste appears to be the opposite of snobbery. Rousseau enjoys simple pleasures. He does not need a lot of servants or extraordinary foods or drinks. Bucolic and voluptuous enjoyments suit his taste best. Rousseau would not imitate other people, rather he would imitate nature. Rousseau sees through and criticizes the pleasures that come from opinion rather than from nature. He sees that it is precisely the pleasure that we seek "to enjoy in others' eyes," that is lost both for the onlooker and the one looked upon (*Emile*, 351; *Pl.* 4:686).

Finally, Rousseau sees only one way of rendering pleasure "pure," that is, "disengaging the pleasures from their pains" (*Emile*, 353; *Pl.* 4:689). One has to remove the exclusiveness of the pleasure. Those pleasures that we can only enjoy so long as someone else is deprived of them will always be those that "are the death of pleasure" (*Emile*, 354; *Pl.* 4:690). The specter of property raises its head and the rich man finds that he is always fleeing himself in order to be happy. Therefore, Rousseau reaches the following logical conclusion: "As for me, when I am rich, I shall act in this respect just as I did when I was poor" (*Emile*, 354; *Pl.* 4:690). Such entertainments "are within the reach of all men and . . . one does not need to be rich to enjoy them" (*Emile*, 354; *Pl.* 4:691). For Rousseau, opinion takes happiness away. Being happy in and of itself is not difficult. Therefore, one only needs to root the "goods of opinions out of his heart" (*Emile*, 354; *Pl.* 4:691).

The description of taste raises a deeper question that this interpretation must resolve. Rousseau states that "this is a kind of essay on *true* taste" (*Emile*, 354; *Pl.* 4:690; emphasis added). It gives the spirit in which one can enjoy himself. "All the rest is only illusion, chimera, foolish vanity" (*Emile*, 354; *Pl.* 4:690). But it has already been noted that true love is a chimera, an illusion, and a lie. Apparently, this latter illusion is necessary. It is the essence of true love. In this case an illusion can make us happy. But other illusions lead us astray. How does one tell the difference? Rousseau answers this by giving accounts of two Sophies, one who falls victim to the illusion and another who thrives because of it.

For true love to flourish between the sexes there has to be an illusion, a lie. There is no true love without enthusiasm, and there is no enthusiasm without perfection, and perfection does not exist in this world. The object of perfection exists only in the imagination. Thus, a man can be led to imagine that a woman is perfect. The reality consists of his sentiments of beauty: "This beauty is not in the object one loves; it is the work of our errors. So, what of it? Does the love any less sacrifice all of his low sentiments to this imaginary model?" (*Emile*, 391; *Pl.* 4:743) Jean-Jacques, the mediator, will create the illusion that brings forth these sentiments in Emile.

THE IMAGINARY SOPHIE

But the path to these sentiments is not straight. Rousseau tells the tale of two Sophies. For a while their stories are the same, but then they split off into diverging paths. We learn first that both Sophies, like Emile, are not prodigies. The description that Rousseau gives the reader is "in accordance with the portrait I [Jean-Jacques] made for Emile" (*Emile*, 393; *Pl.* 4:746). This description forms the basis of his imagining and the readers' as well.

At the age of fifteen, Sophie is given the power by her parents to choose her own husband. Rousseau poses it as a question: "If her character is such as I imagine it, why would her father not speak to her pretty much as follows?" (*Emile*, 399; *Pl.* 4:754) The gist of her father's message is that marriage is the personal union of hearts and minds between a husband and wife. This constitutes the happiness of marriage. He and his wife have enjoyed such happiness, in spite of the fact that this was not the reason why they were conjoined by their families. By a sort of happy chance, the two have grown to love one another. This sort of happiness has been their sustenance in the face of the loss of wealth and position. Her father ends by making the following agreement with Sophie: "You will choose and we will be consulted" (*Emile*, 401; *Pl.* 4:758). The father is unafraid of universal blame should Sophie choose someone of lesser rank. The parents seek her happiness, not public approval.

The address by Sophie's father to Sophie is followed by an address by Rousseau to the reader. This address to the reader has the effect of increasing both intimacy (Rousseau speaks directly to the reader from the pages of the book) and alienation (Rousseau criticizes the reader). Sophie, given the way she was raised, does not resemble "girls raised in your [the readers'] way" (*Emile*, 401; *Pl.* 4:758). The ways of Sophie's parents are not the ways of the readers, and those ways are evil.

The effect of the father's address on Sophie is to make her resolute in being found worthy of her parents' esteem. The effect of the address on the reader is unclear because "it does not belong to everyone to feel what a source of energy the love of decent things can give the soul and what force one can find within oneself when one wants to be sincerely virtuous. There are people to whom everything great appears chimerical, and who in their base and vile reason will never know what effect even a mania for virtue can have upon the human passions" (*Emile*, 402; *Pl.* 4:758). For such people, one can speak only in examples. It is true that they may still deny even the examples, but that is to their own harm. Rousseau places the point of the example he is about to give in the context of examples in general, and this is the context of a book that is meant to be one giant example. For the point is not whether the story is believed to be true to not. The point is that Rousseau is hoping to lead the reader to a great truth by having "told fictions" (*Emile*, 402; *Pl.* 4:759). This is an example of his method; this is the way he pursues his ends.

The Movement Away from the "Other" Sophie

In order to give the example of what effect a mania for virtue may have, Rousseau begins, as the reader learns only later, to go "astray." He goes astray by having "Sophie" go astray.[7] He gives her an "elevated soul," an ardent temperament. Her sentiments are deep and strong enough so that "she would rather die a martyr to her condition than afflict her parents, wed a man without merit, and expose herself to the unhappiness of an ill-matched marriage" (*Emile*, 402; *Pl.* 4:758). The religious language of martyrdom is an important clue as to what is at stake here. Sophie will die, and she will die witnessing some reality. What is that reality? Rousseau writes that she would "die a martyr to her condition." Is that condition virginal chastity? No one has died of that. Rather, she suffers from a desire without object or, more accurately, a desire without a mediator to point out the object of the desire and to make it desirous.[8]

While saying that it does not matter if the story is believed to be true or not, Rousseau also indicates that it may well be based on facts. For although he says "that Sophie is not an imaginary being, that her name alone is of my invention, that her education, her morals, her character, and even her looks have really existed, and her memory still brings tears to every member of a decent family" (*Emile*, 402; *Pl.* 4:759), still the doubters will believe nothing of it. "Sophie"'s story is the story of a martyr, of a victim. It is the one death in *Emile*, and so should be treated very carefully. Rousseau asks what he would "risk in straightforwardly completing the history of a girl so similar to Sophie that her story could be Sophie's without occasioning any surprise?" (*Emile*, 402; *Pl.* 4:759).[9]

What indeed would he risk? He would risk someone's understanding that the story of the "real" Sophie, the Sophie who marries Emile, is the story of a martyr with the killing deferred. A deferred question (for now) is: What prevents the first Sophie's death?

This "other" "Sophie" resembles the real Sophie in all ways, and thus does Rousseau give her that name. This confirms what Rousseau has written: "'Sophie' is not an imaginary being," and "her name alone is of my invention." The stories of the two Sophies differ. The real Sophie will find her lover, she will test him, she will find him worthy of her esteem, and she will give herself to him as her master.

But in this "other" story, "Sophie" is not so fortunate. She hears the speech of her father and so desires to be worthy of her father's esteem. She is sent to her aunt's house in the city to meet eligible men. After a few meetings, "Sophie" makes clear that she does not want any of these men as her beloved. She misses her parents and returns home earlier than scheduled.

But something has changed in her. She desires a sexual union and desires it deeply. She is able to communicate this to her mother, who tells her to take the legitimate solution that is offered: choose a husband. Her fate, as the mother and, through her, Rousseau, emphasizes, "depended on herself alone" (*Emile*, 403; *Pl.* 4:760). Her

mother is puzzled by her lack of willingness to marry. All these men have been presented, all turned away, yet a man is what "Sophie" supposedly wants. "What an
inexplicable contradiction!" (*Emile*, 404; *Pl.* 4:761).

Rousseau tells that the key to this contradiction is simple. Certainly her sexual
desires could be easily satisfied. But she is also looking for a master, and this is much
more difficult. None of the men she meets are really men but are rather "only mon-
keys" who have "no soul" (*Emile*, 404; *Pl.* 4:761).

"Sophie's" contradiction is contained in the following words: "I see not one [man]
who does not excite my desires, and one who does not repel my desires" (*Emile*, 404;
Pl. 4:761). "Sophie" is caught in the double bind of scandal. It appears that the
source of the problem is that the image of the man she desires is imprinted so deeply
on her soul. At first Sophie's soul is no less marked. In a sense, "Sophie" senses who
this man is, and "she prefers to die unhappy and free rather than in despair with a
man she does not love and whom she would make unhappy" (*Emile*, 404; *Pl.* 4:761).

The model that makes all the others pale in comparison is fictional. It is here that
the danger of the course that Rousseau has chosen becomes clear. "Sophie" reveals to
her mother the cause of her "sadness without remedy . . . of her tears that will never
dry up" (*Emile*, 404; *Pl.* 4:762). It is a book.

The particular book is not without significance, but so is the more general reflection that the cause of pain and problems is literature. Rousseau is writing a book to
solve the problem caused by books. In his book, he is depicting the problem books
can cause—a mortal problem that can kill an innocent young girl. Would "Sophie"
have been helped if she had read *Emile*? Does changing her fate in the book change
her fate in reality?

The book that so possesses her is François de Fénelon's *Telemachus, Son of Ulyssses*.
The mother discovers that her daughter, so dismissive of all the men she could have,
is in a rivalry with a fictional character, Eucharis, for the affections of another fictional
character, Telemachus, son of Odysseus.[10] "Sophie," Rousseau writes, "loved him with
a passion of which nothing could cure her" (*Emile*, 404–5; *Pl.* 4:762). Her parents do
not see what Rousseau sees and what he would have the reader see—the seriousness of
passions aroused by literature and the danger of rivalry without mediation.

Slowly, this realization dawns on them too, however, and they fear for their
daughter's sanity. But never has she been so lucid. She does not want a prince, she
does not seek Telemachus, and she can distinguish between fiction and reality. She
seeks a resemblance to the fictional portrait. She loves what does not exist yet holds
that this resemblance must exist, all the while admitting that she is incapable of
discerning who this man is. She says to her parents, "But what sort of man is he?
Where is he? I do not know. He is none of those I have seen. Doubtless he is none I
shall see" (*Emile*, 405; *Pl.* 4:763).

This is a "sad narrative" that Rousseau both brings and does not bring to a conclusion. Using preterition, Rousseau says without saying how the story ends. He
refuses to bring before the reader's eyes "the long disputes which preceded the catastrophe" (*Emile*, 405; *Pl.* 4:763). He does not show the breakdown in the relationship
between the loving parents and their virtuous daughter. He does not depict the girl
growing more attached to her love object the more that she is persecuted for it. He
does not show the reader her "descending into the grave" (*Emile*, 405; *Pl.* 4:763).

Rousseau puts aside these dreadful objects. His point has been made: "Sophie" dies witnessing both the power of fiction and the necessity of a mediator.

Still, even with his point made, questions remain. What is the difference between the Sophie who lives and "Sophie" who dies? Both read *Telemachus, Son of Ulysses*, both are searching for the one who resembles *Telemachus*, and both identify themselves with Eucharis. Is it simply, as Rousseau seems to suggest, that the one who does not die has a more ordinary soul? Rousseau has been at pains to stress the likeness between the two. The one *could be* the other. As Elizabeth Wingrove says, "It is thus difficult to sustain any strong convictions that preventing an illusory excess is the story's moral, given how the characters continue to rely upon an excess of illusion."[11] This "excess of illusion" is the lie that is true love and thus forms the basis of Rousseau's whole theory of romance.

What is the moral of this story then? With regard to "Sophie," Rousseau confesses, "I went astray myself" (*Emile*, 405; *Pl.* 4:763). The difference between the dead "Sophie" and the living Sophie is that Rousseau does not go astray in the case of the second. The difference between the two stories is the presence of the Mentor in the latter case. Jean-Jacques becomes the mediator of the successful union. He transforms the relationship from a simple relationship of two lovers searching for one another into a triangular relationship in which the Mentor indicates to each who the desirable one is. When they do in fact meet, it is the Mentor who, by skillfully telling Sophie that she is Eucharis, indicates to her who her Telemachus is. "Sophie" admits, "Doubtless he is none that I will see" (*Emile*, 405; *Pl.* 4:763)." But the living Sophie "believes she sees Telemachus affected by Philoctetes's misfortune" (*Emile*, 414; *Pl.* 4:775). It will only take a few more minutes for Sophie to be certain: "But in spite of this modest air and these lowered eyes, her tender heart palpitates with joy and tells her that Telemachus has been found" (*Emile*, 415; *Pl.* 4:777).

The role of the mediator is both essential and hidden. Rousseau remarks, "[the mother of the family] smiles at the success of our projects" (*Emile*, 415; *Pl.* 4:776). She too plays a role. It is the mother who sees that "it is time to captivate the heart of the new Telemachus" (*Emile*, 415; *Pl.* 4:776). She has her daughter speak, and the sound of her voice makes Emile surrender. Emile "swallows with deep draughts the poison" of her charms and wishes to observe Sophie without being observed, while Sophie rejoices at her triumph without showing signs (*Emile*, 415; *Pl.* 4:776). For the two young people, it is as if their own desires at last find the objects that they seek. Emile finds his Sophie; Sophie finds her Telemachus. What neither realizes is that they have not found each other. These objects have been designated as such to them by the "other."

This initial identification, while important, is not enough. The "crisis" that the tutor is trying to navigate now is the one that "serves as a passage from childhood to man's estate" (*Emile*, 416; *Pl.* 4:777), that is, to being a citizen. This crisis will be dealt with at length and in detail. Only the first, critical stage has been traversed.

HISTORY AS ROMANCE, ROMANCE AS HISTORY

Rousseau is now going to give the story of the "real" Sophie and her relationship with Emile. It is natural enough for the reader to believe, and indeed Rousseau tells him, that he is about to read the too "naïve and too simple history of their innocent love" (*Emile*, 415; *Pl.* 4:777). Just as this part of the book details the crisis through which Emile must be made to pass, it presents to the reader a crisis involving the genre of the book. Is the book an educational treatise, a history of the species, or a novel, that is, a romance? The question is not academic. Romances corrupt; they are scandalous in the sense of leading people, especially innocent young people, down the wrong path.

Rousseau is anticipating the accusation that "the people" will make. They will say that his book is "a frivolous game" (*un jeu frivole*), that it is "a romance" (*un roman*) (*Emile*, 416; *Pl.* 4:777). But Rousseau's reply is ready, and it is not an argument. Rather, it is a strategy, the strategy that the tutor uses with Emile. Even as the readers begin to formulate the accusation, to bring their complaint before Rousseau, he turns around and accuses them. The readers are the guilty party: "You who deprave it, it is you who make a romance of my book" (*Vous qui la dépravez, c'est vous qui faites un roman de mon livre*) (*Emile*, 416; *Pl.* 4:777). Rousseau did not write a romance. He wrote a history of his species. But the readers have depraved it by making it into something it is not. The readers' own depravity prevents them from reading it correctly, and transforms it into a romance.

In this way, the reader finds himself in the same situation vis-à-vis the author as little Emile found himself vis-à-vis Robert, the gardener. The reader would like to accuse the author of depravity—that is, of causing scandal in the sense of leading young people into sin by writing a titillating account of the couple's romance. This romance is only made worse by the veneer of virtue with which he covers it.

Such is the accusation that Rousseau both fears and desires. Rousseau fears it because this accusation has the power to destroy him as an author who thinks the art of writing as "useful" to others, as contributing to the virtue of the people. Yet he desires it because it is only in the making of this accusation that the reader fully enters into the educational process that *is* this book. Rousseau has so constructed the situation, much like Jean-Jacques constructs it for Emile, that as soon as the reader formulates the accusation, the reader is being accused. It is by means of the accusation that the accuser provides the evidence that convicts her of the very accusation she has formulated. By reading the novel as a romance, one proves not that the text depraves its reader, but that the reader who makes the accusation is guilty of depraving the text. This proof is to accomplish in the reader the same thing it accomplishes in little Emile—the destruction of the seeds of vanity.

Rousseau is writing a treatise intended to be useful, but it will not be useful if he skips over the most important part for fear of being scandalous. According to Rousseau, the most important part is the romance between Emile and Sophie.[12] It is the story or, better, the history of their desire. Were Rousseau to skip over it, the book would fail to realize its objective. The problem is not that the subject matter is scandalous; rather, the problem is in the impure ears of his contemporaries, who succeed in making everything scandalous. On the pretext of avoiding scandal, one covers up what is in fact a scandalous situation—the lack of educating young people about this most important period of their lives.

So Rousseau's purpose is not to talk about romance or about how to romance a woman. Rather, he is trying to show, by example, how the history of the species is marked by a certain form of desire. This desire depends on the "other" for its intensity and even for its existence. For example, Jean-Jacques questions Emile's newfound love interest. This is not for the sake of lessons, or for getting him to think more clearly about why he finds this girl attractive; rather, the questions "only have the effect of giving the young man a new interest in Sophie out of the desire to justify his inclination" (*Emile*, 416; *Pl.* 4:778). For Emile, "this resemblance of names, this meeting (which he believes fortuitous)," even the very reserve of his teacher serve to excite his desires (*Emile*, 416; *Pl.* 4:778). Jean-Jacques is using all the methods at his disposal to give Emile the desire for Sophie and to raise it to a high level.

Emile is "as happy as a man can be" (*Emile*, 419; *Pl.* 4:782). This happiness is human happiness, meaning that it is built on longing and desire, not on accepting and possessing. Over and over again, Rousseau repeats that possession kills love. He says that to grant Emile now the "crown of his happiness" would be to "destroy its greatest charms" (*Emile*, 419; *Pl.* 4:782). This supreme happiness is one hundred times sweeter to hope for than actually to obtain: "One enjoys it better when one looks forward to it than when one tastes it" (*Emile*, 419; *Pl.* 4:782). Therefore, Emile is to enjoy a long time before possessing.

Jean-Jacques prepares Emile carefully. When he explains the mysteries of sexuality to Emile, he also lets him know that he too, like Emile, is vulnerable to the onslaughts of passions. He, too, has to struggle for self-mastery. In the meeting between Emile and Sophie, the Mentor's presence is always there.

The reader is given several indications of the nature of the relationship between the Mentor and Emile. Early in the courtship of Emile and Sophie, Jean-Jacques remarks, "Already Sophie appears too estimable for him not be sure of making *me* love her" (*Emile*, 416; *Pl.* 4:778; emphasis added). The switch is interesting. In fact, Jean-Jacques arranges everything to make Emile love her, but what is most artfully arranged is to have Emile feel that he has to get the Mentor to love her, too. In a footnote to the text, Rousseau describes the second encounter between Emile and the Mentor and Sophie and her family. He writes, "I admit I am rather grateful to Sophie's mother for not having let her spoil with soap hands as soft as hers, hands which Emile will so often kiss" (*Emile*, 420n; *Pl.* 4:784n). The Mentor is grateful here for the favors that Emile will receive. The identification between the Mentor and Emile will grow deeper and deeper.

Jean-Jacques is the mediator of desire for more than just Emile. After the first conversation between Emile and Sophie, Jean-Jacques notes that this encounter has relieved a great weight from the hearts of the young people. They are able to be more relaxed in each other's presence. But Sophie "changes most palpably in her behavior toward me [Jean-Jacques]. She gives evidence of a more eager regard for me. She looks at me with interest; she speaks to me affectionately. She is attentive to what might please me. I see that she honors me with her esteem, and that she is not indifferent to obtaining mine" (*Emile*, 421; *Pl.* 4:785). The first conversation between the two lovers concerns Jean-Jacques, their mediator. The complexity of the mediation increases, as Jean-Jacques makes clear, because it is not just that Sophie will need his approval to win Emile, but also because Emile may well need Jean-Jacques to be in Sophie's good graces to help him win her. Jean-Jacques feels rewarded that Emile's sensitive heart has given him "a great part in his first discussion with his beloved" (*Emile*, 421; *Pl.* 4:785).

Jean-Jacques has become "the confidant of . . . [his] two young people and the mediator of their loves" (*Emile*, 423; *Pl.* 4:788). Just as there are those who would criticize an author for writing a romance, so there are those who would criticize this sort of function for a governor, yet Jean-Jacques claims that it raises him in his own eyes and makes him satisfied with himself (*Emile*, 423; *Pl.* 4:788). He becomes the chaperone, thus Emile is more than usually docile.

As for Sophie, Jean-Jacques remarks, "The little girl overwhelms me with friendliness by which I am not deceived, and I take for myself only what is intended for me. It is thus she compensates herself indirectly for the respect she imposes on Emile" (*Emile*, 423–24; *Pl.* 4:788–89). It is through the mediator that she gives Emile "countless tender caresses" (*Emile*, 423–24; *Pl.* 4:788–89). There is, according to Jean-Jacques, no jealousy here. Emile knows that Jean-Jacques does not want to harm his interests and so is charmed by the fact that these two are on such good terms. In fact, when Sophie takes the governor's arm instead of his, Emile is "consoled" that it is so. As he goes away, Emile grasps the governor's, not Sophie's, hand and says, "Friend, speak for me" (*Emile*, 424; *Pl.* 4:789).

The novel *Telemachus*, is the downfall of "Sophie." "Sophie" is looking for her Telemachus, but her would-be Telemachus does not have a Mentor. There are only the two, Telemachus and Eucharis, searching for each other, and this is not enough for a successful outcome. Rousseau makes the new situation explicit by stating, "Good Sophie, how your sincere heart is at ease when, without being heard by Telemachus, you can converse with his Mentor" (*Emile*, 424; *Pl.* 4:789).

The illusion strengthens; the "intoxication" of the lovers intensifies (*Emile*, 424; *Pl.* 4:790). Emile and Sophie are "weaving flowers and garlands around the happy bond which is going to unite them until the grave" (*Emile*, 424; *Pl.* 4:790). But these images also intoxicate Jean-Jacques. He also suffers from their delirium.

The illusion of love is performing its good office. The two lovers see each other as "perfect" (*Emile*, 426; *Pl.* 4:792). They experience transports, but it is precisely the transports that they must vanquish. In other words, if they do not need to vanquish them, but can simply surrender to them, they will not experience them as transports. In fact, according to Jean-Jacques, though they will someday know the pleasures of sexual intercourse, "for their whole lives they will regret the happy time which they denied them to themselves" (*Emile*, 426; *Pl.* 4:792). Love does not grow but rather wanes. The secret to love is to keep it uncertain, constantly to be won.

The relationship between the tutor and the pupil comes to the fore not only in the moments of romantic sweetness but also in the moments of chastisement. The mother reprimands Emile for kissing in secret the hem of Sophie's dress. The reprimand is addressed "much more" to Jean-Jacques than to Emile. We are meant to recall here the episode with the magician. There is the same dialectic of secrecy and openness, only reversed. There, the little Emile exposes something that should be kept secret; here, he is hiding what must be kept out in the open. Were he to accuse the mother of humiliating him, he knows that, in a way, he has already humiliated her by taking liberties with her daughter far away from the eyes of her parents.

This triangular relationship between the tutor, Emile, and Sophie is always present and never explicated, unlike the more usual triangle of Sophie, Emile, and other rivals. Sophie uses not only a "mixture of reserve and endearment" to keep Emile's passion ardent, but also anxiety to excite it. She even torments Emile with a playfulness toward other suitors that she never dares to indulge in with him.

Here the readers enter into the realm of jealousy. As Rousseau writes, "[this] must be examined, for such digressions enter into the aim of my book and stray very little from my subject" (*Emile*, 429; *Pl.* 4:796). The reason why Rousseau has gone into such detail with the male/female relationship is precisely to address this question. Rousseau refers here to his theory in the *Second Discourse* that in the state of nature humans lived in peace. This is the natural man in society. The union of the sexes is no longer fortuitous and temporary, but rather is exclusive and permanent. Will Emile be jealous?

Rousseau begins by distinguishing the good from the bad within the natural "desire for exclusive possession of what pleases us" (*Emile*, 429; *Pl.* 4:796). When this desire becomes a passion or a whim, an angry fury or a gloomy suspicion of the rival, then the person is in danger of leaving natural desires behind. Turning to the animal world, Rousseau sees a difference between those animals that can get a mate only by conquest, and so must see every other male as "an intrusive competitor," and those species "in which one male bonds exclusively with one female" (*Emile*, 429; *Pl.* 4:797). In the latter case, the male is less anxious in the sight of other males. Rousseau concludes, "Jealousy has its motive in the social passions more than in primitive instinct. In most liaisons of gallantry the lover hates his rivals far more than he loves his mistress" (*Emile*, 430; *Pl.* 4:797–98). Social institutions both influence the passion and render the signs of preference so nugatory that they no longer assure.

True love is another story. Love between the sexes is not as natural as was thought. True love is a lie and an intoxicant. The person can no longer see the love-object as it really is, for "this passion longs only for exclusions and preferences, and it differs from vanity only in that the latter, which demands everything and grants nothing, is always iniquitous, whereas love, which gives as much as it demands, is in itself a sentiment filled with equity" (*Emile*, 430; *Pl.* 4:798). Love, due to its incredulity, has some compensations: it is more easily persuaded. When esteem is added to love, there is confidence in the other.

Rousseau concludes that the passion of jealousy has few seeds in the human heart and is mostly determined by education. He can predict with a fair amount of confidence the kind of jealousy of which Emile will be capable. Emile's focus will be on his love-object and not on his rival. He will be more intent on getting rid of him as an obstacle than "hating him as an enemy" (*Emile*, 431; *Pl.* 4:798). According to Jean-Jacques, "Emile's unjust pride will not be stupidly offended by someone daring to enter into competition with him" (*Emile*, 431; *Pl.* 4:799). He will simply try harder to make himself lovable. Soon the suitors will be dismissed.

Throughout all this, Rousseau emphasizes how artfully he has arranged the situation. Nothing has been left to chance. Jean-Jacques uses obstacles, such as the distance they live from Sophie's house, to increase Emile's desire. "This distance is the bellows of the forge. By means of it I temper the arrows of love" (*Emile*, 433; *Pl.* 4:802).

In the episodes with the gardener and with the magician, Jean-Jacques victimizes Emile without Emile's knowledge. Here he is doing it with full knowledge of Emile. Rousseau reveals the extent to which desire opens us to becoming victims. It may seem unusual to associate desire and victimization, but in fact, they are deeply related. The mimetic desire that leads to rivalry, envy, and conflict often finds its resolution in a victim. In fact, it is when this resolution is not available that desire grows. Girard explains that "desire is what happens to human relationships when there is no longer any resolution through the victim and consequently no form of polarization that is genuinely unanimous and can trigger such a resolution."[13] Rousseau does not want the final resolution of death, as the story of the "other" Sophie makes clear. He hopes to stabilize the condition of desire. The rules for stabilizing this condition are, as he remarks, in his "detailed examples [*mes details*]"(*Emile*, 435; *Pl.* 4:804).

Everything, even such things as the time and the length of the meetings between the lovers, which appear to Emile to be dictated by Sophie, are actually dictated by the tutor in secret. Sophie simply carries them out. All these arrangements accomplish one purpose: Emile experiences pleasures that "are true, pure, and delicious but less real than imaginary, [and] exacerbate his love without effeminizing his heart" (*Emile*, 435; *Pl.* 4:804). This love and these pleasures are the context in which the true identity of Emile emerges. Insofar as he becomes more enmeshed in desire and thus in being a victim, he also becomes the new man, the Christ.

On those days when he is not allowed to or, due to weather, cannot visit Sophie's house, Emile roams the countryside and observes carefully the agriculture. He is ready both to learn and to teach. He tells the farmers of better ways of raising crops and designs a better plow. He uses their tools better than they do. "In a word, he extends his zeal and his care to everything which is of primary and general utility" (*Emile*, 435; *Pl.* 4:805).

Emile goes beyond even this into the realm of evangelical charity. He practices what is traditionally known as the spiritual and corporal works of mercy. He goes to the poorer members of the area. He sees their concrete situation and helps them. He usually does not give them money directly, but he "provides them with work and often pays them wages himself to do the work they need" (*Emile*, 435; *Pl.* 4:805). He gets them to improve their lot, to fix up their houses or clear their land. He reconciles the estranged. He provides care for the sick. He protects the weak against the strong. He helps a couple marry. He consoles the woman who mourns the death of her child. "Finally, he always does as much good with his person as with his money" (*Emile*, 436; *Pl.* 4:805).

Rousseau makes explicit Emile's identity as Christ without scandal by means of his trade. Learning a trade is an essential part of Emile's education, giving him true independence, since he can always earn his own keep no matter what his situation is. The trade chosen for him is carpentry. At least one day each week during the time of the courtship, Emile and Jean-Jacques work at a master carpenter's workshop.

Sophie and her mother learn of this from the father, who sees them at work. He tells them to go see them in order to learn whether or not Emile "despises the condition of the poor" (*Emile*, 437; *Pl.* 4:807). The women learn when he will be working and go to see this spectacle. They enter the shop and see Emile at work, "with a chisel in one hand and the mallet in the other" (*Emile*, 437; *Pl.* 4:808). Rousseau concludes the scene with the following words: "This sight does not make Sophie laugh. It touches her; it is respectable. Woman, honor the head of your house. It is he who works for you, who wins your bread, who feeds you. This is man" (*Emile*, 437; *Pl.* 4:808). This passage has echoes of Genesis (the winning of bread) and Paul's Letter to the Corinthians ("Woman, honor the head of your house"), as well as a direct quotation from the Gospel of John. "*Voila l'homme* [this is man]" is the French version of Pilate's statement about Jesus: "*Ecce homo* [behold the man]." Emile is the new man, the new Christ, and Rousseau is his evangelist.

The mother is so moved by the scene and the news that he works for twenty *sous* a day that she goes to him, embraces him, and, crying, repeats several times, "My son! O my son!" (*Emile*, 438; *Pl.* 4:808). Again, this is an echo of 2 Samuel 18, where David cries for Absalom.

Having presented the New Man, Rousseau now turns to Woman. In the end, they are not different because Sophie becomes Woman similar to the way that Emile becomes Man: through being scandalized by Emile and accusing Emile, only to find that she herself is guilty of that which she has accused him.

Sophie is described as "imperious and exacting" in regard to the attention that should be paid to her by her lover. "She has that noble pride based on merit which is conscious of itself, esteems itself, and wants to be honored as it honors itself" (*Emile*, 439; *Pl.* 4:809). At the same time, she does not want a man who "knows no law other than hers" (*Emile*, 439; *Pl.* 4:810). Like Circe, Sophia will love only the man she cannot change. This pride is both her downfall and salvation, as the following story shows.

Emile and Jean-Jacques are expected one evening. They do not arrive and no one is sent to explain their delay. Sophie's household spends the evening waiting, and she is, of course, tormented by fears of what might have befallen the two. Finally, the next morning, the messenger that her house sent to inquire returns accompanied by the messenger sent by Emile and Jean-Jacques. The messengers inform them that Emile and Jean-Jacques are well and will be there shortly to make their excuses.

Now Sophie is in a rage. "Emile lives and has kept her waiting needlessly," is the way Rousseau expresses it (*Emile*, 439; *Pl.* 4:810). Even the mother's attitude has cooled. Emile is embarrassed and confused by the reception. He finally understands Sophie's anger and stops even trying to look at her, so great is her fury. Jean-Jacques speaks on their behalf, appealing to Sophie's sense of justice. The story of what befalls Jean-Jacques and Emile is a story of Christian charity, modeled somewhat on the story of the Good Samaritan in Luke's Gospel. They are the good Samaritans who come across an injured man. A peasant fell off his horse due to drunkenness and broke his leg. The pain was too great to put him back on his horse, so Emile and Jean-Jacques carried him themselves to his home.

But it does not end there. The man's wife was far along in pregnancy with their third child. At the sight of her husband's injury, she fell into labor. What to do? Emile ran back to get the peasant's horse in order to ride to the city to get the surgeon. Jean-Jacques stayed in the house trying to assist both the man and his wife. It was past midnight before anyone could rest. They proceeded then to their lodgings near Sophie's house and awaited the morning in order to explain what transpired.

At this point, before anyone can respond, Emile makes his own little speech. He acknowledges Sophie as the "arbiter" of his fate, but says that he will not forget the "rights of humanity," for they are more sacred to him than Sophie's rights. He concludes, "I will never give them up for you" (*Emile*, 441; *Pl.* 4:812–13).

Precisely at the moment when Sophie is implicitly accusing Emile of not honoring her as she deserves, Sophie discovers that she has not honored him as he deserves. The result of the revelation is capitulation. She rises, kisses Emile on the cheek, and says: "Emile, take this hand. It is yours. Be my husband and my master when you wish. I will try to merit this honor" (*Emile*, 441; *Pl.* 4:813). She has been scandalized by Emile's behavior, only to find that she herself has acted in a scandalous way. Her response is not to ask for forgiveness, any more than Emile asks forgiveness of Robert or of the magician. Rather, it is to move ahead, to learn the next secret, to move toward marriage.

Now it is Sophie's turn to practice the corporal works of mercy. She asks to see the unfortunate couple that Emile and Jean-Jacques have aided. They go to their lodgings. She puts on an apron and goes about making the sick people comfortable. Without shame, she changes the man's undergarments. "The zeal of charity outweighs modesty" (*Emile*, 441; *Pl.* 4:813). "Wife and husband together bless the lovable girl who serves them, who pities them, who consoles them. It is an angel from heaven that God sends them. She has the appearance and the grace, as well as the gentleness and goodness of an angel" (*Emile*, 441; *Pl.* 4:813–14). Emile contemplates the image of Sophie in silence. Jean-Jacques, or perhaps Rousseau, addresses man: "Man, love your companion. God gives her to you to console you in your pains, to relieve you in your ills." And then he adds, "This is woman" (*voila, la femme*) (*Emile*, 442; *Pl.* 4:814).

WHERE IS EMILE NOW?

The whole of *Emile* is about place—about discovering one's place in the order of the universe, about staying in that place, and even about finding Sophie's dwelling place. All this seems settled now, yet Rousseau tells the reader, "They [Emile and Sophie] are not yet where they think they are" (*Emile*, 442; *Pl.* 4:814). The couple believes that they are ready for marriage. Sophie's scruples have all been removed, but the scruples of the Mentor have been aroused. He has yet to perform his duty precisely as Mentor—taking Telemachus away from Eucharis. There is one last scandal to be perpetrated.

Jean-Jacques enters Emile's room and asks, "What would you do if you were informed that Sophie is dead?" (*Emile*, 442; *Pl.* 4:814) One can well imagine Emile's response. Agitated and frightened, he confronts a strangely cool Jean-Jacques, who asks him to respond to the question. Emile is angry now and says that, although he does not know what he would do, he knows he would never again see the one who informs him of the fact. Jean-Jacques tells him to relax, that she is well and that they are to see her that evening. For now, though, Jean-Jacques would like to speak to him.

This "terrible preamble" was necessary, according to Jean-Jacques, to get Emile's attention (*Emile*, 442; *Pl.* 4:814). He has been too wrapped up in his passion for

Sophie to be able to hear the lesson that the master wishes to give him. And so the master has to use the very passion that is an obstacle as a way to get his attention.

Jean-Jacques reveals to Emile the nature of their search: they seek happiness. They do not know where happiness is, and therefore, instead of seeking it without knowing where it is, they have refrained from acting. This is the negative education of which Rousseau speaks at the beginning of the book. Others make the mistake of pursuing happiness rather than doing nothing, but Jean-Jacques says, "[for humans,] once we have left the place where we can know it, we no longer know how to get back to it" (*Emile*, 442; *Pl.* 4:815). And so Jean-Jacques has stayed on the road of nature until it would reveal the road of happiness. He has found out that they are the same road.

When Jean-Jacques is teaching Emile about taste, they go to the theatre. There, Emile is "scandalized" by the heroes who are "overcome by extreme pains, [who] make the stage reverberate with their senseless cries, grieving like women, crying like children" (*Emile*, 443; *Pl.* 4:816). Emile, like Plato, is indignant that these are "the models we are offered for imitation" (*Emile*, 443; *Pl.* 4:816).[14] In a structure that resembles that of the episodes with Robert and with the magician, Emile accuses the models of the stage of extolling human "weakness under the false image of virtue" (*Emile*, 443; *Pl.* 4:816). And now he finds that he is guilty of the same thing. Jean-Jacques tells him, "Now you have become one of its heroes" (*Emile*, 443; *Pl.* 4:816).

In this way, Emile is being introduced to the world of virtue. Up until now, he has been good in the Rousseauian sense: he has caused no harm. To be virtuous is to conquer the affections, to follow reason and conscience, to do what one ought to do rather than what one desires. For virtue, one needs strength, and one must struggle. Jean-Jacques invites Emile into the realm of true freedom. He tells him that until this point, he has only been "apparently free," like a slave of whom nothing has been commanded (*Emile*, 445; *Pl.* 4:818). To be truly free is to be master of one's domain, to be able to command one's heart. Jean-Jacques will not allow Emile to distinguish between those passions that are permitted, such as his passion for Sophie, and those that are forbidden: "All passions are good when one remains their master; all are bad when one lets oneself be subjected to them" (*Emile*, 445; *Pl.* 4:819).

With the onset of puberty, Rousseau tells the reader that his pupil is now a man. At this point, Jean-Jacques declares this fact directly to Emile and adds a precept: "Be a man. Restrain you heart within the *limits of your condition*" (*Emile*, 445; *Pl.* 4:819; emphasis added). One must already be a man in order to become a man. One has to have been subjected to the limits of the human condition in order to respect them and to choose to remain within them. One has to be victimized in order to choose to be a victim.

Jean-Jacques tells Emile, "the illusions of pride are the source of our greatest ills" (*Emile*, 446; *Pl.* 4:819). The wise man "stays in his place." He does not seek after imaginary estates. Here is Jean-Jacques' advice:

> Do you want, then, to live happily and wisely? Attach your heart only to imperishable beauty. Let your condition limit your desires; let you duties come before your inclinations; extend the law of necessity to moral things. Learn to lose what can be taken from you; learn to abandon everything when virtue decrees it, to put yourself above events

and to detach your heart lest it be lacerated by things; to be courageous in adversity, so as never to be miserable; to be firm in your duty, so as never to be criminal. (*Emile*, 446; *Pl.* 4:820)

Living in this way, Emile will know life's nothingness and see death as the beginning of existence. The Mentor now tells Emile what he has already told the reader: "You have enjoyed more in hope than you will ever enjoy in reality. Imagination adorns what one desires but abandons it when it is in one's possession. Except for the simple Being existing by itself, there is nothing beautiful except what is not" (*Emile*, 447; *Pl.* 4:821).

In other words, the fate of the second Sophie is not entirely different from that of the first. Her being must be annihilated in order for her beauty to exist. The practical outcome of this discourse is that the Mentor tells Emile that he must sacrifice Sophie by leaving her. There is a scandalized reaction. Emile will not let himself become a "traitor, a cheat, a perjurer" (*Emile*, 447; *Pl.* 4:821). The separation is to be temporary, but it will accomplish its purpose.

Where is Emile now? What is his place? By wanting to marry and become the head of a household, he will become a member of the state. Jean-Jacques asks him if he is prepared for that. He goes so far as to say, "You believe you have learned everything, and you still know nothing. Before taking a place in the civil order, learn to know it and what rank in it suits you" (*Emile*, 448; *Pl.* 4:823).

Emile struggles against this advice to leave Sophie. There must be an alternative, and he tries to find it. In the end, Jean-Jacques ends up, for the first time in the novel, having to command him. The tutor calls in the promise to protect Emile from himself that Emile extracted from him earlier. He simply says, "Emile, you have to leave Sophie. I wish it" (*Emile*, 449; *Pl.* 4:824). The tutor is still the mediator and has now achieved a place where he can openly command against the thing Emile most desires.

The obedience to this command is the split in Emile that is mentioned at the beginning of this chapter. Jean-Jacques claims that he is forcing Emile to be free, but I see it as further proof of the fact that Emile only knows what to desire by learning it from his mediator.

As for Sophie, Jean-Jacques admits that she has suffered violence. "An unforeseen blow" has struck her (*Emile*, 449; *Pl.* 4:824). Is it a fatal blow? Perhaps not, but we shall see that the tutor is worried that her fate might still resemble that of the other Sophie. She is afraid of being forgotten by her lover. Again the role of the mediator comes to the fore:

It is I [Jean-Jacques] who receives her complaints, who see her tears, whom she affects to take as her confidant. Women are skillful and know how to disguise themselves. The more she grumbles in secret against my tyranny, the more attentive she is in flattering me. She senses that her fate is in my hands.

I console her. I reassure her. I make myself answerable for her lover, or rather her husband. (*Emile*, 449; *Pl.* 4:825)

In this way, Jean-Jacques consolidates the position he has coveted. Sophie esteems him enough to believe that he would not want to deceive her. Now Jean-Jacques can say, "I am the guarantor of each for the other" (*Emile*, 449; *Pl.* 4:825).

Finally, Rousseau reminds the reader of the story that is being re-enacted. It is the story of Eucharis, Telemachus, and his Mentor. Sophie is in the place of Eucharis, and thus is in the place of the "other" Sophie. And so Jean-Jacques is worried that the "fantastic loves" should not awake during Emile's absence. She is not to suffer the fate of the "other" Sophie. Is it Emile's absence or the absence of the Mentor that suddenly makes the book, *Telemachus*, dangerous to Sophie? She is to give it to Emile; he can read it in the presence of the mediator. When Sophie receives *The Spectator* from Emile, she is to learn from it the "duties of a decent woman" that will soon be hers.[15]

If Sophie is Eucharis, left on the island of Calypso by Telemachus, who is just barely able to be dragged away by his Mentor, then the affair of Emile and Sophie is more dangerous than it appears. Sophie is now to be transformed by her reading from dangerous nymph to "a decent woman." More importantly, Emile is to be transformed from the delusional lover, Telemachus, to the responsible prince. The experience with Eucharis is necessary so that Emile can know firsthand the strength of the passion that no man can totally avoid. At the same time, this passion, like all the others, has to be overcome. In overcoming it, it becomes possible for Emile to enter into the political world, to understand the principles of political right.

CHAPTER 6

THE POLITICS OF SCANDAL

INTRODUCTION

In many ways, the whole of *Emile* has been building up to Rousseau's political philosophy and his particular version of the social contract.[1] Ever since the incident with Robert, the gardener, in which little Emile beginss to learn about property, rights, and agreements, his education prepares him for this moment. Already in the course of the novel several things have appeared that could be considered protocontracts for Emile. With the emergence of his sexuality and his entry into moral relationships, Emile makes an agreement with his tutor. He begs of his teacher, "Make me free . . . force me to be my own master" (*Emile*, 325; *Pl.* 4:652), a statement meant to make the reader think of the famous line from the *Social Contract* in which, when someone is constrained to obey the general will, "he will be forced to be free" (*CW* 4:141; *Pl.* 4:364).

Emile's statement reveals his readiness to enter into civil relations, but still, this agreement to obey the tutor had to be tested by his being ordered to leave Sophie. When Emile is unwilling to leave Sophie, unwilling to listen to reason, Jean-Jacques trumps him by saying, "Emile, you have to leave Sophie, I wish it" (*Emile*, 449; *Pl.* 4:824). It is the only time that the tutor gives his pupil a direct order, the only time that his will explicitly contradicts the pupil's will. Emile's whole education is designed to prepare him for the moment that he can accept the will of another without alienating his own. Finally, right before their departure, Sophie's father takes Jean-Jacques aside and gives him his parting words: "Remember that your pupil has signed his marriage contract on my daughter's lips" (*Emile*, 450; *Pl.* 4:825). While the relationship of marriage is not the same as relationships between citizens, Emile's ability to enter into the former contract prepares him for the latter.

The narrative framework of love and lies will guide the interpretation, not only of this part of *Emile*, the subsection titled, "On Travel," but also of the *Social Contract*, a summary of which is contained therein. The end of the novel is scandalous, but not for the reasons usually brought forward. It is scandalous insofar as the closer Emile approaches his goal of self-mastery, the more this goal recedes. At the climax, he himself puts it out of reach forever, thus rendering his state of scandal permanent. Scandal, understood as the kind of desire that removes the goal ever further with each step one takes toward it, cannot live in the truth. If one grasps the truth, then one either moves toward the object or gives up. But neither can it live in a pure lie. The desire is real. It feeds off the truth, but truth that comes to one through the lie. The truth of the *Social Contract* is such a truth.

I will show how the narrative context sets up scandal as the entry way to the *Social Contract*. Then I will show how scandal forms the very heart of the *Social Contract* itself, and, finally, I will show how the *Social Contract* opens out to a state of permanent scandal, a state illustrated by the fate of Emile.

THE NARRATIVE CONTEXT

The last chapter ended with Emile's taking leave of Sophie. The preparation for this leave-taking has some interesting parallels with the way Jean-Jacques prepares his charge for their journey to find Sophie. Both of these preparations point to the role of fiction, of imaginary models, of exemplars, in leading someone to the truth. Just as Jean-Jacques provides an imaginary model of Sophie to guard Emile as he encounters the silly females of the city, so the real Sophie is to perform this function on these travels. Emile takes the "sad image" of her face at his departure with him, and that should allow the tutor to return his heart to her at any time (*Emile*, 450; *Pl.* 4:826). On the first journey, precisely at the point where Emile is able to enter into an agreement with his tutor, he also needs an outside attachment for his heart in order to protect that agreement. This agreement is the one in which Emile begs Jean-Jacques, "Make me free by protecting me against those of my passions which do violence to me . . . force me to be my own master" (*Emile*, 325; *Pl.* 4:652). Jean-Jacques agrees to the compact, but at the same time, he begins to paint the image of a fictional Sophie for Emile. In this later journey, Emile's contract is with the real Sophie, and it is her image that is to sustain him.

And so, just as before he met her, the image is still a fiction. At the start of their search for Sophie, Jean-Jacques makes the imaginary description and asks, "And what is true love itself if it is not chimera, lie, and illusion?" (*Emile*, 329; *Pl.* 4:656).[2] Jean-Jacques takes Emile away from Sophie precisely at the moment that he has "exhausted [life's] happiness" (*Emile*, 447; *Pl.* 4:821). To actually possess Sophie will only destroy her desirability. Once Emile understands that "there is nothing beautiful except that which is not," then he is ready for the teachings of the *Social Contract*, which occupy the same ontological space (*Emile*, 447; *Pl.* 4:821).

Rousseau grounds his political philosophy in his anthropology that holds that a person needs a lie in order to live the truth, and the greater the truth to be lived, the greater the lie must be. The *Social Contract* demands the kind of human being produced by the structure of romance—a person who lives a truth by believing in a lie. This kind of person is not produced all at once. It is a dynamic process, as symbolized by the tutor instructing Emile in the ideas of political right as they travel. The section "On Travel" is bound by an Emile who is the lord of Sophie on the near side, and an Emile who willingly accepts being her victim on the far side. Only as victim can the dynamic equilibrium of the *Social Contract* be maintained.

The fundamental reason for this is that possessing what one desires would render it undesirable. But this is only one side of the scandalous situation. Even if this were not the structure of human desire, Emile would still be in scandal. Jean-Jacques explains Emile's situation to him in the following terms: Emile is about to reach his majority, to become the head of a household, to take his place in society. Jean-Jacques tells him, "[you need to give thought to] what kind of man you want to be, what you want to spend your life doing, and what measures you want to take to assure yourself and your family of bread" (*Emile*, 456; *Pl.* 4:833). This entry into society is a dangerous moment. Unless Emile chooses wisely, he could end up in relations of dependence with men he despises, or he could end up under the control of others and forced to do evil to avoid evil. All the possibilities offered for Emile to take advantage of his property have their pitfalls. They will "put him in a precarious and dependent state, and force him to adjust his morals, his sentiments, and his conduct to the example and prejudices of others" (*Emile*, 456; *Pl.* 4:834). Even the military is no refuge for the man of honor. Aside from its inherent violence, if Emile wants to be a real soldier, "[he] will be despised, hated, and perhaps driven out" (*Emile*, 456; *Pl.* 4:834).

Emile has an answer for all the obstacles to his happiness that the governor has presented. In line with what he has learned through his education, he will circumvent these obstacles by limiting his wants: "Give me Sophie and my field—and I shall be rich" (*Emile*, 457; *Pl.* 4:835). Emile's scandalous situation becomes clear because, as Jean-Jacques informs him, no mere scaling back of expectations and limiting of desires will do any good in this case. In fact, it only increases the dangers. Each step away from the dangers only brings them closer, and this is the scandalous situation *par excellence*, because scandal refers to the sort of desire in which the very efforts made to satisfy it decrease the likelihood of it being fulfilled. I will have more to say on this form of scandal in the next chapter. In the following quote, the tutor goes on at length about these dangers because he has "more experience" and sees "the difficulties of the project better": "But where is the state where a man can say to himself, 'The land I tread is mine'? Before choosing this happy land, be well assured that you will find there the peace you seek. Be careful that violent government, a persecuting religion, or perverse morals do not come to disturb you there" (*Emile*, 457; *Pl.* 4:835). The very attempt to keep enough influence to avoid these problems will probably cost more than the property that Emile would be trying to protect.

Such is the situation in which Emile finds himself and within which Emile and his tutor depart on their journey. The problem dictates the travel. Their intention is clear—to look for a place where Emile can pursue in peace his dream with Sophie. The reader knows that this place does not exist. It is a chimera, like the true love that is driving him. This chimera, like love, will also have an equally good effect. Emile will learn about governments and public morality. The two years spent searching for a nonexistent place will not be in vain.

THE *SOCIAL CONTRACT* AND THE STATE OF NATURE

The existential state of Emile, scandal, has its theoretical correlative in the space of the *Social Contract*. This is the space between "is" and "could be," between "man as he is" and "laws as they can be" (*CW* 4:131; *Pl.* 3:351). As Rousseau puts it in *Emile*,

"It is necessary to know what ought to be in order to judge soundly about what is" (*Emile*, 458; *Pl.* 4:836–37). The space that is opened up by this distinction could be called the space of "scandal," in the sense that it is the space in which one finds things as they are, but these things are not what they ought to be.

There is no way to get to the doctrine of the *Social Contract* without going through the state of nature. Rousseau begins his summary of it in *Emile* by saying, "For example, by first going back to the state of nature" (*Emile*, 459; *Pl.* 4:837). One can go further and say that the going back in order to look at the change from the state of nature to the state of civil society takes place in the same theoretical space as the *Social Contract*. The function of the state of nature and the text is identical in that each is used as a standard for judgments. As Rousseau puts it in the *Discourse on Inequality*, even if the state of nature has never actually existed, it is still "necessary to have precise Notions in order to judge out present state correctly" (*CW* 3.13; *Pl.* 3:123). The state of nature is the standard according to which we make our judgments. And so is the *Social Contract*. "One must construct a standard to which measurements one makes can be related. Our principles of political right are that standard" (*Emile*, 458; *Pl.* 4:837).

This way of understanding the *Social Contract* is strengthened by Emile's reaction at the conclusion of the summary. Jean-Jacques says that he will not be surprised if his pupil remarks, "Someone might say we are building our edifice with wood and not with men, so exactly do we align each piece with the ruler" (*Emile*, 467; *Pl.* 4:849). This is precisely the purpose of the *Social Contract*, like the state of nature, to establish "right," not what is. Each gives principles. For Rousseau, this distinction between what is and what could be, between fact and right, or, better put, the ability to make this distinction, is absolutely fundamental.

There is further evidence for the ontological status of the *Social Contract* as a fiction that leads to the truth. After their travels are complete and they have returned to Sophie's dwelling, Jean-Jacques asks Emile what he has decided. We will look at his decision in more detail later, but what is interesting here is Jean-Jacques' response to that decision. He asks, "What difference does it make that the social contract has not been observed, if individual interest protected him as the general will would have done, if public violence guaranteed him against individual violence?" (*Emile*, 473; *Pl.* 4:858). The fact that the social contract has never been observed does not change anything.

An even clearer indication of the hypothetical status of the contract is contained in the text of the *Social Contract* itself. As Rousseau gets ready to formulate clauses of the compact that will solve the "fundamental problem" of government and liberty, he tells the reader that "although they may never have been formally pronounced, they are everywhere the same, everywhere tacitly accepted and recognized" (*CW* 4:138; *Pl.* 3:360). The social contract may never have been actually pronounced (that is, like the state of nature, it may never have actually existed), but that is not what is crucial. What is crucial is that each person is tacitly drawn to it, and if they grow attached to it, the attachment will enable them to live according to it. The idea of the social contract allows Emile to have civic virtue, just as his attachment to Sophie allows him to have moral virtue.

The state of civil society as contained in the *Social Contract* shares the same onto-logical status as the state of nature, and that is what makes the transition from the one to the other possible. According to Rousseau, the state of nature ought to determine the state of civil society, and so the conditions of the possibility for the one hold also for the other. The movement is not from one historical fact to another, nor from one arbitrary fiction to another. Rather, it moves from one set of conditions for the possibility of consciousness to another. The first set, as the next chapter shows, is arrived at by looking at humans as if they were abandoned by God; the second set is arrived at by looking at humans as abandoned by God and alienated from them-selves. This alienation allows a human to see himself or herself against the crowd, and, at the same time, as a member of the crowd against some other individual.[3]

SELF-ALIENATION

The central moment of the *Social Contract* is the total self-alienation of each of the members, such that the human subject enters into a double relation with itself. Rousseau formulates it in the following words: "Each of us puts his person and all his power in common under the supreme direction of the general will; and in a body we receive each member as an indivisible part of the whole" (*CW* 4:139; *Pl.* 3:361). Within this single act of association, Rousseau sees a "reciprocal commitment of the public and the individuals" (*Emile*, 460; *Pl.* 4:840). Still, each individual is contract-ing with himself. Rousseau interprets this to mean that "each individual, contracting with himself so to speak, finds himself engaged in a double relation, namely toward the private individuals as a member of the Sovereign and toward the Sovereign as a member of the State" (*CW* 4:139–40; *Pl.* 3:362).[4] Call to mind that Rousseau has just defined "State" as the public person when it is passive. Rousseau is constructing the agreement so that one can both make a promise to oneself and avoid the prob-lem that one can release oneself from the obligation simply because one no longer feels like doing it.

As Rousseau states the commonplace: "No one is held to commitments made only with himself" (*Emile*, 461; *Pl.* 4:840), hence, the necessity of the double rela-tionship of each member to himself. The person is able to see himself as a *member*, as belonging to something larger than himself. He is a member of the Sovereign, and at the same time, he is a member of the State. On the one hand, as a member of the Sovereign, he is against each other member of the State considered an individual; on the other hand, as a member of the State, he is a single member against the Sovereign. One can ask, does the Sovereign include him when he is considered a member of the State? The answer is clearly yes—but under another aspect—or even as another per-son (i.e., the person of the Sovereign). Were this not so, the Sovereign could not oblige the members of the State to do anything. The member is obliged to "a whole of which [he] is a part" (*CW* 4:140; *Pl.* 3:362). More significantly, he is obliged to himself as another. The act of alienation is a true act of alienation. One becomes "other" to himself.

It goes even deeper than this. Something new has emerged with the social con-tract. As discussed earlier, Emile's relationship with Sophie allows a split between his desires and his will, bringing about the necessity for virtue. With the act of alienation, Emile begins to see himself, at one and the same time, as being part of the group against each member, and as being alone against the group. He has entered into a double relationship in which he is both the individual subject who stands against the group (the public, or the Sovereign) of which he is a part, and he is the group that stands against one of its own.

This is the structure of the *Social Contract*. This is the kind of consciousness that it engenders—a consciousness that allows one to see oneself as part of the group confronting one single member of the group, or as the one member who is being so confronted. Rousseau is quite explicit in showing that all the questions about the social contract revolve around grasping the "unique and particular nature" of the social pact (*Emile*, 461; *Pl.* 4:841). It is the people contracting with itself as the people in the meaningful sense that "the people as sovereign body contracts with the individual as subject" (*Emile*, 461; *Pl.* 4:841). This thought can be represented spatially. The formula of the contract demands that each person be on the periphery of a circle with some "other" at the center, and at the same time, that each be in the center with all the "others" on the periphery.

With this a new definition of scandal, a purely formal definition, emerges. To be scandalized means to put oneself simultaneously and permanently both on the periphery and in the center. It is, to make the implicit explicit, to be both victimizer and victim. If one locates oneself only on the periphery, then one is a persecutor and subject to the usual delusions of persecution. One will see oneself as justified and the one in the center as the cause of social problems. One is not troubled by the one in the center. He belongs there. One cannot picture oneself in the center. But if one is only in the center, then one is the victim, and one will see oneself as innocent and persecuted. The world is still split in a dualistic fashion. One cannot picture oneself on the periphery. To vacillate between the two is to find oneself simultaneously already guilty of the crimes one accuses others of, and to find the others guilty of the crimes of which one feels one is being accused. This is the very structure analyzed in the stories of Emile and the gardener, and Emile and the magician.

Another way of viewing this is to recall that Rousseau held that even though it is "not impossible for a private will to agree with the general will on a given point, it is impossible, at least, for this agreement to be lasting and unchanging" (*CW* 4:145; *Pl.* 3:368). The general and private will of the single individual come into a conflict of necessity and force the individual to occupy two standpoints at once.

The single act of association, which constitutes the social contract, creates sovereignty, and this sovereignty shares in the structure of the act that produces it: "The Sovereign, by the sole fact of being, is always what it ought to be" (*CW* 4:140; *Pl.* 3:363). Sovereignty presumes the distinction between "is" and "ought" in overcoming that distinction. The creation of order would seem to be the closing of the gap in which the *Social Contract* exists. In fact, it is a displacement of that space.

The production of the Sovereign is such that the moment it exists, the moment the "is" and the "ought" coincide, they also get separated in the form of the Sovereign and the executive power. The Sovereign is indeed what it ought to be, but it is always threatened with becoming "other." And should the Sovereign become "other," should it possess executive power, the result is not that the "is" and the "ought" are once again separated. Rather, "were it possible for the Sovereign, considered as such, to have the executive power, right [ought] and fact [being] would be so completely confounded that one would no longer know what is law and what isn't" (*CW* 4:194; *Pl.* 3:432). Sovereignty ceases to be sovereignty—it ceases to be, when it ceases to be what it ought to be—and this is when the violence becomes explicit. The body politic falls "prey to the violence against which it was instituted" (*CW* 4:194; *Pl.* 4:432). The unity of the "is" and the "ought," the sacred unity of the Sovereignty, hides the violence that constitutes that unity.

This hidden violence means that the essence of the *Social Contract*, as contained in the terms of the surrender to the general will, is incomplete, or, better put, the *Social Contract* contains even more than is stated in its formulation. "It tacitly includes the following engagement, which alone can give force to the others: that whosoever refuses to obey the general will shall be constrained to do so by the entire body; which means only that he will be forced to be free" (*CW* 4:141; *Pl.* 3:364).

Sovereignty is violence. It is the force that the body politic has to move its members.[5] The tacit engagement concerns this force, and yet the question persists: in what does the particular force of the Sovereign consists. It is not and cannot be simple violence directed toward an individual to force the individual to do something or be killed. There are several reasons for this. Primarily, no act of sovereignty can concern a person as an individual. Secondly, Rousseau is categorical that the maxim that "the government is allowed to sacrifice an innocent man for the safety of the multitude" is "one of the most execrable that tyranny ever invented, the most false that might be proposed, most dangerous that might be accepted, and the most directly opposed to the fundamental laws of society" (*CW* 3:152; *Pl.* 3:256). One should hardly expect to find such a maxim in his writings.

My interpretation of the famous phrase "he will be forced to be free" is both influenced by and formulated against the interpretation offered by Steven G. Affeldt in his article "The Force of Freedom: Rousseau on Forcing to Be Free." Affeldt is correct when he states that the general will "can only exist as a current will,"[6] that the "will exists only in willing," and that "its time is always now."[7] Law has to be continuously willed, and a citizen has to be continuously constituting the general will. Affeldt's formulation that "for Rousseau, genuine society exists only in the continuous origination or in the continuous constitution of a general will among a people" expresses Rousseau's position with great clarity.[8]

This interpretation implies that society is under the constant threat of annihilation. If for a moment one ceases to originate the general will, and instead one becomes a passive but compliant denizen of society, then "one is not an apathetic citizen, or an indifferent citizen, or a bad citizen. One is simply not a citizen at all."[9] The reason for this constant threat to society is the individual will of each person. "The private will tends by its nature toward preferences, and the general will towards equality" (*CW* 4:145; *Pl.* 3:368). I also agree with Affeldt's conclusion that in spite of, or indeed because of, this incessant threat, Rousseau's tacit engagement of the social compact cannot amount to sanctioning social power: "For coercive power is perfectly powerless to address a withholding . . . of participation."[10]

In developing his more positive account of what to "force to be free" means, Affeldt emphasizes that it is an "engagement" or task and that the agency of constraint—those doing the forcing—is the entire body. The engagement is to counteract the threat to society that comes from private wills by "working to constrain to obey the general will those who refuse to do so." Citizens are to function "as agents of constraint."[11] That is, they are to so heed the call of the general will that they will work to "constrain others to heed that call as well."[12]

Affeldt ends by suggesting that the force or power to be used is something other than coercive force. One is an agent of constraint through instruction and attraction. Affeldt raises the fundamental problem that his interpretation faces: "It may seem that this interpretation is unable to take fully literally Rousseau's talk of *forcing* to be free."[13] Affeldt's position points toward an answer to the meaning of force. The "continuous origination" or the "continuous constitution of a general will" suggests a continuous struggle.

Affeldt is surely correct in insisting upon a distinction between private wills and private interests. Private interests do not interfere with the general will and are often discovered only in the context of the general will. But Affeldt does not explore the relationship between common interest and the general will. Perhaps he does not because Rousseau is so clear on this point: "What generalizes the will is not so much the number of votes as the common interest that unites them" (*CW* 4:149; *Pl.* 3:374).[14] The general will "considers only common interest" (*CW* 4:147; *Pl.* 3:371).[15] It is fair to conclude that the task of originating the general will can be defined in terms of originating common interest, and Rousseau tells the reader how that is done.

Once again, a crucial aspect of Rousseau's theory is contained in a footnote. Rousseau quotes the Marquis d'Argenson to the effect that the only way to get the agreement of two private interests is through both opposing the interests of a third. Then Rousseau adds, in his own words, that to form the agreement of all interests, or to form a common interest, that will, in turn, be the object of the general will, one must oppose them all "to the interest of each." The private interests of each one are the "obstacles," the *skandalon*, that both oppose and, in opposing, form the general interest, and thus the general will. Without these private interests, without these obstacles, the common interest "would scarcely be felt" (*CW* 4:147n; *Pl.* 3:371n). The interests of each make the common interest possible at the same time that they prevent it from being realized.[16] This is a scandalous situation.

This interpretation aligns closely with the one offered by Hannah Arendt in *On Revolution*.[17] According to Arendt, Rousseau constructs the one state out of its many members by taking "his cue from the common experience that two conflicting interests will bind themselves together when they are confronted by a third that equally opposes them both."[18] She sees that Rousseau does not restrict himself to forming the unity by opposing the society to some external threat. Rather, there is a "common enemy . . . within the breast of each citizen, namely, in his particular will and interest."[19]

The analysis presented here is closest to Arendt's in the way she sees that the very existence of the general will depends upon "its being opposed to each interest or will in particular."[20] Our analyzes are most far apart in the way that Arendt sees the common enemy, as she puts it, within the breast of each individual rather than between individuals, as I emphasize. I am willing to accept that a single person can bring all (minus one) of his interests into agreement by opposing them to a single interest. But the problem of politics is the problem of people living together and not simply of personal integration. When Rousseau writes that without the different interests, "politics would cease to be an art," he is referring to an interpersonal problem (*CW* 4:147n; *Pl.* 3:371n).

This is, of course, the same structure as that of the basic articulation of the social compact. Each member of the Sovereign joins together in opposing some*one*. Each one finds himself opposed by others. But Rousseau has now made the opposition and the "forcing to be free" explicit.

The structure of the social contract itself and the sovereignty it generates are such that each member is constantly faced with the choice of either joining with the group to oppose and constrain the one, or being the one who is so opposed and constrained. What is not possible in the social contract is choosing to join the one in solidarity against the others. To repeat, the forming of the common interest that is the basis for forming the common will consists precisely in the opposition of all interests against each individual interest. There is no theoretical space for joining with the one. The structure itself forces an act of will, so that the general will can be generated.

As Riley has shown in the article "Rousseau's General Will," the only thing that could be forced here is an act of the will. If one simply yields to force, that would be, according to Rousseau, "an act of necessity not of the will."[21] That is, the social contract is constantly forcing its members to exercise their will, to choose, and this choosing creates the very structure (all against one) that is needed for the social contract to operate. Put in this situation, each is forced by all the others either to oppose someone or to be the one who is opposed. This is where the "force" of the contract is operative.[22]

CIVIL RELIGION

Emile does not contain, in its summary of the *Social Contract*, anything about either the "Legislator" or "Civil Religion" (*CW* 4:154ff; *Pl.* 3:381ff; and *CW* 4:216ff; *Pl.* 3:460ff, respectively). I have tried to indicate in an implicit manner why that is so. Clearly, the tutor functions as the legislator. He slowly prepares the boy Emile to accept the rule of reason, the rule of law.

I have also given a detailed interpretation of the "Profession of Faith" that focuses upon the political dimension of its teaching concerning a violent God. But the audience of *Emile* and the audience of the *Social Contract* are different, so that the treatment of religion in the *Social Contract* is not precisely the same as the treatment in *Emile*. If the overall purpose of religion in the "Profession of Faith" is to ensure the belief of the ordinary person in a God who upholds the moral order, then the purpose of religion in the *Social Contract* is to ensure a supply of victims to reinforce the social order. The delicate balance that lies at the heart of the *Social Contract*, the balance between seeing oneself as part of the group against one member and also seeing oneself as the one member against the group, is inherently unstable. Eventually, the group will need to dispel its tensions and antagonisms on someone. Rousseau gestures toward the victim in this section of the *Social Contract*.

By the time of the *Social Contract*, Rousseau had long avoided giving either a theogony or a genealogy of religion. The development of these anthropological realities is never mentioned in the *Second Discourse*. Rousseau cut out parts that he had written that dealt with this topic.[23] As for the "Profession of Faith," it presumes that various religions exist in various countries and so should always remain. But in the *Social Contract*, Rousseau lifts the veil a bit. According to the *Social Contract*, the gods were originally kings. They ruled because peoples were opposed to each other, because armies that were fighting one another could not follow the same God. Gods were born, then, of conflict, and remained tied to this conflict.

The division of the world into nations resulted in three related things: polytheism, civil intolerance, and theological intolerance. The country's gods were identified with its laws, and all political wars had a theological dimension as well. If a people were vanquished, so were its gods. Gods, too, lived and died by the logic of violence. Gods and their religions were in a state of war with regard to one another, fighting each other on behalf of the people with whom they were associated. According to Rousseau, "there was no other way to convert a people except to subjugate it, nor any missionaries other than conquerors" (*CW* 4:217; *Pl.* 3:460). Thus, the cacophony of gods could become more uniform with the spread of the Roman Empire.

It was into this unity brought about by violence that "Jesus came to establish a Spiritual Kingdom on earth" (*CW* 4:217; *Pl.* 3:462). According to Rousseau, Jesus introduced something both new and terribly unsettling. The theological and the political, whose unity had been testified to through violence, now became separate, and this "brought about the end of the unity of the State and caused the internal divisions that have never ceased to stir up Christian people" (*CW* 4:217; *Pl.* 3:462). The unity of the State up until this point had been a unity in which political wars against other states were also theological wars against other gods. This unity was a unity of the control and direction of violence. But now the political could no longer presume that the spiritual would justify its violence. Hence, there develops internal violence.

The persecutions that were the reaction to the rise of Christianity were due to the fact that Christians would not worship the gods of the government and insisted on keeping their own God with His own heavenly kingdom. The pagans regarded them, then, as rebels, who "beneath a hypocritical submissiveness," were in fact planning to take over the authority they pretended to respect (*CW* 4:217; *Pl.* 3:462).

According to Rousseau, this is exactly what happened. Christians, under a visible leader, became violent. This, in and of itself, was not the problem. As far as Rousseau is concerned, the violence of the pagans and the violence of the Christians are the same thing. The problem is that the Christians were not thorough enough. They kept, rather than overcame, the distinction between the prince's civil power and the priest's religious power. "This double power has resulted in the perpetual conflict of jurisdiction that has made any good polity impossible in Christian states" (*CW* 4:218; *Pl.* 3:462).

In spite of attempts to preserve or re-establish the ancient republics, "the dominating spirit of Christianity" has prevailed (*CW* 4:218; *Pl.* 3:463). What exactly is that "spirit"? It is the spirit that says that the State is not absolute, and that the State serves God rather than the gods serving the state. The spirit of Christianity dissolves the "necessary bond" between the State and its religion (*CW* 4:218; *Pl.* 3:462). A Christian could, conceivably, belong to any civil body.

For Rousseau, it is clear that no state has ever been founded without religion serving as its base. He rejects the thought of those, like Pierre Bayle, who would claim that "no religion is useful to the body politic" (*CW* 4:219; *Pl.* 3:464). This sentiment underlies the "Profession of Faith." Even though this points to the centrality of religion in Rousseau's political thought, it makes equally clear that that religion cannot be Christianity, because "Christian law is fundamentally more harmful than useful to the strong constitution of a State" (*CW* 4:219; *Pl.* 3:464).

When Rousseau begins his categorization of religions, he distinguishes religions through sociological categories. Societies are either general or particular and so religions are either of man or of the citizen. General society and the religion that belongs to it are abstractions. This religion would have no "temples, altars, or rituals," and it would be "limited to the purely internal cult of the Supreme God and to the eternal duties of morality" (*CW* 4:219; *Pl.* 3:464). It is "true Theism," "the pure and simple Religion of the Gospel" (*CW* 4:219; *Pl.* 3:464). On the other hand, the religion of the citizen is prescribed by the laws of the country in which it exists and has all the concrete things that the other religion does without. This religion regards everything outside of it as "infidel, foreign, barbarous" (*CW* 4:219; *Pl.* 3:464). Finally, there is a third type of religion, which is neither that of man nor of citizen but is "bizarre" because it gives its adherents "two legislative systems, two leaders, and two fatherlands, subject[ing] them to contradictory duties, and prevent[ing] them from being simultaneously devout men and Citizens" (*CW* 4:219; *Pl.* 3:464). Roman Catholicism is an example of this third kind.

Each of these three presents the political philosopher with problems. The third clearly puts man in contradiction with himself and so can be ruled out. But so can the first and the second. The second is bad because it leads to uncontrolled violence in that it makes a people bloodthirsty and intolerant. It can make the murder of someone who does not accept the God into a holy act. The first is disqualified for problems that are not unlike those of the third kind. Because true theism detaches its adherents "from all worldly things" including the State, it is contrary to the social spirit. Without going into all the details, I wish to underline what Rousseau holds about Christianity: "Christianity preaches nothing but servitude and dependence" (*CW* 4:221; *Pl.* 3:467). Christianity is the opposite teaching from that contained in *Emile*.

Rousseau has not simply condemned this or that particular religion. He has gone much further and called into question all of the religions that were available to him at the time. None of his options will fulfill the needed function. So now Rousseau must do something quite radical; he must develop his own notion of religion—a true civil religion. In order to do this, Rousseau abandons the sociological considerations that have guided his investigation up to this point and turns to the question of "right" in order to determine principles. He reaffirms and specifies the importance of religion to the Sovereign. The religion of the citizen has one purpose—that of forming a set of opinions important to the well-being of the community as follows: "Now it matters greatly to the State that each Citizen have a Religion that causes him to love his duties, but the dogmas of that Religion are of no interest either to the State or to its members; except insofar as these dogmas relate to morality, and to the duties that anyone who professes it is obliged to fulfill toward others" (*CW* 4:222; *Pl.* 3:468). This principle establishes a "purely civil profession of religion" (*CW* 4:222; *Pl.* 3:468).

The Sovereign, the force that moves the members, establishes the articles of faith, "not exactly as Religious dogmas, but as sentiments of sociability without which it is impossible to be a good Citizen and a faithful subject" (*CW* 4:222; *Pl.* 3:468). The power that the Sovereign possesses is positive in this regard, but it is only prohibitive, not prescriptive. It cannot force belief, but it can punish disbelief. The Sovereign can banish those who do not believe because they are *ipso facto* unsociable. It is impossible for them to love the laws without religion. It is impossible for them to give their lives for the State. But there is a worse offense than disbelief, and that is hypocrisy: "If someone who has publicly acknowledged these same dogmas behaves as though he does not believe them, he should be punished with death. He has committed the greatest of crimes; he has lied before the laws" (*CW* 4:223; *Pl.* 3:468).

Let me draw attention to the fact that, quite consistently, Rousseau is not concerned with the person's private beliefs. It is not as if the citizen were to publicly proclaim the prescribed beliefs and then privately tell people that *really* he does not accept them. His actions are what condemn him. He may even think that he does believe, but if he gives evidence that his actions do not match his beliefs, he is to be killed. The reader does not yet know, in the text, what exactly these dogmas are, but she already knows the punishment for not being true to them.[24] This at least suggests that the content of the dogmas is less important than the structure. A judgment can be rendered by the government that the *behavior* of one of its members does not coincide with these beliefs, and then that member can be killed.

The dogmas of the civil religion are simple and few: they include the existence of God, and the existence of an afterlife in which the just are rewarded with happiness and the wicked are punished. Further, the civil religion includes the sanctity of the social contract and the laws. It is this holiness that makes the crime of acting against the professed beliefs so serious. To lie before the laws is the "greatest of crimes" because of the sanctity of the laws. This profession contains one negative dogma— the prohibition of intolerance. If one asks what behavior would qualify as evidence that one does not believe these dogmas, a concrete answer in the text is difficult to find. A lack of belief means that one is "incapable of sincerely loving the laws, justice and of giving [one's] life, if need be" (*CW* 4:223; *Pl.* 3:468). Who is to judge the sincerity of someone else's love? It is easy if the person simply says that he or she does not believe, for then he or she is banished. Much more difficult is the case of the person who does believe but who "behaves as if he does not believe them" (*CW* 4:223; *Pl.* 3:468). These are the people who must be killed for lying before the laws.

The Narrative

To return to the novel and draw our discussion together, let me point out that Rousseau emphasizes the importance of the lie and illusion for Emile's entry into the

Social Contract only at the end of the section in which its summary is contained. This ending sheds a light backward on the section "On Travel," and in this way it also helps the reader to understand the *Social Contract*, whose summary it contains.

The passage to which I am referring is Jean-Jacques' defense of his strategy of having Emile fall in love before embarking on these travels. Jean-Jacques holds that Emile is safe from the "contagion" of loose morals that he will encounter due to the "attachment [to Sophie] he bears in his heart" (*Emile*, 470; *Pl.* 4:853). Jean-Jacques believes in the power of "true love" to effect the inclinations of young people. In fact, he is apodictic: "A young man must either love or be debauched" (*Emile*, 470; *Pl.* 4:853). As for those who appear virtuous without being in love, they appear to be what, in fact, they are not. Most people will be satisfied with this appearance of virtue; Jean-Jacques, of course, is not. He says, "I seek reality, and I am mistaken if there are other means of getting it than those I give" (*Emile*, 470; *Pl.* 4:853).

In order to back up this claim, the tutor states, "The idea of getting Emile to fall in love before making him travel is not my invention. Here is the incident which suggested it to me" (*Emile*, 470; *Pl.* 4:853). With this sentence, the author moves from romance to history, from novel to confession. While Rousseau is in Venice he visits a young Englishman, Lord John, and his governor. The governor is rereading aloud a letter from the mother of the young man. Although Rousseau cannot understand the contents of the letter, he observes Lord John stealthily tearing off his cuffs and putting them in the fire. This puzzles Rousseau, and so he shows the young man's bare wrists to his governor and asks what it might mean.

With Lord John's consent, the governor explains the situation and translates the contents of the letter. It seems that Lord John is promised to a Miss Lucy back in England. She has been stitching cuffs for him. The letter relates how a female friend comes to visit and insists on helping her with the cuffs. Miss Lucy allows her to do that but then awakes early the next morning and undoes all the stitching done by her friend. She does this because, so the letter runs, "she does not want a single stitch in her gift to be done by a hand other than her own" (*Emile*, 470; *Pl.* 4:854). Hearing this causes the young man to destroy the cuffs he is wearing, because they are a gift from a female admirer in Venice.

Rousseau suspects that the letter is deliberately arranged as "an expedient . . . against the lady of the cuffs" (*Emile*, 471; *Pl.* 4:854). Not so, says the governor. Rather, he feels that God has blessed his work, which he does with "simplicity and zeal" (*Emile*, 471; *Pl.* 4:854). This could be considered simply a historical incident used to strengthen the author's claim that his fictional account is based on real experience and so should be considered reliable. But Rousseau goes on: "It is time to finish. Let us take Lord John back to Miss Lucy—that is to say, Emile back to Sophie" (*Emile*, 471; *Pl.* 4:854). This identification of the two historical figures with the two fictional characters tells the reader about what has been going on throughout the whole romance of Emile and Sophie.

The fictional characters are real and real characters are now part of a novel. That is, all of them share the ontological status of true love, which is a lie. This is a critical hermeneutical reminder of Rousseau's project. The incident is reported in order to give weight to Rousseau's means of getting at the "reality" of virtue and duty. The means are "true love," the love of Emile and Sophie, and the love of Lord John and

Miss Lucy. The readers are meant to recall here that true love is a fiction, even and especially in real life. The only means that Rousseau has, the only means that there is, to get to the reality he seeks is a fiction. This gives the readers a way to read not just Emile's and Jean-Jacques' travels, but the *Social Contract* as well. The *Social Contract* contains the "true" principles of political right, and it is a fiction.[25] The political philosophy of Rousseau leads to the conclusion that some lies are "worth more than truth," precisely because they make living the truth possible.

CONCLUSION

Even if Rousseau's political philosophy can be viewed as the highpoint of the novel, the book does not end with the summary of the *Social Contract*. The novel itself has a denouement, and this denouement is intimately connected with the teachings of the *Social Contract*. This scene has been a source of discomfort and embarrassment for some commentators on *Emile*.[26] It is not the marriage of Emile and Sophie, which is not really recorded; instead, it is the moment between the marriage and its consummation, the moment when their mediator takes the couple away from the crowd and guides them to another contract, a "treaty," as it is called (*Emile*, 477; *Pl.* 4:863). This treaty is intended to keep the wedding contract viable. Basically, the agreement is that Emile will not exercise his "rights" over the body of his spouse but will always receive her sexual favors as that—favors that are not owed.

At this point in the story, it is fair to say that Emile is burning with desire to exercise his rights, and so is loath to give up what seems to be easy access to their fulfillment. Jean-Jacques and Sophie join together to force Emile to choose to put himself in the state of someone who has to choose constantly to obey the law to which he himself has agreed. Sexuality here stands for the kind of human desire that can constantly be fanned and so used as a motive for choice. Emile threatens violence before acquiescing. Rousseau emphasizes the violence that underlies and gives force to the agreement. Sophie's last words in the novel are, "the ingrate." These are words that are to communicate to us her love for Emile and his lack of understanding of the way in which she loves him. The Sovereign might say the same thing to most citizens whom it forces to be free.

But guided by the tutor and encouraged by Sophie, Emile agrees to the limitation. Two things happen in the story because of this acquiescence. First, as Emile kneels before Sophie to renounce his rights, we overhear Jean-Jacques' unspoken thoughts: "Good Emile, reassure yourself: Sophie is too generous herself to let you die a victim of your generosity" (*Emile*, 477; *Pl.* 4:864). For the reader, the relevant point is that the denouement of the novel has Emile not simply being victimized, but also actually willing himself freely to be put in the position of the victim—a victim with a suspended sentence to be sure, but a victim nonetheless. The other thing that happens is that Jean-Jacques offers to take Emile away at the very moment that Emile is to consummate his marriage. Jean-Jacques makes this offer "in the gravest tone possible" (*Emile*, 477; *Pl.* 4:864). Emile is close to violence. Jean-Jacques then asks, "And you, Sophie, what do you say about it? Should I take him away?" (*Emile*, 477; *Pl.* 4:864). Sophie assents. As Jean-Jacques puts it, "The liar . . . says yes. How charming and sweet a lie, worth more than the truth" (*Emile*, 477; *Pl.* 4:864). The moment of entering into the treaty is still a moment of untruth, but a lie that is used in the service of truth. *Emile* is Rousseau's alternative account of salvation.

As discussed in the last chapter, Rousseau raises the question concerning the genre of the text. Is this a history of the species or a romance? This question reflects the way the book is structured. If the reader accuses the book of being a romance and so a text that depraves, this only proves that the reader has depraved the text by making it a romance. So I end this chapter and this part of the book with a suggestion. Perhaps the reader does not need to decide the genre of the book.[27] The reader should refrain from doing this not in the sense of simply leaving it "undecidable," but rather in the sense of letting the alternatives, texts that victimize by being scandalous and texts that are victimized by being accused of being scandalous, give him the opportunity to read *Emile* as inscribing the struggle between them. Read in this way, *Emile* becomes what Rousseau intended it to be: "the history of [his] species" (*Emile*, 416; *Pl.* 4:777). That is, it becomes the history of humankind staggering between killing the victim and repenting it.

By reading *Emile* in this way, the reader succeeds both in not judging it and in letting it be what Rousseau intended. If, in *Emile*, Rousseau presents a text that allows for, indeed calls for, both the killing of the victim and repentance, then there is also a need for a myth that both justifies that killing and calls for that repentance. In other words, there is a need for a text that both embraces and rejects the Gospel. The *Discourse on Inequality* is such a text.

PART III

THE *DISCOURSES*

CHAPTER 7

THE SCANDAL OF ORIGINS

INTRODUCTION

In the *Discours sur l'origine et les fondements de l'inégalité parmi les hommes* (1755; *Pl.* 3:),[1] Rousseau is contesting the prevalent account of origins—the Book of Genesis. The Judeo-Christian Scriptures are both absent and yet present in the *Second Discourse*; it is a discourse from which they have been expelled and yet, by the act of expulsion, are also somehow included within the *Discourse*. It is striking that, for a piece of writing that expressly sets the Scriptures aside, Starobinski could, with reason, write, "Rousseau has rewritten *Genesis* as a work of philosophy, complete with the Garden of Eden, original sin, and the confusion of tongues. This is a secularized, 'demystified' version of the origins of mankind, which *repeats the Scriptures that it replaces in another tongue*. Rousseau's language is that of philosophical speculation, and all mention of the supernatural has been eliminated. Yet Christian theology, though not present explicitly, *shapes* the structure of Rousseau's argument."[2] I wish to specify the way in which theology "shapes" the argument. I will show that the *Second Discourse*, like the Christian Scriptures it both imitates and replaces, causes scandal.[3] And so I can join Starobinski in affirming that the *Second Discourse* "is a thoroughly religious work, but of a very particular kind, a substitute for sacred history."[4]

I wish to show that, according to the text of the *Second Discourse*, it is precisely the Christian Scriptures, or the very source of scandal, that originate the state of nature. The Scriptures, and therefore scandal, make the state of nature both necessary and impossible. These writings have been "set aside," but this act of setting scandal aside constitutes the *Discourse on Inequality* itself and, therefore, constitutes it as scandalous.

I will analyze the *Discourse on Inequality* in this chapter and the next, concentrating in this chapter on the front matter of the *Discourse* (the "Preface," the "Notice on the Notes," and the "Exordium"). The next chapter will look to the body of the *Discourse*. My overall argument that Rousseau constructs the *Second Discourse* as both a rejection and an imitation of the Scriptures has four parts. This chapter will deal with the first two. First, through a careful analysis of the methodological considerations that comprise the "Preface" and the "Notice on the Notes," I make clear that Rousseau characterizes the search for origins as a scandalous enterprise. Second, by an examination of the "Exordium," I will show that it is Sacred Scripture that makes the state of nature first impossible, then necessary, and in this sense scandalous. The next chapter will show how the very obstacles that render discourse impossible in the first part make it necessary in the second, and, finally, that the *Discourse on the Origin of Inequality* is itself an origin.

THE "PREFACE"

After its "Epistle Dedicatory," the *Second Discourse* has a "Preface," a "Notice on the Notes," and an "Exordium." Apparently it is not an easy task to begin to speak about the beginning of human society. In fact, it is impossible. Perhaps the reason why Rousseau judges that this "most useful" of all human knowledge is also the "least advanced" is due to the fact that it cannot be begun (*CW* 3:12; *Pl.* 3:122). In these methodological considerations, Rousseau does not resolve this problem of beginning; rather, he deepens it. Rousseau clearly places this quest for the origin of human inequality in the philosophical and hermeneutical world by his opening reference to the inscription on the Temple at Delphi. This inscription is "more important and more difficult than all the thick Volumes of the Moralists" (*CW* 3:12; *Pl.* 3:122). Particularly in these methodological considerations, but also through the whole of the *Second Discourse*, Rousseau will show the reader that this knowledge is both necessary and impossible; in a word, it is scandalous.

I begin with a reading of the "Preface" in order to show that this work is structured by scandal in that it is structured by a human desire that renders the object it seeks unattainable in the very seeking after it. Two aspects of scandal will emerge in this analysis. First, the way in which scandal grounds the discourse about origins in the sense that the problem of origins is methodologically impossible is made clear, and then, secondly, the way in which scandal is the necessary condition for this kind of thinking. Rousseau is developing the conceptual possibilities of Biblical scandal. More concretely, I shall argue that in the "Preface," Rousseau is able to reduce the question about the origin of inequality "to its genuine state" only through a careful construction of the text around a relationship between being scandalized and being able to see (*CW* 3:13; *Pl.* 3:123).[5] The echoes between the way Rousseau thinks about the problem of origins and his position on scandal are too numerous and profound to be accidental.

THE FIRST HALF OF THE QUESTION: THE ORIGIN OF INEQUALITY

The "Preface" is constructed in two parts that correspond to the two parts of the question posed by the Academy of Dijon: the question of the origin of inequality, and the question of whether this inequality is authorized by natural law. In each part, scandal, in distinct but related forms, plays a decisive role. Also in both parts, the same pattern emerges. Rousseau first indicates the scandal involved in the question, then he gestures toward that which is easy to see, and finally he uses this to open up that which is more difficult to see. He concludes by stating in each case that his are the only means for resolving the difficulties in the question. He concludes the whole of the "Preface" by saying that, in following this path, one will gain a vision of how the things that seem destined to cause misery actually serve human happiness. In effect, he offers salvation by means of scandal.

The first form of scandal in the "Preface" revolves around the methodological impossibility of the problem. The origin of inequality is undecidable.⁶ This methodological impossibility opens up two roads. The first road takes the reader to those things that are easily perceived, and Rousseau goes far enough down this road to provide a clear answer to both halves of the question posed by the Academy. Rousseau does this not in order to resolve the question, but rather to show that to go deeper into the question, the reader must share scandal with him.

Rousseau accepts that the question posed by the Academy is "one of the most interesting that Philosophy might propose," but he raises an objection to it that will remain unanswered (*CW* 3:12; *Pl.* 3:122). It is a question of sight, a question of vision, as follows: "For how can the sources of inequality among men be known unless one begins by knowing men themselves? And how will man manage to see (*voir*) himself as Nature formed him, through all the changes that the sequence of times and things must have produced in his original constitution, and to separate what he gets from his own stock from what circumstances and his progress have added to or changed in his primitive state?" (*CW* 3:13; *Pl.* 3:122). There follows the famous comparison with the statue of Glaucus, a comparison taken from the *Republic* by Plato, but which Rousseau uses to heighten the undecidabilty of the question.

Starobinski notes Rousseau's enigmatic use of the image and asks, "Has Glaucus's face been eaten away by time? Has it lost forever the form it possessed when it first left the hands of the sculptor? Or has it merely been encrusted with salt and algae, beneath which the divine physiognomy preserves its original shape, with no loss of substance?"⁷ Starobinski holds that Rousseau cannot decide between the contradictory answers.⁸ Instead, Rousseau deepens the enigma and makes clear its scandalous character. The problem here is two-fold. Not only does the problem seem to invite question-begging, in that one would need to know in advance a human's original constitution in order to pass judgments on what is "his own," or what is original and what has been added on or changed. But also, "crueler" and therefore more scandalous, is the very structure of the human condition. The more knowledge that the human species accumulates, even if the knowledge concerns its own history, the further it moves itself away from its primitive state and deprives itself of the means of acquiring this knowledge, "so that it is, in a sense, by dint of studying man that we have made ourselves incapable of knowing him" (*CW* 3:12; *Pl.* 3:123).

Although he does not use the word, Rousseau is describing the scandalous situation, devoid of its religious context. The very means that are to bring someone toward what she desires form simultaneously a barrier or obstacle to the object. The person becomes more obsessed with and more blocked from the object with each step she takes. One can either enter into the process itself, which is a form of being scandalized without, perhaps, explicit knowledge of this, or one can stand apart and be scandalized at the human condition.

But then Rousseau seems suddenly to change tact and, instead of giving up an impossible quest, he states that "it is easy to see (*voir*)" that the first origin of differences distinguishing men is in the successive changes of the human constitution (*CW* 3:12; *Pl.* 3:123). In other words, at its beginning, the human species possessed an animal equality, but various physical causes would have changed an individual while the others remained longer in their original state. Rousseau is clearly answering the Academy's question here because he echoes their wording and not his own: "And such was the first *source* of inequality among men" (*CW* 3:12–13; *Pl.* 3:123; emphasis added).[9] The first part of the Academy's question has been answered.

And yet this version of the Academy's question is not the true one. Rather, the true question has to do with "what appears . . . so difficult to see (*voir*)" (*CW* 3:13; *Pl.* 3:123). Rousseau makes his intent clear when he states that he does not seek to resolve the question. Resolving the question of the origin of inequality would be to slacken the tension, to dissolve the scandal. Instead, Rousseau will seek, by means of conjectures,[10] to clarify the question and to reduce it to its "genuine state" (*CW* 3:13; *Pl.* 3:123). To repeat, its genuine state is undecided. Rousseau wants to help people to live with this contradiction and not to be able to escape from it. The question's genuine state becomes the reader's genuine existential state. This is the scandal-inducing state in which each step toward resolving the question only serves to increase the difficulty. Accordingly, "others," those who come after Rousseau and grasp the logic of scandal, will have no difficulty in going "farther on the same road" (*CW* 3:13; *Pl.* 3:123). The technique of scandal is not so difficult to master.

At the same time, Rousseau tells the reader, it will "not be easy for anyone to reach the end" of this road (*CW* 3:13; *Pl.* 3:123). In fact, one must conclude that it will be impossible. This is the road to the state of nature, to the origin of the human species; this is the road whose end is its beginning, and whose beginning moves further away insofar as it is approached. The end this road never reaches is not, at this point, named by Rousseau. He does not tell us where we are going. Rather, he defines it by means of an activity. One will have reached the goal when one has separated "what is original from what is artificial in the present Nature of man" (*CW* 3:13; *Pl.* 3:123). And yet this act of separation is clearly an art, a making or re-creating of what once was by nature, thereby destroying the natural. This is "no light undertaking" precisely because it is a contradictory one and yet it is also "necessary" (*CW* 3:13; *Pl.* 3:123). An understanding of the task as both necessary and yet impossible, that is, as scandalous, allows one to understand why the as-yet-unnamed state of nature is described as a "state which no longer exists, which perhaps never existed, which probably never will exist" (*CW* 3:13; *Pl.* 3:123).

To reduce the possibilities of interpreting this sentence to the alternative of historical existence or nonexistence of the state is to impoverish the possibilities of interpretation. Certainly one can argue in the spirit of Leo Strauss that censorship can induce a form of writing in which small disclaimers take on large significance.[11] But the truly great writers that Strauss analyzes used this challenge not simply to conceal the truth, but also to reveal it in its concealment. Rousseau was one of these great writers. It is not such a straightforward problem that one could conjecture that if the ecclesial and civil authorities had been more tolerant, then Rousseau would have clearly stated, "yes, indeed, this is the historical truth." The fact that he says the opposite—"The Researches which can be undertaken concerning this Subject must not be taken for historical truths" (*CW* 3:19; *Pl.* 3:132–33)—should not be dismissed as a rhetorical posture. The fact that a few lines later he affirms in unambiguous language the historical nature of the enterprise—"O Man, . . . here is your history" (*CW* 3:19; *Pl.* 3:133)—should not be ignored. Perhaps Rousseau has something to teach about the nature of the historical, especially when that history precedes history as such.[12]

Rousseau is beginning to develop the consequences of his "ontological scandal."[13] The activity that he is undertaking, separating what is "original from what is artificial" has ontological consequences in that it reveals "a state which no longer exists, perhaps never existed, which probably never will exist" (*CW* 3:13; *Pl.* 3:123). Take away the "perhaps" and the "probably" from that sentence, and one is left with a state of nature that is either a simple fact or a mere fiction. As a fact, it will simply be part of humanity's "present state" and so will not allow anyone to judge that state. As a fiction, it will simply be other than humanity's present state and so will not allow it to be judged correctly. But for Rousseau, human beings need to have "precise Notions" about this state "in order to judge our [humanity's] present state correctly" (*CW* 3:13; *Pl.* 3:123).

Rousseau's response to the problem that he has posed is to pose yet another challenge: "What experiments would be necessary to achieve knowledge of natural man? And what are the means for making these experiments in the midst of society?" (*CW* 3:13; *Pl.* 3:123–24; emphasis original) The question is not raised in vain.[14] Rousseau's response to this question is the *Second Discourse* itself. The word translated here as "experiments" can also mean "experiences." The experiment/experience needed to achieve the knowledge of natural man is the experience Rousseau has on the way to Vincennes, the experience he renews in the forests of St. Germaine, where he composed the *Second Discourse*.[15] The means for making these experiments is reading a new kind of writing: the *Second Discourse*. Rousseau is convinced of the uniqueness of what he has done. He writes, "These researches, so difficult to conduct and so little thought of until now, are nevertheless the only means we have left to remove a multitude of difficulties that hide from us knowledge of the real foundations of human society" (*CW* 3:13; *Pl.* 3:124). That these researches are the text of the *Second Discourse* Rousseau makes clear in the concluding paragraphs of the "Preface." His own study of "original man, of his true needs, and of the fundamental principles of his duties" is the "only good means" that will remove the difficulties concerning the true foundations of the body politic and will teach human beings to respect those foundations (*CW* 3:15; *Pl.* 3:126).

THE SECOND HALF OF THE QUESTION: NATURAL LAW

In Rousseau's treatment of the second part of the question, that is, whether the inequality is authorized by natural law or not, the scandal now becomes explicit. Up until now, he has expressed it indirectly through his description of the methodological problems confronting the person who undertakes to understand human origins. Now he writes, "It is not without surprise and scandal that one notes the little agreement which prevails on this important matter [e.g., natural right] among the various Authors who have discussed it" (*CW* 3:13; *Pl.* 3:124). The force of this double negative, "not without surprise and scandal," is stronger than it might first appear. Rousseau is not simply asserting that scandal necessarily accompanies one's thoughts or that it is a necessary by-product from this lack of agreement. Rather, he is saying that without scandal, one cannot think the way that he is proposing. Scandal in its second form is the necessary condition for the possibility of this kind of thinking. It is still methodological but it is directly concerned with language.

The source of Rousseau's scandal is the lack of agreement among authors and "serious Writers" (*CW* 3:13; *Pl.* 3:124). It is a scandal about and mediated by language. Ultimately, language makes the split between appearance and reality possible. Here is particularly egregious case. Each author defines "the [natural] Law in his own fashion" (*CW* 3:14; *Pl.* 3:125). And yet the natural law is precisely that which should mean the same thing to everyone. Still, these writers do manage to achieve a kind of spurious unity in this disagreement. Rousseau writes, "So that all the definitions of these learned men, otherwise in perpetual contradiction to one another, agree only in this, that it is impossible to understand the Law of Nature and consequently to obey it without being a great reasoner and a profound Metaphysician: which means precisely that men must have used, for the establishment of society, enlightenment which only develops with great difficulty and in very few People in the midst of society itself" (*CW* 3:14; *Pl.* 3:125). Rousseau's scandal destroys this agreement and reveals the viciousness of the circle.

Thus, the scandal, which was caused by the lack of agreement among writers and philosophers, not only exposes this lack of agreement concerning the definitions of natural law, but it also reveals them to be trapped in the same scandalous circle. Thus, and again, Rousseau turns to what can be clearly seen.

> All that we can see (*voir*) very clearly concerning this Law is that, for it to be Law, not only must the will of him who is bound by it be able to submit to it with knowledge; but also, for it to be natural, it must speak directly by Nature's voice (*CW* 3:14; *Pl.* 3:125).

Nature does not scandalize. Its meaning is clear. Law in itself does not scandalize, if it comes from nature, if it is spoken by nature's voice. Human language scandalizes in that humans can use the same word to mean different things.

In order to deepen the second part of the Academy's question, it is not enough that Rousseau be scandalized by the way language operates. He has to draw the reader into his scandal as well, and he does this by drawing a conclusion from what he has clearly seen. It is a scandalous conclusion borne of a scandalous situation. Rousseau says that he is "leaving aside therefore all scientific books" (*CW* 3:14; *Pl.* 3:125). His reason is that they impart a vision, but it is not a vision of nature; "they teach us only to see (*voir*) men as they have made themselves" (*CW* 3:14; *Pl.* 3:125). Rousseau is going to impart a different vision, and these kinds of books will only interfere. They will be obstacles. This conclusion is scandalous because it has the two characteristics of necessity and impossibility. As the "therefore" in the quote indicates, this sentence is a conclusion, a necessary conclusion of Rousseau's scandal at academic writing. At the same time, it is impossible to leave aside all scientific books, since the book Rousseau is writing is such a scientific book. This form of scandal will again be explicit at the end of the *Discourse on Inequality*.

Rousseau provides an answer to the second half of the Academy's question, much the way he provided one for the first half—provisionally. Rousseau meditates[16] and thus he perceives in the human soul two principles that are anterior to reason. One is self-preservation and the other is a form of natural pity such that humans are reluctant to see any sensitive being suffer. These principles enable Rousseau to answer the second half of the question. Every person is naturally equal to the other in the sense that "as long as he does not resist the inner impulse of commiseration, he will never harm another man or even another sensitive being, except in the legitimate case where, his preservation being concerned, he is obliged to give himself preference" (CW 3:15; Pl. 3:126).[17] The second half of the Academy's question has also been answered.

But Rousseau concludes that "this same study of original man," which he has conducted in these few page of the "Preface," is "the only good means one could use to remove those crowd of difficulties which present themselves" (CW 3:15; Pl. 3:126), meaning the answers he has so far provided have only succeeded in making the difficulties clear. These difficulties present themselves concerning the deeper question, Rousseau's question, which is not to be resolved but rather to be considered in its genuine state: the problem of "the origin of moral inequality" (CW 3:15; Pl. 3:126).

Rousseau ends the "Preface" by promising to deliver us from scandal. First, he makes clear that if the reader will join him in looking at human society "with calm and disinterested attention (regard)" he will be scandalized (CW 3:15; Pl. 3:126–27). Rousseau's reader will be shown "only the violence of powerful men and the oppression of the weak: the mind revolts against the harshness of the former; one is prompted to deplore the latter" (CW 3:15; Pl. 3:127). The realities that scandalize are mediated by a language in which they are "called weakness or power, wealth or poverty" (CW 3:15; Pl. 3:127). One has to look more closely and then one will learn a new language: the language of blessing. Instead of seeing as the scandalized person sees, namely, that the intended good results in evil, the reader will see something new. "By considering what we would have become abandoned to ourselves, we ought to learn to bless him whose beneficent hand, correcting our institutions and giving them an unshakeable base, has prevented the disorders that must otherwise have resulted from them, and has created our happiness from the means that seemed likely to heighten our misery" (CW 3:16; Pl. 3:127). The starting point and method of Rousseau are considerations of what has never existed and could never exist: humanity abandoned to itself. To move out of superficial scandal, the offense at a coarse expression in a play by Molière, by means of scandal is possible at the price of looking at humanity as being outside of the economy of sin and grace, salvation and damnation. Thus, the reader learns how to bless the beneficent hand.

By saying that considerations of humanity abandoned to itself would lead a person to bless the one who corrects our institutions, Rousseau opens up an ambiguity. One can read it as referring to God, especially since Rousseau has mentioned "what divine will has done" shortly before, and uses a quote referring to God to end the "Preface" (CW 3:16; Pl. 3:127). But Rousseau is not asking the reader to consider what God has done; in fact, he is asking the reader to do the opposite: to consider what would have happened had God abandoned humanity to itself. Then the reader will learn to bless Rousseau, whose task it is to correct human institutions and give them an unshakable base, to prevent disorders and to create human happiness out of the very means that seem likely to heighten misery. It will not be the last time that Rousseau puts himself in the place of the Almighty.

Although the word "scandal" is only used once in the entire "Preface," it is, in fact, the basis of the entire text. The impossibility of ever reaching the origin that we seek, combined with the necessity of seeking it, can be characterized as scandalous. Further, the words that are used to describe the state of nature are unstable in their meaning and lead only to further attempts at explanation with more words that are equally unstable. This is yet another scandalous fact. It leads Rousseau to set aside the scientific books that he needs in order to reach the state of nature.

AVERTISSEMENT SUR LES NOTES

The "*Avertissement sur Les Notes*" usually receives comment only to show that in it, Rousseau asks the reader to read the *Second Discourse* at least twice.[18] It is seen as further evidence of Rousseau writing for the "few" while allowing the "many" or the "vulgar" to also misread his work. In this sense, the "Notes" are necessary to the work. But the notes are "not good to read with the text" (*CW* 3:16; *Pl.* 3:128). This would seem to hold no matter how often one reads it. They are relegated by Rousseau to the end of the *Discourse*, but according to the "Preface," the *Second Discourse* never comes to an end.[19] Rather, as the "*Avertissement*" explicitly states, to read this text is always to "begin again" (*CW* 3:16; *Pl.* 3:128), rendering these necessary notes impossible to read, and making the impossibility of finishing and even really beginning this necessary task even more explicit.

THE EXORDIUM

In the "Exordium," Rousseau finally begins the *Second Discourse*, and this beginning will constitute it as discourse.[20] Rousseau is able to begin by famously "setting aside all the facts," these facts being primarily the facts of Scripture (*CW* 3:19; *Pl.* 3:132). He is not merely able to set these facts aside, but, because of the way in which he has reduced and clarified the question of the *Second Discourse*, he is impelled to set them aside. The question that Rousseau has constructed will control the whole of the *Discourse*, but this question is, in turn, controlled or determined by the Scriptures.

The "Preface" and the "Notice on the Notes" have not only shown the deep connection between looking for an origin and scandal, but they have also demonstrated the impossibility of ever reaching "*la véritable origine* [the genuine origin]" (*CW* 3:19; *Pl.* 3:135). In the "Exordium," Rousseau does not contradict or fall behind this extreme position. The search for the origin remains both necessary and impossible. In fact, he states quite clearly that the researches undertaken here are not appropriate for finding the true origin (cf.. *CW* 3:19; *Pl.* 3:135). And yet the "Exordium" goes beyond the "Preface" in that Rousseau does show how to begin: "Let us therefore begin by setting all the facts aside, for they do not affect the question" (*CW* 3:19; *Pl.* 3:132).[21] This beginning is itself a conclusion, as the word "therefore" clearly indicates. What argument does it conclude? It is generally acknowledged that the facts being set aside here are primarily the facts of Sacred Scripture. In order to understand how they can be set aside and why they do not affect the question, the question itself has to be clarified. Whatever it is, it is central to the whole of the *Discourse on Inequality*.

The question does not concern natural inequality. One cannot even ask what the source of natural inequality is, "because the answer would be enunciated in the simple definition of the word" (*CW* 3:19; *Pl.* 3:131). Neither does the problem concern whether there is an essential link between natural inequality and the conventional inequality. Rather, Rousseau gives two versions of the question with which this *Discourse* occupies itself. The first is, "Precisely what, then, is at issue in this Discourse? To indicate in the progress of things the moment when, Right taking the place of Violence, Nature was subjected to Law; to explain by what sequence of marvels the strong could resolve to serve the weak, and the People to buy a repose in ideas at the price of real felicity" (*CW* 3:18; *Pl.* 3:132). And yet this form of the question only serves to bring up exactly the same problems already faced in the "Preface."

There is no way back to the state of nature, and this has everything to do with the use of language. As Rousseau writes, "The philosophers who have examined the foundations of society have all felt the necessity of going back to the state of Nature, but none of them has reached it" (*CW* 3:18; *Pl.* 3:132).[22] And the reason why they have not been able to arrive is due to language. They have used words without explaining how the primitive person could have acquired the concepts. The philosophers have used words without seeing how the meaning of the words could exist. Rousseau sees these authors as "carrying over" into the state of nature ideas they have acquired in society (*CW* 3:19; *Pl.* 3:132). Not only does civil man have to be stripped of these in order to create the natural man, but the creator of the natural man also has to be stripped if he is to arrive at the state of nature. How is this to happen?

According to Rousseau, there is only one way to get back to the state of nature. It is a way that is mediated by a specific language, and it is an indirect way through the Christian Scriptures. The failure on the part of all the other philosophers up to Rousseau has been due to the fact that it has not entered their minds

> to doubt that the state of Nature had existed, even though it is evident from reading the Holy Scriptures that the first Man, having received enlightenment and precepts directly from God, was not himself in that state; and that giving the Writings of Moses the credence that any Christian philosopher owes them, it must be denied that even before the Flood Men were ever in the pure state of Nature, unless they fell back into it because of some extraordinary Event: a Paradox that is very embarrassing to defend and altogether impossible to prove. (*CW* 3:19; *Pl.* 3:132)

This sentence is not an aside. It is a central methodological step for Rousseau. The Scriptures teach us to doubt the actual, historical existence of the state of nature, and by so doing, they open up the possibility of getting on the road to this same state of nature. At the same time, this methodological step logically entails setting aside these same Scriptures once they have performed their task of instructing its readers as to the actual nonexistence of the state of nature.

Thus, Rousseau reaches the conclusion that the Scriptures are to be set aside. He uses the Scriptures, and in using them sets them aside. The very thing he needs in order to get to where he wants to go gets rejected in its very use.

Rousseau has now reached the question that he seeks, and he formulates again what the *Discourse* is about as follows: "[Religion] does not forbid us to form conjectures, drawn solely from the nature of man and the Beings surrounding him, about what the human Race might have become if it had remained abandoned to itself. This is what I am asked, and what I propose to examine in this Discourse" (*CW* 3:19; *Pl.* 3:133). The question that the setting aside of the Scriptures has opened up is what the human race might have become if it had been abandoned to itself. Implicit is the theological question of what the human race might have become if it had been abandoned *by God*. Again, Rousseau does not mean abandoned in its sin or its lostness. That would be the vision that he rejects: the vision of the innocent man crucified. Rather, Rousseau proposes humanity as abandoned to itself without the Cross, and without the sin and the redemption that the Cross implies.[23] This is an interpretation that can only be arrived at by one who has given into the temptation of scandal, that is, by one who rejects the way God has saved humanity and the vision of sin that the act of salvation founds.

What Rousseau rejects here is not some story of something that happened some two thousand years ago. What he rejects is the present reality of salvation being offered in the form of a particular person from a particular race at a particular time. The specific question Rousseau raises is hypothetical. One cannot get to *this* question without going through the Scriptures, because the Scriptures tell that in fact God did not abandon humanity. If one replaces this question with the factual question, "what has become of the human race, since it was abandoned to itself," one has not only a different question, but one has also lost the motivation for answering. What is, is, simply what is. To ask Rousseau's question, one needs the motivation of scandal at the present situation. And this scandal is theological scandal at the way God has chosen to save the human race.

Rousseau uses Scripture to make possible his thinking on the state of nature, and in this very use, he rejects Scripture. Only this reading can make sense of Rousseau's logic, in which he so forcefully reminds Christian philosophers of the implications of the Scriptural account and explains their failure to reach the pure state of nature on the basis of their ignoring what Scripture teaches, followed immediately by a setting aside of all the "facts," since they do not affect the question—the question that Rousseau has been at pains to make clear. He has carefully removed the question from the realm of Scriptures, except at that one point in which the question itself gets opened.

If one, like Rousseau, is scandalized by Christ, then one is scandalized by the way God has acted to save humanity. This form of scandal results in—is the origin of— the state of nature, because the state of nature is what is reached when one abstracts from God's saving action. After this, the state of nature becomes the origin of everything else.

The state of nature is the state that humans would have been in if humans had not, in fact, sinned, and if God had not, in fact, acted to save them. Thus, the kind of thinking that lies at the base of the *Second Discourse* is: "If it were not for the fact that." To go further and specify that what Rousseau means, one could say, "If it were not for the fact of human sin and God's response"—not of what might have been if humans had not sinned and remained in grace, but what might have been if there had been neither sin nor grace. In other words again, what would be the case, if the scandal had not occurred.[24] Rousseau must set the Scriptures aside in order to provide a truly alternative account and because it is the one source that can provide a challenge to his alternative account. The Scriptures that have made the scandal possible also challenge Rousseau's giving of scandal. This kind of contrafactual thinking, thinking of what might have been, characterizes a scandalized consciousness.

The origin of the scandal is the origin of Rousseau's system; to this extent, Rousseau needs Christ and the Christian Scriptures. At the same time, he rejects where Christ and the Scriptures lead. In this way, the origin of Rousseau's system is the rejection of its own origin (Christianity), and the *telos* or goal of the system is the avoidance of the *telos* of the rejected origin. This rejected origin and avoided *telos* frame the *Second Discourse* in the sense that they lie outside of its theoretical space, while giving that space the particular shape that it has. Borrowing from Soren Kierkegaard, one could sum it up in the following way: the Gospel is the result of a faith that annuls the possibility of scandal, and Rousseau's *Second Discourse* is the result of a scandal that annuls the possibility of faith.[25] In the next chapter, Rousseau's undermining of the discourse of the *Discourse on Inequality* by his analysis of the history and use of discourse will be made clear.

CONCLUSION

The state of nature has haunted the consciousness of modernity. A paradise lost that never really existed, it is a kind of modern myth. Combine the state of nature with its inhabitant, the noble savage, and the power that Rousseau continues to exercise, even on the untutored is manifest. This power comes from somewhere. Without taking anything away from Rousseau's genius, I do not think that it is due solely to this. The depth and the power of his thought come from the depth and the power of the reality against which he is struggling. Unlike other thinkers of the French Enlightenment, he did not simply reject Christianity and pursue something else. He offered a real alternative. If *Emile* was to be the modern replacement of Plato's *Republic*, then the *Discourse on the Origin Inequality* was meant to be a new Old Testament. Rousseau was nothing if not bold.

CHAPTER 8

THE ORIGIN OF SCANDAL

INTRODUCTION

The previous chapter demonstrated that Rousseau makes methodical use of the Christian Scriptures to open up a theoretical space, which he calls the state of nature, and, once he opens this space, he sets aside them aside. In order to continually constitute that space, the Scriptures will have to be present throughout the *Second Discourse* even in their absence. As rejected, they continue to be in the text. Their presence is not one of inspiring the composition of the state of nature. The *Second Discourse* does not really "resemble" the Scriptures. The natural man is not Adam. The state of nature is not Eden. Rather, the *Second Discourse* resembles the Scriptures by communicating in the same way that they do. And so the reader must look for a certain kind of logic—the logic of scandal. This is the way in which obstacles become bridges, or the way in which the very thing that makes something impossible ends up being its necessary condition. The obstacles in the state of nature render discourse first impossible and then necessary. More than that, the discourse that emerges from this impossible and yet necessary situation produces the closest thing to a God that appears in the *Second Discourse*.

In Rousseau's treatment of the emergence of discourse, the same obstacles that render the emergence of language and hence (scandalized) consciousness impossible in the "First Part" are precisely those that render it necessary in the "Second Part." The paradoxical nature of the origin of the *Discourse* operates throughout the text, appearing first as obstacles that prevent and then as obstacles that necessitate the development of mind. These considerations reflect in turn on the text of the *Second Discourse* as discourse, rendering it an impossible but necessary text.

Further, the *Discourse on Inequality* is not simply an account of origins; rather, it is itself an origin. Therein lies not only its originality but also its scandal. It originates an impossible but necessary inequality between the reader and the natural man, and thus enacts in the reading what it is being written about. It describes the emergence of scandalized consciousness, and in so doing, it engenders that consciousness in the reader.

Rousseau writes of three aporias in his considerations of the "metaphysical" side of natural man. These are the very things that block the development of language in the "First Part" and then become the necessary conditions of its growth in the "Second Part." Finally, they result in a "discourse within the *Discourse*" that functions to found society and the sacred.

THE "FIRST PART" OF THE DISCOURSE

The Christian Scriptures are capable at any time of being the occasion of scandal. If it is correct that scandal is the necessary condition for the possibility of thinking about the state of nature in the way that Rousseau thinks about it, then this rejected actuality, which makes necessary the impossible, should be present as a constitutive factor in the description of the state of nature. I believe that it is. The Scriptures are present in the space opened up by their absence. Rousseau, as he begins the "First Part," repeats again the gesture that to enter into the state of nature requires the setting aside of the Scriptures. This time he holds that both the reader and the being, who is the object of this investigation, be stripped of all supernatural knowledge. While excusing himself from examining the human in a more primitive physical form, Rousseau repeats that his considerations will be "without having recourse to the supernatural knowledge that we have on this point" (*CW* 3:20; *Pl.* 3:134).

Once Rousseau and the reader have separated themselves from the supernatural source, it is possible and necessary to perform the same operation on the man who is being considered: "Stripping the Being, so constituted, of all the supernatural gifts he could have received and of all the artificial faculties he could only have acquired by long progress" (*CW* 3:20; *Pl.* 3:134). At the very end of the *Second Discourse*, Rousseau repeats this once more, saying, "I have tried to set forth the origin and progress of inequality, the establishment and abuse of political Societies, insofar as these things can be deduced from the Nature of man by the light of reason alone, and independently of the sacred Dogmas which give to Sovereign authority the Sanction of Divine Right" (*CW* 3:67; *Pl.* 3:193). Thus, Rousseau frames the *Discourse* itself with the setting aside of theological knowledge, and religion does not make an appearance in his account of the human movement to social life.

Still, the source of the sacred is present in the form of the "obstacles" to language and society. By focusing on Rousseau's discussion of the obstacles to language in the "First Part" and the story of its emergence in the "Second Part," I hope to make clear that the state of nature makes discourse itself both impossible and then necessary. The impossible becomes the other side of the necessary, and this seemingly strange structure is rooted in the logic of scandal out of which the *Discourse* is written.

When Rousseau turns from the physical aspects of the human animal to its metaphysical aspects,[1] his main consideration deals with the interplay between the human and nature. Rousseau uses the machine image (*CW* 3:25; *Pl.* 3:141) to emphasize that while man and other animals are capable of recovering from an imbalance, they always return to their former state. Rousseau is allowing for movement within nature, but not for real change or development. The needs and the capacities to meet these needs are in balance in the natural man. Development or progress of mind occurs due to needs (*CW* 3:27; *Pl.* 3:143). Rousseau emphasizes in the "First Part" that nature does not progress, it does not offer new and different circumstances to the savage, thus removing from him "the temptation and means of ceasing to be savage" (*CW* 3:28; *Pl.* 3:144). Nature changes, but the changes themselves are always the same, which is almost like not having any change at all.[2] Rousseau describes it in this way: "The spectacle of Nature becomes indifferent to him by dint of becoming familiar. There is always the same order, there are always the same revolutions; he does not have mind to wonder at the greatest marvels; and one must not seek in him the Philosophy that man needs in order to know how to observe once what he has seen every day" (*CW* 3:28; *Pl.* 3:144).

Rousseau turns now toward "the obstacles to the origins of Languages" (*CW* 3:29; *Pl.* 3:146). His purpose in this part of the *Discourse* is to show the difficulties that the state of nature presents to the development of language.[3] In other words, the whole of the state of nature is conceived of as an obstacle. Still, is it an obstacle in the sense of a *skandalon*, both preventing access and yet making the object more and more necessary? As shall become clear, the story of the development of the natural man in the "First Part" meets the requirement of the impossible.[4]

First, according to Rousseau, it is impossible to imagine how language in the state of nature could ever become necessary, and if it were not needed, then it simply would never have developed. Rousseau's principle is that all "progress of mind has been precisely proportioned to the needs that Peoples had received from Nature" (*CW* 3:27; *Pl.* 3:143). But nature does not give this particular need. On the contrary, as Rousseau points out in his conclusion to the discussion: "From the little care taken by Nature to bring Men together through mutual needs and to facilitate their use of speech, one at least sees how little it prepared their Sociability, and how little it contributed to everything men have done to establish Social bonds" (*CW* 3:33–34; *Pl.* 3:151).

For Rousseau, speech is already an "interpreter of things they [primitive people] had to say to each other" (*CW* 3:30; *Pl.* 3:147), and with this conception of speech, the question becomes, how does one enter the world of interpretation—the world in which interpretation becomes necessary? But the question is not explicit yet, and so at this point, Rousseau does not give any solution. Instead, he simply supposes that the need is there and then tries to look at how a certain kind of interpretation, namely conventional signs, could have been established. This leads to the second aporia: "Let us seek, assuming them [conventional signs] to be necessary, how they could begin to be established. New difficulty, worse still than the preceding one. For if Men needed speech in order to learn to think, they had even greater need of knowing how to think in order to discover the art of speech" (*CW* 3:30; *Pl.* 3:147). To get to the point in which articulations of the voice substitute for signs, a universal consent would be necessary, and this is "even more difficult to conceive in itself, since that unanimous agreement must have had a motive, and since speech seems to have been highly necessary in order to establish the use of speech" (*CW* 3:31; *Pl.* 3:148–49).

Rousseau goes on to consider not just the basic invention of sounds standing for the ideas of things, but also the establishment of the "Division of Discourse" (*CW*

3:31; *Pl.* 3:149). His basic principle is that there are no general ideas in the mind without the aid of words, and these ideas are only understood when they occur in propositions. "It is therefore necessary to state propositions, hence to speak, in order to have general ideas; for as soon as the imagination stops, the mind goes no further without the help of discourse" (*CW* 3:32; *Pl.* 3:150).

At this point, Rousseau interrupts his own considerations. His concern all along has been to the show the obstacles, not to solve them. Languages are not simply unnecessary in the state of nature; rather, they are impossible. Even if their necessity is presumed, it is impossible to establish speech without first presuming its existence. And finally, as a third aporia, in considering the relationship between society and language, Rousseau is again led to formulate the problem without pretending to offer a solution: "For myself, frightened by the multiplying difficulties, and convinced of the almost demonstrated impossibility that Languages could have arisen and been established by purely human means, I leave to whomever would undertake it the discussion of the following difficult Problem: Which was most necessary, previously formed Society for the institution of Languages; or previously invented Languages for the establishment of Society?" (*CW* 3:33; *Pl.* 3:151).[5] Rousseau's point, as he makes clear in the "Preface," is not to resolve the question, but to clarify it. The clarity he has reached is that "one sees" how little Nature has done to bring men together or to make speech necessary. If there are social bonds between men, clearly this is not Nature's doing. "In fact it is impossible to imagine why, in that primitive state, a man would sooner have need of another man than a monkey or a Wolf of its Fellow creatures; nor, supposing this need, what motive could induce the other to provide for it, nor even in this last case, how they could agree between them on the conditions" (*CW* 3:34; *Pl.* 3:151).

THE "SECOND PART" OF THE DISCOURSE

One is tempted to say that Rousseau has overstated his case, so clear has he been about the impossibility of the emergence of language and abstract thought in the state of nature. Each problem is brought to its most acute form, only to let the next one emerge in an even more acute form. But from this impossibility, Rousseau will now describe its necessity. Rousseau will narrate a story that is necessary, because "one could not conceive of any other system that would not provide [him] with the same results, and from which [he] could not draw the same conclusions" (*CW* 3:42; *Pl.* 3:162).[6] In other words, anyone and everyone would have to draw the same conclusions that Rousseau does. The impossibility of the emergence of language has changed into the necessity of its emergence.

How does one move from impossibility to necessity? How does one cause to happen what has been ruled out? There is no smooth transition here. James Swenson describes Rousseau's view of historical progress as "catastrophic—which is to say, discontinuous."[7] The obstacles that prevent progress in the "First Part" now show their other dimension and cause progress. The reader would search in vain for a *reason* for the change in the obstacles.[8] He or she must simply accept, first, that there was a state in which this development was impossible, and, second, that the development took place. Rousseau will connect these two facts *via* a narrative.

Indeed, this is how he begins the "Second Part" of the *Discourse*. He tells a story that is already part of a larger story. "The first person who, having fenced off a plot of ground, took into his head to say *this is mine* and found people simple enough to believe him, was the true founder of civil society" (*CW* 3:43; *Pl.* 3:164).[9] The problem here is that for some reason, people are not scandalized by this act. They accept it and, in accepting it, open the door to far worse scandals: "What crimes, wars, murders, what miseries and horrors would the human Race have been spared by someone who, uprooting the stakes or filling in the ditch, had shouted to his fellows: Beware of listening to this impostor; you are lost if you forget that the fruits belong to all and the Earth to no one!" (*CW* 3:43; *Pl.* 3:164) But this beginning is actually the end of one story, the "last stage of the state of Nature" (*CW* 3:43; *Pl.* 3:164).

Accordingly, Rousseau begins again. This time the starting point is the same as that described in the "First Part": "The life of an animal limited at first to pure sensations and scarcely profiting form the gifts Nature offered to him" (*CW* 3:43; *Pl.* 3:164). However, this time, "difficulties soon arose; it was necessary to learn to conquer them" (*CW* 3:43; *Pl.* 3:165). Human beings begin to develop. Here is progress of the mind. But the progress is always against nature; it is in this sense unnatural, artificial, violent. It is against nature in the specific sense that the obstacles belong to, are a part of, nature: "He learned to surmount Nature's obstacles, combat other animals when necessary, fight for his subsistence even with men, or make up for what had to be yielded to the stronger" (*CW* 3:43–44; *Pl.* 3:165). As the race spreads, the difficulties multiply. This dealing with difficulties develops the human, and the human became thereby somewhat enlightened not only about these difficulties, but also about his own position vis-à-vis the other species and his own fellows.

I do not wish to simply repeat Rousseau's narrative of the development. Rather, I wish to point to the way that he overcomes, almost by fiat, one is tempted to say, the very aporia he is at pains in the "First Part" to make clear. Humans have begun to live in simple huts as families. The "first difference" is thus introduced between the way of life of the two sexes. Rousseau tells that here, one can catch a "slightly better glimpse of how the use of speech was established and perfected imperceptibly in the bosom of each family; and one can conjecture further how various particular causes could have spread language and accelerated its progress by making it more necessary" (*CW* 3:46; *Pl.* 3:168). It is due to natural disasters, such as floods and earthquakes, then, that would have left some areas surrounded by water and cut off from other land masses. "Revolutions of the Globe detached and broke up portions of the Continent into Islands" (*CW* 3:46–47; *Pl.* 3:168). From this, humans are forced to live together and devise a common idiom that is then brought fully developed to the continent.

My interest here is not so much the scientific theory as the fact that Rousseau uses the word "revolutions" to talk about the kind of transformation that could have brought about this kind of dramatic, need-inducing change.[10] In the "First Part," Rousseau states that nature is always the same, and he expresses this, by saying that it is "always the same revolutions" (*CW* 3:28; *Pl.* 3:144). There is no explanation given for why the word "revolutions" means one thing at one time and then means something totally different, almost opposite, at another. The lack of explanation is itself a kind of explanation. Rousseau is pointing to the way that language functions—to the scandalous aspect of language that he mentions in his "Preface." The same word has various meanings for different authors and is capable of being defined in a variety ways. The scandal of the aporia concerning the origin of language is being overwhelmed by the scandal of language itself.

When language, which can be used in this way, and which is the interpretation of what people want to say, is introduced into the world, "everything begins to change its appearances" (*CW* 3:47; *Pl.* 3:169). This is the source of the fatal gap between appearance and reality. Rousseau sums up the progress and its relation to the *skandalon* in the following manner: "People grow accustomed to consider different objects and to make comparisons; imperceptibly they acquire ideas of merit and beauty which produce sentiments of preference. By dint of seeing one another, they can no longer do without seeing one another again. A tender and gentle sentiment is gradually introduced into the soul and at the least obstacle becomes an impetuous fury. Jealousy awakens with love; Discord triumphs, and the gentlest of the passions receives sacrifices of human blood" (*CW* 3:47; *Pl.* 3:169).[11] This is Rousseau's account of the emergence of scandalized consciousness. By this, I mean a consciousness formed by obstacles and capable of taking offence. This is a consciousness that causes "the offended man" to see in a voluntary wrong "contempt for his person which was often more unbearable than the harm itself" (*CW* 3:48; *Pl.* 3:170).

Once Rousseau has dilated a little on the role of metallurgy and agriculture in this process, he tells that "it is easy to imagine the rest" (*CW* 3:51; *Pl.* 3:174). The destruction of natural equality brings about violence as follows: "Thus the usurpations of the rich, the brigandage of the Poor, the unbridled passions of all, stifling natural pity and the as yet weak voice of justice, made man avaricious, ambitious, and evil. Between the right of the stronger and the right of the first occupant there arose a perpetual conflict which ended only in fights and murder" (*CW* 3:52; *Pl.* 3:176). The world has reached the Hobbesian state of war. Discourse, made possible by the overcoming of natural obstacles, soon leads to human obstacles that bind humans together while driving them apart.[12]

At this point, the pattern reverses, in that the very forces that threaten to attack the person are to be turned to his favor, but nothing new is introduced into the system. Just as before, when the very forces that prevent language from originating turn out to be its cause, so here the violence that threatens to destroy the nascent human society will be redirected toward its preservation. It is discourse that is capable of effecting this transformation, because it itself is the result of such a transformation. Nothing has changed, and everything has changed. The chains are interpreted to mean freedom for the people, and so they are embraced.

This is not all. It is at least suggested here that discourse also makes a God, and so also makes religion. This dimension has been notable by its absence from Rousseau's account of how society came about. The logic of the *Discourse* is clear: "Instead of turning our forces against ourselves, let us gather them into one supreme power (*un pouvoir suprême*)," a God, and He will protect us (*CW* 3:54; *Pl.* 3:177). To this newly created God, even the rich have to "sacrifice" a part of their freedom so that it can maintain them in "eternal concord" (*CW* 3:54; *Pl.* 3:178). The text has moved from the engendering of the state of nature through the rejection of the Christian

Scriptures to the engendering of discourse through the state of nature, and then further to the engendering of transcendence through discourse. In each of these cases, the impossible yet necessary structure gets repeated.

Again, I do not believe that it is necessary to detail Rousseau's narrative. It is enough to point out that, both when society gets founded on the specious discourse within the *Discourse*, and also when Rousseau leaves the narrative voice to test "facts by right" (*CW* 3:59; *Pl.* 3:182) and founds the state in that way, both these scenarios end in the situation that they were founded to remedy. The state is institutionalized scandal. It is necessary, but the "vices that make social institutions necessary are the same ones that make their abuse inevitable," that is, render them impossible. (*CW* 3:62; *Pl.* 3:187). Rousseau is clear that the very things that draw humans together, such as the universal desire for reputation, also makes them competitors and thus causes "reverses, successes, and catastrophes"—the very stuff of scandals (*CW* 3:63; *Pl.* 3:189).

CONCLUSION

The whole of the *Second Discourse* is addressed to the reader. In its conclusion, Rousseau makes explicit the meaning that the *Second Discourse* is to originate for "every attentive Reader" (*CW* 3:65; *Pl.* 3:192). This meaning is both necessary and impossible. What the reader finds by means of this *Discourse* is a great difference, an inequality, between the natural and the civil, between the original man and the artificial man, between the savage and the civilized. The readers will learn that these are not superficial differences that cover over a deeper essential unity. Rather, human nature itself has changed, and the savage and the civilized differ "in the bottom of their Hearts" (*CW* 3:66; *Pl.* 3:192). While it still may be true that all desire happiness, the word no longer means the same thing: "What constitutes the supreme happiness of one would reduce the other to despair" (*CW* 3:66; *Pl.* 3:192). The savage does not give any meaning to the words "power" and "honor." The consideration of others means nothing to him.

Many themes, with which Rousseau has been dealing, converge here: the impossibility of reaching or even understanding the state of nature due to a change in humans that renders all seeking for that state vain; the turning away from books, both scientific and sacred, that are "other" and yet purport to tell humans who they are; and the way in which language, rather than enabling communication, actually blocks it due to the different meaning that words hold for different people. Rousseau summarizes it in the following way: "The genuine cause of all these differences: the Savage lives within himself; the sociable man, always outside himself, knows how to live only in the opinion of others; and it is, so to speak, from their judgment alone that he draws the sentiment of his own existence" (*CW* 3:66; *Pl.* 3:193). These are not two separate but equal conditions.

Rousseau leaves it to the reader to conclude that living within oneself and not drawing the sentiment of one's existence from others is a superior way of life. The message of the *Second Discourse*, then, is that one should not live in the opinions of others. This is the impossible and yet necessary position of the reader of this text. He or she hears from Rousseau that he or she should not listen to the opinion of others. To live according to Rousseau is to reject Rousseau. To accept him is to deny his teaching. Only Rousseau can teach us that.

But it does not end there. It is from listening to the opinions of others, from living outside oneself, from drawing one's sentiment of existence from the judgment of others, that so much "indifference to good and evil arises, along with such fine discourse on morality" (*CW* 3:66; *Pl.* 3:193). The reader has been reading one such "fine discourse." At this point, the book drops from one's hands; one sees that the *Second Discourse*, because it is so deeply rooted in scandal, undermines itself in its attempt to communicate its scandal.

The *Second Discourse* is itself an origin; it originates a world. This origin is an imitation of Scripture and thus it can be called scandalous in a double sense. First, it is scandalous in that it imitates the source of scandal and attempts to arouse the same passion in the reader that Rousseau himself felt. And second, it is scandalous in a postmodern sense. An imitation that is an origin is the erasure of what seem to be self-evident differences. Whatever an imitation is, it is not an original. And whatever an origin is, it is not an imitation. Rather, it is imitation that first causes an origin to be an origin, since before it is imitated, it is isolated and singular, the source of nothing. The origin and the copy are bound together in a way that deconstruction loves to deconstruct.

The *Second Discourse* appears to be written in a composed, scientific style. And yet, the *Second Discourse* is scandalous. The *Second Discourse* is not scandalous in the sense of provoking outrage, but rather scandalous in the sense in which all real art can form a stumbling block for its beholder. I am not arguing that all art is necessarily scandalous; even in art that is so judged, the scandal may well lie more in the eye of the beholder. But art can be scandalous and it can have as its aim to give scandal. Certainly, Rousseau was cognizant of this fact. Rousseau chose not to shock in any obvious way in the *Second Discourse*. He chose to write for the few, and for these few, to originate a world, a state, that would act as a stumbling block, a critique of the present, and a dread to the future.

CHAPTER 9

THE LOGIC OF SCANDAL

INTRODUCTION

In the *Dialogues,* through the character of the Frenchman, Rousseau's advised reading his works in the reverse order of publication. *Emile* revealed the first principles of his system—the forming of consciousness through victimization. The *Discourse on Inequality* built on this and moved into the world of scandal by postulating a humanity abandoned by God. Only with the *Discourse on the Sciences and Arts* (*Discours sur les sciences et les arts,* 1750) and its attendant Controversy does the depth of Rousseau's scandal reveal itself.

On the surface, Rousseau is scandalized by the fact that the very things held in such esteem by eighteenth century European society, the arts and sciences, were the cause of that society's decadence. His response was to write the *Discourse on the Sciences and Arts.* Using scandal as a hermeneutical key, the reader can arrive at a deeper understanding of this *Discourse.* At the same time, he or she can also deepen an understanding of the philosophical import of the biblical notion of scandal. The paradoxical nature of the *First Discourse* is well-known. By viewing it as both the *result* and the *origin* of scandal, this paradoxical nature gets specified. By reflecting on its specific nature, one grasps the way scandal can form thought. Approached in this way, some of the hermeneutical difficulties of the *First Discourse* resolve themselves, while some of the deeper dimensions of Rousseau's system are revealed.

I begin by establishing from the writings of the Controversy that Rousseau experienced scandal on the road to Vincennes. His scandal led him to give scandal. Secondly, I will use the writings from the Controversy to trace the meaning of scandal for Rousseau. Several different but related meanings will emerge from an analysis of the texts. To summarize: Active scandal is doing something offensive. Passive scandal results from an encounter with something offensive, like hypocrisy. This is Rousseau's scandal. It is good or proper scandal. There is also bad passive scandal. It is the scandal the corrupt take at small indiscretions in order to hide their corruption. Here, scandal itself becomes not a reaction to, but rather a source of, hypocrisy. In addition, there is the back-and-forth of Rousseau being scandalized by hypocrisy, and the hypocrites being scandalized by his blunt honesty.

This interplay of scandal as a result and an origin opens up to an analysis of the text as inscribed within this dynamic. The "Prosopopoeia of Fabricius," as that part of the *First Discourse* is known, is the immediate result of Rousseau's experience of scandal and is the textual origin of the *First Discourse*. The analysis of the "Prosopopoeia" moves the argument along by revealing that in the attempt to give scandal, Rousseau hopes to create a new order, or perhaps better put, to restore an order that has been lost. He hopes to move from nothingness or vanity to being. The means for this movement are violent. The *First Discourse* is not intended to be vain; rather, it is a call to action, a call to expel those things or people who are responsible for expelling virtue from the republic.

The penultimate section of this paper will examine the way in which the structure of the *First Discourse* itself, especially in the practical solution it proposes, reflects the structure of scandal as being both a result and a source. Briefly put, the solution to the problem of depravity caused by the arts and sciences is the proper use of the arts and sciences coupled with distinguishing those who can use them properly from those who cannot. This analysis of scandal will aid in the understanding of the logic of this solution.

In the final section, I conclude with a few reflections upon the tensions that exist between the Christian sources of the notion of scandal and Rousseau's use of it. I hope to show that scandal can help in placing Rousseau's thought vis-à-vis the Gospel.

THE SYSTEM AS GROUNDED IN SCANDAL

Although the word "scandal" never occurs in the *First Discourse*, one can easily sense Rousseau's reaction to the fact that the depravity he sees is being caused by the very things, the sciences and the arts, that are held in such honor and should be contributing to the felicity of humankind. The writings of the Controversy will help specify this general sense. Although the texts of the Controversy are, of course, chronologically later than the *First Discourse* because they are a defense of the position he takes in the *First Discourse*, they often shed light on its premises and origins. These texts present direct evidence of Rousseau's experience of scandal, his wish to scandalize, and his thoughts on scandal.

First, Rousseau's system is rooted in the experience of scandal. In the *Letter to Grimm*, Rousseau notes that one of his critics, Joseph Gautier, is struck by the fact that people could not speak a more decent language than that of their century. He considers the French of the eighteenth century to have been purified of any rusticity. For Rousseau, this is also striking, but he sees "more (*je vois encore*)": "But I see further that people could not have more corrupt morals, and that is what scandalizes me" (*CW* 2:87; *Pl.* 3:63). This ability to see further, or to see more, and its resulting scandal is a reference to the content of Rousseau's illumination on the road to Vincennes.[1]

Rousseau's experience on this road was an experience of vision and of transformation. "I saw another universe and I became another man," is how Rousseau himself describes it in his *Confessions* (*CW* 5:294; *Pl.* 1:351). His task after the vision was to realize a way of transmitting this vision and this experience of transformation to others. The experience itself, the experience of being scandalized to one's depths by the way in which the very things that seem to promise weal actually cause woe, is, in a certain sense, intolerable. The following is Rousseau's first written account of it, in which he switches for a moment to the present tense: "I feel my head seized by a dizziness similar to drunkenness. A violent palpitation oppresses me, makes me sick to my stomach; not being able to breathe anymore while walking, I let myself fall under one of the trees of the avenue, and I pass a half-hour there in such agitation that when I got up again I noticed the whole front of my coat soaked with my tears without . . . having felt that I shed them" (*CW* 5:575; *Pl.* 1:1135).

The violence and intolerability of the experience itself seeks relief in written expression. It is, then, from the very intolerability of the scandal that a system is born, a system that seeks to remedy the evil it has seen. Everything in his "[three] main works" stems from this experience (*CW* 5:575; *Pl.* 1:1136). In it, Rousseau saw "all the contradictions of the social system," that is, he saw the contradiction between appearance and reality (*CW* 5:575; *Pl.* 1:1135).[2] This contradiction becomes, as is well-known, the theme of the *First Discourse*. Rousseau's reaction in this experience can be specified by saying that he is scandalized. As the whole of the *First Discourse* makes clear, he sees not merely the depravity of human's morals, but further, that the more moral a people appears, the worse the morals actually are.

But Rousseau is not simply scandalized. He, in turn, gives scandal. After confessing his scandal at corrupt morals, he writes: "He [M. Gautier] seems to me above all very offended (*très scandalisé*) by the way I spoke of the education at Colleges" (*CW* 2:87; *Pl.* 3:63). Rousseau has caused scandal. Now he is caught in the circle of being scandalized and giving scandal in return, and it is this circle that his writings exemplify.

Rousseau shows in other writings from this period that in writing the *First Discourse*, he was aware that he would both cause scandal and that such scandal was of a sinful nature. In the *Preface to Second Letter to Bordes*, he writes about how much worse it could have been, and about how much "scandal would have happened had [he] from the first instant developed the entire extent of a System that is true but distressing, of which the question treated in this Discourse is only a Corollary" (*CW* 2:184; *Pl.* 3:106).

These considerations forced him to mitigate some of what he might have said, while still compelling him to invite divine punishment for the sin of what he does say. For Rousseau was aware that to praise ignorance is a scandalous act. Rousseau defends this by distinguishing a ferocious and brutal ignorance "born of a wicked heart and a false mind" (*CW* 2:51; *Pl.* 3:54), from a "modest ignorance, which is born from a lively love of virtue and inspires only indifference toward all things that are not worthy of filling a man's heart and do not contribute to his betterment; a sweet and precious ignorance, the treasure of a soul that is pure and content with itself, which places all its happiness in turning inward, bearing witness to its own innocence, and has no need to seek a false and vain happiness in the opinion others might have of it" (*CW* 2:51–52; *Pl.* 3:54). Rousseau states, "That is this ignorance I praised and the one I request from Heaven as punishment for the scandal I caused to the scholarly by my stated scorn for the human sciences" (*CW* 2:52; *Pl.* 3:54).[3]

Values are being reversed here, insofar as the causing of scandal is still a "sin" that deserves divine punishment but its punishment is in fact a "treasure." Thus, there is both an acknowledgment of the traditional Christian teaching (to avoid giving scandal) and its reversal. Rousseau makes the reversal completely clear when he states, in a footnote in his *Observations*,[4] that the early Christians, who not only wrote in defense of the faith, but also provided the witness of their blood, "Would be rather scandalous Authors today, for they upheld precisely the same sentiment as I do" (*CW* 2:45n; *Pl.* 3:46n).

THE MEANING OF SCANDAL

Rousseau is aware, then, of both being scandalized and giving scandal in return. What precisely is scandal and how does it operates in his thought? It is not simple. Rousseau implicitly distinguishes between "good" scandal and "bad" scandal. Rousseau's own scandal is good or proper scandal, but the scandal he causes others is not necessarily good. People should not be (but will in fact be) scandalized by what he has to say. It is one more sign of their depravity.

This kind of thinking is most clearly expressed in a footnote that deals with scandal toward the beginning of Rousseau's *Final Reply*. The footnote is attached to the following sentence: "The more the interior is corrupted, the more the exterior is composed" (*CW* 2:111–12; *Pl.* 3:73). The more the morals of a society have been depraved, the less it can allow unseemly or scandalous displays.

The footnote begins on a note of irony when Rousseau states that he cannot attend a comedy "without admiring the delicacy of the spectators" (*CW* 2:112n; *Pl.* 3:73n). Their delicacy means that the least indiscretion in language wounds their ears. He continues, "And I have no doubt whatever that the most corrupt are always the most scandalized" (*CW* 2:112n; *Pl.* 3:73n). The most corrupt are then both the most exteriorly composed in the sense of never openly causing scandal and the most easily scandalized. The most corrupt are the most outwardly scandalized by the smallest things, thereby both trying to hide and nonetheless revealing their depravity. Accordingly, Rousseau cautions against taking this increase in delicacy as a sign of a higher morality. Scandal is on the rise, but the very increase in being scandalized signals more corruption. The corruption has now reached the imagination, and "once the imagination has been sullied, everything becomes a subject of scandal for it" (*CW* 2:112n; *Pl.* 3:73n).

The economy of being scandalized and sharing that scandal becomes a source of energy. "When nothing good is left but the exterior, all efforts are redoubled to preserve it" (*CW* 2:112n; *Pl.* 3:73). The corrupted interior cannot allow its truth to be revealed. It must appear never to give scandal, even in minor things, although it can take scandal in them. The state of having a corrupted interior and a composed exterior, which is the *result* of corruption, becomes a *source* of energy for those who are in society. Rousseau makes this clear by the way he connects the footnote, which contains this thought, with the main text. The latter continues after the footnote, "*In this way* the cultivation of Letters imperceptibly engenders politeness" (*CW* 2:112; *Pl.* 3:73; emphasis added). In what way, precisely?

The principle of interior corruption and exterior composure in and of itself does not engender anything. But the energy created by letting everyone know that one is scandalized by banalities, while hiding the true scandal under a composed exterior, does create politeness, taste, style, and urbanity, for all these things presume showing one's scandal at the use of a coarse word, and hiding one's own truly scandalous actions. It is true that this is the world of the "supplement"—"All these things will be, if you will, the supplement of virtue" (*CW* 2:112; *Pl.* 3:74). But the world of the supplement is the world of scandal,[5] and this is the world that is the subject of the *First Discourse*.

At the same time, what is not said is as important as what is. Rousseau himself has a pure interior and an exterior that is never accused of being composed. He is scandalized, but his scandal is the polar opposite of the kind he is criticizing. In fact, the more composed the exterior of society is, the more violently Rousseau will have to attack it. In this way, his own dependence on society is made clear. Rousseau, especially in this writing, shares in the split between appearance and reality that he so denounces. It is only in his withdrawal from society that he can begin to have the calm exterior that will mirror his pure interior.

The arts and sciences play the role in society of hiding a corrupt interior. While this is the theme of the *First Discourse*, Rousseau gives a particularly clear formulation of this in his "Preface to Narcissus" as follows: "The sciences have therefore not done all the evil, they have only done their good part of it; and above all what specifically belongs to them is to have given our vices an agreeable color, a certain honest appearance that prevents us from being horrified by them" (*CW* 2:190n; *Pl.* 3:964n).

The more the sciences succeed in masking the vices, the more Rousseau will have to attack them. At the same time, the interplay between the efforts at keeping a composed exterior and the horror of seeing the corruption of humanity's true interior provides a source of energy to society. In this same essay, Rousseau compares the arts and sciences to a varnish that prevents the evils they have hatched from becoming worse; that is, the arts and sciences help prevent scandal. "It is vice that takes the mask of virtue, but not as a hypocrisy to deceive and betray" (*CW* 2:196n; *Pl.* 3:972n); rather, it does so as an "escape from the horror" (*CW* 2:196n; *Pl.* 3:972n) that occurs when vice sees itself uncovered. "[The arts and sciences] destroy virtue but leave its public simulacrum which is always a fine thing" (*CW* 2:196; *Pl.* 3:972).

Rousseau does not consider the arts and sciences hypocritical because they each reach truth. This is the same reason that he does not oppose them in and of themselves. They have other positive effects. Again, the system of supplement. To look on unmitigated vice would be a "horror" that humans cannot bear (*CW* 2:196n; *Pl.* 3:972n). "A certain softness," "a certain appearance of order that prevents horrible confusion," as well as "a certain admiration of beautiful things" constitute a "public simulacrum" that allows people to live in society (*CW* 2:196n; *Pl.* 3:972).[6] It represents a kind of faded image of the society that people would like to have.

THE PROSOPOPOEIA OF FABRICIUS

The meaning of scandal is related to the central theme of the *First Discourse*, in that the corruption caused by the arts and sciences causes scandal. Rousseau's system originates in his experience of scandal. It should not surprise then to learn that this experience results in a text that is the textual origin of the *First Discourse*. Rousseau wrote the text directly out of his experience of being scandalized, and he wrote it to cause scandal.

The text is known as the "Prosopopoeia of Fabricius." It was written "in pencil under an Oak"[7] directly following the experience of enlightenment (*CW* 5:295; *Pl.* 1:351). It is, as Starobinski puts it, "the sole remaining witness of the illumination on the road to Vincennes."[8] It is not merely an expression of the experience, but it is also a part of the experience itself; it is a "vestige of the force" of the illumination.[9] The immediate result of the experience on the road is the origin of the *First Discourse*. That the origin of this text is the result of an experience of scandal, and that this result is yet another origin, is part and parcel of the experience itself. This is a part of the dynamic of scandal.

The prosopopoeia is a calling back to this world the shade of the ancient Roman, Fabricius. Again to quote Starobinski, "Fabricius himself is a dead man returned to life in order to inveigh against a scandalous world."[10] The scandal goes deep. Starobinski terms it an "ontological scandal."[11] It has reached the ontological level in that Fabricius unites in himself virtue and eloquence, and this is as it should *be*. But the "Rhetoricians" whom he sees now governing Rome have an eloquence that lacks truth or virtue. As Starobinski writes, "The specious speech, the speech which has ceased being the speech of being and has reduced itself to the song of flute player is a non-being, a vain breath, a substitute for essential plenitude and virtuous will. The scandal is in the conjunction of effective power and weak speech, without the content of the truth, which exercises an illegitimate fascination (*charme*)."[12]

Rousseau, through the prosopopoeia, begins to reverse this by calling forth Fabricius, who has an uncorrupted interior, since he is virtuous, while his exterior is not composed. He is scandalized. Through Fabricius, Rousseau rails against the "vain talents" and "vain pomp" that are the source of his scandal (*CW* 2:11; *Pl.* 3:15). Fabricius is scandalized by what he sees and hears, by "the pompous appearances" and by the "strange language" (*CW* 2:11; *Pl.* 3:14). It is not so much that appearances deceive (Fabricius is not deceived), as it is a matter of what they reveal. They reveal that moderation and virtue no longer dwell in the land. Rousseau does not attempt in this prosopopoeia to prove that "disastrous splendor [succeeding] Roman simplicity" is the same as vice succeeding virtue(*CW* 2:11; *Pl.* 3:14). This is assumed. Instead, one could say that he uses his outrage to try to shock others by having Fabricius say offensive things to the Romans.

Against this vanity, this empty show of appearances, stands not just the figure of Fabricius, but also the figure of the prosopopoeia. Rousseau explicitly states, "It was not in vain that I called up the shade of Fabricius" (*CW* 2:11; *Pl.* 3:15). Through Fabricius, Rousseau will accomplish what otherwise he should not. Fabricius is to scandalize the reader. He is to call forth "odious pictures which offend our delicacy" (*CW* 2:11; *Pl.* 3:15). When Rousseau returns to his own voice, he lets the reader set these aside (cf.*CW* 2:11; *Pl.* 3:15).[13]

The prosopopoeia is written not only to cause scandal; this scandal is, in turn, to result in violence. Fabricius calls those he addresses "Madmen (*Insensés*)" (*CW* 2:11; *Pl.* 3:14) in order to rouse them. He accuses them of becoming slaves. Then he commands them to destroy: "Romans, hasten to tear down these Amphitheatres, break these marble statues, burn these paintings, chase out these slaves who subjugate you and whose fatal arts corrupt you" (*CW* 2:11; *Pl.* 3:14–15).

The prosopopoeia can be characterized in the following way to interpret the whole of the *First Discourse*: the result of being scandalized is a text of a scandalized man scandalizing others and thus leading them to violence.[14] Further, one can call this text "pagan" in the sense that Rousseau calls up a pagan Roman whose first word is "gods."[15] Rousseau has to do this because the text is a conscious turning away from the Biblical imperative not to be scandalized or to give scandal. Rousseau's scandal means that he has to employ a pagan calling on pagan gods, since a Christian is allowed neither to be scandalized nor to cause scandal.[16] The text is practical, not vain, and its practicality consists in its call to violence. The reader is called on to expel those people (or things) that have expelled virtue. With this characterization in mind, it becomes possible to offer a comprehensive interpretation of the *First Discourse*.

THE FIRST DISCOURSE

By analyzing the *First Discourse* from the viewpoint of scandal, one can, in contrast to the immediate reaction to it and the even later interpretation of it, see that Rousseau is offering a practical solution to a practical problem. The *First Discourse* is almost always viewed primarily as a critique of culture, a critique of the arts and sciences, a writing whose form (as an academic discourse) contradicts its content (calling for the abolition of the arts and sciences). It has been criticized since the time of its publication for its lack of a practical program.[17]

The interpretation offered here brings out what Rousseau himself insists upon throughout the Controversy: he is not opposed to the arts and sciences *per se*, and his *Discourse* offers a practical program. At the same time, this viewpoint allows one to see why these other interpretations have been put forth. I wish to suggest that, given the nature of his texts and the logic they embody, this phenomenon should hardly be surprising. It is this logic, as contained in the *First Discourse*, that I wish to investigate now.

In order to understand the practical program that Rousseau offers, a clear grasp of the problem it is meant to resolve is necessary. As is well-known, the basic problem for Rousseau is the split, in sense of a lack of correspondence, between appearance and reality that the arts and sciences allow and foster.[18] But this split is further specified by Rousseau. It takes the form of a split between "power" (*la puissance*, the political power of princes) on one side and "intellect and wisdom" (*les lumiéres et la sagesse*) on the other (*CW* 2:22; *Pl.* 3:30).

According to Rousseau, the ultimate cause of this gap is the fact that all the sciences have their origin in human pride. Pride is the "passion to gain distinction" (*CW* 2:14; *Pl.* 3:19) that leads to an inequality among humans. It introduces the "distinction of talents" (*CW* 2:18; *Pl.* 3:25). Ultimately, it is the envy generated by this distinction of talents that makes humankind unhappy, because, due to this envy, wisdom gets separated from power. That is, it becomes profitable to appear wise even if one is not, and so appearances begin to be mistrusted. Those with power do not know to whom to turn, so they turn to no one. No doubt, the distinction of talents and its resulting envy are also responsible for a kind of progress, the growth of knowledge, but Rousseau wants to distinguish between real and apparent progress. Real progress would be to overcome the pride that is the source of human vices and unhappiness.[19] But Rousseau understands that all attempts to root out pride are themselves rooted in pride and therefore cannot ultimately solve the problem. A proud intellect cannot overcome pride. Rousseau realizes that he does not have within himself, nor does humanity have within itself, the resources to overcome this problem. He can only rearrange the available forces.

To overcome the split between power and wisdom, Rousseau proposes a very straightforward solution. Princes need to allow that "learned men of the first rank find honorable asylum in their courts. . . . Only then will one see what can be done by virtue, science, and authority, animated by noble emulation and working together for the felicity of the human Race" (CW 2:22; Pl. 3:30). Without this union, "the People will continue to be vile, corrupt, and *unhappy*" (CW 2:22; Pl. 3:30; emphasis added).

It would seem that Rousseau has reached the solution for the fundamental practical problem of the *Discourse*. Humans can become happy by combining power and wisdom. This can be accomplished when those in power allow men who are both learned and virtuous into their councils. It should be clear also that if this were the extent of Rousseau's ideas, the *First Discourse* would be as forgotten as the other twelve answers to the Academy's question.[20] Still, what the first phase of the solution makes evident is Rousseau's *affirmation* of the arts and sciences. He affirms the role that they are to play in bringing about human happiness. Interpreters of Rousseau often overlook this fact. Any interpretation that simply sees the *First Discourse* as a condemnation of the arts and sciences will be inadequate, even if it grasps the dialectical nature of the artistic condemnation of the arts.[21]

For Rousseau, it is not enough to combine power with wisdom and virtue. He is both too honest and too profound to be satisfied with this solution. He knows that through his solution, he has reintroduced the "distinction of talents" by which "disastrous inequality" gets introduced to human society and virtue gets debased (CW 2:18; Pl. 3:25). An elite will be formed, this will foment jealousy, and the whole problematic, which he is trying to solve, will simply be displaced. The combination of power with wisdom and virtue, good in itself, will necessarily produce an unwanted consequence: envy. This problem, in turn, leads to the second step in the solution.

Before looking at this step, I want to emphasize that this envy is not some minor inconvenience or slight moral failing for which a reader might be tempted to take it. Rousseau sees it as capable of undoing any good his first step might produce. Since it manifests the underlying pride, he sees it as the root of all the problems in society. He proposes to overcome it by establishing a new distinction. Instead of power being separated from wisdom and virtue, Rousseau wants those who form the councils of power to be separated from the people. There will be those destined for immortality and "the rest." In order to prevent envy from occurring, Rousseau wants "the rest" to understand itself as being part of a "glorious distinction" between those who know how to speak well and those who know how to act well. Quoting in full what he says:

"This [a love of virtue] is true Philosophy, let us know how to be satisfied with it; and without envying the glory of those famous men who are immortalized in the Republic of Letters, let us try to put between them and us that glorious distinction noted between two great Peoples long ago: that the one knew how to speak well, the other to act well" (*CW* 2:22; *Pl.* 3:30). The "two great Peoples" refer to the republics of Athens and Sparta.

THE ATHENS/SPARTA CONTRAST

These final words of the final sentence of the *First Discourse* call the reader's attention to a literary device that runs as a kind of leitmotiv not only through the whole of the *Discourse* but also even into the Controversy—the Athens/Sparta contrast. Athens is an example of a "sort of civility," which is "the semblance of all the virtues without the possession of any" (*CW* 2:5; *Pl.* 3:7). Sparta, on the other hand, is the republic of "happy ignorance," the republic of wisdom and virtue. While both serve as exemplars of a sort, Sparta functions rhetorically in the same way as Fabricius and Rousseau himself. Sparta puts to shame the "vain doctrine" (*CW* 2:9; *Pl.* 3:12) that the arts and sciences promote virtue, just as Fabricius combats the vanity of corrupt Rome. The example of Sparta is intended to scandalize Rousseau's readers.[22]

Sparta also parallels the figure of Fabricius in that it functions as a call to violence. Sparta's virtue is due to the fact that it "chased the Arts and Artists, the Sciences and Scientists away" (*CW* 2:9; *Pl.* 3:12). Sparta is only an example, even if it is the premiere one, of "those few Peoples who, . . . have by their own virtues created their own happiness" (*CW* 2:8; *Pl.* 3:11). The one consistent criterion used in the *First Discourse* for judging whether a people is depraved or not is their capacity for violence against outsiders.[23] The problem with the arts and sciences, the specific sense in which they are dangerous to politics, is that they weaken military virtues (*CW* 2:17; *Pl.* 3:24). Cultivated people are defeated in battle by barbarians. Therefore, reasons Rousseau, their corruption is made manifest. The degeneracy of modern society is not so much a lack of violence when compared with robust republics, but is rather due to the fact that the people exercise hidden violence within the group.

Rousseau expresses the same thought on the individual level through the following metaphor. "The good man is an Athlete who likes to compete (*combattre*) in the nude. He disdains all those vile ornaments which would hamper the use of his strength, most of which were invented only to hide some deformity" (*CW* 2:6; *Pl.* 3:8). Virtue, like corruption, is known by "signs," but here the signs are nudity and fighting. There are for Rousseau only two choices. Either one accedes to being complicit in the hidden violence of modern society, or one fights against this hidden violence by advocating open violence.[24] The beauty of open violence is that then the appearances and the reality coincide, and thus virtue is maintained. The *First Discourse* has been understood, from the moment of its publication, as being a part of the very thing, namely the arts and sciences, that it attacks. But this is to miss the deeper point, which is that the *First Discourse* is, first and foremost, not an academic treatise but rather an *open attack* on the arts and sciences. It is here that its appearance (rhetoric) corresponds to its reality (content) and it becomes for Rousseau an act of virtue.

The Logic of Rousseau's Position

In spite of its violence, Rousseau's solution is not radical.[25] The re-invoking of the distinction between the two republics means that the split between appearance and reality is not overcome but rather perpetuated by being used as part of the solution. The world of the split between appearance and reality is the world that Rousseau critiques, but it is also the one he imitates. He criticizes Athens because he sees the depth of the problem, and he imitates the opposition between it and Sparta because he has no other options. In order to prevent the emergence of envy, which will destroy political unity, Rousseau has to argue for instituting once again the "glorious distinction" in which two entities simultaneously threaten each other while guaranteeing one another's existence. Thus, Rousseau uses the cause of the problem as its own solution.

One could schematize it in the following way. The source of vice is the arts and sciences. The source of the arts and sciences is pride, which is the primary vice. There is no escape from this circle, nor does Rousseau try to escape. Rather, he rearranges the available forces. But this means that, if one accepts his analysis of the problem, then one cannot accept his solution; and if one accepts his solution, then one has to find a problem with his analysis. On the one hand, this logic makes Rousseau invulnerable and, in that sense, powerful. One reads the writings of the Controversy and is struck only by the spiritlessness of his opponents.[26] On the other hand, this logic makes him isolated.[27] It precludes from the start any possibility of human solidarity, because to agree with Rousseau is to necessarily disagree with him, and to disagree with him is to prove him correct. In the logic of this *Discourse*, there is no giving scandal without first being scandalized, there is no calling up the spirit of Fabricius without a corrupt Rome to tirade against, and there is no Sparta without Athens. Most critiques of the *First Discourse* only serve to prove the authors' self-interest.

Rousseau is trying to control or confine the basic human problem of pride so that some progress will be possible without too much evil. In order to overcome the split between power and wisdom, scholars are to assist princes. If that comes about, the people will be envious of the powerful elite. This envy is a threat to civil order, so that a new distinction becomes necessary. Rousseau understands that the best way to prevent the emergence of envy is through strong distinctions. Humans only become rivals of those whom they view as being on their level. A clear and sharp distinction prevents this. The division into "them" and "us" will ensure the peace.

This split between Athens and Sparta, between those who know how to speak well and those who know how to act well, is ultimately only a dim reflection of the fundamental split that constituted the blinding illumination on the road to Vincennes. Rousseau expresses this division in his "Preface" as follows: "I foresee that I will not be easily forgiven for the side I have taken" (*CW* 2:3; *Pl.* 3:3). Rousseau is alone on the side he has taken against everyone else.

The depth and power of Rousseau are rooted in the strength and conviction with which he perceives the problem. Rousseau's greatness is to see that all human endeavors, especially the highest and noblest, are tainted with pride. Nothing escapes this poison. This kind of insight sometimes leads to a religious conversion. More often than not, however, the insight itself is prevented by a contraction of consciousness that can only see the good or at least shies away from seeing the way in which even our best efforts bring forth evil. Rousseau is criticizing just this kind of smugness, which was a mark of Enlightenment thinking. In it, technical progress was all too easily equated with moral progress. But if this insight is attained without conversion, it leads to a desperate attempt to claim innocence. Rousseau makes this attempt.

THE KING'S OBJECTION

In his *Reply to the Discourse*, Stanislaus Leszinski, the King of Poland,[28] poses the most direct question to Rousseau concerning his thoughts on scandal. The king asks whether Rousseau would have the veneer of society simply thrown out, since it often serves as a mask for hypocrisy. "Would he wish then for vice to appear openly, for indecency to be joined to disorder and scandal to crime?" (*CW* 2:34; Launay 2:49). Rousseau is quite certain that he would prefer to have vice appear openly, since it would result in a safer society. But as to whether scandal should be joined to crime, Rousseau's answer is, "I do not know" (*CW* 2:49; *Pl.* 3:51).[29] This admission of ignorance is not without its importance for my overall interpretation, since it indicates an insuperable objection that forces Rousseau to grow more circumspect in causing scandal.

The issued raised by the King is one of major political import, for it concerns how to deal with violence. In a way, Rousseau has already indirectly answered the question by his way of writing the *First Discourse*. This presents the reader with the paradoxical situation of the king, who does not wish to cause scandal, bringing about a situation in which it will be caused by asking openly for the position on scandal that Rousseau has indicated, but not proclaimed, precisely because it is scandalous.

In fact, the *First Discourse* is a frontal, public, scandal-inducing attack on the arts and sciences, but Rousseau cannot say this. Instead Rousseau gives, in a very lapidary form, his position concerning scandal. Because of its importance I will quote it in full:

> I prefer to have my enemy attack me with open force than to come up treacherously and strike me from behind. What then! Must scandal be combined with crime? I do not know, but I surely wish that deceit were not combined with it. All the maxims about scandal to which we have been treated for so long are very convenient for the vicious: if one wished to follow them rigorously, one must allow himself to be robbed, betrayed, and killed with impunity, and never punish anyone; for a scoundrel on the rack is a very scandalous thing. (*CW* 2:49; *Pl.* 3:51)

If the King's question reveals the depth of the political implications of scandal, Rousseau's answer reveals its theological and even Christological dimensions.

Placed beneath the admission of his inability to answer the objection, Rousseau's answer allows for two interpretations. The first interpretation runs along the following lines: The King's objection presupposes that scandal is to be avoided in order to assure public order. Rousseau accepts this presupposition and argues that, since the "scoundrel on the rack is a very scandalous thing" (*CW* 2:49; *Pl.* 3:51), one could not even punish criminals if one were to follow the maxims on scandal rigorously. But if criminals cannot be punished, much more disorder would ensue. This contradicts the presupposition, and so the presupposition that scandal must be avoided is false. In this way, the maxims on scandal can be set aside, even by a good citizen.

SCANDAL AS BOTH FORBIDDEN AND NECESSARY

Another interpretation is possible and even demanded by the text. I say "demanded" due to the presence of the word "betrayed" in the passage quoted above. Its presence needs to be accounted for. Normally, the criminals who would rob and kill someone do not "betray" the person. Rather, the word leads the reader necessarily to think of a particular case of scandal, and in this way reveals Rousseau's thought on the issue.

One should not build too much on a single word, but the preceding analysis has prepared the reader for my conclusion. Recall that most of Rousseau's comments on scandal occur within the context of what could be broadly termed "moral theology." He understands it as deserving of punishment, he asks for forgiveness, he compares himself with martyrs, and so on. Further, in a passage of the *First Discourse*, which has not yet been quoted, he also indirectly raises the question of why so many "shameful monuments" are prepared for posterity "by Printing under the reign of the Gospel" (*CW* 2:20n; *Pl.* 3:28n). It is reasonable to expect even more of an effect from Christianity? Finally, and decisively, Rousseau himself justifies this attention to his vocabulary. He writes, "It was only gradually and always for few Readers that I developed my ideas. It is not myself that I treated carefully, but the truth, so as to get it across more surely and make it useful I have often taken great pains to try to put into a Sentence, a line, a word tossed off as if by chance the result[s] of a long sequence of reflections" (*CW* 2:184; *Pl.* 3:106).

The presupposition of the argument in the second interpretation remains the same as in the first: scandal is to be avoided to assure public order. And again, due to the scandal of the punished criminal, criminals cannot be punished. But the result this time is not the increase in disorder. Rather, it is the fact that Rousseau understands that he will have to allow himself to be made like Christ, for example, to be robbed, betrayed, and killed with impunity as Christ was. This Rousseau is not prepared to do. Thus, the presupposition must be false.

In other words, the seemingly innocuous rejection of some maxims on scandal involves a refusal on Rousseau's part to be made like Christ. Rousseau is trying to ensure that the distinction between him and the "scoundrel on the rack" is fixed, otherwise he could end up in the same position. I am not arguing here about the moral status of this refusal; I am trying rather to show the level at which Rousseau's argument operates and the necessity of multiple interpretations for his texts. I am not reducing the text to a theological level, but rather I am expanding the possibilities of interpretation. Thus, it is not merely a political debate over which maxims lead to greater stability, although this is one moment in the argument. It is also not just a question of why such apparently moral societies produce so many candidates for the rack, although this, too, is a question that troubles Rousseau. Rather, it is a question of what is involved politically in following Christ. Rousseau sees deeper than many believers.

There is, however, a still deeper element that underlies both interpretations. The ultimate reason why the maxims about scandal will cause disorder (the emphasis of the first interpretation) or will cause one to become like Christ (the emphasis of the second interpretation) is contained in the final phrase "for a scoundrel on the rack is a very scandalous thing" (*CW* 2:49; *Pl.* 3:51). That is, Rousseau is scandalized by this sight and it is important to note that this is not a self-evident reaction. The question needs to be raised, even if Rousseau did not, why "a scoundrel on the rack" is such a scandalous thing. "A scoundrel on the rack" is not, in and of itself, "a very scandalous thing" (*CW* 2:49; *Pl.* 3:51). It is only so in a culture that has been touched by the Gospels. Otherwise, and often enough even there, "a scoundrel on the rack" is a rather satisfying sight.[30] It only becomes scandalous because Christ himself was once that "scoundrel on the rack,"[31] and with that act, he identified himself with the outcast, the criminal, and the marginalized. It is only when the scoundrel ceases to be seen as a scoundrel and becomes a human being, and as such the brother or sister of Christ, that the sight of him stretched out on the rack becomes capable of producing scandal. In this way, Christ himself creates the possibility of scandal.

Rousseau brings into relief something that is difficult even for Christians to grasp—the relationship between Christ as the cause of scandal and the moral maxims forbidding scandal. How is it that Christians can admit that the Cross of Christ is a scandal, and yet forbid the causing of scandal? Through Rousseau's text, the linkage between these two responses and scandal comes into focus. Everything, including the prohibition of causing scandal, flows out of the "essential scandal"[32] that the Cross is. God does not "cause" scandal, and yet the Cross of Christ is an occasion of scandal. It remains such an occasion, and yet there is another possible response to it—faith. As Kierkegaard so aptly expresses it, scandal must always remain "as an annulled possibility . . . an element in faith."[33] Rousseau is ultimately scandalized, not merely by a society in which appearances do not match reality, but also by the fact that the Son of God chose to appear as "a scoundrel on the rack."

In Rousseau's answer to the question about whether scandal will be joined to crime, Christ appears twice: once as the ultimate origin of scandal, the "scoundrel on the rack," and secondly as embodying the final result of the one who follows the maxims on not causing scandal (for example, the one who is robbed, betrayed, and killed with impunity). Here, Christ occupies both the places of origin and of result. He is the origin and end of the system in a negative sense. Christ functions in this way insofar as He is the origin that gets rejected, and the result it is designed to avoid. In this way, He is the figure in which all the other figures of Rousseau will be inscribed.

Thus, the ultimate origin of Rousseau's system is indeed scandal, but it is scandal in a theological and even Christological sense. And yet its ultimate goal is to avoid being made like this Christ, from whom it takes its origin. Thus, scandal means that which is both necessary to the system and yet, at precisely the same moment, is impossible. Rousseau needs the scandal of the Cross to generate his system, and yet he must at the same moment reject the Cross, rendering it impossible. These two marks have appeared and reappeared throughout this investigation, but now their ultimate source is clear.[34] This is both the ultimate meaning of my initial claim that Rousseau's system is grounded in scandal and, at the same time, a definition of what I mean by scandal. Rousseau finds Christ on the Cross scandalous and rejects him. This rejection has political implications but is rooted in the theological.

To return here to Rousseau's admission that he does not know how to answer the King. Rousseau does not have an answer to the King's objection as to whether it is permissible or not to cause scandal because either to affirm or to deny the objection would destroy his system. The question remains at the basis of his system as an "undecidable."[35] This means that it is undecidable between the two extremes of necessity and impossibility. If Rousseau were to answer, as it seems his performance in the *First Discourse* would warrant, "yes, it is allowed," this would involve contradicting the teaching of the Church, both Protestant and Catholic, leaving him open to charges of causing social unrest. This is something that Rousseau does not want to have happen.[36] This is the obvious meaning of scandal being forbidden.

But this surface reason occludes the deeper truth. Scandal is forbidden to Rousseau because it opens a serious political objection to his system. That is, the forbiddenness of scandal or its impossibility is not due to some external force like the ecclesiastical authorities. Rather, the system itself renders it forbidden. Still, in giving into the essential scandal, Rousseau cannot ever completely free himself from scandal without running the risk of giving up that which drives his whole system. Rousseau is *scandalized* and ultimately this scandal is rooted in the fundamental Christological scandal. But he refuses to become like Christ, and in this way turns away from the fundamental scandal, cutting himself off from his own source. If he were to accept the essential scandal in all of its implications, he would no longer be scandalized and again his system would be no more. Rousseau then has to continue to find the "scoundrel on the rack" a scandalous sight and yet deny both the source and the consequences of that vision.

PART IV

AUTOBIOGRAPHY

CHAPTER 10

THE CONFESSION OF SCANDAL

THE EMERGENCE OF AUTOBIOGRAPHY

Two factors inherent in Rousseau's system dictate his turn to autobiography. First, as I pointed out in the previous chapter, the logic of scandal isolates the scandalized person, making himself the only thing about which he can write. Second, Rousseau writes his autobiography due to the self-reflexive character of his system. Each of Rousseau's texts reflects back upon itself; it enacts what it is about. In enacting its content, that the *First Discourse* is an artistic and scientific work about the arts and sciences. In an analogous way, the *Second Discourse* is not only about an origin but is itself an origin, and *Emile* is not only an educational treatise, but it is also an education.

Rousseau structures these texts in this way because the whole system is built upon scandal, that is, upon the rejection of rejection, or the expulsion of expulsion. The system heads toward the *Confessions* because this expulsion of expulsion both expels and re-enacts the original expulsion of the other. Rousseau is finally left with only the self doing the expulsion. The *Confessions* is the dramatic rendering of this principle. His system gradually and inexorably works toward revealing itself as a system that contains and, in the end, *is* a single self—Jean-Jacques Rousseau.

The *Confessions*, then, both reverses and confirms the pattern in his writings that has been apparent up to this point. Rather than saying that the *Confessions* is not only about scandal, but is itself a scandal, it would be closer to the truth to say that it is not just a scandalous work, but it also reveals what scandal is. The scandalous aspects of the *Confessions* are well-known: Rousseau's childish sexual proclivities, his lie about the stolen ribbon that condemns innocent Marion, his initiation into sexual relations by Madam de Warens, which he himself compares with incest, and the abandonment of his children. There is something to offend everyone.

Had his works been treated in their chronological appearance, the movement toward autobiography would have been visible in its broad outlines. The *First Discourse* contains little of Rousseau. He has a virtuous, ancient Roman, Fabricius, speak to decadent Rome, in order that he himself might deliver a message to modern-day Paris. The "Preface" and the frontispiece are really the only places where Rousseau himself comes explicitly to the fore.[1] The *Second Discourse* contains Rousseau's famous "Epistle Dedicatory" to his homeland, and in general, the language of the *Discourse* is much more openly self-referential. Recall its opening line, "The most useful and least advanced of all human knowledge seems *to me* to be that of man" (*CW* 3:12; *Pl.* 3:112; emphasis added). In this *Discourse*, Rousseau places himself, and not some virtuous, ancient Greek, in the Lyceum of Athens, with "the human Race for an audience" (*CW* 3:19; *Pl.* 3:135).

In *Emile*, the movement toward confessional literature is clear. Rousseau makes Jean-Jacques a character in his own novel. While the character of the tutor cannot be simply equated with Rousseau, there are certain passages that are clearly autobiographical, such as the vignettes in which the character of Jean-Jacques purports to tell the reader about something he has experienced in his own past.[2] The fictional biography of Emile is laced with the autobiography of Jean-Jacques Rousseau. Paul Zweig summarizes it in this way, "Little that he wrote, after the first *Discourses*, is not closely concerned with the separate, idiosyncratic character of Jean-Jacques. Even the *Social Contract* is curiously rooted in autobiography."[3] This suggests what is clear from the reading of the *Dialogues* in Chapter 2: Rousseau has tied the fate of his thought to that of his own self.

But the logic that leads to autobiography can also be discerned in the approach used in this study. At the most profound level of his system, Rousseau rejects Christ, the *arche* (principle) and the *telos* (goal) of the system. Something or, more properly, someone must be put in his place. This someone is Jean-Jacques.

THE CONCEPTION OF THE SELF IN THE *CONFESSIONS*

As many commentators have noted, Rousseau intends the text of the *Confessions* to be to stand in the place of his own self. Holding the text of the *Confessions* in his hands when he appears before God, Jean-Jacques says, "Behold what I have done, what I have thought, *what I have been*" (*CW* 5:5; *Pl.* 1:5; emphasis added). There is no reason to restrict this identity to the level of content. The constitution of the text, as text, gives a clue to the constitution of the self of Jean-Jacques. Looking not only at the content of the various stories, but also at the way Rousseau makes the work function, the reader gets an idea of Rousseau's conception of his own self.

The first thing to notice is that Rousseau begins the *Confessions* by inviting the reader, both human and divine, to judge him.

> Whether nature has done well or ill in breaking the mold in which it cast me, is something which cannot be judged until I have been read.
> 3. Let the trumpet of the last judgment sound when it will; I shall come with this book in my hands to present myself before the Sovereign Judge. (*CW* 5:5; *Pl.* 1:5)

The second thing to notice is that at the very end of the *Confessions*, Jean-Jacques, the self that the reader is to judge, condemns to death the person who misjudges him. His condemnation of such a person is expressed in the following: "As for me, I declare it loudly and without fear: Anyone who, even without having read my readings, will examine with his own eyes my natural disposition, my character, my morals, my inclinations, my pleasures, my habits, and will be capable of believing that I am a dishonest man, is himself a man fit to be strangled" (*CW* 5:550; *Pl.* 1:656; translation altered).

The third things to notice is that between the call to judgment and the condemnation of those who misjudge is the declaration and explanation that all errors in judgment are due to the reader's fault. The totality of the elements that make up Jean-Jacques will be given in the text, but their final result is left up to the reader. The reader is to "assemble the elements" that are presented in the book and "to define the being made up of them" (*CW* 5:147; *Pl.* 1:175). This being, Jean-Jacques, will be the result of the reader's work, and this is as it ought to be, because then any errors will also be the reader's own and not Rousseau's. In short, the author charges the reader to create a self that has been true to itself, and if it has not been true to itself, this error is due to the reader. The existence of this autonomous self depends upon the judgment of the reader. For this to work, there is one condition that Rousseau must fulfill—perfect transparency to the reader.[4]

Everything that comes between the invitation to judge and the condemnation of misjudgment serves to make both the judging and the condemnation possible. The self that the reader has judged into existence now judges that reader. He is a self that condemns those who condemn him. So the reader's judgment, if correct, has created a self that is capable of murder, and if it is incorrect, the reader is condemned to strangulation.[5]

Rousseau is using Christianity against itself. No matter how badly it has been historically fulfilled, Christianity is premised on not judging others. "Therefore you have no excuse, whoever you are, when you judge others; for in passing judgment on another you condemn yourself, because you, the judge, are doing the very same things" (Rom. 2:1). It is this logic, as expressed by St. Paul, that Rousseau wants to use and take advantage of. By putting the reader in the position of judging, Rousseau has put the reader in the position of being condemned, *whether the judgment rendered is positive or negative*. By beginning with a call to judgment, Rousseau guarantees that he will reach the end of condemnation.

In light of this beginning and this end, my thesis is that a consciousness scandalized by the reality it encounters results in and serves to unite the opening invitation to judgment and the closing condemnation to death. For his part, Jean-Jacques is unable to either accept or reject the reality that scandalizes him, and by this, I mean primarily the human other. Going beyond scandal in one direction would mean accepting this other for who he or she is and for the grace he or she offers. It would mean to cease judging. Going beyond it in the opposite direction would be to join the mob in putting the other to death. Rousseau's place does not lie in either of these directions; rather, *he makes the other reject him*. This rejection constitutes the roots of the plot that begin to occupy Jean-Jacques' thoughts toward the end of the *Confessions* and reach their fullness in the *Dialogues*.

THE INVITATION TO JUDGMENT

Rousseau wrote the *Confessions* so that the reader could judge him, thereby involving her in his system, regardless of whether the judgment she renders is positive or negative. The form of judgment is absolute or total. The reader is to pronounce Jean-Jacques guilty or innocent; there is no middle ground. The charge against Jean-Jacques is the charge of dishonesty, in the sense of his being untrue to himself. The *Confessions* only makes sense when read as a defense against this accusation, and as an appeal for a verdict. The innocence of Jean-Jacques is never the innocence of a child; rather, it is innocence in the sense of an acquittal of an accusation.[6]

In order that the reader may judge whether Jean-Jacques is true to himself or not, Rousseau's presentation has to be total, it has to be complete. Rousseau promises to provide the reader of the *Confessions* with "a portrait of a man painted exactly according to nature" (*CW* 5:3; *Pl.* 1:3). More than that, Rousseau will present a complete picture of himself, telling everything without any gaps. Rousseau talks of a complete disclosure: relating "everything that has happened, everything I have done, everything I have thought, everything I have felt" (*CW* 5:146–47; *Pl.* 1:175). More famously, he writes, "I would like to be able to render my soul transparent to the eyes of the reader in some fashion, and to do so I seek to show it to him under all points of view, to clarify it by all lights, to act in such a way that no motion occurs in it that he does not perceive so that he might be able to judge by himself about the principle which produces them" (*CW* 5:146; *Pl.* 1:175).

Thus, the active involvement of the reader in the project of the *Confessions* is essential, for the reader is to judge.

The claim to total revelation seems improbable. How can anyone tell anyone else everything? But Rousseau has found a way around this problem. In the prayer that comes at the beginning of the *Confessions*, he states, "I have unveiled my interior as Thou hast seen it Thyself" (*CW* 5:5; *Pl.* 1:5). In other words, the reader is being given a divine, that is, an absolute viewpoint. Having read the book, he should be able to give a divine, absolute judgment. Everything does not need to be said, because the point of view as such is all-revealing. Such is the plan. How does one, in fact, give another human a divine viewpoint? How does one make an infinite revelation with finite means?

Rousseau does it by imitating the Scriptures. But this time, in contrast to the *Discourse on Inequality* and his alternative account of creation, one could say that Rousseau writes in parables.[7]

A parable is a genre that has its roots in the Christian Gospels and the sayings of Jesus. It is a short narrative; that is, it tells a story and relates an action. The story is meant to both obstruct the understanding, and to reveal the Kingdom of God. Parables are, in short, like the kingdom they reveal: capable of producing both faith and scandal. But the salient feature of the genre is that one parable can serve as a total revelation of the mystery of the kingdom. Still, the *telos* of the biblical parable is not to help one judge, but rather to bring one into the kingdom where there is no longer any judgment. For Rousseau, his parables are meant to help us judge him. This is another example of Rousseau's subversive use of biblical patterns. To put the situation of the reader in its most pointed form, if she judges Jean-Jacques innocent, she has cooperated in bringing into existence a murderous self, who at the end of the *Confessions* can condemn everyone who does not agree with the reader. Most, if not all readers, will refuse to acquiesce in bringing this self into existence. If she judges negatively, however, then Rousseau condemns her. The important point is that either way, it leaves everyone against Jean-Jacques Rousseau.

To summarize: both the claim to provide a divine viewpoint and the demand for judgment are the dialectical opposites of Augustine's *Confessions*, which Rousseau's *Confessions* is designed to replace. As is well-known, Augustine begins and sustains his *Confessions* as a prayer that the reader is allowed to overhear. The whole of Augustine's *Confessions*, including its most famous line, "Our hearts are restless until they rest in Thee," is an affirmation of the difference between God and humans. Augustine did not write the *Confessions* for the sake of human judgment, but rather in order to praise God. As he wrote, "Have I not openly accused myself of 'my faults', my God, and 'you forgave me the iniquity of my heart' (Ps. 31: 5). I do not 'contend with you in a court of law' (Job 9: 3), for you are the truth. I do not deceive myself, 'lest my iniquity lie to itself' (Ps. 26: 12). Therefore, I do not contend with you like a litigant because, 'if you take note of iniquities, Lord, who shall stand?'" (Ps. 129: 3).[8]

It would expand this chapter out of proportion to go through each story and demonstrate the way in which it contributes to the formation of the reader's judgment, and thereby to his or her condemnation. Instead, the exemplary story that Rousseau claims reveals Jean-Jacques to the full—the story of the encounter with the Venetian courtesan, Zulietta—will serve as the basis of this exploration. In this story there are a variety of ways in which Rousseau scandalizes the reader in order to get him to render a judgment. Finally, this way of reading the *Confessions*, as a story of theological scandal, reveals that the obscure plot against Jean-Jacques that emerges in the "Second Part" is a counterpoint to the system's obscure beginnings in scandal.

THE STORY OF ZULIETTA

The reason for choosing this particular passage for analysis should be clear. Rousseau announces to the reader in the strongest possible terms that the whole of his identity is contained, not even in the relatively short story of the whole encounter, but just in the few pages that tell the story of his meeting with Zulietta in her quarters following their introduction the night before, and of his going to try to see her on the third day.

Rousseau points to the importance of the story in three steps. He interrupts the narrative in order to address the reader, saying, "If there is one circumstance in my life that depicts my natural disposition well, it is the one I am about to recount" (*CW* 5:269; *Pl.* 1:320). Secondly, he gives notice that the story's contribution to achieving the goal of the *Confessions* is so great that this overrides any scandalous element in it. "The strength with which I recall the object of my book at this moment will make me despise the false decorum that could prevent me from fulfilling it here" (*CW* 5:269; *Pl.* 1:320). Finally, he dares the reader to continue reading as follows: "Whoever you may be who wishes to know a man, dare to read the two or three pages that follow; you are about to know J.-J. Rousseau to the full" (*CW* 5:269; *Pl.* 1:320).[9]

Knowing Jean-Jacques Rousseau to the full entails an act of interpretation. In this single story there are several layers of meaning, each with their own form of scandal.

The story parodies Biblical stories in that it can, and indeed must, be interpreted on several levels at the same time. I distinguish four and call them: the literal, the psychological, the philosophical, and the theological.[10] What holds for the *Confessions* as a whole holds for this episode and each of its levels: not only is it scandalous itself, but it is also about scandal.

Zulietta, a prostitute, is provided to Jean-Jacques by a French ship's captain in return for help that he has received from Jean-Jacques, who was at the time the secretary of the French Embassy. The core section, the real parable, begins the day after Jean-Jacques and Zulietta's first meeting aboard the ship, when Jean-Jacques goes to see her in her quarters. There he tries to make love to her, but he is unable to consummate the affair. He tries to understand the reason for this unwillingness, but in the process, ends up hurting her feelings. He takes his leave of her, but asks for another rendezvous. She grants the request. In fact, though, she leaves town before they can meet again. Thus, on a literal level, it is a story of prostitution, passion, sexual failure, miscommunication, and, being a bit more detailed, a malformed nipple. This is not exactly the conversation of polite society.

Accordingly, on this level, the story is scandalous in the most widely accepted usage of the word: it offends society's mores, especially society's sexual mores. Just the telling of it is scandalous, and yet Rousseau defends the telling in terms of the great revelation and, therefore, the great good that can come from it.

Already on the literal level the story has something to say about the nature of scandal. The story is about Jean-Jacques' relationship with one of society's outcasts. The narrative implies that the most revelatory thing about his own self is contained in the story of his relationship with one of society's victims. This takes us beyond scandal in its usual sense. Of course, his relationship with her is enigmatic. He is completely smitten with her and yet constantly uneasy. He pushes her away at the moment that he longs to embrace her. He is dying to please her and yet offends her.

Remaining on the literal level, Jean-Jacques does not join with the rest of society in rejecting her. Rather, he so arranges things that she rejects him. This could be termed Rousseau's rejection of rejection, his scandal at scandal. He will not join the victimizers. But his rejection of rejection is problematic in that rejecting rejection ends up re-enacting the rejection it rejects.

To understand this story as scandalous and therefore as revelatory on a psychological level, the nature of the story and its characters must be more deeply considered. As Madeleine B. Ellis, in her study of Rousseau's stay in Venice, astutely points out, there is an identification between Zulietta and Jean-Jacques. "Her sentiments are his. Her indifference to money is his own. . . . Moreover, Zulietta's demand for respect corresponds . . . to the demands of his own pride for deference to his person and place."[11] Rousseau's conclusions about Zulietta are his conclusions about himself.

In addition to this, Rousseau himself gives the reader a clear indication of what the parable is meant to elucidate about his personality immediately before the direct address to the reader, in which he makes clear that this story will reveal his personality. In trying to describe the delights that await him in Zulietta's quarters, he warns the reader, "Do not try to imagine the charms and graces of that girl enchantress; you would remain too far from the truth" (*CW* 5:269; *Pl.* 1:320). In fact, according to

Rousseau, "never has such sweet enjoyment been offered to the heart and senses of a mortal" (*CW* 5:269; *Pl.* 1:320). But Jean-Jacques is not made to enjoy. He says that he "killed" these delights, "as if without cause" (*CW* 5:269; *Pl.* 1:320).

And yet Jean-Jacques, the one who kills them, is also a victim. "Nature did not make me to enjoy" (*CW* 5:269; *Pl.* 1:320). Rather, nature, which can do no wrong, gave him a head "that has the poison for that ineffable happiness, the appetite for which it put into [his] heart" (*CW* 5:269; *Pl.* 1:320). Rousseau simply juxtaposes his heart and his head, his appetite and his poison. The question presents itself whether there is any evidence that he seeks precisely those delights that he knows his heart will poison; whether the happiness is ineffable precisely because it will be killed.

This personality trait can be understood as the psychological form of scandal. Jean-Jacques himself renders impossible the happiness that is necessary to him. The closer that Jean-Jacques approaches the goal of his desires, the more inaccessible it becomes, due to the poison he carries around within him. Jean-Jacques only obtains what he does not desire, and desiring anything renders it dead and therefore unattainable.

How does this occur in the story? Rousseau gives a detailed account of his thinking. As already mentioned, he was utterly smitten by Zulietta's vivacity. Now he is alone with her. At the very moment that he is to "pluck" the fruit, something happens. "Suddenly instead of the flames which were devouring me, I feel a mortal coldness running through my veins; my legs shake me, and ready to faint, I sit down, and weep like a child" (*CW* 5:269; *Pl.* 1:320). He is struck by two different things that he cannot reconcile. One is her perfection and the other is her condition. On the one hand, she is "the masterpiece of nature and of love; the mind, the body, everything about it is perfect; she is as good and generous as she is lovable and beautiful" (*CW* 5:269; *Pl.* 1:321). On the other hand, she is a wretched trollop. Jean-Jacques concludes, "There is something inconceivable in this" (*CW* 5:269; *Pl.* 1:321).

Rousseau's evidence for the unintelligibility of the situation is not just Jean-Jacques' feelings. The presence of "others" is critical to a proper understanding of the story. Their attraction to Zulietta is the only way of confirming her worth. It cannot be without reason that men are not in a contest over Zulietta. There are, then, two possible explanations for these facts. One could be that Rousseau's heart fools him, fascinates him, and makes him "the dupe of a worthless slut" (*CW* 5:269; *Pl.* 1:321). Then he must simply send her away and get on with his life. But this option is not even deemed worth exploring by Rousseau. His heart is not so corrupt. His eyes are not so weak. The only other possibility is, "Some hidden flaw of which I am unaware must destroy the effect of her charms and make her odious to those who ought to contend over her" (*CW* 5:269; *Pl.* 1:321). This is the only truly plausible explanation, and so Jean-Jacques begins "to look for this flaw with a singular application of mind" (*CW* 5:269–70; *Pl.* 1:321).

Jean-Jacques finds the hidden flaw for which he is searching, but it is not so hidden. It is not, he is convinced, venereal disease that drives the men away. Rather, it is a visible flaw that is normally invisible. Zulietta has a malformed nipple. But even this is not, in fact, the hidden flaw. Rather, the deformity itself "depended on some notable natural vice" (*CW* 5:270; *Pl.* 1:321). Jean-Jacques finds himself "turning and returning [to] this idea" (*CW* 5:270; *Pl.* 1:321). This leads him to the conclusion, "In the most charming person I could imagine, I was holding in my arms only a sort of monster, the outcast of nature, men and love" (*CW* 5:270; *Pl.* 1:321–22).

How does Jean-Jacques react to this outcast? He does not join society in rejecting her, but neither does he embrace her. He shares his own revulsion in a mild manner, talking of the malformed nipple with Zulietta, who first takes it as a joke. There is no clear resolution; Jean-Jacques can neither accept nor reject her. Rather, he maintains an "undercurrent of uneasiness" that is not hidden from her (*CW* 5:270; *Pl.* 1:322).

Zulietta's flaw gives a clue as to why this story is so central to the project of the *Confessions*. In another passage, Rousseau admits that part of the motivation for his frankness in the *Confessions* is to make them "interesting" (*CW* 5:433; *Pl.* 1:516). This "truthfulness without precedent" grounds the book's uniqueness (*CW* 5:432; *Pl.* 1:516). Rousseau then writes, "I had always laughed at the false naïveté of Montaigne who, while making a pretence of admitting his flaws, takes great care to give himself only amiable ones: while I, who always believed myself to be and who still believes myself to be, taking everything into account, the best of men, felt that there is no human interior as pure as it can be, that does not harbor some odious vice" (*CW* 5:432; *Pl.* 1:516–17). Zulietta has some hidden flaw that makes her "odious to those who ought to contend over her," but so does everyone else, including Rousseau himself. The *Confessions* would not have been written without this belief in the odious vice that could be exposed. The search for this in the Zulietta figure, who has been identified with the Jean-Jacques figure, is the very heart of the project of the *Confessions*. Rousseau has to get this out in the open. He has presented himself as someone who has to look for hidden causes to explain the reality he is unable to accept. He will not fail to find the hidden causes.

If the psychological scandal is Jean-Jacques' offense at the condition of Zulietta, then the philosophical scandal becomes clear in his offending her. Throughout most of the encounter, Jean-Jacques maintains "an undercurrent of uneasiness" with her. He mentions the nipple, at first as a "joke." But Zulietta is sensitive to his discomfort and becomes offended. She moves away from him when he tries to approach her. Finally, she rejects him, telling him "in a cold and disdainful tone," "*Zanetto, lascia le Donne, e studia la matematica*" [leave the women and study mathematics] (*CW* 5:270; *Pl.* 1:322). This enigmatic statement can begin to make sense if the Zulietta figure is interpreted in yet another way. Beyond the historical figure, and beyond being an aspect of Jean-Jacques' psyche, Zulietta stands for Eros.

It is helpful to recall here Rousseau's Platonism. The philosophical scandal is dramatized by the fact that Jean-Jacques, after offending Eros, is instructed by Eros herself to give up the erotic and to pursue the mathematical. Stanley Rosen writes that the movement from the erotic to the mathematical is a movement toward the "general and thus anonymous enterprise" of mathematical philosophy.[12] According to Plato, this kind of philosophy is necessary for a correct political philosophy, and thus, this is intended as a movement toward that. In the story, Zulietta is pushing Jean-Jacques out of her private quarters and into the public square. But, also according to Plato, mathematical philosophy and abstract, general considerations of justice do not suffice. The push from the erotic to the mathematical has to include the erotic for there to be justice. The mathematical only teaches general rules, but to be just one also needs to know human nature. And this is precisely what Rousseau has told the reader she we will learn from this story. In the expulsion of Jean-Jacques from the erotic, the reader gains exactly the erotic insight she needs to complete her more general considerations of political philosophy.

We can see this in another way. According to Plato, mathematics is the most "apt to summon thought" (*The Republic of Plato*, trans. Allan Bloom [New York: Basic Books, 1968], 524d). He argues as follows:

> For if the one is adequately seen, itself by itself, or is grasped by some other sense, it would not draw men toward being. . . . But if some opposition to it is always seen at the same time, so that nothing looks as though it were one more than the opposite of one, then there would now be need of something to judge; and in this case, a soul would be compelled to be at a loss and to make an investigation, setting in motion the intelligence within it, and to ask what the one itself is. And thus the study of the one would be among those apt to lead and turn around toward the contemplation of what *is*. (*Republic*, 524d–25a)

It is not surprising that the dramatic scene in Zulietta's quarters contains echoes of this passage. For Jean-Jacques, Zulietta is never simple, although she is the one. There is an opposition to her that is always seen at the same time, so that there is a need for judgment. Jean-Jacques' soul is at a loss, and it will have to make an investigation in order to find out what *is*. The parallel movement of soul is going on in the reader concerning Jean-Jacques.

Zulietta, the figure of Eros, is also then a figure of mathematics, number, [*arithmos*]. Eros never totally leaves Jean-Jacques. She is enshrined in his heart in the unending "senseless regret" that is the result of this encounter (*CW* 5:271; *Pl.* 1:322).

The theological scandal in the story emerges through the relationship of Jean-Jacques and Zulietta when the reader interprets Zulietta as a Christ figure. Jean-Jacques begins the tale by telling that he enters Zulietta's room as a "sanctuary." He writes that he realizes he is in the presence of the divinity, and in fact states, "I believe I saw the divinity in her person" (*CW* 5:269; *Pl.* 1:320). The predominance of theological language describing this encounter needs to be accounted for in any interpretation of this passage. Rousseau speaks of Zulietta in language that is normally reserved for Christ, the incarnate Son of God. But Jean-Jacques' encounter with the incarnated deity is troubled. The crisis, and clearly it is a crisis, that he has with Zulietta finds its ultimate meaning as the crisis of theological scandal raised by an encounter with Christ.

Let me emphasize that Rousseau does not present the reader here with the conflict, which is so prevalent in Rousseau's writings from the *First Discourse* on, between reality and appearance. It goes much deeper than that. Zulietta does not just appear to be good, she *is* good, and yet she *is also* a whore. This has already been emphasized on the philosophical level. Zulietta is herself and her opposite. This conflict is the crux of Rousseau's scandal, *and* it is the same conflict as having a crucified God. The language of Zulietta's divine-like goodness links her to Christ, but so does her lowly status. She, too, is a slave and finds herself in that position. For Jean-Jacques, Zulietta has to be one or the other—a divinity or a monster, but he has no reliable criterion for making the judgment. He cannot accept that this is what it means to be human. Thus, he condemns society for not contending over her. She is now the basis of his system, the basis of his critique, and so he cannot reject her without the system collapsing. But neither can he accept her in the sense of overcoming the perceived duality. Rather, he needs her to reject him so that he can occupy the place of the one that is most "apt to summon thought" (*Republic*, 524d). From this the plot grows.

The theological issues do not end here. Rousseau cannot understand how this woman, so lovely and so precious, can throw herself at him, "whom she knows has nothing" and "whose *merit*—which she cannot know—must be nothing in her eyes" (*CW* 5:269; *Pl.* 1:321; emphasis added). This is another indication that the highlighted incident is to be interpreted in terms of theological scandal. In one sentence, Rousseau is writing about the incongruity of her perfection and her state, and in the next, he is describing her self-giving and love for Jean-Jacques without there being the possibility of any merit on his side. Are these facts unrelated? In a theological context they are not. Only faith can annul the scandal of a humble God and accept his unmerited love. Ultimately, faith is the acceptance of this love and scandal is its rejection.

The story continues with Rousseau delineating how Jean-Jacques reacts to the inconceivability with which he is confronted. The category of the inconceivable need not be limited to rational or philosophical scandal. Kierkegaard points out that that which contains the possibility of offense does not fit into the category of human understanding. The figure of Zulietta is such a scandalous object.

Having offended her by his crass comments on her deformity and being dismissed by her, Jean-Jacques takes his leave. He asks for yet another meeting. The request is granted, but the scandal does not pass. Jean-Jacques passes the time "ill at ease" (*CW* 5:270; *Pl.* 1:322). He is still smitten by her charms and her graces. He regrets using his time with her so poorly and, while he is impatient to "repair the loss," there is no talk of forgiveness (*CW* 5:270; *Pl.* 1:322). He is "still uneasy in spite of everything [he] could do to reconcile the perfections of that adorable girl with the unworthiness of her condition" (*CW* 5:270–71; *Pl.* 1:322). He goes to her to prove his merit, but she is not there, having left for Florence the day before.

That which he cannot have suddenly becomes precious to him. He only really feels his love for her in losing her. This "senseless regret" is all that he is left with (*CW* 5:271; *Pl.* 1:322). He ends the episode with these words: "Entirely lovable, entirely charming though she was to my eyes, I could console myself for losing her, but I admit that I could not console myself for the fact that she carried off only a contemptuous memory of me" (*CW* 5:271; *Pl.* 1:322). Certainly, the reader is jarred by this conclusion. Given what has occurred before this, the repetition of "entirely" and the emphasis on "to my eyes" is incongruous at best and dishonest at worst. Is this not the Zulietta with the malformed nipple, the one who was precisely not "entirely lovable, entirely charming," but rather a flawed specimen whose deformity signaled depravity? Is the point of the whole story to get the reader to accuse Jean-Jacques of dishonesty and thereby suffer his condemnation?

Not for the careful reader. Rousseau is saying that Zulietta is quite literally "entirely" lovable and charming. Her lovability and charm not only include but also are predicated upon her flaw. That is, the kind of lovability that Zulietta embodies is the fascination of scandal. It is the attractiveness of that which someone wants precisely because he cannot have it, the fascination of the paradox, the magnetism of a humbled God.

It is in the "senseless regret" that the first glimpse of the plot against Jean-Jacques makes an appearance (*CW* 5:271; *Pl.* 1:322). As Zulietta exits the scene, Jean-Jacques is sure that she carries away with her a contemptuous memory of him. This leaves him disconsolate. If Jean-Jacques could have overcome his scandal and accepted Zulietta as both a prostitute and a sign of the divinity, he would not have had to condemn the society that sees her state as her only reality, nor would he have forced her to reject him. He is forced to have her reject him because he cannot follow society's solution, nor can he reconcile the two realities she embodies.

Jean-Jacques can console himself for losing Zulietta. He can find substitutes and supplements for her. In this sense, his loss of her is not irreparable. But what is irreparable is Jean-Jacques' anxiety over his reputation with her. Aside from the author's conviction, there is no reason for believing that Zulietta in fact "carried away a contemptuous memory" of Jean-Jacques. He, as well as the reader, has no way to test the accuracy of the conviction. This reveals something profound about Rousseau. The one whom he does not accept will become for him the one who rejects him. There is a desolation in the heart of Jean-Jacques, and it is there because of his belief that Zulietta hates him. That is, Jean-Jacques is convinced that the historical woman, Zulietta, the object of his desire, Eros, and Christ all hold him in contempt.

ZULIETTA AND THE ROAD TO VINCENNES

There is something puzzling about the way Rousseau has shaped his *Confessions*. Clearly, his life-transforming event was his experience on the road to Vincennes in 1549. There, he "saw another universe" and he "became another man" (*CW* 5:294; *Pl.* 1:351). The content of the experience is not discussed at all in the *Confessions*, and Rousseau priveleges the encounter with Zulietta as the moment of revelation. Instead of recounting in the *Confessions* his experience on the way to visit Diderot in prison, Rousseau refers to another, earlier account he wrote about in one of his four letters to M. de Malesherbes.[13] Instead he gives the reader a meditation on memory, on how it serves him, and on how it does not.[14]

This short but highly meaningful account of the relationship between his memory and his writing serves both to emphasize the importance of the experience on the road to Vincennes and to link it with the encounter with Zulietta. Rather than looking to this experience as some sort of resolution to the encounter with Zulietta, it is more accurate to say that Vincennes confirmed Rousseau in his experience that there is no resolution. At Vincennes, he generalized his experience with Zulietta; he saw *all* the contradictions of the social system. He did not resolve the contradictions; he lived them, and the *Confessions* is the story of how he did that: he wrote and forgot and then remembered through the writing.

The story about Zulietta ends with the words, "*un souvenir méprisant*" (*CW* 5:271; *Pl.* 1:322). The levels upon which this thought reverberates have already been detailed. Through a strange alchemy, the contemptuous feelings that Jean-Jacques has for the person of Zulietta, for the object desired, for Eros, and for Christ get split off and projected onto their object. I am not reducing this to a psychological mechanism—although it does have a psychological component. It is also a philosophical move and a theological reality.

The desolation of these contemptuous memories is what accompanies Rousseau on the way to see his friend Diderot. They are what causes the "instant" in time that has its inevitable effect on "all the rest of [his] life and misfortunes," and not Diderot's suggestion that he compete for the prize, as might be inferred from the report of the incident in the *Confessions* (*CW* 5:295; *Pl.* 1:351). As he is recounting the illumination on the road to Vincennes, Rousseau tells the reader that memory serves "only as long as he has relied on it" (*CW* 5:294; *Pl.* 1:351). For Rousseau to "entrust the deposit" of his experience to paper means that this experience will abandon him (*CW* 5:294; *Pl.* 1:351). Once he has written it, he "no longer remember[s] it at all" (*CW* 5:294; *Pl.* 1:351).

According to the *Confessions*, one act in this life-changing experience was to write the "Prosopopoeia of Fabricius" "in pencil under an Oak" (*CW* 5:295; *Pl.* 1:351). The very experience is one of writing and therefore one of forgetting, but not just forgetting. Rousseau remembers through the writing what has been forgotten through the original writing. The experience abandoned him as he was having it. As memory goes away, the identity of the person is lost, and this is why it is the experience itself that constitutes the instant of Rousseau's fall and not Diderot's later suggestion to compete for the prize. Already under the oak, Rousseau could say, "From that instant I was lost". Rousseau's experience that day was not the experience of Saul on the road to Damascus. In that experience, Saul is confronted with his violence, with his victim, and so found a new identity—Paul. Rousseau, according to his own testimony, lost himself that day.

Writing does not just cause him to forget; it also helps him to remember. As part of his description of the Vincennes experience, Rousseau explains his "peculiar manner" of working (*CW* 5:295; *Pl.* 1:352). He tells the reader that he dedicated the time that he could not sleep to formulating the *Discourse*. He meditated, he shaped and reshaped passages until he was satisfied. But his memory would not serve him. By the time he got up, prepared himself, and sat at his writing table, he could no longer recall the material he had worked on in bed. So he took the mother of this mistress, Therese Levasseur, as a secretary. She would arrive early, light the fire in his room, and then Jean-Jacques would dictate the night's work from his bed. This practice, he tells the reader, "saved [him] from forgetting many things" (*CW* 5:295; *Pl.* 1:352). The very thing, writing, that has caused the experiences to abandon him, now keeps him from forgetting them.

The experience on the road to Vincennes represents a generalizing of the experience Rousseau delineates in his description of his encounter with Zulietta. The experience is a generalizing of the inconceivability at the heart of reality. Zulietta, like Christ, is both divine and a slave. Reality at its deepest level is not simply contradictory; it also requires one to make a choice.[15] Rousseau understood at Vincennes that society solves this problem through a complex transformation. In society, Zulietta's goodness simply disappears, and her station becomes the absolute reality by which she is judged, condemned, and cast out. Those who reject her create their identities through this rejection of her. They become the "good" people of society, but it is a relative goodness, the goodness of amour-propre. Rousseau sees through their appearances to the rejection that makes these appearances possible. He refuses to join in with that rejection. He rejects their rejection. But in doing this he also joins them. Thus, he refuses any solidarity with Zulietta.

For Rousseau, the solution to the situation is to get that which has been rejected by the others to reject him. In this way, he becomes the isolated victim, with everyone else arrayed against him. The important relationship becomes his relationship to himself. By getting Zulietta to reject him, he does not have any need for forgiveness. Rousseau has succeeded in bringing the encounter to a conclusion without ever having to choose a side. Rousseau never rejects Zulietta as a monster, although he does see her as that, nor does he ever join with her in love, which the sexual act could symbolize. He can always maintain to himself that he would have done that, but he has removed the possibility of that ever being put to the test. He is left with senseless regret, which he deposits on paper to forget and to remember.

THE PLOT

At the very beginning of Book VIII, shortly before relating his experience on the road to Vincennes, Rousseau writes, "I was obliged to make a pause at the end of the preceding book. With this one begins the long chain of my misfortunes in its first origin" (*CW* 5:293; *Pl.* 1:349). As we have already seen, Jean-Jacques himself feels that from the instant that he decides to compete for the Academic Prize, he is "lost" (*CW* 5:295; *Pl.* 1:351). By understanding this experience in the light of what has gone before in the encounter with Zulietta, it is possible to make some sense of the plot that comes to dominate Rousseau's thinking and writing from this point on.

The plot has significance on many different levels, and the way that the Zulietta story has been interpreted can help in differentiating these levels. Obviously, there is the personal, literal, and historical level. Without trying to affix any blame, Rousseau did in fact go from being one of the lionized figures of the Paris literary scene to being an outcast. Again, without affixing responsibility, there is the fact that he was threatened with arrest by the *Parliament* of Paris, condemned by the Archbishop of Paris, and expelled from several places, and the fact that his house was stoned and pamphlets were written against him.

The psychological level of the plot has already been fairly well explored. Rousseau suffered bouts of paranoia with varying degrees of intensity. Whatever literal truth there is to the actions done against him, his own imaginings made them all worse. At times, even Rousseau can admit this.

Philosophically, the plot is a mirror image of his system. David Gauthier writes that it is gross distortion of Rousseau's thought to see the plot as an expression of his theory of the general will.[16] I agree, but for a different reason. As Gauthier says, the general will cannot have a determinate individual for its object, whereas the plot clearly does. One can add to that that the general will is always the will of "a people" and never the will of all of humanity. But the plot clearly involves everyone. Its structure is all against one, Jean-Jacques. Rousseau emphasizes this fact as follows: "It was necessary to divert the whole world away from me, not leave me a single friend, either small nor great. What do I say? it was necessary not to let a single word of truth pierce through to me. If a single generous man came to say to me, 'You are playing the virtuous man, nevertheless this is what they are saying about you, what do you have to say?' truth triumphed, and Grimm was lost" (*CW* 5:413; *Pl.* 1:493). This *universality* does not correspond to the general will of Rousseau's political philosophy, but to that other "*universe*" that he saw on the road to Vincennes, and this universe was a universalizing of his experience with Zulietta. The system is universal because its deepest level is not political, but rather philosophical and theological.

The plot is the outcome of Jean-Jacques' search for the hidden flaw. He will inevitably find one, and it will be not just the flaw of the historical person of Zulietta, the famous or infamous "malformed nipple," but also the flaw of Eros, the flaw of philosophy. The dilemma that Jean-Jacques faces with Zulietta needs to be kept before our eyes here. Either his heart is fooled and he is the "dupe of a worthless slut," or some hidden flaw "must destroy the effect of her charms and make her odious to those who ought to contend over her" (*CW* 5:269; *Pl.* 1:321). Neither of these alternatives is good. Rousseau's experience with Zulietta and its generalization at Vincennes consist in this search for and finding of the hidden flaw in everything that renders all odious. From his descriptions of both experiences, the one in the courtesan's quarters and the other on the road to Vincennes, it is clear that they are terrible, wrenching experiences of sadness and desolation. The tears shed in both places are the tears of inconsolable sorrow.

At the very heart of reality, Rousseau discovers an inconceivability. Zulietta's condition does not match her adorableness, and neither does the crucified condition of Christ match his divinity. This is the obscurity, the darkness that gets reflected in the plot. Rousseau's system cannot reach into the theological scandal in which it originates. It reacts to it. In a parallel fashion, it cannot explain the plot in which it terminates.

CHAPTER 11

"AT THE BOTTOM OF THE ABYSS"

INTRODUCTION

Rousseau continues to scandalize. Each new generation finds his work outrageous, provoking, and controversial. He constructed his system to help both individuals and societies keep order, even when neither forgiveness nor violence was a possibility. *Les Rêveries du Promeneur Solitaire* leads to the very heart of Rousseau's scandalized consciousness and gives a final image of how this works, of the tensions it keeps in balance. Sometimes in striking lyrical prose, other times in a kind of tired repetition, Rousseau delineates the ontological extremes he continues to unite as he approaches death. He is completely alone, yet completely dependent upon the other. He is like God, yet the plot against him seems divinely sanctioned, and thus, he is God and he is the victim; he is violent and he is violated. In his new-found peace, he uses the language of classic Christian spirituality to describe an interior life devoid of Christ.[1]

Scandal does not appear to be the most helpful concept for interpreting the *Reveries*. Rousseau uses the word "scandal" only once.[2] If we substitute the word "indignation" for scandal, the text begins to open up. Even with the declaration of a new-found peace, Rousseau often admits that indignation is only "a sign, a gesture, a glance from a stranger" away (*CW* 8:85; *Pl.* 1:1094). He continues, "I am my own only when I am alone. Apart from that I am the plaything of all those around me" (*CW* 8:85; *Pl.* 1:1094). The only way for him to maintain his calm is by making sure that his expulsion from society is complete. In this aloneness, Rousseau begins to use some of the most intensely religious language of all his writings. The religious language tells us little about God, but it does illuminate Jean-Jacques.

Society has expelled Jean-Jacques and he has expelled society. These mutually opposed expulsions not only structure the text of the *Reveries* but also define the relations within it. Precisely by expelling and being expelled, Rousseau attains his God-like state, and, at the same moment, the "others," the members of the "*complot*," achieve their divine status also. In fact, we find in the *Reveries*, not at all unlike what we saw in the *Dialogues*, two mutually opposed systems, Rousseau's and the others', both of which depend upon the other for their continued existence.

Although each of these specular realities will claim that it is simply a justified response to the other, they are coeval. They are both systems of victimization. In victimizing, each produces the divinity of itself and of the other. When these systems seem most opposed, they are, in fact, most alike. In reading the *Reveries* in this way, a deeper understanding of the discussion of truth and lying in the "Fourth Walk" emerges, as well as a better grasp of the concept of nature and its connection with the central topics of reverie and botany.

VIOLENT EXPULSION

Rousseau begins the *Reveries* with his conclusion, "I am now alone on earth" (*CW* 8:3; *Pl.* 1:995).[3] Violence has brought about this being alone. Rousseau writes that they, that is, everyone else, "have violently broken all ties which attached me to them" (*CW* 8:3; *Pl.* 1:995). Rousseau responds to this violent expulsion with violence. "I struggled for a long time as violently as I did in vain" (*CW* 8:4; *Pl.* 1:996).

This mutual violence leads to a mutual expulsion, in fact, to a mutual annihilation. After they have violently broken all ties with him, Rousseau says that they are "now strangers, unknowns, in short, nonentities (*nul*)" to him (*CW* 8:3; *Pl.* 1:995). Just a few pages later, he also writes the following: "I am henceforth nothing (*nul*) among men, and that is all I can be, no longer having any real relations or true society with them" (*CW* 8:7; *Pl.* 1:1000).

The *Reveries* are justly famous for the lyrical accounts Rousseau gives of his reveries. He also describes many things in this work besides peaceful reverie. He speaks of being "dragged, [he] know[s] not how, out of the order of things," and he goes on to write, "I have seen myself cast into an incomprehensible chaos where I distinguish nothing at all" (*CW* 8:3; *Pl.* 1:995). He claims to be spit upon and to be buried alive. Thus, much of the text conveys violence.

Rousseau's state of scandal has now become chronic. He recalls how it began as follows: "I fell into all the snares they placed along my path; indignation, fury, delirium took possession of me. I was completely disoriented. My mind was overwhelmed" (*CW* 8:70; *Pl.* 1:1076). At the same time, the present generation has been scandalized by him. "I saw myself suddenly misrepresented as a dreadful monster the likes of which has never existed. . . . I struggled violently and only entangled myself more" (*CW* 8:71; *Pl.* 1:1076).

And yet, out of this violent struggle, peace emerged. The unanimity of the plot and Rousseau's peace are coeval. Only when he realizes that the league is "universal, without exception," can Rousseau recover his equilibrium (*CW* 8:71; *Pl.* 1:1077). Everyone is against him and that is what gives him peace. In the text, it is exactly the moment when he has concluded his unsuccessful search for even one exception to the universality of the plot that he finds "serenity, tranquility, peace, even happiness" (*CW* 8:71; *Pl.* 1:1077). Why? It is simple: "We want to be esteemed by the people we esteem; and as long as I could judge men, or at least some men, favorably, the judgments they held about me could not be uninteresting to me" (*CW* 8:71; *Pl.* 1:1077). Rousseau achieves peace when he is able to judge unfavorably, or to condemn, everyone else.

The peace that Rousseau finds is the peace of what I term hyper-scandal. This is scandal raised to such a level that it is no longer distinct episodes of scandal, but rather a permanent state, a habit of being. In this habit, the plot is constantly being confirmed as unanimous. The unanimity of the plot, in turn, renders reality itself hostile. As it has been throughout this work, so here my interest is less in Rousseau's psychological condition than in the metaphysics that underlie it. There is no one nor anything that can speak a welcoming word to Rousseau. Benevolence is not to be found except in feeding from his own substance. Rousseau says, "If I recognize anything around me, it is only objects which distress me and tear my heart asunder; and I cannot cast my eyes on what touches and surrounds me without forever finding some disdainful object which makes me indignant or a painful one which distresses me" (*CW* 8:6; *Pl.* 1:999). The active animosity of his generation is "ever perceptible and ever active," and the indignities with which they overwhelm him are incessant (*CW* 8:26; *Pl.* 1:1023).

Rousseau is certain of one thing: his enemies make "everything appear only false and deceptive . . . an occasion for virtue is never anything but a lure they hold out to draw me into the snare they want to enlace me in" (*CW* 8:50; *Pl.* 1:1051; cf. also *CW* 8.53; *Pl.* 1:1055). Again, he writes, "[I am certain] that I am not allowed to see things as they are, I abstain from judging according to their given appearances; and with whatever lure the motives for acting are covered, it is enough that these motives be left within my reach for me to be sure they are deceitful" (*CW* 8:53; *Pl.* 1:1056). Human beings can live their lives such that the only thing they really want is that which they cannot have. The person can recognize that he desires the unattainable precisely because it is unattainable, and he can even see that should he attain it, he would no longer want it. When a person reaches this stage of sickness, then the very desire for something is the sign that he should not strive for it. Every attractive thing, by dint of being attractive, becomes repulsive. Rousseau has reached that state about everything "external." Everything is reversed. All opportunities become snares, friends become enemies, the promise of joy is a lie.

This fall "into another order" is marked by stumbling, and Rousseau is oppressed by the "thousand cruel ways they stare at" him (*CW* 8:54; *Pl.* 1:1057). Nature does remain a refuge. Nature provides a safe haven because it appears to be untouched by human hands. As a refuge, it does not solve or transform Rousseau's problems. It allows him to escape, to find temporary respite. Rousseau forgets the others and feels like they also forget him.

Two Deities

Rousseau feels that all, "without exception," are participating in the plot against him(*CW* 8:71; *Pl.* 1:1077). They are all condemning him as a monster. He, in turn, condemns them. At the same time that Rousseau and the others become *nul* for each other, a kind of divinization by each side of the other occurs. Turning first to Rousseau's tranformation to a divinity, Rousseau claims in the "First Walk," that having expelled everyone, with nothing more to hope for or to fear, he is now "tranquil at the bottom of the abyss, a poor unfortunate moral, but unperturbed, like God

Himself" (*CW* 8:6; *Pl.* 1:999). Scandal has led Rousseau to the bottom of the abyss. Even more, it has led him to contentment at the bottom of the abyss.

This contentment is present in reverie also. In the state of reverie, the soul finds "a solid enough base to rest itself on entirely and to gather its whole being into" (*CW* 8:46; *Pl.* 1:1046). In that state, the person is sufficient unto him or herself, "like God" (*CW* 8:46; *Pl.* 1:1047). "Such is the state in which I often found myself during my solitary reveries" (*CW* 8:46; *Pl.* 1:1046). The descriptions of reverie make clear that peacefulness and the God-like status are grounded in the self being isolated from everything else. When Rousseau says he is at the bottom of the abyss, he means that the abyss is his own self, and that there he rests content.

Rousseau's God-like status has echoes beyond self-sufficiency. In his reveries, he is a creator. He can assimilate reality to his fictions, so that the line between fiction and reality is blurred (cf. *CW* 8:47–48; *Pl.* 1:1048).

The experience of being "delivered from all the earthly passions the tumult of social life engenders" founds the claim to self-sufficiency and its peace (*CW* 8:48; *Pl.* 1:1048). Rousseau becomes free for transcendence, so that his soul can "soar up above this atmosphere and commune in advance with the celestial intelligences" (*CW* 8:48; *Pl.* 1:1049). Reverie even realigns the ontological order so that Rousseau in reverie is more in the midst of the charming images that elude his senses than when he is really there (cf. *CW* 8:48; *Pl.* 1:1049). Still, all of this is based upon the expulsion of Rousseau. He himself sees his reveries as a gift of his persecutors. "Those moments of rapture, those ecstasies, which I sometimes experienced in walking around alone that way, were enjoyments I owed to my persecutors" (*CW* 8:9; *Pl.* 1:1003). The experience in which Rousseau is most enclosed in himself is an experience that he owes to the others.

Rousseau is not alone in having divine characteristics. According to Rousseau, the plot against him has gone beyond being "only a fruit of the wickedness of men" (*CW* 8:15; *Pl.* 1:1010). The evidence pushes Rousseau beyond his previous conclusion "that [his] personal fate and that of [his] reputation have been so fastened by the connivance of the whole present generation that no effort on [his] part could free [him], since it is completely impossible for [him] to transmit any bequest to other ages without making pass in this age through the hands of those interested in suppressing it" (*CW* 8:15; *Pl.* 1:1009). In addition, everyone who is against Rousseau, all those who "have some secret animosity against" him, have been raised up and placed in positions of authority (*CW* 8:15; *Pl.* 1:1009–10). They have all banded together with the one end of persecuting Rousseau. "This universal agreement is too extraordinary to be purely fortuitous" (*CW* 8:15; *Pl.* 1:1010). He grounds this claim upon the fact that so very little would have been able to stop the plot dead in its tracks. "A single man, . . . a single event, . . . a single unforeseen circumstance . . . would have been enough to make it fail" (*CW* 8:15; *Pl.* 1:1010).

Exactly like Rousseau in the state of reverie, the plot comes up against nothing "which had been an obstacle to it" (*CW* 8:15; *Pl.* 1:1010). Just one obstacle and it would have been ended. This is a sign of transcendence, of divinity. On account of it, Rousseau cannot "doubt that its complete success is written among the eternal decrees" (*CW* 8:15; *Pl.* 1:1010). Rousseau feels that he must regard it "as one of those secrets of Heaven impenetrable to human reason" (*CW* 8:15; *Pl.* 1:1010).

According to the logic that Rousseau is employing here, the violence against him is the violence of the totally other. Rousseau has done nothing to bring this violence upon himself. He is innocent. He is good. This violence now has a transcendent source and sanction, and that consoles Rousseau and helps him to resign himself. He admits that he does not go as far as "St. Augustine who would have consoled himself to be damned if such had been the will of God" (*CW* 8:16; *Pl.* 1:1010). Rousseau believes that since God wills his suffering, and since God knows that he is innocent, he can learn to suffer without murmur. Rousseau's peace is an act of submission to the God of this violence. He surrenders to this God because he is sure that ultimately this God will violently avenge him against his enemies. He concludes, "In the end everything must return to order and my turn will come sooner or later" (*CW* 8:16; *Pl.* 1:1010).

Rousseau's condemnation of those involved in the plot, its divine status, and his serenity are intertwined. Not only is the plot divine, but so is Rousseau's peace. Being completely cutoff—on the island or in the city—has its counterpart in being self-sufficient like God. The only way, however, to achieve this kind of self-sufficiency is for God Himself to be behind the violence. How does the complete condemnation of Rousseau by everyone and the condemnation of everyone by Rousseau yield a God? It does so because this structure of the victim surrounded by his persecutors gives each side extraordinary power. Clearly, a mob of persecutors has a kind of raw power to kill, but its fascination with the victim is a sign of the victim's power, also. Why are people fascinated with Jean-Jacques Rousseau? In part because he demands it. But being able to have people respond to that demand is also testimony to his genius. Rousseau realizes that being completely alone as the result of a unanimous expulsion is terrible in the full sense of the word—horrible but also awesome—sacred. Rousseau experiences a kind of negative power. He is completely unable to act, unable to do good, but he is also no longer the patient of any act by others. This theme will be examined in the "Conclusion."

TWO SYSTEMS

The ultimate result of these mutual exclusions and mutual divinizations is the emergence of two opposed systems. Rousseau tells the story of his own system in the "Third Walk" by giving a synopsis of his spiritual autobiography. Rousseau begins the story by writing that he had been "born into a family in which morals and piety reigned" (*CW* 8:19; *Pl.* 1:1013). He ends it several pages later with the affirmation, "[The] result of my painful seeking was approximately that which I have since set down as the 'Profession of Faith of the Savoyard Vicar'" (*CW* 8:22–23; *Pl.* 1:1018). The religious nature of this synopsis should not be overlooked. Rousseau uses the language of Christian asceticism—"I forsook the world and its pomp . . . I eradicated from my heart the cupidity and covetousness which give value to everything I was forsaking . . . My complete renunciation of the world" (*CW* 8:20; *Pl.* 1:1015). This is not an isolated text. Rousseau uses the language of Christian spiritual writing of the eighteenth century throughout.

In the *Reveries*, Rousseau claims to have achieved "*indifférence.*"[4] This indifference is not the normal indifference of apathy.[5] Rather, Rousseau uses the term in the manner that St. Ignatius uses it in the "First Principle and Foundation" of the *Spiritual Exercises*.[6] The following quote from the *Reveries* is practically a paraphrase from the *Spiritual Exercises*: "Is it nothing at my age to have learned to view life and death, sickness and health, wealth and misery, glory and infamy with the same indifference?" (*CW* 8:74; *Pl.* 1:1080–81).[7] For Ignatius, indifference is the utterly personal response by the human who realizes her creaturehood, who realizes that she is not God. Rousseau inverts the indifference so that it is his response to his experience of being divine. Ignatian indifference results from a profound experience of being gifted by the Triune God with everything—sickness as well as health, a long life or a short one—each is a gift. The true meaning of this indifference is revealed in what the person cares about. The man or woman of Ignatian spirituality cares only about giving greater glory to God. For Rousseau, this indifference is for the sake of his own self. So, I do not mean to imply that Rousseau has become a Jesuit, but rather to show the religious quality of the text. Rousseau is adapting this language for his own ends.

His end is to give a description of a developed interior life without Christ. If one were to look either at the Gospels directly or at eighteenth-century handbooks of Christian piety, one would find many of the same things that Rousseau has claimed to accomplish laid out as the ideals to which Christians should aspire. Rousseau's interior life, his resignation, his simplicity, and his goodness all closely resemble the Christian ideal.

The difference lies in both the "unshakable principle" (*CW* 8:22; *Pl.* 1:1018) and the "principle fruit" (*CW* 8:24; *Pl.* 1:1020) of Rousseau's spirituality. The system's "unshakable principle" is innocence. By innocence, Rousseau means such good faith that any errors cannot be held against him. He has chosen what to believe "with all the maturity of judgment one can put into it," and so even if he were to fall into error, he is convinced that "we could not justly suffer the penalty, since we would not be at fault" (*CW* 8:22; *Pl.* 1:1018). The "principle fruit" is the vision and the certainty of "the great . . . compensation" for any ordeal undergone, in other words, recompense (*CW* 8:24; *Pl.* 1:1020). After he has outlined this system, Rousseau poses the following question: "Do not this deliberation and the conclusion I drew from it seem to have been dictated by Heaven itself to prepare me for the fate which awaited me and to enable me to endure it?" (*CW* 8:23; *Pl.* 1:1019) Rousseau specifies the fate of which he speaks. It is a violent one—"implacable persecutors, traitors silently entwined me with nets forged in the pits of Hell . . . dragged through the mud, . . . Thrust into the abyss of ignominy, enveloped in horrific darkness" (*CW* 8:23–24; *Pl.* 1:1019). It is the plot.

Christianity does not begin with human innocence. Nor, contrary to popular belief, does it begin with human guilt. It begins with the person of Jesus Christ and his death and resurrection. In the light of that person, forgiveness becomes visible. Thus, the fate that awaits Christians is not a violent one. Even if violence is practiced against them, Christianity allows them to give it another "spiritual" interpretation.

This spiritual interpretation allows the literal interpretation, the violence itself, to stand. It does not try to whitewash it, or wish it away. But neither does it stay there. The violence becomes an opportunity to forgive.

Still, the "unshakable principle" and the "principle fruit" of Rousseau's system and Christianity do not stand diametrically opposed to each other. If they did, then Christianity would simply be on the same level as the plot. Rousseau stands against Christianity, but Christianity does not stand against him. Christianity takes Rousseau's system and finds the good, the truth, in it, and allows that to be seen.

Rousseau's deliberation and conclusion, his system, comes out of and leads to violent expulsion. Accordingly, it simultaneously calls forth the awful fate he describes, while providing the means to endure it. By Rousseau's own words, it is not his system alone that "has been dictated by Heaven" (*CW* 8:23; *Pl.* 1:1019). The plot of his enemies is also "one of those secrets of Heaven" (*CW* 8:15; *Pl.* 1:1010). The plot and its response issue forth from one source—the sacred.

Rousseau has deliberated, reached a conclusion, and formed a system. But this system was not formed in isolation; it emerged simultaneously with the system that opposes it. His system is kept in place through its opposition to another sacred system. Even in being overwhelmed and in the knowledge of the objections to his system, Rousseau is always able to see the other system as well. He writes, "The whole present generation sees only errors and prejudices in the sentiments with which I alone nourish myself. It finds truth and evidence in the system *opposed to mine*" (*CW* 8:24; *Pl.* 1:1020; emphasis added). Further, Rousseau makes clear that he does not base his adherence to his system primarily on its inner coherence or his conviction that it is correct. He states quite plainly that his system has "insurmountable difficulties which are impossible for me to resolve" (*CW* 8:24; *Pl.* 1:1020). On the other hand, Rousseau sees his only other option, were he to abandon his system, as that of "adopting the doctrine of my persecutors" (*CW* 8:26; *Pl.* 1:1022). This is the tragedy of Rousseau. He could only see two options and they were always opposed to one another. He will not adopt the position of his enemies. His is the system of innocence and theirs is the system of wickedness. Better to run the risk that he might be "only a dupe, a victim, a martyr of a vain error" (*CW* 8:25; *Pl.* 1:1021). Anything is better than undoing the opposition between himself and the other.

This opposition is Rousseau's link to the other. The universality of the participation in the plot against him gives him peace. The system opposed to his is "the most iniquitous and absurd system an infernal mind could invent" (*CW* 8:72; *Pl.* 1:1077), and every member of his generation, "without exception," participates in it (*CW* 8:71; *Pl.* 1:1077). Rousseau describes the situation as follows:

> Then I began to see myself alone on earth and I understood that in relation to me my contemporaries were nothing more than automatons who acted only on impulse and whose action I could calculate only from the laws of motion. Whatever intention, whatever passion, I might have supposed in their souls would never have explained their conduct with respect to me in a way I could have understood. Thus their interior dispositions ceased to be of any importance to me. I no longer saw in them anything but randomly moved masses, destitute of all morality with respect to me. (*CW* 8:72; *Pl.* 1:1078)

For Rousseau, the ultimate outcome of structuring the world in terms of Jean-Jacques versus everyone else is that Jean-Jacques ends up "alone on earth," the very words with which he started the *Reveries*. He finds himself surrounded by humans who have ceased to be human. They are now a mob and they are intelligible in terms of the impersonal forces that moves the mob.

There is then a structure of two divine and yet opposed realities—Rousseau in his reveries and the others in their plot. Each of these divine beings demands a victim. Rousseau makes abundantly clear that he is the victim of the plot, and the humanity of the others is the victim of Rousseau as self-sufficient. It does not, however, end there. On a more profound level, each is a victim of itself. Rousseau is the victim of his own deification and he seems to be aware of that danger. In speaking of the "ring of Gyges" and the power it would give him, Rousseau finally decides to throw the ring away. His fear of the ring stems from his weakness against sexual temptations. He concludes, "Anyone whose power puts him above other men ought to be above human weakness; otherwise, this excess of strength will in effect serve only to put him below others and below what he himself would have been had he remained their equal" (*CW* 8:56; *Pl.* 1:1058). By putting himself above all others, Rousseau has, in effect, put himself below them. He becomes the victim of his own system. Insofar as people join together against Jean-Jacques, they are becoming the mob that he accuses them of being, and are so losing their humanity.

TRUTH, REVERIE, AND BOTANY

By viewing the text as structured according to two sides in violent conflict, two sides who first mutually expel one another, and then take on divine attributes and produce mutually opposed systems, a deeper insight emerges into Rousseau's notion of the truth in the "Fourth Walk," his notion of reverie, and, perhaps, even his practice of botany.

TRUTH

The mutual opposition of the systems dictates the truth each can admit. Rousseau, in his self-sufficient condition, finds that his commitment to truthfulness is "founded more on a feeling of uprightness and equity than on the reality of things" (*CW* 8:39; *Pl.* 1:1038). Reality takes a backseat to a feeling of uprightness against an accusation. Since the two systems mirror each other in such a way that each is the condemnation of the other, the evidence that they admit seems both the same and reversed. The evidence is the same in that it points *to the identical guilt* of each side. At the same time, the evidence is reversed in that it proves this identical guilt of *the other side*. Thus, for Rousseau, truth and lying are determined by whether the accusation is accurate or not.

The main question that the "Fourth Walk" pursues bears this interpretation. It is not, primarily, a question of an abstract definition of truth and falsehood. Rousseau begins the reverie by describing his feeling of being accused by a short dedication that Fr. Rozier wrote on the title page of a journal he sent to him: "*Vitam vero impendenti, Rosier.*" The dedication is a variation on the motto that Rousseau adopted from

Juvenal for himself: "to consecrate one's life to truth." Rousseau feels that the dedication has only the semblance of politeness. Rozier intends "to be cruelly ironic" (*CW* 8:28; *Pl.* 1:1024). It is "sarcasm" (*CW* 8:28; *Pl.* 1:1024). Rousseau resolves to examine himself on what he might have done to deserve this treatment. He begins his promenade as one accused.

Rousseau recalls then the "dreadful lie" of his youth and its "victim" (*CW* 8:28; *Pl.* 1:1024). This lie inspired Rousseau with a "horror for lying," and yet he is surprised to discover how often, and how gaily, he has lied since then. Rousseau formulates the problem of the reverie in this way:

> Moral instinct has always guided me well; my conscience has preserved its initial integrity; and even if it had been altered by bending to my interests, how—having preserved all its rectitude on those occasions when a man, forced by passions, may at least excuse himself for his weakness—does it lose its rectitude only with regard to indifferent matters for which there is not excuse for vice? I saw that the accuracy of the *judgment I had to make about myself* on this point depended upon a solution to this problem and, after having thoroughly examined it, this is the manner in which I managed to explain it to myself. (*CW* 8:29; *Pl.* 1:1025–26; emphasis added)

The whole reverie on truth and lying concerns an accusation made against Jean-Jacques and the judgment he feels he must render about himself.

This is the context that determines the kind of truth about which Rousseau is concerned. Truth can only be real, valuable, and worthwhile when someone's good name or reputation is at stake. Then, truth becomes sacred. Rousseau writes that the "holy truth his heart adores does not consist in indifferent deeds and useless names, but in faithfully rendering to each one what is owed in things which are genuinely his own, in imputing good or bad, in making retributions of honor and blame, praise and disapproval" (*CW* 8:34; *Pl.* 1:1032). Truth unconnected with accusation is indifferent, and lies in this realm are fiction. Outside the world of charge and counter-charge, there is no truth that matters.

REVERIE AND BOTANY

In reverie, Rousseau manages to escape from the passions that the "tumult of social life engenders" (*CW* 8:48; *Pl.* 1:1048). This is the negative description of reverie. Rousseau also gives a positive description of the state as follows: "These hours of solitude and meditation are the only ones in the day during which I am fully myself and for myself, without diversion, without obstacle, and during which I can truly claim to be what nature willed" (*CW* 8:9; *Pl.* 1:1002). "To be what nature willed" is a lapidary formulation of the highest goal of Rousseau's system. What does nature will him to be, and how does Rousseau describe it? Here again the feeling of self-sufficiency emerges. He says that when he is fully himself and for himself, he finds that he has nothing more to hope for or to fear in this world (cf. *CW* 8:6; *Pl.* 1:999). For Rousseau, nature has the same theoretical status as the principle of natural goodness. It is not simply given, it does not exist "out there." Rather, nature results from Rousseau being expelled and from his expelling others. Nature becomes a refuge in the face of expulsion.

Rousseau ends the "Seventh Walk" by saying that he is "attached to botany by the chain of accessory ideas" (*CW* 8:67; *Pl.* 1:1073). Two of these accessory ideas are remembering and forgetting. "Botany gathers together and recalls to my imagination all the ideas which gratify it more" (*CW* 8:67–68; *Pl.* 1:1073). The natural scenes and peacefulness are "retraced in [his] memory" (*CW* 8:67–68; *Pl.* 1:1073). At least one reason for the botany is to make sure that his indignation over the ignominy and insults does not embitter him against humans (Cf. *CW* 8:62; *Pl.* 1:1066).

Rousseau wants to forget and be forgotten. Walks and botany provide images to replace those that his memory pushes away. It is a double movement. Rousseau finds pleasure in escaping his persecutors by getting into the woods, and then the "pleasure of going into an uninhabited area to seek new plants blots out" that former pleasure (*CW* 8:65; *Pl.* 1:1070). The pleasure of expulsion is itself expelled.

But Rousseau also wants to remember. An essential element in the reverie is memory. Botany, especially the herbarium, plays a special role here. "All my life I will remember a plant excursion," begins one such story (*CW* 8:65; *Pl.* 1:1070). And yet, precisely in the middle of this story, Rousseau also notes, "Dominated by the strong impression of the surrounding objects, I forgot botany and plants" (*CW* 8:66; *Pl.* 1:1071). The following statement succinctly expresses the role of botany in both forgetting and remembering: "Botany makes me forget men's persecutions, their hatred, scorn, insults, and all the evils with which they have repaid my tender and sincere attachment for them. . . . It recalls to me both my youth and my innocent pleasures" (*CW* 8:68; *Pl.* 1:1073).

Thus, nature is not some objective fact, but is rather deeply connected with Rousseau's memory and forgetfulness. For Rousseau, reverie, promenades, and botany are the ways that he remembers and forgets. He writes,

> I clamber up rocks and mountains, I go deep into vales and woods in order to slip away, as much as possible, from the memory of men and from the attacks of the wicked. It seems to me that in the shade of a forest I am as forgotten, free, and peaceful as though I had no more enemies or that the foliage of the woods must keep me from their attacks just as it removes them from my memory; and in my foolishness I imagine that by not thinking about them, they will not think about me (*CW* 8:65; *Pl.* 1:1070).

Rousseau cannot afford to recall evil, either his own or that of others. All too soon, he would be simply overwhelmed. He has no experience, as is clear from his recollection of the lie that makes a victim out of Marion, of remembering a sin as forgiven. Without this realm of grace, then nature becomes the place of escape, and nature wills that one simply forget both evils done and evils endured to concentrate on finding a "refuge where persecutors will not unearth" him. Rousseau's unusual use of the word "unearth [*disinter*]" points to the kind of refuge that nature has become. It is a tomb; it is being "tranquil at the bottom of the abyss" (*CW* 8:6; *Pl.* 1:999).

CONCLUSION

Rousseau's character, his person, was formed by something besides pure nature. His soul received its form from a human being, Mme de Warens. He tells the reader,

"This first moment of encounter determined my whole life and by an inevitable chain of events shaped the destiny of the rest of my days" (*CW* 8:89; *Pl.* 1:1098). He repeats a few sentences later that his return to her "determined [his] fate" (*CW* 8:89; *Pl.* 1:1098). Rousseau recalls the brief time that he was with her as the time in which, in his words, "I was myself, fully, without admixture and without obstacle, and when I can say that I genuinely lived" (*CW* 8:89; *Pl.* 1:1098–99). That is, he lived then as he was able to live later in the hours of solitude and meditation, those hours in which he was "what nature willed" (*CW* 8:9; *Pl.* 1:1002). Somehow in Rousseau's youth, Mme de Warens was able to play the role that nature was to play later in Rousseau's life. She was, for this brief period, the transcendent object of Rousseau's existence. He says, "I lived only in and for her" (*CW* 8:89; *Pl.* 1:1098).

Rousseau explains what he means by saying, "I lived." This short period of time gave him a certainty about himself that he might have otherwise lacked. This is how he describes himself: "For, weak and without resistance all the rest of my life, I have been so troubled, tossed about, plagued by the passions of others that, almost passive in such a stormy life, I would have difficulty in unraveling what there is of my own in my own conduct" (*CW* 8:89; *Pl.* 1:1099). Rousseau goes on to say that the essential quality of those few years was that "[he] did what [he] wanted to do, [he] was what [he] wanted to be" (*CW* 8:90; *Pl.* 1:1099). This makes it sound as if Rousseau achieved a high degree of autonomy, but he prefaces this statement with its metaphysical condition: he was "loved by a woman full of desire to please" (*CW* 8:89; *Pl.* 1:1099). Rousseau ceased to be tossed about, ceased to be "plagued by the passions of others," when he found the one in whom and for whom he could live (*CW* 8:89; *Pl.* 1:1099). The fullness of her desire to please filled him. He was no longer plagued because it was this single person's desire he could now imitate. The very point that Rousseau felt that he could unravel what was his own in his conduct, and felt that he did what he wanted to do and was who he wanted to be, was a time of living the desire of another. This was a time during which he worshiped a woman and bowed before the other. The scandal of being plagued by the passions of others gave way to the idolatry of romantic love. Rousseau had found peace.

This last case of divinity raises the question of whether this idol, too, demands sacrifice. All too quickly, this could become an exercise in assigning blame about who was responsible for ending the relationship. Rousseau protests, "Ah! if I had sufficed for her heart as she sufficed for mine, what peaceful and delightful days we might have spent together" (*CW* 8:89; *Pl.* 1:1098). But this is not the question I wish to pursue. Rousseau himself gives some clues in the text about what was offered on that Palm Sunday by the act of worship that determined the rest of his life.

Rousseau tells that in his relationship with Mme de Warens, he "saw this delicious but fleeting state in which love and innocence inhabit the same heart prolonged . . . for a long time" (*CW* 8:89; *Pl.* 1:1098). He makes it clear that this state ended with the consummation of their relationship. After that, love and innocence no longer inhabited the same heart. The reader's first inclination is to assume that innocence has been lost. But it is clear from all Rousseau's writing in general, and from the *Reveries* in particular, that innocence has never left his heart. This leaves only one option: love was sacrificed. Given the whole of the text of the *Reveries*, this latter interpretation makes much more sense. The end of Rousseau's life is marked by the inability to do good. No charity is possible. In part, he blames this on the plot, which makes all of reality into a snare. But in the "Sixth Walk," he also makes clear that of his own, he often refuses to do good because from the "first good deed . . . were forged chains of subsequent liabilities I had not foreseen and whose yoke I could no longer shake off" (*CW* 8:50; *Pl.* 1:1051). This is the ultimate result of his adoration of Mme de Warens.

The "Sixth Walk" tells the story of Rousseau's encounter with a small handicapped boy. The boy begs from him and chatters a bit, and Rousseau kindly gives him a coin. At some point, without consciously thinking about it, Rousseau changes his route so that his walk no longer takes him by the boy. The chatter has become annoying and Rousseau is feeling the chain of duty beginning to form. He is in danger of becoming the boy's benefactor, and this would give the boy a claim on his charity. More generally, Rousseau does not want anyone to have an expectation of receiving something from him. Constraint takes away his desires. "After so many sad experiences, I have learned to anticipate the consequences of my first constant impulses and I have often abstained from a good action I had the desire and the power to do, frightened of the subjection I would submit myself to afterward if I yielded to it without reflection" (*CW* 8:52; *Pl.* 1:1054). Rousseau abstains from good. And yet, he signals to the reader that he understands well the price that he pays for the detour that he makes. In order to avoid meeting the "lame little boy," Rousseau could not pass through "*la barriére d'enfer*," the exit from Hell (*CW* 8:49; *Pl.* 1:1050).

PART V

CONCLUSION

FORGIVING ROUSSEAU

Throughout this work, I have showed how interpreting Rousseau's writings in the light of scandal helps increase understanding of each work's inner unity as well as its interconnectedness with the other works. I would like to draw together some of the aspects of that interconnectedness in order to strengthen my claim that this approach reveals Rousseau's system most clearly.

Rousseau made various remarks about his system. First, in one of his autobiographical "Letters to Malesherbes" he writes that the system consists primarily in the three writings, the *Discourse on the Sciences and Arts*, the *Discourse on the Origin of Inequality*, and *Emile*. Together, he says, they form "the same whole" (*CW* 5:575; *Pl.* 1:1136). Second, in the *Dialogues* the Frenchman remarks that he has found that the systematic order of these writings is the reverse of their order of publication.

With regard to the first point, I maintain that these three writings, *Emile*, the *Discourse on Inequality*, and the *Discourse on the Sciences and the Arts*, answer, respectively, the three questions any philosophical anthropology has to answer: Who are we? Where did we come from? What are we to do? They form the "same whole" in the sense that if the reader sufficiently understands the implications of the answer to any one of these questions, she will be able to answer the other two. To understand the second point more deeply, I would like to begin by explaining the relationship between the parts, starting with that which is easier: the relationship between the two *Discourses*.

One way to understand the *Second Discourse* is to consider the way that it functions as an origin. One of the most surprising ways in which it realizes this function can be formulated paradoxically as follows: the *Second Discourse* is the origin of the *First Discourse*.[1] Rousseau states quite clearly in his unpublished *Preface to a Second Letter to Bordes* that the question treated in the *First Discourse* is "only a corollary" of "a System that is true but distressing" (*CW* 2:184; *Pl.* 3:106). Further, he tells in the *Confessions* that he had the occasion to develop the principles of his system "completely in a work of greatest importance" (*CW* 5:326; *Pl.* 1:388). This work is, of course, the *Second Discourse*. Thus, the relationship between the *First Discourse* and the *Second Discourse* is best understood as the relationship between a work in which systematic principles have been completely developed and a corollary or a treatment of a proposition that follows without need of separate proof. The order of their appearance and writing is the reverse of what one would normally expect. The *First Discourse* logically depends upon the *Second*. It presumes a proof that does not yet exist.

Still, one might think that the only reason that the *First Discourse* appeared before the *Second Discourse* was due to the accidents of history. But Rousseau himself gives a further indication of the necessity of their appearing in reverse order: scandal.

> If the Discourse of Dijon alone excited so many murmurs and caused so much scandal, what would have happened if I had from the first instant developed the entire extent of a System that is true but distressing, of which the question treated in this Discourse is only a Corollary? A declared enemy of the violence of the wicked, I would at the very least have passed for the enemy of public tranquility; and if the zealots of the opposite party had not labored charitably to ruin me for the greater glory of philosophy, it is at least beyond doubt that, discussing an unknown man, they would easily have succeeded in turning to ridicule the work and its author, and that beginning by ridiculing my System, this method validated by much experience would have dispensed them from the inconvenient effort of examining my proofs. (*CW* 2:184; *Pl.* 3:106)

Scandal is not only the ground of Rousseau's system, but it is also a controlling factor in the way the system is formulated; it affects its expression. The whole system is scandalous to the point of being able to cause public unrest. Avoiding this determines how it will be made known. The origin of the system is scandal, and it itself is also scandalous and therefore can only be made known in a careful manner. In this sense, the unwritten *Second Discourse* engenders the *First Discourse* to prepare its own way.

The *Second Discourse* could be written because a public body, once again the Academy of Dijon, had had the courage to pose "this great question": "*Quelle est la source de l'inégalité parmi les hommes, et si elle est autorisée pa la loi naturelle?* [What is the source of the inequality among humans and whether it is authorized by natural law]" (*CW* 5:326; *Pl.* 1:388).[2] This is the historical occasion for the writing of the *Second Discourse*. Chapter 9 examined in detail the historical occasion of the *First Discourse*. The shattering event on the road to Vincennes gave birth, however, to more than the "Prosopopoeia of Fabricius" and the *First Discourse*. There were "crowds of great truths," and what he was able to retain from these truths has been "weakly scattered about in . . . [his] three principle writings, namely that first discourse, the one on inequality, and the treatise on education, which three works are inseparable and together form the same whole" (*CW* 5:575; *Pl.* 1:1136).

Given this, the *Second Discourse* can easily be view as being in direct continuity with the *First Discourse*, answering objections that were raised in connection with the former. In the *First Discourse*, Rousseau has already seen inequality as the basis of all other evils: "What brings about all these abuses if not the disastrous inequality introduced among men by the distinction of talents and the debasement of virtues" (*CW* 2:18; *Pl.* 3:25). Still, the *First Discourse* was often criticized during the Controversy precisely on this point: it did not make clear the proper order of cause and effect regarding the relationship between the arts, sciences, and depravity.

Rousseau's thought on this point remained unclear and was often criticized, since he seemed, on the one hand, to maintain that the arts and sciences corrupted humans, and on the other, that the origin of the arts and sciences was vice.[3] In the course of the Controversy, he was forced to clarify his thought. Already in the *Reply by the King of Poland*, the following criticism can be read:

> How many incontestable testimonies, august monuments, immortal works there are by which history attests that the sciences contributed everywhere to the happiness of men, the glory of empires, the triumph of virtue.
>
> No, it is not from the sciences, but from the bosom of wealth that softness and luxury have always been born (*CW* 2:33–34; Launay, 2:74).

Did the arts and sciences themselves actually cause depravity, or was it rather depravity itself that ruined the arts and sciences? Rousseau replies in the following manner: "This is how I would arrange the genealogy. The first source of evil is inequality. From inequality comes wealth, for those words poor and rich are relative, and everywhere that men are equal, there are neither rich nor poor. From wealth are born luxury and idleness. From luxury come the fine Arts and from idleness the Sciences" (*CW* 2:48; *Pl.* 3:49–50). Rousseau's genealogy is clearer here, if still incomplete, for the question it raises is the question that the Academy will pose: whence the inequality?

Still, Rousseau gives here an important indication of the direction his investigation will take. Inequality is fundamental and somehow coeval with language. It is words that create the reality of wealth; the words "rich" and "poor" are not inscribed in nature. Accordingly, wealth does not create inequality as a doctrinaire socialist might have it. To simply divide the pie differently, more equitably, will not make humans equal. The causality flows in the reverse direction. The creation of a language of relations is the creation of "wealth" and "poverty." This line of thought is what Rousseau will develop in the *Second Discourse*. As Patrick Coleman puts it, "The originality of Rousseau's analysis [in the *Second Discourse*] lay in the way he demonstrated how inequality functioned, not only in the course of human history, but in the genesis of the conceptual vocabulary that made social communication possible and in turn could justify social inequality."[4] Before language, one human might have had more than another without this being a form of "wealth" that made him "rich" and at the same time made someone else "poor." For Rousseau, it would be possible to imagine a world in which possessing more did not make humans unequal, anymore than being taller made them unequal. But to do this, one would need a new language.

Viewing the *Second Discourse* as the origin of the *First* gives the reader a way of comprehending their similarities and differences. It is not difficult to accept a certain unity of thought and a common intention in the two works, and most commentators easily join them together as they pass from the one to the other in a seamless sort of way. And yet, the differences are to be noted. If the general themes of the two *Discourses* are not so very apart, still, on a stylistic level, the two works sometimes seem as if they could have come from two different hands. Their tones are as different as night and day. The prophetic attempt to denounce evil is mostly absent from the *Second Discourse* and is replaced with a much more scientific tone. Starobinski describes the *First Discourse* with these words: "Suffused with pathos, the antithesis of appearance and reality gives the [*First*] *Discourse* its dramatic tension. What had been merely a well-worn figure of rhetoric now expresses a pain, a rending of the soul."[5] The *Second Discourse* is not suffused with pathos, and it is not a rending of the soul.

Instead, the *Second Discourse* is a calling into being. It is not that this calling into being is absent from the *First Discourse*, or, for that matter, from the "Prosopopoeia." In fact, this is the deepest level of their unity. The effect of the experience of scandal was a text in which Rousseau calls to life the dead Fabricius. Rousseau makes the ontological import of this rhetorical figure clear when he states, "It was not in vain that I called up the shade of Fabricius" (*CW* 2:11; *Pl.* 3:15). Rousseau restores Fabricius to life and questions him. He "calls" Fabricius by name and then has Fabricius call upon his fellow Romans. "Madmen (*Insensés*)" (*CW* 2:11; *Pl.* 3:14) is the vocative he uses. Such is the central vision of the Prosopopoeia, as well as the whole of the *First Discourse*, and, indeed, the system that results from the experience of scandal—there is a madness afoot.

When Rousseau recalls, in his *Confessions*, the genesis of the *Second Discourse*, he relates how he traveled to St. Germaine and how, on his walks, he entered deep into the forest. He continues, "I sought, I found the image of the first times whose history I proudly traced; I made a clean sweep of the petty falsehoods of men, I dared to strip naked their nature, to follow the progress of time and things that have disfigured it, and comparing the man of man with the natural man, to show them the genuine source of his miseries in his pretended perfections" (*CW* 5:326; *Pl.* 1:388). There, he saw anew the vision of Vincennes, the "contradictions of the social system" (*CW* 5:575; *Pl.* 1:1136). Rousseau's soul raised itself close to the divinity. In the imaginary address to his fellows, the first word he puts into his own mouth is the very word that he has Fabricius use: Madmen (*Insensés*). He continues, "Learn that all your ills come to you from yourselves" (*CW* 5:326; *Pl.* 1:389). It is the same vision at the base of each of these *Discourses*.

The *First Discourse* remains, in spite of its very practical proposal, a stinging denunciation of the split between appearance and reality. The *Second Discourse* examines how this split is possible, the way in which it begins. And it is here that the enormity of the choice that Rousseau has made begins to make itself felt. In rejecting being made like Christ crucified and electing to cause scandal, Rousseau will have to offer an alternative to Christianity. Rousseau does not immediately develop an alternative account of salvation. Rather, Rousseau begins by contesting the prevalent account of origins. In so doing, the question gets raised, has Rousseau then ceased to scandalize? The answer must be "no." Certainly, the *Second Discourse* is not the rhetorical blast that the *First Discourse* is. Instead, it is a carefully modulated attempt to lead the reader into scandal. Rousseau is going to indirectly scandalize the reader or invite the reader to share in his scandal.

In his study on the notion of origin in the tragedies of Pierre Corneille, entitled *The Tragedy of Origins*, John D. Lyon offers some pertinent reflections on the import of offering an account of origins in seventeenth-century France. I quote at length:

> There were enormous interests at stake in any investigation of origins. In a society that conveyed nobility, privilege, and power according to heredity, both the origin of a person and the origin of the family as a whole were paramount. Other institutions besides

the family . . . claimed foundations in a distant past. Challenges to these institutions, notably from religious reformers, often took the form of challenging the account of origin that had been given. This variant of the humanist discovery of the past has the typical humanist pattern of the recovery of something lost and of a break with the immediate past, judged as fallen and in rupture with the origin, and a revalorization of the earlier, "true" past.[6]

With Rousseau, all this is further radicalized. The institutions being challenged by Rousseau are the most basic institutions of European culture, and the break is not simply with the immediate past and its account of origins, but also includes an attempt to replace the ancient account of origins—the Jewish and Christian Scriptures.

The relationship between *Emile* and the *Second Discourse* is different from that between the two *Discourses*. Rousseau states that he was able, in the *Second Discourse*, to develop his principles "completely" (*CW* 5:326; *Pl.* 1:388). So it cannot be that this *Discourse* would depend upon some other principles in *Emile*. Still, there is a sense that it does. James Alison tells us that, theologically speaking, "it is from an understanding of the end, or purpose, of the act [of creation] that its beginnings are understood."[7] To give some formulation, not necessarily of creation, but of the original event by which humans became humans, depends on an understanding of the end or purpose of the human race. Alison goes on to point out, in agreement with Eric Gans, that there is no other access to any originary, foundational event except through a purely hypothetical construct. Humans cannot remember that which gave rise to memory. Our beginnings are shrouded in darkness. Still, humans can construct an account of how things began based upon the present structure of consciousness. "This construct is not a piece of original knowledge about what has happened, which has somehow mysteriously been maintained alive by some form of traditional transmission, for, by definition, that which constitutes and structures consciousness and which was not, at the time, part of a human representational order is not something of which the newly conscious humans can be conscious. Rather, the construct is an a posteriori approach in the light of what we know now."[8] *Emile* represents the light of what Rousseau knows now, and it is this light that gave him access to construct the origins of the human. I do not need to belabor the point that this light is not the light of the Cross; it is not the light of forgiveness, and so Rousseau had no access to knowledge of original sin.

For Rousseau, the place of the human is the victim (*Emile*) and the event is an accident (*Second Discourse*). Because Christians think that human origins are revealed in Christ, they understand that foundational event to be one in which the birth of human awareness is the occultation of something.[9] Because Rousseau thinks that human origins are revealed in Emile/Jean-Jacques/himself, he sees the foundational event to be one in which the birth of human awareness is a "fatal accident" or a happening in which God originally left humankind to itself (*CW* 3:48; *Pl.* 3:171).

In this way, it is not that the *Discourse on Inequality* explains why Emile's education has to be carried out in the way it is presented in the novel. Rather, Rousseau's anthropological position in *Emile*, that the place of the human is the place of the victim, demands a story of origins in which the cause of the human predicament is a "fatal accident." In a paradoxical fashion, if the *Discourse on Inequality* assigned responsibility for human devolution to anything other than an accident, then the tutor of Emile would be revealed as a victimizer and not simply Emile's covictim.

ROUSSEAU AND CHRISTIANITY

Rousseau claimed to be a Christian, at the same time he made clear that he did not accept many of Christianity's central dogmas. Generally speaking, one finds two reactions to this double reality. The interpreter could hold that Rousseau was not a Christian and claimed this simply because of the society in which he lived, that is, out of fear of persecution by ecclesiastical or civil authorities. This interpretation is hard to accept, given the way Rousseau boldly proclaimed so many other "dangerous" truths. He signed his works; he attached his name. This interpretation implies that he did not want to cause scandal.

The other interpretation allows Rousseau's claims to stand and holds that he is correct about what Christianity is. That is, it is the religion of the heart that he describes, without the dogma, without the structures of authority. This would be a Christianity that does not cause scandal.

My position is that Rousseau is telling the truth when he claims to be a Christian, and he makes that claim because he has grasped the absolute centrality of the victim. As I have tried to make clear throughout the book, Rousseau cannot live with Christianity and he cannot live without it. With Christianity, Rousseau would have to accept forgiveness, which includes a moment of admission to one's own complicity in victimizing. He could no longer claim the innocence that he sees as essential to his identity. Without Christianity, it is better that one man die for the people than that the whole nation perishes.

WHY IS THIS IMPORTANT?

This book is a philosophical study of Rousseau's thought. It presents interpretations that are based on a close reading of the texts, and offers these interpretations to its readers in the hope that they will deepen their understanding of Rousseau, but also with the knowledge that the readings themselves will be subjected to critical analysis. I welcome that. I am prepared to learn from the criticism where appropriate and to answer it with counterarguments when I deem it necessary.

Still, there was a claim, made at the very beginning and sustained on each page of the work, that the light of the Cross makes some realities accessible that otherwise remain in darkness. I have claimed that Rousseau rejected that light and, therefore, claimed that I have not. Again, this does not mean that I think that my arguments are "above" or "outside" of rational criticism. The usual rules of rational discourse apply.

The problem lies in another direction. I also claim at the beginning of the book that Rousseau seeks a "forgiving" reader, and that I would try to be that reader. Here, at the end, I am brought to the realization that I am seeking the same thing for myself.

The problem is the following: I believe that not just the human community, but human rationality itself is constituted through the expulsion of the victim. The light that salvation brings redeems this rationality, but like the Cross itself, it has to do it by sharing in the same violent situation it is bringing to end. This makes for an inherent ambiguity. People can continue to interpret Christianity as a religion that promises violent retribution against evildoers instead of a religion that presents a God who "causes His sun to rise on the evil and the good, and sends rain on the righteous and the unrighteous" (Matt 5:44).

In an analogous way, a reader can interpret my work as yet another accusation against Rousseau. One could read it as accusing him of misunderstanding the doctrine of original sin and refusing the salvation offered to him. My work also appears to accuse him of causing scandal. Further, there are other accusations made. I claim that the Archbishop of Paris understands the doctrine as little as Rousseau. I also appear to accuse various commentators of falling into the same kind of logic of accusation as Rousseau, and so on. Of course, by the same token, I fall into that logic also.

But this would be to misread me. If I am arguing for forgiveness, then, yes, the sin will have to appear, but it will appear only as it is passing out of existence. What makes it appear is the new creation coming into existence—the illuminating source now appearing at the heart of Rousseau's system. If I am correct in my interpretation that Rousseau took scandal at the salvation offered in Christ, then Christ stands in the center of Rousseau's thought. That he stands there rejected, I do not deny—but for whom is that not in some sense true? The only true Christ is the crucified one. The deep grace of Rousseau's writing, the new interpretation it receives here, is that it succeeds in being a luminous testimony to the centrality of the one whom it has rejected. Why is Rousseau's thought so significant, why is it so central? Because behind every page, every work, and behind the whole system stands Christ crucified. This is the truly amazing thing—Rousseau can lead a reader to Christ. More than that, in his muted request for forgiveness, when he writes, "I foresee that I will not easily be forgiven for the side I have dared to take," Rousseau avers that on some level, he wants to lead the reader there (*CW* 2:3; *Pl.* 3:3).

That there is both beauty and power in Rousseau's writings has never been in dispute. This beauty and power is again rooted in Christ. Rousseau's thought not only continually circles around this forgiving figure, but it also points toward it.

John the Baptist also pointed toward Him, and Christ addressed to him the words, "Blessed is the one who does not take scandal at me" (Matt 11:6). The comparison between John the Baptist and Jean-Jacques Rousseau is not arbitrary. Rousseau shares John's prophetic stance. No one in his age was clearer in denouncing its evils. No one saw as acutely the way pride infects precisely the highest human accomplishments. And yet, all this vision was blind to the possibility of redemption.

In a sense, contrary to what I stated about original sin in the first chapter, Rousseau sees the sin with great clarity without seeing the redemption. But ultimately, this is not to really see the sin. Thus, Rousseau develops incredible critiques of society, of the theater, and of amour-propre that lead nowhere. In fact, they only serve to spread Rousseau's outrage and thus lead to consequences that are as bad as the evils that he denounces. In a sense, he propagates the very vices against which he protests.

Let that stop here. There need be no more outrage against Rousseau. And yet precisely this brings up the paradoxical problem of our age: there is no more outrage against Rousseau. No Christian has raised his or her voice against him since Jacque

Maritain. Deconstructionists find Rousseau's logic to be exemplary. The educational techniques of *Emile*, the revelation of sexual depravity in the *Confessions*, and the claim that he is like God in the *Reveries* no longer seem to scandalize, and this might appear to be a good thing. Still, if the reader is incapable of scandal at Rousseau, then he or she is equally incapable of forgiving him. So again, my hope is that this book can help the reader "annul" his or her scandal at Rousseau and find his or her way to Christ through him.

Notes

CHAPTER 1

1. Robert J. Ellrich, *Rousseau and His Reader: The Rhetorical Situation of the Major Works* (Chapel Hill: University of North Carolina Press, 1969). In *Rousseau and His Reader*, Ellrich sees this sentence as evidence of Rousseau's "fundamental posture in the work, his presentation of himself to the reader as the virtuous outsider" (28).
2. I use "Controversy" with a capital letter here as a technical term to refer to those writings by Rousseau and his "opponents" that followed the publication of the *First Discourse*. The Controversy lasted until the publication of *Discourse on the Origin of Inequality* (1755).
3. All of these quotes are taken from the entries, "**Scandale**" and "**Scandaleux,**" in *The Encyclopedia of Diderot & d'Alembert*, trans. Jason Kusnicki, vol. 14 (Ann Arbor: Scholarly Publishing Office of the University of Michigan Library, 2002), 741, available at http://quod.lib.umich.edu/d/did/. Cf. *Encyclopédie ou dictionnaire raisonné des sciences, des arts et des métiers, Paris, Neuchâtel, 1751–1765*.
4. *The Encyclopedia of Diderot & d'Alembert* s.v. "scandale."
5. *Dictionnaire de l'Académie française* (first edition, 1694) s.v. "scandale," available at http://colet.uchicago.edu/cgi-bin/dico1look.pl?strippedhw=scandale&dicoid=ACAD1694.
6. Gouhier has some very enlightening reflections on Rousseau's rejection of this dogma in Henri Gaston Gouhier, *Les méditations métaphysiques de Jean-Jacques Rousseau* (Paris: J. Vrin, 1970). He sees it has Rousseau's "troisième refus fondamental," the other two being the historical revelation and the idea of church that would interpret that revelation (37).
7. Christophe de Beaumont quotes this sentence as a proof text (*CW* 9:4).
8. A translation of Beaumont's Pastoral Letter is conveniently printed in the *Collected Works*. The original French text is available in Rousseau, *œuvres complètes*, vol. 3, ed. Michel Launay (Paris: Editions du Seuil, 1977).
9. Ernst Cassirer, *The Question of Jean-Jacques Rousseau,* 2nd ed., ed. Peter Gay (New Haven, CT: Yale University Press, 1989), 74.
10. The full title is *Jean-Jacques Rousseau, Citoyen de Genève, à Christophe de Beaumont, Archevêque de Paris, Duc de St. Cloud, Pair de France, Commandeur de l'ordre du St. Esprit,, Proviseur de Sorbonne, etc.* (Amsterdam: Marc Rey, 1763). For the significance of Rousseau naming himself in the title, or rather making his name a title, see Christopher Kelly, *Rousseau as Author: Consecrating One's Life to the Truth* (Chicago: University of Chicago Press, 2003), 16–19.
11. My discussion of this misconception is based upon the interpretation of the dogma of original sin in James Alison, *The Joy of Being Wrong: Original Sin through Easter Eyes* (New York: Crossroad, 1998). Hereafter cited as *Joy*.

12. Alison explains the "foundational mentality" as the "need to shore up identity, to justify oneself . . . in the ordinary human way of seeking a fundamental (foundational) cause for things. . . . The foundational mentality has managed to turn original sin into a way of accounting for our present evil by blaming someone: Adam or, sometimes, the serpent" (*Joy*, 170).

13. Again, as Alison so nicely puts it, "original sin was discovered as it became possible to leave it" (*Joy*, 221).

14. In commenting on Rousseau's statement in the "Preface to *Narcissus*," in which Rousseau claims to have showed "that all these vices do not belong so much to man as to man poorly governed," J. H. Broome sees this as Rousseau's "defence against the doctrine of original sin." See J. H. Broome, *Rousseau: A Study of his Thought* (New York: Barnes and Noble, 1963), 32. This understanding of the doctrine has to be called into question.

15. For a somewhat different reading of the argument between Rousseau and Beaumont that concentrates more on the historical situation, see André Ravier, "Le Dieu de Rousseau et le Christianisme," *Archives de Philosophie* 41, no. 1 (1978): 408–11.

16. I must part ways with Arthur Melzer in his contention that Rousseau, "going beyond Enlightenment efforts to 'manage' religion found in Locke, Hume, Voltaire, and others, . . . made an earnest effort to revive and reinvigorate Christianity, if in a new, more politically salutary form" (344). Rousseau is not reviving Christianity. He does not trust in the power of forgiveness to form a society, yet he will not simply go back to the unadorned violence that founded pagan society. The quote is taken from Arthur M Melzer, "The Origin of the Counter-Enlightenment: Rousseau and the New Religion of Sincerity," *American Political Science Review* 90, no. 2 (1996): 344–60.

17. I do not wish to appear to be nitpicking when I criticize Richard Boyd's otherwise excellent article, "Pity's Pathologies Portrayed," for one time using the expression "forgiving society" in reference to what pity may or may not be able to accomplish. The reason I point this out is that Rousseau never aimed toward a forgiving society. Forgiveness is totally absent from his world. Richard Boyd, "Pity's Pathologies Portrayed: Rousseau and the Limits of Democratic Compassion," *Political Theory* 32, no. 4 (2004): 519–46.

18. One could use the language of grace here, and then one would have to concur with Robert Derathe's conclusion that Rousseau's religion "ne faite aucune place à la grace [has no place of grace]." "Jean-Jacques Rousseau et le Christianisme" (400).

19. Christopher Kelly, *Rousseau's Exemplary Life: The Confessions as Political Philosophy* (Ithaca, NY: Cornell University Press, 1987), 243.

20. Ibid.

21. Ibid., 245.

22. Ibid., 246.

23. Ibid., 244.

24. Pierre Burgelin writes the following concerning *Julie*: "A certains égards, l'histoire de Julie est celle d'une conversion. . . . Elle devient vraiment un être nouveau. Mais cette conversion n'implique en rien ce que les spirituels chrétiens appellent sentiment du péché, c'est-à-dire d'offense à Dieu (où est ici la loi divine?), ni au sentiment du pardon." Pierre Burgelin, *Jean-Jacques Rousseau et la religion de Genève* (Geneva: Labor et Fides, 1962), 45.

25. The very fine and balanced article by Gustav Lanson, "L'unité de la pensée de Jean-Jacques Rousseau," was written as a corrective to three intemperate interpretations by Faquet, Lemaître, and Espinas, all of whom attacked Rousseau as being incoherent. His conclusion is worth quoting: "Voilà, comment m'apparaît l'oeuvre de Rousseau: très diverse, tumultueuse, agitée de toute sorte de fluctuations, et pourtant, à partir d'un

certain moment, continue et constante en son esprit dans ses directions successives."
Gustave Lanson, "L'unité de la pensée de Jean-Jacques Rousseau," *Annales de la Société Jean-Jacques Rousseau* 8 (1912): 28. Lanson does not ever use the concept of scandal, but it does seem that his explanation for the text that causes readers to react so violently can be reconciled with my interpretation. Robert Derathé sees Rousseau as so taken by a vision of civic virtue that it makes him aware of the natural goodness that remains unchanged at the bottom of the human heart. Derathé argues that Rousseau's thought is "double," but not contradictory. Robert Derathé, "L'unité de la pensée de Jean-Jacques Rousseau," in *Jean-Jacques Rousseau* (Neuchâtel: Editions de la Baconnière Switzerland, 1962), 218. By "double," Derathé means that Rousseau offers the choice between two options, that of natural man in a domestic society, or that of a "denatured" citizen in a political society modeled on the *Social Contract.*

26. Arthur M. Melzer, *The Natural Goodness of Man: On the System of Rousseau's Thought* (Chicago: University of Chicago Press, 1990), 4.

27. Ibid., 6.

28. Ibid., 7.

29. Ibid.

30. Ibid.; emphasis original.

31. Ibid.

32. Ibid., 9; emphasis original.

33. Ibid.

34. Ibid.

35. Ibid.

36. *Merriam Webster's Collegiate Dictionary*, 11th ed., s.v. "Desultory."

37. Melzer, *Natural Goodness*, 12.

38. In his *Rousseau's Exemplary Life: The* Confessions *as Political Philosophy*, Christopher Kelly touches on the religious nature of Rousseau's thought through a careful delineation of Rousseau's comparisons between Cato, Socrates, and Jesus, as well as the comparison between each of these figures and himself. But, as Kelly sees, this comparison between figures is not enough. He cannot avoid looking at Rousseau's "understanding of the true message of Christianity" (66). The context for Jesus' message is the impossibility of civic virtue, and the exemplary life of civic virtue is not found in any of the figures named so far, rather, it is the elder Brutus who put his children to death. Kelly comments, "This sort of action is precluded by Jesus' gentleness. Christianity embraces self-sacrifice, but it leaves sacrifices of sons to God the Father" (66). More important, it seems to me, is the fact that Christianity does not allow for self-sacrifice and the sacrifice of others to be equated. Kelly is simply explicating Rousseau's position here, but one cannot simply allow to pass without comment the thought that for Jesus, Brutus represents a no longer attainable ideal, and that even for depraved Christianity, he represents a "splendid vice" (66). Rather, it needs to keep clearly in mind that Jesus came to overturn the thinking of Brutus and those who would hold them up as virtuous. Such is the primary anthropological contribution of the Judeo-Christian tradition. Any attempt to turn back from this should be resisted. Kelly sees that Brutus's murders have a purpose, and the purpose is "inspiring an active spirit of sacrifice for the community," but Kelly fails to fully register that Christian self-sacrifice unmasks this justification of murder through a higher purpose by destroying the myth that justifies it.

39. John McManners, "The Religion of Rousseau," *The Journal of Religious History* 5 (1969): 349.

40. Jacques Maritain, *Three Reformers: Luther—Descartes—Rousseau*, new ed. (London: Sheed and Ward, 1944), 160.

41. In the context of his excellent study, *The Religious Dimension in Hegel's Thought* Emil Fackenheim notes that "right- and left-wing interpretations are often more profound and exciting than mediocre attempts at impartial exposition" Emil L. Fackenheim, *The Religious Dimension in Hegel's Thought* (Bloomington: Indiana University Press, 1968), 76n. I mention this because my choice of these two commentators, while not being right or left wing, are also not mediocre attempts at impartial exposition. I am indebted to them both.

42. Maritain, *Three Reformers*, 141.

43. Ibid., 141. One can sometimes feel that Maritain overshoots his mark in his attempt to discredit Rousseau's claim to being a Christian. In *La famille et la jeunesse de J.-J. Rousseau*, Eugene Ritter is more measured and perhaps more insightful in his remark that, in spite of fifteen years of association with Catholics, attending their liturgies, and so on, Rousseau did not have "*l'imagination catholique.*" Eugene Ritter, "La famille et la jeunesse de J.-J. Rousseau," *Annales de la Société Jean-Jacques Rousseau* 16 (1924–25): 233.

44. Maritain, *Three Reformers*, 144; emphasis original.

45. Ibid., 144.

46. Ibid., 141.

47. Ravier, "Le Dieu de Rousseau," 428.

48. Jean Starobinski, *Jean-Jacques Rousseau: Transparency and Obstruction* (Chicago: University of Chicago Press, 1988), 5.

49. Jacques Derrida, *Of Grammatology*, 1st American ed. (Baltimore: Johns Hopkins University Press, 1976), 151.

50. Burgelin, *Jean-Jacques Rousseau et la religion de Genève*, 57.

51. René Girard, Jean-Michel Oughourlian, and Guy Lefort, *Des choses cachées depuis la fondation du monde* (Paris: Grasset, n.d.), 573–92; see also René Girard, *I See Satan Fall Like Lightning* (Maryknoll: Orbis Books, 2001). Girard's references to Rousseau are quite limited; see, for example, René Girard, *The Scapegoat* (Baltimore: Johns Hopkins University Press, 1986), 53, 115.

52. René Girard, *Things Hidden since the Foundation of the World* (Stanford, CA: Stanford University Press, 1987), 426.

53. For a basic understanding of the biblical notion of scandal, the following titles are helpful: Gustav Stählin, *Skandalon: Untersuchungen zur Geschichte eines biblischen Begriffs* (Gütersloh, Germany: C. Bertelsmann, 1930); Gustav Stählin, "*Skandalon, skandalizo,*" in *Theologisches Worterbuch des Neuen Testaments*, ed. Gerhard Kittel and Gerhard Friedrich, 7:339–58; Jean Calvin, *Concerning Scandals* [*De scandalis*] (Grand Rapids, MI: Eerdmans, 1978); Helmut Bintz, *Das Skandalon als Grundlagenproblem der Dogmatik. Eine Auseinandersetzung Mit Karl Barth* (Berlin: de Gruyter, 1969); David McCracken, *The Scandal of the Gospels: Jesus, Story, and Offense* (New York: Oxford University Press, 1994); James Alison, *The Joy of Being Wrong: Original Sin Through Easter Eyes* (New York: Crossroad, 1998), 140–46; Gil Bailie, *Violence Unveiled: Humanity at the Crossroads* (New York: Crossroad, 1995), 207–10.

54. Girard, *Things Hidden*, 246; emphasis original.

55. Tzvetan Todorov, *Life in Common: An Essay in General Anthropology, European Horizons* (Lincoln: University of Nebraska Press, 2001), 38. See also J. H. Broome, *Rousseau: A Study of his Thought* (New York: Barnes and Noble, 1963). In this work, Broome gives the following description of amour-propre: "This form of self-seeking *relative to others*

is, for Rousseau, the beginning of conflict and competition between men" (40; emphasis original).

56. Girard, *Things Hidden*, 416.

57. There would be little debate about P. Riley's claim that the "Profession of Faith" is "the very heart of *Emile*." See Patrick Riley, *The General Will Before Rousseau: The Transformation of the Divine into the Civic* (Princeton, NJ: Princeton University Press, 1986), 101. Nevertheless, for being the heart, the "Profession of Faith" creates difficult problems concerning the coherence of the book. It is not at all self-evident how the "Profession of Faith" fits into the overall structure of *Emile*. This problem will be treated in Chapter 3.

58. Timothy O'Hagan, *Rousseau* (New York: Routledge, 1999). O'Hagan quotes Peter Jimack in pointing out that the order of the two parts of the "Profession of Faith," is significant. As Jimack notes, "The usual version of deism started from the challenging and rejection of . . . fundamental features of Christian revelation . . . and then proceeded nevertheless to defend the existence of God" (294–95). The quote is taken from Peter Jimack, *Rousseau, "Emile"* (London: Grant & Cutler, 1983), 39–40. The significance that Jimack sees is that Rousseau's starting point is not the rejection of Christianity, but rather of atheism. As I make clear in Chapter 3, Rousseau is disguising his real intent here, which is to render mute the New Testament's witness to the nonviolence of God.

59. Melzer, *Natural Goodness*, 19.

60. Gouhier rightly sees, besides the theological, a properly philosophical influence in this myth-making impulse, one that has its roots in Plato (*Les méditations métaphysiques*, 18).

61. Girard, *Things Hidden*, 426.

62. Thus, I have to disagree with B. Groethuysen's analysis in Bernhard Groethuysen, *J.-J. Rousseau* (Paris: Gallimard, 1983). His conclusion runs as follows: "Voilà comment la religion se place dans l'ensemble des idées et des sentiments de Rousseau. Ce n'est pas sa philosophie qui est chrétienne, c'est l'homme en lui qui est chrétien, malgré le philosophe" [So this is the way that religion has its place in the ensemble of idea and sentiments of Rousseau. It is not that his philosophy is Christian, rather the man in him is Christian in spite of the philosophy] (310). The distinction is too facile. The man and his philosophy are not so easily separated, especially on this point. Rousseau and his philosophy are both Christian in and to the same degree: they embody scandal at forgiveness and yet embrace the centrality of the victim.

63. This is where I take issue with Derathé. See Robert Derathé, *Le Rationalisme de Jean-Jacques Rousseau (Paris: Presses Universitaires de France*, 1948). He sees Rousseau as being much nearer to a pagan religious sensibility. He poses the question, "what remains of the Christian doctrine in the religion of Jean-Jacques?" His answer is: "Nothing or almost nothing" (410). But this is to overlook the importance of the victim for Rousseau. Derathé's analysis remains at the level of seeing Rousseau's system as a rejection of original sin and replacing it with the principle of natural goodness (410–11).

CHAPTER 2

1. Due to the nature of the *Dialogues*, "Jean-Jacques" will refer to the character of that name, as will the "Frenchman." The difficulty is with the name Rousseau. In those cases in which the context renders it ambiguous, I will state whether the text is referring to either Rousseau the character, or Rousseau the author.

There is not an abundance of secondary literature on the *Dialogues*. Masters and Kelly's "Introduction" to the work in the *Collected Works* is helpful, as is Foucault's in the edition he edited (*Rousseau Juge de Jean-Jacques*, Paris: Librairie Armand Colin,

1962). James F. Jones gives a sympathetic reading in his article, "The *Dialogues* as Autobiographical Truth," and his book, *Rousseau's "Dialogues": An Interpretative Essay* (Geneve: Libraire Droz, 1991). There is much to recommend about Eugene Stelzig's article, "Autobiography as Resurrection: Rousseau's *Dialogues*." He reads them as "autobiography written in extremis" (40). The *Dialogues* raise the "dilemma faced by all autobiographers: how can they succeed in communicating to anybody . . . who and what they are, what they have been, thought, done" (40). He also understands the lucidity of the *Dialogues*. But his use of the word "resurrection" in the title holds out more promise than Stelzig can actually deliver. If the "essence of his [Rousseau's] being was a function of how others looked at him, and his three autobiographies are a thoroughly calculated attempt to control and manipulate those books," then resurrection is just resurrection of damaged reputation, nothing more, no matter how hard Rousseau may try to puff up his existence (49). If resurrection has, in Rousseau's text, a deeper meaning, then Stelzig has failed to find it.

2. See Stanley Rosen, *Plato's Sophist: The Drama of Original and Image* (New Haven, CT: Yale University Press, 1983). As Rosen reminds us regarding Plato, "The dialogue, regarded as a dramatic unity, is thus an image, albeit one of a peculiar kind, of the author's comprehensive intentions. It is via the dramatic form of the dialogue that the author accommodates its doctrines to the natures of different readers" (2).

3. Cf. James F. Jones, *Rousseau's Dialogues: An Interpretive Essay* (Geneva: Librairie Droz, 1991), 108. He writes: "The triumph of the truth over those patent falsehoods that comprise the mirage of the evil "Jean-Jacques" will ultimately hinge upon an act of faith, the case for the good "Jean-Jacques" being consequently formulated in such a way that the Frenchman will come to believe the truth. The latter will undergo the requisite conversion in a distinctly religious sense." In general Jones is sensitive to the theological underpinnings of the work. He speaks again about the Frenchman's "conversion." He also says that the Frenchman accepts the truth of Jean-Jacques, as that truth is "revealed through the latter's writings as through a religious system's sacred texts" (133). However, he never uses these religious echoes in a systematic way. In *Rousseau and His Reader: The Rhetorical Situation of the Major Works* (Chapel Hill: University of North Carolina Press, 1969), Ellrich also refers to the Frenchman's "radical conversion" (86). More importantly, according to Ellrich, the Frenchman's conversion does not consist in simply changing from being against Jean-Jacques and in favor of the Gentlemen to the reverse position; the radicalness of the conversion consists in the Frenchman becoming Rousseau. "We see here a prolongation of Rousseau's desire to serve as model, to see those he addresses incorporated into himself. The breakdown in the distinction between Self and Other will insure perfect understanding" (86).

4. All parenthetical references refer to the *Dialogues* unless otherwise noted.

5. Frédéric Eigeldinger, "Ils Ne Me Pardonneront Jamais Le Mal Qu'ils M'ont Fait," *Etudes Jean-Jacques Rousseau* 10 (1998): 77–89. In his very fine article, Eigeldinger gives considerable textual evidence to show that this notion, namely, of never receiving forgiveness for the wrongs that others have done to him, is a theme running through much of Rousseau's writings and correspondence. In 1768, Rousseau hung an inscription titled, "Sentiments of the Public towards Me in the Various Estates That Compose It" in his lodgings. Twice, in reference to the magistrates and the Swiss, he uses the formulation, "[they] hate me because of the wrong they have done me" (*CW* 11:67; *Pl.* 1:1185). A similar expression occurs in the *Letter to Beaumont as follows*: "I have been surrounded by spies and by the malicious; and the world is full of people who hate me because of the harm they have done me" (*CW* 9:49; *Pl.* 4:963). Further, this interpretation of not being forgiven is

connected with Rousseau's thoughts on scandal. He writes to Mylord Maréchal that the ministers of the Gospel, "après avoir établi en principe leur compétence sur tout scandale, . . . excitent le scandale sur tel objet qui leur plait, et puis en vertu de ce scandale qui est leur ouvrage . . . s'emparent de l'affaire pour la juger":

> [. . .]Les brouillons de ministres [de Neuchâtel] me haïssent encore plus à cause du mal qu'ils n'ont pu me faire. (Eigeldinger, "Ils Ne Me Pardonneront," 86. He is quoting the letter of 6 avril from *Correspondance complete de Jeqn-Jacques Rousseau*, 51 vols., ed. R. A. Leigh (Geneva: Institute et Musée Voltaire, 1965–95)

6. I do not intend this to restrict forgiveness to Christianity, but we can join Hannah Arendt in seeing in Jesus of Nazareth the historical embodiment of a human practice known as forgiveness. Cf. Hannah Arendt, *The Human Condition, Charles* (Chicago: University of Chicago Press, 1958), 236–43.

7. One of the ways that Rousseau accomplishes this is by turning the accusations made by his enemies against them. For an interesting analysis of how this is accomplished through the use of figurative language, see Timothy Scanlon, "Aspects of Figurative Language in Rousseau's 'Dialogues,'" *Essays in French Literature* 13 (1976): 13–27. The article suffers by limiting itself to giving a psychological explanation for Rousseau's accusations.

8. I agree with Masters and Kelly, when they highlight for the reader in their "Introduction" to the *Dialogues* Rousseau's warning "one should be careful about attributing to 'Jean-Jacques' opinions expressed by characters in his work" (*CW* 1:xxii–xxiii; they refer to pages 69–70 in the text for Rousseau's warning). Still, in this work, the author makes clear that all of these opinions contribute to a single portrait. It is the reader's task to construct that portrait.

9. Interpreters tend to take individual statements from the *Dialogues* to back up their assertions concerning other works or their overall interpretation of Rousseau.

10. Michael O'Dea argues persuasively for the importance of the text's status as fiction in Michael O'Dea, "Fiction and the Ideal in *Rousseau Juge de Jean-Jacques*," *French Studies* 40 (1985): 141–50. Further, he emphasizes the way that the fictionality of the text undercuts any claim by Rousseau to have realized the ideal of communication.

11. The only article that I have read that pays much attention to the motif of portraits is Suellen Diaconoff, "Identity and Representation in the Prose and Painted Portrait," in *Autobiography in French Literature* (Amsterdam: Rodopi, 1985), 61–70. Unfortunately, this article is marred by a serious underestimation of the control that Rousseau exercises in his writing. She writes, "The relationship between the problems of identity encountered by both autobiography and the painted portrait is underscored, unwittingly, by Rousseau in one key section of the 'Deuxième Dialogue' in which he discusses what he calls a 'cabale de portraits' directed against him" (61). There is nothing unwitting about it, as I will show. In her study of Rousseau's descriptive technique, Margaret Buchner has a chapter titled, "Rousseau's Style of Portraiture," but she never mentions the *Dialogues*. See Margaret Louise Buchner, *A Contribution to the Study of the Descriptive Technique of Jean-Jacques Rousseau* (New York: Johnson Reprint, 1973).

12. Jean Starobinski, "The Accuser and the Accused," in *Jean-Jacques Rousseau*, ed. Harold Bloom, 173–93 (New York: Chelsea House, 1988). Starobinski's article deals with more than the *Dialogues*; it treats Rousseau's writings as the "logical consequences of his first intervention as a self-appointed prosecutor" (174). Starobinski analyzes the periods of Rousseau's life, dividing them according to which of the following conditions predominates: accusation (as in the *First* and *Second Discourse*, the *Letter to d'Alembert*, and much of his writing on music), justification of the accusations (as in *Julie* and *Emile*), or defense

against accusations (as in his autobiographical works). Starobinski accentuates the way that scandal led to Rousseau's success, and both the similarities and the differences between Rousseau and more properly theological writers, such as Francois de Fénelon and Blaise Pascal. The newness here is that Rousseau "takes upon himself the task of moral preaching which, up to now, exclusively and almost professionally belonged to the Church" (180). He summarizes, "*Accuser*, rejecting injustice and suspicious authority, Rousseau is the first to fill with a sacred fascination the theoretical model of a society or of an education able to repair harm done. *Accused*, seeking within himself justification and compensation, he is again the first to show the full range of autobiography, in which a life's truth is expressed in the 'chain of one's secret feelings'" (192).

13. The Frenchman discovers the "unpardonable crimes" of Jean-Jacques in his writings. Rousseau comments, "He knew that the Nobles, the Viziers, the Lawyers, the Financiers, the Doctors, the Priests, the philosophers, and all the sectarian people who truly plunder society would never forgive him for having seen and shown them as they are" (*CW* 1:206; *Pl.* 1:926).

14. In Ronald Grimsley, *Rousseau and the Religious Quest* (Oxford: Clarendon Press, 1968), Grimsley astutely notes that this world is built upon banishment: "The very idea of paradise as a self-contained abode presupposes the need to banish all those dark and sinister forces that threaten to disturb the peace and innocence of its happy inhabitants" (125).

15. Toward the end of the "First Dialogue" there is a similar discussion. Rousseau expounds to the Frenchman why he feels he can doubt what is so certain for everyone else. At this point, he is stilled worried by the accusations, but he is not convinced. In order to get to the truth, Rousseau must "reject all human authority in this matter, all proof that is dependent on the testimony of someone else" (*CW* 1:85; *Pl.* 1:769). As Burgelin points out in *Jean-Jacques Rousseau et la religion de Genève*, the certitude Rousseau has that his life is a sort of imitation of Christ is very strong in the whole of the *Dialogues*, and it shows Rousseau himself searching for the truth about Jean-Jacques in the same manner as the Vicar searches for the truth about religion. See Pierre Burgelin, *Jean-Jacques Rousseau et la Religion de Genève* (Geneva: Labor et Fides, 1962).

16. I am referring here to the following words of Virgil addressed to Dante as they enter the Inferno: "'Here must all fear be left behind; here let all cowardice be dead. We have come to the place where I have told you you will see the wretched people who have lost the good of intellect.'" Alighieri Dante, *Inferno, Princeton/Bollingen Paperbacks*, ed. Charles Southward Singleton (Princeton, NJ: Princeton University Press, 1980), Canto III, 14–18. The reader enters into this abyss with the same purpose as Dante: "To treat of the good that I found in it" (Canto I, 8).

CHAPTER 3

1. Judith Shklar, *Men and Citizens: A Study of Rousseau's Social Theory, Cambridge Studies in the History and Theory of Politics* (London: Cambridge University Press, 1969), 235.

2. *Emile et Sophie, ou Les Solitaires, Pl.* 4:881–924.

3. All parenthetical references refer to *Emile* unless otherwise noted.

4. Pierre Burgelin, "L'idée de place dans l'*Emile*," *Revue de littérature compare* (octobre–décembre 1961): 529–37.

5. Janie Vanpée, "Rousseau's *Emile ou de l'éducation*: A Resistance to Reading," *Yale French Studies* 77 (1990): 156–76. In her article, Vanpée emphasizes the "pedagogical mission" of *Emile* and criticizes those interpreters who focus primarily on the pedagogical theory and practice as an object of analysis rather than "an engagement that implicates the

reader" (158n). Hers is a very insightful reading, but it does not address Rousseau's use of scandal to draw the reader in.

6. Cf., *Emile*, 98, 175; *Pl.* 4:330, 440.

7. Cf. *Emile*, 136; *Pl.* 4:386. About his experience of fetching the Bible in the dark, Rousseau writes: "One might ask if I tell this story as a model to follow and as an example of the gaiety which I exact in this kind of exercise? No, but I give it as proof that nothing is more reassuring to someone frightened of shadows in the night than to hear company, assembled in the neighboring room, laughing and chatting calmly." Both immediately preceding and immediately after the "Profession of Faith," Rousseau tells the reader that he is not giving this "as a rule" (*Emile*, 260, 313; *Pl.* 4:558, 635).

8. This should be read carefully, for it is fairly clear that the child in these two episodes is not the real Emile, but one that is more like a normal child and thus serves as a better example.

9. Rousseau refers to the conversation with Robert on p. 111 (*Pl.* 4:350), and to how he had laid a foundation for all the ideas of exchange in this episode on p. 189 (*Pl.* 4:461). He implicitly refers to the episode with the magician a few pages later when he says that the one who is "taught as his most important lesson to want to know nothing but what is useful interrogates like Socrates" (*Emile*, 179; *Pl.* 4:446). The magician had been referred to as "our magician-Socrates" (*Emile*, 175; *Pl.* 4:440). And when talking about how to disabuse someone of vanity, Rousseau remarks that "the adventure with the magician would be repeated in countless ways" (*Emile*, 245; *Pl.* 4:537).

10. Cf. *Emile*, 101; *Pl.* 4:334, where Rousseau writes: "Here we are in the moral world." These words come immediately following the story of Emile's encounter with Robert (the gardener) and its aftermath.

11. This theme gets picked up by Rousseau in several other works, most notably in the *Reveries of a Solitary Walker as follows*: "In all the evils which befall us, we look more to the intention than to the effect. A shingle falling off a roof can injure us more, but does not grieve us as much as a stone thrown on purpose by a malevolent hand. The blow sometimes goes astray, but the intention never misses its mark" (*CW* 8:72; *Pl.* 1:1078).

12. Rousseau comments, "And surely this possession is more sacred and more respectable than that taken of South America when Núñez Balboa in the name of the King of Spain planted his standard on the shore of the South Sea" (*Emile*, 98; *Pl.* 4:330–31). Rousseau first used this example in the Geneva manuscript when he wrote: "To what extent can the act of taking possession establish property? When Núñez Balboa, standing on the shore, took possession of the South Sea and all of South America in the name of the Crown of Castile, was this enough to dispose all the inhabitants and exclude all the princes of the world?" (*Geneva Manuscript, CW*, 4:93; *Pl.* 3:301; cf. also *Social Contract, CW*, 4:143; *Pl.* 3:366–67 for the parallel passage). Thus, there are two types of planting, one that constitutes a legitimate claim through labor, and another that is simply the hegemony of violence.

13. In his peroration against foresight, Rousseau sees humans extending themselves not only temporally into the future, but also spatially: "Our individual persons are now only the least part of ourselves. Each one extends himself, so to speak, over the whole earth and becomes sensitive over this entire large surface" (*Emile*, 83; *Pl.* 4:307).

14. Awakening to the moral world as already guilty would correspond to many people's conception of the dogma of original sin. A more correct understanding would be to awaken to a new creation through forgiveness. Part of this awakening would be a view of the old creation as it passes out of existence.

15. In case the reader, like the author of *Anti-Emile* (Jean-Henri-Samuel Formey, *Anti-Emile* [Berlin: Pauli,1763]), does not understand this, Rousseau adds the following note for the next edition: "I could not keep from laughing in reading a subtle critique of this little tale by M. de Formey. 'This magician,' he says, 'who prides himself on his emulation with a child and gravely sermonizes his teacher is an individual of the world of Emiles.' The clever M. de Formey was unable to suppose that this little scene was arranged and that the magician had been instructed about the role he had to play; for, indeed, I did not say so. But on the other hand, how many times have I declared that I did not write for people who have to be told everything." Quoted by Bloom in his notes to his translation of *Emile* (*Emile*, 487n6).

CHAPTER 4

1. The best critical edition of the "Profession of Faith" remains *La "Profession de foi du vicaire savoyard" de Jean-Jacques Rousseau*, ed. Pierre Maurice Masson (Fribourg: (Suisse) Librairie de l'Université (O. Gschwend); Paris: Hachette, 1914). The phrase "*clef de voûte* [keystone]" is from Albert Schinz, *La Pensee de Jean-Jacques Rousseau* (Paris: Librairie Félix Alcan, 1929), 451. He cites no fewer than eight other authors, as well as himself, who hold this position. Still, he feels that the question of *how* it is the keystone still needed to be examined. Over seventy-five years later, I agree.

2. Rousseau refers to the two parts of the "Profession of Faith." The first part begins with the title typographically set off from the preceding part. At one point, the vicar interrupts his discourse in order to see how the young man is reacting. Then there is a brief narrative concerning his reaction. After this, the vicar picks up his profession. The part that follows this interruption is the second part. In the Plèiade edition, the first part extends from page 565 through page 606, and the second part extends from page 607 to page 635.

3. "*Philosophes*" is the named used for the group of thinkers at the vanguard of the French Enlightenment. The name includes, but is not limited to, Jean Le Rond d'Alembert, Denis Diderot, Friedrich-Melchior Grimm, and Paul-Henri Thiry, baron d'Holbach. Rousseau arrived in Paris as someone seeking entrance into this group. Having achieved that he became the Enlightenment's most profound critic. The best study on Rousseau's relationship with the *philosophes* is Mark Hulliung's *The Autocritique of Enlightenment: Rousseau and the Philosophes* (Cambridge, MA: University of Harvard Press, 1994).

4. In *La Pensée*, Schinz argues in a somewhat similar fashion that the "Profession" functions in Rousseau's system as a coercive power that goes beyond not only the individual human, but also human society. Only God is powerful enough to guard humans against themselves (cf. 456).

5. To Rousseau's way of thinking, the fact that the "Profession of Faith" is a transcription increases, rather than lessens, its value. As he writes in his *Dictionary of Music* on the entry "Copyist," "there are many intermediaries between what the Composer imagines and what the Listeners hear. It is for the *Copyist* to bring these two end points as close together as possible, to indicate clearly everything that should be done so that the performed Music renders to the Composer's ear exactly what he depicted in his head when composing it" (*CW* 7:384; *Pl.* 5:742). The importance Rousseau gives to the position of the copyist came to my attention in Michèle Crogiez's *Rousseau et le Paradoxe* (Paris: Honorâe Champion Editeur, 1997), 297.

6. This is not the only place that Rousseau uses himself rather than Emile as an example that should be closer to the reader. At times Emile is simply too different from the reader to

serve as an example that can be easily grasped. See, for example, his discussion on taste (*Emile*, 344–54; *Pl.* 4:678–91).

7. Cf. Patrick Riley, *The General Will Before Rousseau: The Transformation of the Divine into the Civic, Studies in Moral, Political, and Legal Philosophy* (Princeton, NJ: Princeton University Press, 1986), 193ff, for a discussion of how Rousseau sees most "miraculous" happenings as a combination of human conceit and magic.

8. For samples of this sentiment, cf. *Emile*, 292, 312, 314; *Pl.* 4:603, 632, 636.

9. This interpretation is confirmed by the *Letters Written from the Mountain*. In the "Fifth Letter," one reads the following: "Consider the religious condition of Europe at the moment I published my Book, and you will see that it was more than probable that it would be welcomed everywhere. Religion, discredited everywhere by philosophy, had lost its ascendancy even over the people. The Clergy, obstinate about propping it up on its weak side, had let all the rest be undermined, and, being out of plumb, the entire edifice was ready to collapse. Controversies had stopped because they no longer interested anyone, and peace reigned among the different parties, because none cared about his own anymore. In order to remove the bad branches, they had cut down the tree; in order to replant it, it was necessary to leave nothing but the trunk" (*CW* 9:227; *Pl.* 3:802).

10. In J. H. Broome, *Rousseau: A Study of his Thought* (New York: Barnes & Noble, 1963), Broome devotes a chapter to the "Profession." There, he says that the underlying structure of Rousseau's religious theory as a whole

> may not be apparent at a first reading of the Profession de foi, because in relating his ideas to the particular context, Rousseau has modified the usual order of exposition and made the main body of constructive thought precede the main body of criticism. Consequently, for the reader who wishes to trace the central current of religious ideas and relate them to his philosophy as a whole, the simplest procedure is to reverse the order and consider the first phase of the text as the outcome of the second. If this is done, the entire work falls into place as a further exercise in the familiar fall-and-redemption perspective, modified by the sense of human evolution towards enlightenment. (108–9)

Two comments need to be made here. First, to reverse the order is to give up a major textual clue as to what Rousseau is about here. Second, and this applies to the whole of Broome's treatment, Broome's too-easy assimilation of Rousseau's thought to the Christian pattern of fall-and-redemption means that the scandal of Rousseau's thought gets lost, and with it, the scandal of the Gospel. It is unfortunate because Broome was so close to seeing the implications of his own interpretation. He opens the chapter on the "Profession" by writing, "With the convergence of his political theory and his moral and educational doctrines, it might now be asserted that Rousseau has outlined a complete social philosophy, capable of replacing a religious conception of life" (105). Broome does not actually assert this, and yet this is the truth. Rousseau is offering an alternative, not to some abstract religious conception of life, but to the Christian conception of life. John T. Scott also points out, in a footnote to his article, "Politics as the Imitation of the Divine in Rousseau's *Social Contract*," that Broome is a "prominent example" of those scholars who, while they have interpreted Rousseau's thought from a theological perspective, hold interpretations that "usually remain impressionistic." John T. Scott, *Polity* 26, no. 3 (1994): 479.

11. With the expression "*le fer et le feu* [the fire and the sword]," Rousseau could also be referring to the Roman Empire, in connection with the phrase "with fire and with steel." which is sometimes used.

12. My concern here is not to accuse Rousseau of anti-Semitism. There are passages in the "Profession of Faith" that claim equal rights for Jews and Muslims to practice their religion, to believe their own doctrines (Cf. *Emile*, 304; *Pl.* 4:621). What interests me more is the fact that he felt his passage was weakened when these parts were left out. Further, he sees these anti-Semitic remarks as being something said "so wholeheartedly in favor of Religion" (*CW* 9:72; *Pl.* 3:992). It suggests that he wants to restore a certain logic at work in the passage that gets destroyed if the derogatory remarks are removed. Thus, Rousseau's approach to the Gospels turns them into something other than what they truly are. The archbishop is wrong not to explicitly recognize and repudiate this.

13. Robert Derathé, "Jean-Jacques Rousseau et le Christianisme," *Revue de Métaphysique et de Morale* 53 (1948): 379–434. In his article, Derathé points out very clearly the way in which Rousseau refuses any sort of blind belief and insists on judging the divine character of any revelation on the basis of its content. On the basis of this, Rousseau judges the Gospels to be divinely inspired, but he also perverts them into a text of persecution. Rousseau refuses anything in the Scriptures that he judges is unworthy of God, that is, anything that does not confirm his idea of God. In the "Profession," the vicar claims that he maintains a respectful skepticism before the things in the Gospel that "shock" his reason. As Derathé points out, this "respectful skepticism" is actually closer to indifference (393). But the reaction to the scandals in the Scripture should be faith, not indifference.

14. Henri Gaston Gouhier, *Les Méditations Métaphysiques de Jean-Jacques Rousseau* (Paris: J. Vrin, 1970), 39.

15. Susan Meld Shell, in her "*Emile*: Nature and the Education of Sophie," in *The Cambridge Companion to Rousseau*, ed. Patrick Riley (Cambridge: Cambridge University Press, 2001), 272–301, sees Rousseau's political teaching as speaking to "private, post-Christian men," offering them a modern version of what Lycurgus, the law-giver, offered the Spartans (278).

CHAPTER 5

1. Some may wonder about the way that I have divided the novel, treating the latter half of Book IV together with the first part of Book V. This division corresponds more closely to the educational plan of Rousseau than his own division of the books. Books I through III deal with childhood, while Books IV and V deal with the crisis of puberty. The "Profession of Faith" has a special role in preparing for that crisis.

2. René Girard, *Things Hidden since the Foundation of the World* (Stanford, CA: Stanford University Press, 1987), 416.

3. In Book III, Chapter XVI of the *Social Contract*, Rousseau writes, "If it were possible for the Sovereign, considered as such, to have the executive power, right and fact would be so completely confounded that one would no longer know what is law and what isn't; and the body politic, thereby denatured, would soon fall prey to the violence against which it was instituted" (*CW* 4:194; *Pl.* 3:432).

4. In *Love and Friendship* (New York: Simon and Schuster, 1993), Allan Bloom makes a similar point. He writes, "Up to now Emile has lived according to his inclination, doing what comes naturally, and has never been asked to bind himself in such a way that duty conflicts with inclination and divides him. Now he will become divided, but on the basis of his own inner recognition that it is really for his own deepest satisfaction" (90). Emile cannot know "his own deepest satisfaction," unless and until the tutor indicates it.

5. Laurence Mall, '*Emile*' ou les figures de la fiction, *SVEC, 2002:04* (Oxford: Voltaire Foundation, 2002). Mall astutely notes the "ubiquity" of the "I" mediators in Book V. By this, she means that the tutor not only mediates Emile's desire, but also the desire of others, such as Sophie. The "I" in the text takes up a shifting series of alliances—with

Sophie, with her father, and with her mother. At the same time, the "I" of the author also "establishes a climate of complicity" with the reader (170).

6. In *Deceit, Desire, and the Novel: Self and Other in Literary Structure* (Baltimore: Johns Hopkins University Press, 1965), Girard distinguishes between external and internal mediation according to the distance separating the mediator from the subject. In external mediation, the distance is great enough that there is no possibility of rivalry between the two. With internal mediation, that possibility emerges. Thus, this part of *Emile* could be viewed as describing the movement from external to internal mediation.

7. Rousseau, while writing the romance of two fictional characters, Emile and Sophie, inserts a subplot about another Sophie, who is also fictional but is perhaps closer to a historical model than the first Sophie. The story of the first Sophie and the second Sophie are the same up to a certain point but then begin to go in different directions. The former ends up marrying Emile and the latter dies before she meets Emile or someone like him. For the sake of clarity, whenever referring to the second Sophie the name will be enclosed in quotations marks.

8. Elizabeth Rose Wingrove gives a very fine commentary on this "several page digression" in *Rousseau's Republican Romance* (Princeton, NJ: Princeton University Press, 2000). Not only in this section, but also throughout the book, Wingrove gives a sophisticated reading of Rousseau's political philosophy through its philosophy of sexual interaction. Her concept of "consensual nonconsensuality," meaning the condition in which one wills the circumstances of one's own domination" (5), is brilliant and brings both the realms of sexual relations and political relations into a common light. But as the whole thrust of my presentation is trying to make clear, to ignore the religious underpinnings of both sexuality and politics is to leave unexposed another, deeper, layer of unity. I think one good example of this lack is her analysis of the present digression. Her cautions about the difficulty of deriving a simple point from the story are well taken and indicate again the great care with which she approaches the text. But to say one is to suspect *any* lessons from a double and discarded Sophie is to go too far. One has to say that by Wingrove's reading, Rousseau could have left out the digression and still reached his conclusion that "the recognition of sexual identity is a recognition of political forms" (84). One has to see what difference there is between the situation of the two Sophies and explore the significance of that difference. Their situations are not identical, and in spite of Rousseau's misleading comments, the differences are not limited to character traits.

9. Thus, I disagree with Mira Morgenstern's analysis in *Rousseau and the Politics of Ambiguity: Self, Culture, and Society* (University Park: Pennsylvania State University Press, 1996), that the major difference between the Sophie who dies and the one who lives is the ordinariness of the latter. Morgenstern is aware of how the tutor uses Sophie, but the way he mediates the desires of Sophie and Emile is not brought out.

10. Pierre Burgelin, "Sur l'éducation de Sophie," *Annales historiques de la Révolution Française* 35 (1959–62): 126–27; Wingrove, *Rousseau's Republican Romance*, 83.

11. Wingrove, *Rousseau's Republican Romance*, 83.

12. Rousseau's language makes clear that he is thinking about the charge of causing scandal: "If I have been able to make these essays useful in some respect, it is especially by having expanded at great length on this essential part [the romance of Emile and Sophie], omitted by all others, and by not letting myself be rebuffed in this enterprise by false delicacies or frightened by difficulties of language" (*Emile*, 416; *Pl.* 4:777).

13. Girard, *Things Hidden*, 288. Girard means by "unanimous" a situation of "unanimity minus one," the one being the victim.

14. For a penetrating analysis of Plato's theory of mimesis and its relationship to his feelings on tragic drama, with occasional references to Rousseau, see Stephen Halliwell,

The Aesthetics of Mimesis: Ancient Texts and Modern Problems (Princeton, NJ: Princeton University Press, 2002).

15. Rousseau mentions his own reading of *The Spectator* in his *Confessions* as something that pleased him and did him some good (*CW* 5:92–93; *Pl.* 1:110–11). *The Spectator*, edited by Joseph Addison, appeared for a period of two years beginning in 1711. After that it was available in book form. A French translation, *Le Spectateur* or *Le Socrate moderne* first appeared in 1714. The periodical promoted what might be referred to today as "family values."

CHAPTER 6

1. The title of this chapter is an obvious play on the title "The General Will and the Scandal of Politics" in Tracy B. Strong, *Jean-Jacques Rousseau: The Politics of the Ordinary* (Thousand Oaks, CA: Sage, 1994), 67–103. Strong sees the scandal there as being created for Rousseau by Hume's writing on politics. Humans' lack of knowledge of the other undermines any trust one might have in another. Strong sees "Rousseau's political thought . . . as a solution—or an attempt at a solution—to a stance that was, one might say, 'destructive of political philosophy'" (73).

2. Cf. also *Emile*, 391; *Pl.* 4:743, where Rousseau writes, "In love everything is only illusion."

3. These texts, *Emile* and the *Discourse on Inequality*, are being treated in this order due to their order of publication, as was indicated in the introductory chapter, but more profoundly because the movement from *Emile* to the *Second Discourse* is a movement from first principles, which ought to be more or less self-evident, to deeper principles. Human beings are alienated from themselves; this is easy to grasp. The concept that humanity is abandoned by God, though, is far more difficult.

4. The parallel passage in *Emile* is as follows: [. . .] "this act of association contains a reciprocal commitment of the public and the individuals, and that each individual, who is, so to speak, contracting with himself, is committed in two respects—as a member of the sovereign, to the individuals, as member of the state, to the sovereign" (*Emile*, 460–61; *Pl.* 4:840).

5. As Rousseau puts it in Chapter IV of Book II, the state is a moral person whose most important concern is its own preservation, therefore "it must have a universal, compulsory force to move and arrange each part in the manner best suited to the whole. Just as nature gives each man absolute power over all his members, the social compact give the body politic absolute power over all its members, and it is this same power, directed by the general will, which as I have said bears the name sovereignty" (*CW* 4:148; *Pl.* 4:372).

6. Steven G. Affeldt, "The Force of Freedom: Rousseau on Forcing to Be Free," *Political Theory* 27, no. 3 (1999): 305.

7. Ibid., 306.

8. Ibid.

9. Ibid., 308.

10. Ibid., 314.

11. Ibid.

12. Ibid.

13. Ibid., 324.

14. In Patrick Riley, "Rousseau's General Will: Freedom of a Particular Kind," in *Rousseau and Liberty*, ed. Robert Wokler (Manchester: Manchester University Press, 1995), 1–28, Riley says that he will discuss how Rousseau generalizes the will, but he never adverts to

the forming of common interests or to the footnote in which he describes the process. Rather, he sees it as a process of "doing away with will's particularity and selfishness and 'willfulness,'" while not destroying it (8).

15. Patrick Riley's other outstanding study, *The General Will Before Rousseau: The Transformation of the Divine into the Civic, Studies in Moral, Political, and Legal Philosophy* (Princeton, NJ: Princeton University Press, 1986) is essential reading on the topic of the general will. He shows himself to be quite sensitive to the theological background of the concept. He fails to see that Rousseau's desacralizing of this concept is still a move within Christianity and not a move outside of it.

16. Strong, in *Jean-Jacques Rousseau: The Politics of the Ordinary*, draws attention to scandal and its connection to Rousseau's political philosophy. He also analyzes this footnote to the effect that the obstacle that the general will is set against is the particular will. Thus, the opposition between the two is "one of kind and not one of substance" (82). While I agree with him as far as he goes, I think that he fails to see the critical importance of this idea of opposition of all against one to form the general will.

17. Hannah Arendt, *On Revolution* (London: Penguin, 1963), 76–78.

18. Ibid., 77.

19. Ibid., 78.

20. Ibid. This parallel was brought to my attention by Wolfgang Palaver in his article "Mimesis and Scapegoating in the Works of Hobbes, Rousseau, and Kant," *Contagion* 10 (Spring 2003): 126–48.

21. Cf. Patrick Riley, "Rousseau's General Will. " The quote from Rousseau is from the *Social Contract* (*CW* 4:133; *Pl.* 3:354).

22. For a different interpretation of this phrase, see John Hope Mason, "'Forced to Be Free,'" in *Rousseau and Liberty*, ed. Robert Wokler (Manchester: Manchester University Press, 1995). He interprets the phrase to mean that those who do not obey the general will, "'will be forced to [pay] the penalty for violating that rule of law which alone enables everyone (including him) to be free.'"

23. These fragments have been printed in Heinrich Meier's bilingual edition: *Diskurs über die Ungleichheit / Discours sur l'inégalité*, 3rd ed. (Padernborn: Schöningh, 1993), 386–401.

24. See Felicity Baker, "Eternal Vigilance: Rousseau's Death Penalty," in *Rousseau and Liberty*, ed. Robert Wokler (Manchester: Manchester University Press, 1995). Felicity Baker's suggestive, but sometimes impenetrable, article deserves more extensive treatment than a footnote, but allow me to limit myself to the following observations:

She is one of the few interpreters to notice and comment on the strangeness of this rather sudden appeal to the death penalty in the *Social Contract*. As she writes, "Readers do not usually reach the passage describing the civil religion, however, fully alerted to the possibility of Caligula. On the contrary, the emotional impact of the death penalty comes not from the violence it might avert or punish, but from the violence of the penalty itself, for which the reader feels totally unprepared. . . . He . . . means to repel readers by the brutal insertion of death into the religious dimension of social reality, where we might rather expect to find gentleness" (160).

She asserts at several points "that Rousseau's thinking is normally opposed to violence" (160). This seems overly facile. Beginning with the *First Discourse*, Rousseau often supports violence, even violence that is extreme. Think of the injunction to murder in the footnote on the opening page of *Emile*.

Her suggestion that the death penalty in the *Social Contract* is intended for the prince who can destroy the community is valuable. However, she fails to draw the consequences from the connections that she sees. She is sensitive to the topic of persecutory violence, to the founding of the community, and to the possibility of the king being killed, but she fails to see how these are all basically the same thing. Persecutory violence founds the city and the king is simply, as Gil Bailie has remarked, "the victim with a suspended sentence."

Finally, she links the existence of the community with the consciousness of death and claims that "if ever that reality saw one single powerful exception, disaster would ensue" (182). I would claim that reality did see one single powerful exception in the resurrection of Christ and the gathering of a community around the forgiving victim. Whether one would call that a disaster or not, I will leave open.

25. Rousseau puts it this way in the *Geneva Manuscript*: "There are a thousand ways to bring men together; there is only one way to unite them. That is why in this work I give only one method for the formation of political societies, although in the multitude of aggregations that now exist under this name, there may not even be two that were formed in the same manner and not one according to the manner I establish. But I seek right and reason, and do not argue over facts" (*CW* 4:88–89; *Pl.* 3:297).

26. Cf. Madeleine B. Ellis, *Rousseau's Socratic Aemilian Myths: A Literary Collation of* Emile *and the* Social Contract (Columbus: Ohio State University Press, 1977), 372, 382n67.

27. Cf. Laurence Mall, Emile *ou les figures de la fiction, SVEC, 2002:04* (Oxford: Voltaire Foundation, 2002), 9–44, for a very intelligent and enlightening look at the question of the genre of *Emile*.

CHAPTER 7

1. For the text, I have also consulted Heinrich Meier's bilingual edition: *Diskurs über die Ungleichheit / Discours sur l'inégalité*, 3rd ed. (Padernborn: Schöningh, 1993).

2. Starobinski, *Jean-Jacques Rousseau: Transparency and Obstruction* (Chicago: University of Chicago Press, 1988), 290; emphasis added.

3. For a discussion of the way that the Scriptures can be an occasion of scandal, see David McCracken, *The Scandal of the Gospels: Jesus, Story, and Offense* (New York: Oxford University Press, 1994), 14–31.

4. Starobinski, *Rousseau*, 290.

5. The importance of the use of the verb "to see" is not limited to the "Preface." In Richard L. Velkley, *Being After Rousseau: Philosophy and Culture in Question* (Chicago: University of Chicago Press, 2002), Velkley remarks, "The focus on the moment at which man had his present physical form, but reason only latently, or *in nuce*, [at the beginning of Part I] is an imaginative construction. This fact is emphasized by the repeated use of the verb "to see" in the second paragraph. . . . This use of imagination . . . points to relation of [the] form of the *Discourse* to its content, a relation that tends to be invisible. The power of theoretical vision or imagination is hidden behind what it makes visible" (41). Both this chapter and the next could be read with profit in conjunction with Velkley's work.

6. One can consult the "Preface" by John P. Leavey to the English translation of Jacques Derrida, *Edmund Husserl's Origin of Geometry, an Introduction* (Lincoln: University of Nebraska Press, 1989), for a helpful discussion of this concept. I emphasize that I am using the concept to indicate that the origin occupies a place in the system that is both impossible and yet necessary.

7. Starobinski, *Rousseau*, 16.

8. Starobinski, *Rousseau*, 15.

9. Rousseau changed the wording of the Academy's question from the "source" to the "origin" of inequality. While I cannot find any consistent difference in his usage of these two

terms, he may have done it to help distinguish these two forms of the question, that which is easy to see and that which is more difficult.

10. Cf. Mark Hulliung, *The Autocritique of Enlightenment*, 52–75. Hulliung gives a excellent account of the intellectual motivation that underlying this type of thinking about origin. "Ultimately what the philosophes wanted to unearth was the origin of religion, buried under the ignorance and fear of natural forces so characteristic of primitives and children" (54).

11. Here I am arguing against the position taken by H. Meier both in the introductory "essay" to his excellent edition of the *Discourse* and to his development of this position in his article entitled: "The *Discourse on the Origin and the Foundations of Inequality Among Men*: On the Intention of Rousseau's Most Philosophical Work," *Interpretation* 16, no. 2 (1988–89): 211–27. The interpretation by Victor Gourevitch, in his article, "Rousseau's Pure State of Nature," *Interpretation* 16, no. 1 (1988): 23–59, is much closer to the position I am outlining here.

12. As Gouhier comments in *Les Méditations Métaphysiques De Jean-Jacques Rousseau* (Paris: J. Vrin, 1970): "If the state of nature is not an historical epoch, but a hypothesis of the work [of the *Discourse on Inequality*] it is a hypothesis of the work that allows one to understand the historical human" (14). Gouhier goes on to say that Rousseau proceeds like a theologian in defining the human before history, but then leaves aside everything that the theologian says that is properly theological (14). This is true as long as it is understood that leaving aside all that is properly theological is itself a theological move.

13. Jean Starobinski, "La Prosopopée de Fabricius," *Revue de Sciences Humaines* 41, no. 161 (1976): 93.

14. It is worth noting that in his own answer to the question, Rousseau is signaling a move away from the practical proposal he made in the *First Discourse*. There, he suggests that enlightened princes allow the truly wise a place on their councils and in their counsels (cf. *CW* 2:22; *Pl.* 3:30). Here, he admits that such cooperation "is hardly reasonable to expect, especially with the perseverance or rather the succession of enlightenment and good will necessary on each side to achieve success" (*CW* 3:13; *Pl.* 3:124).

15. I analyze the experience on the road to Vincennes in Chapter 9. Cf. *Confessions, CW* 5:326; *Pl.* 1:388 for the reference to the time in the forest of St. Germaine.

16. The use of this particular word here is another example of the way in which Rousseau is undercutting his own thought. Rousseau's famous dictum reads, "I almost dare affirm that the state of reflection is a state contrary to Nature and that the man who meditates is a depraved animal" (*CW* 3:23; *Pl.* 3:138). Naturally, the "almost" weakens the statement, but the fact that Rousseau deliberately uses the word is meant to create a tension in the text.

17. In James Swenson, *On Jean-Jacques Rousseau: Considered as One of the First Authors of the Revolution* (Stanford, CA: Stanford University Press, 2000), Swenson states that "the passion of pity would seem, in some measure, to represent the social within nature and the natural within society" (100). This is true as far as it goes, but ultimately, pity represents the sympathy for victims that Rousseau needs in his system and yet has made difficult to include due to his rejection of the Scriptures. Thus, it gets brought into the state of nature to function "*as if* it were an instinct" (102; emphasis original).

18. Cf. Meier, *Diskurs über die Ungleichheit*, 128–29.

19. While the impossibility of reaching an end of the discourse will remind the reader of Derrida, it is also good to note that Kant's antinomies involve questions (many about origins) that are necessary to pose and impossible to answer. My thanks to Prof. Richard Schenk, O. P., for pointing this out to me.

20. "Exordium" is the way most scholars refer to the part of the discourse after the title and before the "First Part." Rousseau does not use the word.

21. Victor Goldschmidt, *Anthropologie et Politique: Les principes du systèm de Rousseau* (Paris: J. Vrin, 1974), gives a long analysis of the formula "Commençons donc par écarter tous les faits [Let us therefore begin by setting all the facts aside]" (125–67). I would agree with him that commentators are more or less unanimous in agreeing that the facts referred to here are "theological" facts in general and the creation account of Genesis in particular. He does point out C. E. Vaughan's early rejection of this restrictive interpretation (125–26), and he himself develops a more comprehensive interpretation of the meaning of the word "facts" for Rousseau. Although I am emphasizing the role of Scripture here, I, too, do not take the meaning of "facts" here to be restricted to the Biblical account. Rather, it is connected with Rousseau's use of "fiction" in the *Second Discourse*.

22. "Mais aucun d'eux n'y est arrivé" (*CW* 3:18; *Pl.* 3:132). This quotation is perhaps the clearest evidence that Rousseau sees the return to the origin as, at one and the same time, necessary and yet impossible. Rousseau does not claim to arrive there himself; rather, he disavows it.

23. Raymond Trousson sees this in his article, "Le Christ dans le pensée de J.-J. Rousseau, 7, 1977," in *Problems d'histoire du Christianisme* (Brussels: Editions de l'universitae de Bruxelles, 1978), 31–56, when he writes, "Alors que le christianisme raconte l'histoire de l'homme tombé et sauvé par la grâce miséricordieuse de Dieu, Rousseau, dès le *Discours sur l'origine de l'inégalité*, a laïcisé cette odyssée" (43).

24. Cf. the discussion by Spaemann in his "Zur Vorgeschichte von Rousseaus Naturbegriff" in which he states that Rousseau, in developing his own version of the state of nature, uses the "*status naturae purae*" of the theologians. This concept of a state of pure nature was developed in the context of controversies concerning grace in the sixteenth century. See Robert Spaemann, *Rousseau—Büger ohne Vaterland: Von der Polis zur Natur* (Munich: Piper, 1980), 63–67. See also Jeremiah Alberg, *Die Verlorene Einheit: Die Suche Nach Einer Philosophischen Alternative Zu Der Erbsündenlehre Von Rousseau Bis Schelling* (Frankfurt: P. Lang, 1996), 48.

25. Cf. Søren Kierkegaard, Howard Vincent Hong, and Edna Hatlestad Hong, *The Sickness Unto Death: A Christian Psychological Exposition for Upbuilding and Awakening* (Princeton, NJ: Princeton University Press, 1980), 116n.

CHAPTER 8

1. Cf. Victor Goldschmidt, *Anthropologie et Politique: Les principes du système de Rousseau* (Paris: J. Vrin, 1974), 268, where Goldschmidt points out that for the scholars of Rousseau's day, the problem of the genesis of ideas from sensation in human knowing was considered to be a properly metaphysical problem.

2. Goldschmidt, *Anthropologie et Politique*, 240. As Goldschmidt points out, the permanence of the state of nature is neither history nor myth, but rather is a reflection of the ahistoricity of the consciousness of the natural human.

3. Jean Starobinski in the editorial notes for the Pléiade edition (*Pl.* 3:1322n2); Paul de Man, *Allegories of Reading: Figural Language in Rousseau, Nietzsche, Rilke, and Proust* (New Haven, CT: Yale University Press, 1979), 142; Heinrich Meier, *Diskurs über Die Ungleichheit = Discours sur l'inéâegalité* (Paderborn, Germany: F. Schöningh, 1984), 117n149; and James Swenson, *On Jean-Jacques Rousseau: Considered as One of the First Authors of the Revolution* (Stanford, CA: Stanford University Press, 2000), 111, all point

out that Rousseau's viewpoint is not to explain the *origin* of language, but rather the *obstacles* to its emergence.

4. It would have been possible to include here a discussion of the aporia that exists in the relationship between freedom and *perfectibilité* or perfectibility, that is that each presumes the other as its cause. But this relationship has been well explored by Paul de Man in *Allegories of Reading*, especially in the chapter titled, "Metaphor." My own analysis differs from his in that he sees freedom of the will as simply "pitted against the ever-present obstacle of a limitation which it tries to transgress" (139). I am trying to show the origin of this "ever-present obstacle."

5. Again, this is the same circle that scandalized Rousseau in the "Preface."

6. Several scholars, including Goldschmidt (see Goldschmidt, *Anthropologie et Politique*, 400), have pointed out the different tenses in which the "First Part" and the "Second Part" are written. The "First Part" is mostly description, while the "Second Part" uses the historical past to narrate a story. From the viewpoint being developed in this work, one could put it this way: it is possible and even necessary to describe an impossible situation, but to move from that to necessity, one has to narrate.

7. Swenson, *On Jean-Jacques Rousseau*, 95. Much of my interpretation coincides with Swenson's. He is sensitive to many of the same points in the narrative that I am. He is a very good critic of any attempt to read Rousseau from a logic of linear causality, but because he does not reach the theological level of Rousseau's discourse, certain transitions in the *Discourse* remain less unexplained than uninterpreted. Thus, I would disagree with his characterization of the discussion of language as primarily providing "a model demonstration of a conceptual dead end" (111). Rather, Rousseau is setting up his scandalous logic of an impossible but necessary development.

8. Swenson, *On Jean-Jacques Rousseau*, 109, mentions that population growth is given as a reason for the development. This is correct, but it is not given in the narrative until later. The concrete difficulties and obstacles are the height of trees and competition of animals, certainly factors that were present in the "First Part" (cf. *CW* 3:43; *Pl.* 3:165).

9. It is of significance that in this passage, Rousseau himself seems to contrast being scandalized versus believing. The problem is that the people believed the man who made a claim to property. I also find it of interest that Goldschmidt, when referring precisely to this passage, that is, to the words "Ceci est à moi, [This is mine]" characterizes it as "le noyau d'irrationalité et de scandale [the nucleus of irrationality and scandal]." (*Anthropologie et Politique*, 533).

10. The best study on Rousseau's use of the word "revolution" remains Nagao Nishikawa, "Concept de révolutionnaire chez J.-J. Rousseau," in *Etudes Sur J.-J. Rousseau*, ed. Takeo Kuwabara (Kyoto: Iwanami, 1970), 195–296 (text in Japanese).

11. This seems to be a good description of what René Girard calls "mimetic desire." As I stated in my introduction, Todorov draws the parallel in a parenthetical remark in Tzvetan Todorov, *Life in Common: An Essay in General Anthropology*, European Horizons (Lincoln: University of Nebraska Press, 2001): "the mimetic desire of Girard is only another name for the amour-propre of Rousseau" (38).

12. Goldschmidt, *Anthropologie et Politique*, 579n65, makes the point that the political institutions are not established to defend humans from the obstacles of nature, but rather from obstacles that emerge from other humans. The obstacles are human relations.

CHAPTER 9

1. The classic interpretation of Rousseau's recollection is Ernst Cassirer, "*Das Problem Jean-Jacques Rousseau,*" in *Drei Vorshläge, Rousseau Zu Lesen,* ed. Ernst Cassirer, Jean Starobinski, Robert Darnton (Frankfurt: Fischer, 1989), 7–78; originally in *Archiv für Geschichte der Philosophie* 41 (1932): 15–16. The English translation is *The Question of Jean-Jacquest Rousseau,* 2nd ed., ed. Peter Gay (New Haven, CT: Yale University Press, 1989: 46–47.

2. For the problem of appearance and reality, consult Starobinski, *Jean-Jacques Rousseau: Transparency and Obstruction* (Chicago: University of Chicago Press, 1988), esp. chap. 1; and Judith N. Shklar, *Men and Citizens: A Study of Rousseau's Social Theory* (London: Cambridge University Press, 1969), 50–51.

3. Rousseau is referring here to the following prayer in the *First Discourse*: "Almighty God, thou who hold all Spirits in thy hands, deliver us from the enlightenment and fatal arts of our forefathers, and give back to us ignorance, innocence, and poverty, the only goods that can give us happiness and are precious in thy sight" (*CW* 2:21; *Pl.* 3:28).

4. The full title is: *Observations by Jean-Jacques Rousseau of Geneva on the Reply Made to his Discourse* (October 1751).(*CW* 2:37–54; *Pl.* 3.35–57)

5. The theme of scandal is touched upon in Derrida's analysis of Rousseau in Jacques Derrida, *Of Grammatology,* 1st American ed. (Baltimore: Johns Hopkins University Press, 1976). Still, the primary reality seems to be the supplement that contains all else, including scandal. I am arguing for a reversal of this ordering.

6. Cf. Robert Spaemann, "Von der Polis zur Natur—Die Kontroverse um Rousseaus ersten 'Discours,'" in *Rousseau—Bürger ohne Vaterland: Von Der Polis Zur Natur.* (Munich: Piper, 1980), 50–51, in which he comments on the notion of "doux" as a sign for Rousseau of the simultaneous domestication and decadence of virtue.

7. *Confessions, CW* 5:295; *Pl.* 1:351.

8. Jean Starobinski, "La Prosopopée de Fabricius," *Revue de Sciences Humaines* 41, no. 161 (1976): 83.

9. Ibid., 85.

10. Ibid., 86.

11. Ibid., 93.

12. Ibid., 93.

13. It is worth pointing out that this gesture of setting aside these images is typical of Rousseau. He identifies himself with the harshness and violence of Fabricius as a citizen. But his own voice is almost always softer and more given to enjoyment of the arts.

14. L. Strauss and J. Shklar both have given serious attention to the *systematic* role that violence plays in the *First Discourse.* Cf. Leo Strauss, *Natural Right and History* (Chicago: University of Chicago Press, 1971), 258–59; and Judith N. Shklar, *Men and Citizens: A Study of Rousseau's Social Theory* (London: Cambridge University Press, 1969), 14–15.

15. Prof. Christopher Kelly pointed out to me that Rousseau writes that he could have put this speech "into the mouth of Louis XII or Henry IV," two Christian monarchs (*CW* 2:11; *Pl.* 3:15).

16. Cf. Matt 18:17, 11:6.

17. The very first published reaction to the *First Discourse* was "Observations on the *Discourse* which was awarded the first prize at Dijon." It was published (anonomously, but presumably by the editor, Abbé Guillaume-Thomas-François Raynal) in the June 1751 issue of the *Mercure.* In it, one reads the following: "In the end, this what they object. What practical conclusion can be reached from the thesis the author upholds? . . . But what use can one draw from it? How can this disorder be remedied, either on the side of the

princes or that of private individuals?" (*CW* 2:23). Spaemann points out that the supposed "lack of a therapy" was one of the main criticisms of the *First Discourse*. Robert Spaemann, *Rousseau—Bürger Ohne Vaterland: Von Der Polis Zur Natur.* (Munich: Piper, 1980), 50–51.

18. Cf. Starobinski, *Jean-Jacques Rousseau: Transparency and Obstruction*, 6–11.

19. Cf. Strauss, *Natural Right and History*, 258–59.

20. For the historical background to the Academy's question, cf. Spaemann, *Rousseau*, 34–37. Spaemann covers much of the same ground in this article as I do here, but from a different viewpoint. That is, he traces the development of Rousseau's thought during the Controversy, especially in regard to its critique of bourgeois society. This critique leads to a consideration of inequality, and that is the theme of the *Second Discourse*.

21. An example of this is Yomoya Yoshioka, *Jan-Jakku Rusoh ron* [Jean-Jacques Rousseauology] (Tokyo: Tokyo University Press, 1988). This is perhaps the best overall study of Rousseau's thought in Japanese. But he interprets the *First Discourse* solely from the viewpoint of a "critique of knowledge" (cf. 12–39). Christopher Kelly, "Rousseau and the Case against (and for) the Arts," in *The Legacy of Rousseau*, ed. Clifford Orwin and Nathan Tarcov (Chicago: University of Chicago Press, 1997), 20–42, is balanced overall (witness the title), but the case against the arts is developed almost wholly from the *First Discourse*, while the case for the arts comes from other writings. It might have been different if he had expanded his considerations to include science as well.

22. Cf. *Final Reply*, *CW* 2:119; *Pl.* 3:83, in which Rousseau states that his adversaries are embarrassed each time that Sparta is mentioned. "What wouldn't they give for this deadly Sparta never to have existed."

23. Cf. Spaemann, *Rousseau*, 51.

24. Rousseau elaborates on this in footnote 9 of the *Second Discourse as follows*: "Let us therefore penetrate, through our frivolous demonstrations of good will, what goes on at the bottom of our Hearts, and let us reflect on what the state of things must be where all men are forced to flatter and destroy one another, and where they are born enemies by duty and swindlers by interest" (*CW* 2:75; *Pl.* 3:203). The whole footnote should be consulted.

25. Burgelin makes a similar point in Pierre Burgelin, *La philosophie de l'existence de J.-J. Rousseau* (Paris: Presses universitaires de France, 1952), 283.

26. The king's *Reply* (*CW* 2:28–36) and Bordes's *Discourse on the Advantages of the Sciences and Arts* (*CW* 2:93–109) escape this criticism somewhat.

27. The theme of isolation grows in importance in Rousseau's writings, but it is present from the very beginning.

28. Formerly known as Stanislaus I (1677–1766), he was the deposed King of Poland. It was published anonymously. Rousseau assumed that it was written, at least in part, by his Jesuit advisor, Father de Menou (cf. *Confessions* 5.307; *Pl.* 3:606).

29. I know of no other objection raised in the Controversy to which Rousseau admits that he does not have an answer. The following passage explains why: "Before explaining myself, I meditated on my subject at length and deeply, and I tried to consider all aspects of it. I doubt that any of my adversaries can say as much. At least I don't perceive in their writings any of those luminous truths that are no less striking in their obviousness than in their novelty, and that are always the fruit and proof of an adequate meditation. I dare say that they have never raised a reasonable objection that I did not anticipate and to which I did not reply in advance. That is why I am always compelled to restate the same things" (*CW* 2:110n; *Pl.* 3:71–72n).

30. I believe that the most philosophically rigorous proof of this is offered by F. Nietzsche in *Genealogy of Morals*. See Friedrich Wilhelm Nietzsche, *The Birth of Tragedy; and, the Genealogy of Morals*, 1st ed. (New York: Anchor Books, 1990).

31. There may be some who object to what they see as a too easy identification between the rack and the Cross. Pictures from the period, however, show while that the word Rousseau uses refers to a circular rack, the prisoners on it resemble the corpus on a crucifix, since their arms are outstretched and legs are together. It is this *image* that Rousseau finds scandalous.

32. Søren Kierkegaard, Howard Vincent Hong, and Edna Hatlestad Hong, *The Sickness unto Death: A Christian Psychological Exposition for Upbuilding and Awakening* (Princeton, NJ: Princeton University Press, 1980), 116.

33. Kierkegaard, Hong, and Hong, *The Sickness unto Death*, 116n.

34. David McCracken, *The Scandal of the Gospels: Jesus, Story, and Offense* (New York: Oxford University Press, 1994). This way of looking at scandal accords well with recent thought on the issue. As McCracken summarizes it, Lévi-Strauss, Derrida, and Eco have all found scandal to be at the point that erases "what seem to be self-evident differences" (10). For Lévi-Strauss, it is the self-evident difference between nature and culture. For Derrida, it is the founding concepts of the philosophical tradition. For Eco, it is the way metaphor brings together the disparate. Cf. Claude Lévi-Strauss, *The Elementary Structures of Kinship [Les structures élémentaires de la parenté]*, rev. ed. (London: Eyre and Spottiswoode, 1969); Jacques Derrida, *Writing and Difference* (Chicago: University of Chicago Press, 1978), 282–89; and Umberto Eco, "The Scandal of Metaphor: Metaphorology and Semiotics," *Poetics Today* 4, no. 2 (1983): 217–53.

35. By the use of this word, I intend to draw attention to a similarity between the thought of Rousseau and that of Derrida. At the same time, I wish to emphasize the difference. Whereas Derrida emphasizes that there is no choice (cf. Derrida, *Writing and Difference*, 292), I am trying to show that Rousseau's undecidability is the result of a decision.

36. Recall what Rousseau wrote in the unpublished *Preface to a Second Letter to Bordes*, referred to earlier: "If the Discourse of Dijon alone excited so many murmurs and caused so much scandal, what would have happened if I had from the first instant developed the entire extent of a System that is true but distressing, of which the question treated in this Discourse is only a Corollary? A declared enemy of the violence of the wicked, I would at the very least have passed for the enemy of public tranquility" (*CW* 2:184; *Pl.* 3:106).

CHAPTER 10

1. The "Preface" was added to the *Discourse* after Rousseau was awarded the prize from the Academy of Dijon. In it, he speaks of himself in the following terms: "I foresee that I will not easily be forgiven for the side I have dared to take. Running counter to everything that men admire today, I can expect only universal blame" (*CW* 2:4; *Pl.* 3:3). As for the frontispiece, which depicts the god Prometheus offering the gift of fire and, at the same time, warning the satyr about its deleterious effects, Rousseau explicates its meaning in his *Letter to Lecat*. He writes, "Prometheus who cries out and warns them of the danger is the Citizen of Geneva" (*CW* 2:179; *Pl.* 3:102). In Thomas M. Kavanagh, *Writing the Truth: Authority and Desire in Rousseau* (Berkeley: University of California Press, 1987), Kavanagh comments, "Rousseau, as he interprets this image, implicitly casts himself as a victim sacrificing himself for all mankind" (126).

2. The episode of fetching the Bible out of the temple in Book II, as well as the story of the lesson he learns from the governor of Lord John in Venice are just two examples of this.

3. Paul Zweig, *The Heresy of Self-Love; a Study of Subversive Individualism* (New York: Basic Books, 1968), 144.

4. For Starobinski's enlightening commentary on Rousseau's attempt at full self-disclosure, see Jean Starobinski, *Jean-Jacques Rousseau: Transparency and Obstruction*, 188–200.

5. Starobinski discusses this same problem in terms of trying to translate a truth whose proof is intuitive into a form that will allow the other to make the equally intuitive act of judgment. As he writes, "A 'circuit of words' intervenes between Rousseau's initial sentiment— that he is not guilty—and the final judgment, in which others will recognize his innocence" (*Jean-Jacques Rousseau: Transparency and Obstruction*, 188).

6. In *Heresy of Self-Love*, Zweig defines Rousseau's sense of innocence in the following way: "'To the pure all is pure,' and Rousseau sets out, in his confessional works, to demonstrate this 'grace' at the core of his being: a grace not of God but of nature, of pure intentions and impulsive energies. By thus proving his 'innocence' Rousseau recomposes his life in terms of the until-then-ineffable purity, and delights in it" (151). This kind of description demonstrates the danger of nontheologians taking up uncritically the language of theology. To speak of a "grace of nature" in this context is obscure, rather than illuminating.

7. I am not the only one who sees the Zulietta story as a parable. Ellis writes, "The parable of Zulietta, for it is really a parable, is one of the most terrible indictments of society in the whole of Rousseau's work." See Madeleine B. Ellis, *Rousseau's Venetian Story* (Baltimore: Johns Hopkins University Press, 1966), 132. She also subtitles the section dealing with this episode, "The Zulietta Parable."

8. Augustine, *Confessions*, ed. Henry Chadwick (Oxford: Oxford University Press, 1991), 6.

9. It is a matter of amazement to me how often this story is simply overlooked in spite of Rousseau's insistence on its revelatory power. Happily, this is not always the case. Christopher Kelly, *Rousseau's Exemplary Life: The Confessions as Political Philosophy* (Ithaca, NY: Cornell University Press, 1987), gives a detailed and illuminating interpretation of this encounter. Kelly follows this same quotation by saying, "With this Rousseau asserts that this section most clearly reveals the subject of the *Confessions* as a whole. This section of two or three pages and its surrounding context should be considered the heart of the *Confessions*" (174). Kelly himself latter corrected this view, so that even though there are very good hermeneutical reasons for exploring the "surrounding context" of the story, a strict reading would still say that the two or three pages are the "heart" of the book.

10. Although I will not build my argument on it, I do believe that the larger story of the encounter with Zulietta is structured as a parody of, and an antithesis to, the Passion of Christ. It begins with an evening meal. During the Last Supper, the "enemy" of Christ, Judas, leaves the meal. In the middle of Jean-Jacques' meal, Zulietta enters and, as she does, he is warned by the ship's captain, "By my faith, Sir, . . . watch out for yourself, here is the enemy" (*CW* 5:267; *Pl.* 1:318). The following day is the encounter between Zulietta and Jean-Jacques that reveals who he is, in the same way as the events on the day following the Last Supper definitively reveal Christ. One could argue that Rousseau offers the artistic opposite of the Crucifixion as two passionate lovers making love. That is what is supposed to happen with Jean-Jacques and Zulietta, and parody consists in the lack of consummation. Finally, Jean-Jacques asks for a meeting for the next day but reports that "she put off until the third day" (*CW* 5:270; *Pl.* 1:322). The third day is the day that Christ encounters the women who come seeking him. In the parody, it is the man who seeks out the woman, but she is not there. No meeting actually occurs.

11. Ellis, *Rousseau's Venetian Story*, 137.

12. Stanley Rosen, *The Quarrel between Philosophy and Poetry: Studies in Ancient Thought* (New York: Routledge, 1988), 109.

13. The four letters are often printed in editions of the *Confessions*. They can be found in English at *CW* 5:572–83 and in French at *Pl.* 1:1130–47.

14. For people looking for parallels between St. Augustine's *Confessions* and Rousseau's *Confessions*, this discussion of memory could fruitfully be compared with St. Augustine's in *Confessions*, Book Ten.

15. Kierkegaard tells that the offense involves "the most terrible decision" in *Philosophical Fragments, or, a Fragment of Philosophy; Johannes Climacus, or, De Omnibus Dubitandum Est* (Princeton, NJ: Princeton University Press, 1985), 34.

16. David Gauthier, "*Le Promeneur Solitaire*: Rousseau and the Emergence of the Post-Social Self," *Social Philosophy & Policy* 8(1): 41.

CHAPTER 11

1. In *Poetics of the Literary Self-Portrait*, Michel Beaujour points out the religious dimension of the *Reveries*. After noting that others, in particular Marcel Raymond and Jean Grenier, have also noted "the affinities between Rousseau's "reverie" and religious meditation," he goes on to see more in them than the mere secularization of meditation. He writes, "At any rate, *secular* should be understood in the sense of 'nontheological,' 'nondogmatic,' or, even 'nonnormative.' If the *Rêveries* speak of God, he is neither the God of Abraham, nor Christ, nor even the philosophers' divine clockmaker, but a deity who is responsive to Jean-Jacques' feelings" (61).

2. Cf. *CW* 8:56; *Pl.* 1:1059. In the "Fourth Walk," while discussing Montesquieu's *Temple of Gnide*, Rousseau makes clear reference to the teaching on scandal when he says that "it is necessary to distinguish between the learned public and the hordes of simple, credulous readers whom the story of the manuscript, narrated by a serious author with the appearance of good faith, really deceived and who fearlessly drank from a goblet of ancient form the poison of which they would at least have been suspicious had it been presented to them in a modern vessel" (*CW* 8:32–33; *Pl.* 1:1030).

3. Consult Eli Friedlander, *J.J. Rousseau: An Afterlife of Words* (Cambridge, MA: Harvard University Press, 2004), for a slightly different take on this opening line.

4. Cf. *CW* 8:5; *Pl.* 1:998; *CW* 8:8; *Pl.* 1:1001; *CW* 8:70; *Pl.* 1:1076; *CW* 8:71; *Pl.* 1:1077; *CW* 8:74; *Pl.* 1:1081. The word is variously translated in English. In Marcel Raymond, *Jean-Jacques Rousseau: La Quête de soi et la Rêverie* (Paris: Librairie José Corti, 1962), Raymond draws attention to another parallel between the *Reveries* and Ignatius's *Spiritual Exercises*: the composition of place. Taking up this suggestion, Beaujour sees the order of the *Reveries* as following that of "the composition of place" (*Poetics of the Literary Self-Portrait*, 60).

5. Marcel Raymond holds in his editorial note in the Pleiade edition the following: "Dans le *2e Dialogue*, l'idée se présentait sous une forme plus religieuse, l'indifférence se ramenant à la résignation à la volonté divine" (*Pl.* 1:857). He extends this to a use in the "Third Dialogue" as well. The use in the *Reveries* is at least as religious, if not more so, than in the *Dialogues*.

6. There are several very reliable translations of *the Spiritual Exercises* by St. Ignatius of Loyola. By convention, the text is referred to by paragraph numbers that were inserted in the text. I follow this convention. The "First Principle and Foundation" is paragraph 23.

7. The text of the *Spiritual Exercises* runs as follows: "It is therefore necessary that we should make ourselves indifferent to all created things, in so far as it is left to the liberty of our

free-will to do so, and is not forbidden; in such sort that we do not for our part wish for health rather than sickness, for wealth rather than poverty, for honor rather than dishonor, for a long life rather than a short one" (SpEx. No. 23).

CHAPTER 12

1. In this context, it is of great interest to follow Schinz's argument about the relationship between the two *Discourses* in Albert Schinz, *La Pensée de Jean-Jacques Rousseau* (Paris: Librairie Félix Alcan, 1929), and what it says about Rousseau's relationship to Christianity. The interest comes from the ineluctable logic that leads to scandal.

   At first, Schinz seems to be saying, similar to my own position, that the *Second Discourse* is the philosophical foundation of the *First Discourse.* something very similar to the position I have outlined above. He writes, "Et c'est cette conclusion justement, qui fit voir dans le *Second Discours* sur l'origine de l'inégalité un écrit parent du *Discours sur les Sciences et les Arts*—voire comme un fondement philosophique au pessimisme exprimé dans le premier écrit" (171). But he follows this up by saying that this conclusion is a misunderstanding based on appearances. There is a "radical opposition" between the two *Discourses* in that the earlier one is a plea for virtue, while the later one is no longer preoccupied with the idea of renouncement for the sake of virtue.

   To explain this discrepancy between the two *Discourses,* Schinz holds that Rousseau let slip, by way of error, the idea of "*vertu chrétienne*" into that of Roman virtue. Rousseau is guilty of "une grave confusion" (173). The Romans did not have the idea of renouncement as did the Christians. True, men like the ancient Romans, Fabricius and Cato, disciplined their appetites, but they did it to gain something. It was never renouncement for the sake of renouncement. There was never an idea of giving up present happiness for future happiness.

   Schinz sees the problem being resolved for Rousseau later on the basis of his rejection of the dogma of original sin. By allowing for Christian virtue in the *First Discourse,* Rousseau has allowed for this dogma to enter in by the back door. He implicitly adopts the idea of human being perverse. Only this "theory" can justify Rousseau's enthusiasm for the virtue of renouncement, "la vertu qui a comme objet l'expiation" (174).

   With the change of viewpoint between the *First* and *Second Discourse,* for which Schinz is arguing, this dogma, which implicitly condemns happiness in the world, is no longer needed, in fact it is "une pierre d'achoppement" (174).

   And so Schinz is led to seeing that Rousseau has being scandalized by Christianity. In this, he is correct. Still, the scandal does not begin with the *Second Discourse.* There is no error, no grave confusion between Christian and Roman virtue in the *First Discourse.* The dogma of original sin is no less a stumbling block then, than later. Rather, as I have tried to demonstrate, Rousseau needs the idea of original sin in the sense of an original victim at the basis of social order in order to occupy that original place. Without that, his system collapses, and if that space is filled by Christ, then his system simply becomes Christianity.

2. There is the historical problem of how directly this question was aimed by the Academy at Rousseau personally. In other words, the *First Discourse* may have been publicly, and not merely privately, successful in preparing the way for the *Second.*

3. Spaemann points out that Lessing had, in a review of the *First Discourse,* already pointed out the weakness of Rousseau's argument that parallel existence does not establish causality. Robert Spaemann, *Rousseau, Bürger Ohne Vaterland: Von Der Polis Zur Natur* (Munich: Piper, 1980), 49–50.

4. Patrick Coleman, *Rousseau's Political Imagination: Rule and Representation in the Lettre à d'Alembert, Histoire des Idées et Critique Littéraire; V. 220* (Geneva: Librairie Droz, 1984), 9. Coleman has put his finger on a very important point, but it goes deeper than his formulation allows. For Rousseau, not only does the conceptual vocabulary make social communication possible and justify social inequalities, but it also *creates* social inequality. The metaphysical power of language is underestimated by Coleman here.

5. Starobinski, *Jean-Jacques Rousseau: Transparency and Obstruction*, 4.

6. John D. Lyon, *The Tragedy of Origins: Pierre Corneille and Historical Perspective* (Stanford, CA: Stanford University Press, 1996), 20.

7. James Alison, *The Joy of Being Wrong: Original Sin through Easter Eyes* (New York: Crossroad, 1998), 99.

8. Ibid., 66. At this point in his argument, Alison is engaging Gans's account of the foundational event in the latter's work, *Science and Faith*.

9. Cf. *ibid.*, 67.

BIBLIOGRAPHY

Académie française Paris. *Le dictionnaire de l'académie française*. Paris: chez la veuve de J. B. Coignard et chez J. B. Coignard, 1694.

Acher, William. *Jean-Jacques Rousseau: écrivain de l'amitié*. Paris: Editions A. G. Nizet, 1971.

Affeldt, Steven G. "The Force of Freedom: Rousseau on Forcing to Be Free." *Political Theory* 27, no. 3 (1999): 299–333.

Alberg, Jeremiah. "The Place of the Victim." In *The Victim in French Literature*, edited by Norman Buford, 111–18. Amsterdam: Rodopi, 2005.

———. "Rousseau and Original Sin." *Revista Portuguesa de Filosofia* 57, no. 4 (2002): 773–90.

———. "Rousseau's *First Discourse* and Scandal." *International Philosophic Quarterly* 41, no. 161 (2001): 49–62.

———. "The Scandal of Origins." *Contagion: Journal of Violence, Mimesis, and Culture* 11 (Spring 2004): 1–14.

———. *Die Verlorene Einheit: Die Suche Nach Einer Philosophischen Alternative Zu Der Erbsündenlehre Von Rousseau Bis Schelling*. Frankfurt: P. Lang, 1996.

Alison, James. *The Joy of Being Wrong: Original Sin through Easter Eyes*. New York: Crossroad, 1998.

———. *Raising Abel: The Recovery of Eschatological Imagination*. New York: Crossroad, 1996.

Ansell-Pearson, Keith. *Nietzsche Contra Rousseau: A Study of Nietzsche's Moral and Political Thought*. Cambridge: Cambridge University Press, 1991.

Arendt, Hannah. *The Human Condition, Charles R. Walgreen Foundation Lectures*. Chicago: University of Chicago Press, 1958.

———. *On Revolution*. London: Penguin, 1963.

Aricò, Santo L. *Rousseau's Art of Persuasion in "La nouvelle Héloïse."* Lanham, MD: University Press of America, 1994.

Augustine. *Confessions*. Edited by Henry Chadwick. Oxford: Oxford University Press, 1991.

Babbitt, Irving. *Rousseau and Romanticism*. Austin: University of Texas Press, 1977.

Bailie, Gil. *Violence Unveiled: Humanity at the Crossroads*. New York: Crossroad, 1995.

Baker, Felicity. "Eternal Vigilance: Rousseau's Death Penalty." In *Rousseau and Liberty*, edited by Robert Wokler, 152–85. Manchester: Manchester University Press, 1995.

Banerjee, Amal. "Rousseau's Conception of Theatre." *British Journal of Aesthetics* 17 (1977): 171–77.

Barras, Moses. *The Stage Controversy in France from Corneille to Rousseau*. New York: Institute of French Studies, 1933.

Barth, Hans. "Über die Idee der Selbstentfremdung des Menschen bei Rousseau." *Zeitschift für philosophische Forschung* 13, no. 1 (1959): 16–35.

Barth, Karl. *Die Protestantische Theologie Im 19. Jahrhundert. Ihre Vorgeschichte Und Ihre Geschichte*. Zollikon, Switzerland: Evangelischer Verlag, 1947.

Bartlett, Anthony W. *Cross Purposes: The Violent Grammar of Christian Atonement*. Harrisburg, PA: Trinity Press International, 2001.

Barzilai, Shuli. *Lacan and the Matter of Origins*. Stanford, CA: Stanford University Press, 1999.

Baud-Bovy, Samuel. *Université ouvrière et faculté des lettres de l'université de Genève. Jean-Jacques Rousseau*. Neuchâtel, Switzerland: La Baconniáere, 1962.

Beaudry, Catherine A. *The Role of the Reader in Rousseau's Confessions*. New York: Peter Lang, 1991.

Beaujour, Michel. *Poetics of the Literary Self-Portrait*. New York: New York University Press, 1991.

Bernardi, Bruno, Florent Guénard, and Gabriella Silvestrini. *La religion, la liberté, la justice: un commentaire des Lettres écrites de la montagne de Jean-Jacques Rousseau*. Paris: J. Vrin, 2005.

Bernasconi, Robert. "No More Stories, Good or Bad: De Man's Criticisms of Derrida on Rousseau." In *Derrida: A Critical Reader*, edited by David Wood, 137–66. Oxford: Blackwell, 1992.

Bintz, Helmut. *Das Skandalon als Grundlagenproblem der Dogmatik: Eine Auseinandersetzung mit Karl Barth*. Berlin: de Gruyter, 1969.

Blanchard, William H. *Rousseau and the Spirit of Revolt; a Psychological Study*. Ann Arbor: University of Michigan Press, 1967.

Bloom, Allan David. *Love and Friendship*. New York: Simon and Schuster, 1993.

Bloom, Harold. *Jean-Jacques Rousseau: Modern Critical Views*. New York: Chelsea House, 1988.

Blum, Carol. *Rousseau and the Republic of Virtue: The Language of Politics in the French Revolution*. Ithaca, NY: Cornell University Press, 1986.

Bonhôte, Nicholas. *Jean-Jacques Rousseau: vision de l'histoire et autobiographie*. Lausanne, Switzerland: Editions L'Age d'Homme, 1992.

Boss, Ronald Ian. "Rousseau's Civil Religion and the Meaning of Belief: An Answer to Bayle's Paradox." *Studies on Voltaire and the Eighteenth Century* 84, no. 13 (1971): 123–93.

Bosshard, Peter. *Die Beziehungen Zwischen Rousseaus Zweitem Discours Und Dem 90.Brief Von Seneca*. Zurich: Juris Verlag, 1967.

Bouchard, Marcel. *L'academie de Dijon et le premier Discours de Rousseau*. Paris: Société Les Belles Lettres, 1950.

Boyd, Richard. "Pity's Pathologies Portrayed: Rousseau and the Limits of Democratic Compassion." *Political Theory* 32, no. 4 (2004): 519–46.

Bretonneau, Gisáele. *Valeurs humaines de J.-J. Rousseau*. Paris: La Colombe, 1961.

Broome, J. H. *Rousseau: A Study of His Thought*. New York: Barnes and Noble, 1963.

Bucher, Gérard. *L'imagination de l'origine*. Paris: L'Harmattan, 2000.

Buchner, Margaret Louise. *A Contribution to the Study of the Descriptive Technique of Jean-Jacques Rousseau*. New York: Johnson Reprint, 1973.

Burgelin, Pierre. "L'idée de place dans l'*Emile*." *Revue de littérature compare* (October–December 1961): 529–37.

———. *Jean-Jacques Rousseau et la religion de Genève*. Geneva: Labor et Fides, 1962.

———. *La philosophie de l'existence de J.-J. Rousseau*. Paris: Presses universitaires de France, 1952.

———. "Sur l'éducation de Sophie." *Annales historiques de la Révolution Française* 35 (1959–62): 113–37.

Calvin, Jean. *Concerning Scandals*. Grand Rapids, MI: Eerdmans, 1978.

Canovan, Margaret. "Arendt, Rousseau, and Human Plurality in Politics." *The Journal of Politics* 45, no. 2 (1983): 286–302.

Carroll, Robert C. "Muse and Narcissus: Rousseau's *Lettres à Sara*." *Studies on Voltaire and the Eighteenth Century* 137, no. 6 (1975): 81–107.

Cassirer, Ernst. "Das Problem Jean-Jacques Rousseau." In *Drei Vorshläge, Rousseau Zu Lesen*, by Ernst Cassirer, 7–78. Frankfurt: Fischer, 1989.

———. *The Question of Jean-Jacques Rousseau*. 2nd ed. Edited by Peter Gay. New Haven, CT: Yale University Press, 1989.

———. *Rousseau, Kant, Goethe; Two Essays*. Hamden, CT: Archon Books, 1961.

Charvet, John. *The Social Problem in the Philosophy of Rousseau, Cambridge Studies in the History and Theory of Politics*. Cambridge: Cambridge University Press, 1974.

Chauvet, Louis Marie. *Symbol and Sacrament: A Sacramental Reinterpretation of Christian Existence*. Collegeville, MN: Liturgical Press, 1995.

Cherry, Christopher. "Meaning and the Idol of Origins." *Philosophical Quarterly* 35, no. 138 (1985): 58–69.

Citton, Yves. "La preuve par l'Emile." *Poetique* 100 (1994): 413–25.

Cladis, Mark Sydney. *Public Vision, Private Lives: Rousseau, Religion, and 21st-Century Democracy*. Oxford: Oxford University Press, 2003.

Cobban, Alfred. *Rousseau and the Modern State*. 2nd ed. Hamden, CT: Archon Books, 1964.

Cochin, Augustin. *Les sociétés de pensée et la démocratie moderne*. Paris: Copernic, 1978.

Cohen, Paul M. *Freedom's Moment: An Essay on the French Idea of Liberty from Rousseau to Foucault*. Chicago: University of Chicago Press, 1997.

Coleman, Patrick. "Characterizing Rousseau's *Emile*." *Modern Language Notes* (1977): 761–78.

———. *Rousseau's Political Imagination: Rule and Representation in the Lettre à d'Alembert*. Genève: Librairie Droz, 1984.

Condillac, Etienne Bonnot de. *An Essay on the Origin of Human Knowledge; Being a Supplement to Mr. Locke's Essay on the Human Understanding*. Gainesville, FL: Scholars' Facsimiles and Reprints, 1971.

Cooper, Laurence D. *Rousseau, Nature, and the Problem of the Good Life*. University Park: Pennsylvania State University Press, 1999.

Coreth, Emerich. *Trinitätsdenken in Neuzeitlicher Philosophie*. Salzburg: Anton Pustet, 1986.

Cottret, Monique, and Bernard Cottret. *Jean-Jacques Rousseau en son temps*. Paris: Perrin, 2005.

Cranston, Maurice William. *Jean-Jacques: The Early Life and Work of Jean-Jacques Rousseau, 1712–1754*. Chicago: University of Chicago Press, 1991.

———. *The Noble Savage: Jean-Jacques Rousseau, 1754–1762*. Chicago: University of Chicago Press, 1991.

———. *The Solitary Self: Jean-Jacques Rousseau in Exile and Adversity*. Chicago: University of Chicago Press, 1997.

Cranston, Maurice William, and R. S. Peters. *Hobbes and Rousseau: A Collection of Critical Essays*. 1st ed., *Modern Studies in Philosophy*. Garden City, NY: Anchor Books, 1972.

Crocker, Lester G. *Jean-Jacques Rousseau*. New York: Macmillan, 1968.

Crogiez, Michèle. *Rousseau et le paradoxe*. Paris: Honorâe Champion Editeur, 1997.

———. *Solitude et méditation: étude sur les rêveries de Jean-Jacques Rousseau*. Paris: Champion, 1997.

Dante, Alighieri. *Inferno*. Edited by Charles Southward Singleton. Princeton, NJ: Princeton University Press, 1980.

Dauphin, Claude. *Musique et langage chez Rousseau, SVEC, 2004:08*. Oxford: Voltaire Foundation, 2004.

Davis, Michael. *The Autobiography of Philosophy: Rousseau's The Reveries of the Solitary Walker*. Lanham, MD: Rowman and Littlefield, 1999.

de Man, Paul. *Allegories of Reading: Figural Language in Rousseau, Nietzsche, Rilke, and Proust*. New Haven, CT: Yale University Press, 1979.

————. *Blindness & Insight; Essays in the Rhetoric of Contemporary Criticism.* New York: Oxford University Press, 1971.

————. *The Resistance to Theory.* Minneapolis: University of Minnesota Press, 1986.

————. *The Rhetoric of Romanticism.* New York: Columbia University Press, 1984.

De Mijolla, Elizabeth. *Autobiographical Quests: Augustine, Montaigne, Rousseau, and Wordsworth.* Charlottesville: University Press of Virginia, 1994.

Deguy, Michel, and Jean Pierre Dupuy. *René Girard et le problème du mal.* Paris: Grasset, 1982.

Dent, N. J. H. *A Rousseau Dictionary.* Oxford: Blackwell Reference, 1992.

Derathé, Robert. "Jean-Jacques Rousseau et le Christianisme." *Revue de Métaphysique et de Morale* 53 (1948): 379–434.

————. *Jean-Jacques Rousseau et la science politique de son temps.* 1st ed. Paris, Presses Universitaires de France, 1951.

————. *Le rationalisme de Jean-Jacques Rousseau.* Paris: Presses, Universitaires de France, 1948.

Derrida, Jacques. *De la grammatologie.* Paris: édtions de Minuit, 1967.

————. *Dissemination.* Chicago: University Press, 1981.

————. *La dissémination.* Paris: éditions du Seuil, 1972.

————. *Edmund Husserl's Origin of Geometry, an Introduction.* Lincoln: University of Nebraska Press, 1989.

————. *The Gift of Death, Religion and Postmodernism.* Chicago: University of Chicago Press, 1995.

————. "La linguistique de Rousseau." *Revue internationale de philosophie* 82 (1967): 443–62.

————. *Monolingualism of the Other, or, the Prosthesis of Origin, Cultural Memory in the Present.* Stanford, CA: Stanford University Press, 1998.

————. *Of Grammatology.* 1st American ed. Baltimore: Johns Hopkins University Press, 1976.

————. *Of Spirit: Heidegger and the Question.* Chicago: University of Chicago Press, 1989.

————. *Writing and Difference.* Chicago: University of Chicago Press, 1978.

Derrida, Jacques, and Stefano Agosti. *Spurs: Nietzsche's Styles = Eperons: les styles de Nietzsche.* Chicago: University of Chicago Press, 1979.

Derrida, Jacques, and John D. Caputo. *Deconstruction in a Nutshell: A Conversation with Jacques Derrida, Perspectives in Continental Philosophy.* New York: Fordham University Press, 1997.

Derrida, Jacques, and Collège international de philosophie. *De l'esprit: Heidegger et la question.* Paris: Galilée, 1987.

Derrida, Jacques, and Thomas Dutoit. *On the Name.* Stanford, CA: Stanford University Press, 1995.

Diaconoff, Suellen. "Identity and Representation in the Prose and Painted Portrait." In *Autobiography in French Literature,* 61–70. Columbia: University of South Carolina, 1985.

Domenech, Jacques. *Les Confessions Rousseau.* Paris: Ellipses, 2000.

Duchet, Michèle, and Michel Launay. "Synchronie et diachronie: *l'Essai sur l'origine des langues* et le *deuxième Discours.*" *Revue internationale de philosophie* 21 (1976): 421–42.

Dumouchel, Paul. *Violence and Truth: On the Work of René Girard.* Stanford, CA: Stanford University Press, 1988.

Eco, Umberto. "The Scandal of Metaphor: Metaphorology and Semiotics." *Poetics Today* 4, no. 2 (1983): 217–57.

Eigeldinger, Frédéric. "Ils ne me pardonneront jamais le mal qu'ils m'ont fait." *Etudes Jean-Jacques Rousseau* 10 (1998): 77–89.

Eigeldinger, Marc. *Jean-Jacques Rousseau: univers mythique et cohérence.* Neuchatel, Switzerland: Editions de la Baconniáere, 1978.

Ellenburg, Stephen. *Rousseau's Political Philosophy: An Interpretation from Within.* Ithaca, NY: Cornell University Press, 1976.

Ellis, Madeleine B. *Rousseau's Socratic Aemilian Myths: A Literary Collation of Emile and the Social Contract.* Columbus: Ohio State University Press, 1977.

———. *Rousseau's Venetian Story.* Baltimore: Johns Hopkins University Press, 1966.

Ellrich, Robert J. *Rousseau and His Reader: The Rhetorical Situation of the Major Works.* Chapel Hill: University of North Carolina Press, 1969.

Encyclopédie ou dictionnaire raisonné des sciences, des arts et des métiers. 17 vols. Paris, Neuchâtel: 1751–65.

Fackenheim, Emil L. *The Religious Dimension in Hegel's Thought.* Bloomington: Indiana University Press, 1968.

Fauconnier, Gilbert. *Index-Concordance d'Emile et Sophie et de la Lettre à Christophe de Beaumont.* Geneva: Slatkine, 1993.

———. *Index du* Discours sur l'économie politique *et fragments politiques.* Geneva: Slatkine, 1992.

Fauconnier, Gilbert, and Etienne Brunet. *Index-Concordance de* Julie, ou, la nouvelle Héloèise. 2 vols. Geneva: Slatkine, 1991.

Fauconnier, Gilbert, and Michel Launay. *Index-Concordance des Rêveries du promeneur solitaire.* Geneva: Slatkine; Paris: Champion, 1978.

Fénelon, François de Salignac de La Mothe. *The Education of a Daughter.* Bedford, MA: Applewood Books, 1995.

———. *Telemachus, Son of Ulysses.* Edited by Patrick Riley. Cambridge: Cambridge University Press, 1994.

Ferrara, Alessandro. *Modernity and Authenticity: A Study in the Social and Ethical Thought of Jean-Jacques Rousseau.* Albany: State University of New York, 1993.

Fetscher, Iring. "Rousseau und die Folgen. Ethik und Politik." *Neue Hefte für Philosophie* 29 (1989): 1–23.

———. *Rousseaus Politische Philosophie: Zur Geschichte des Demokratischen Freiheitsbegriffs.* Frankfurt: Suhrkamp, 1975.

Formey, Jean-Henri-Samuel. *Anti-Emile.* Berlin: Pauli, 1763.

Franke, William. *Dante's Interpretive Journey, Religion and Postmodernism.* Chicago: University of Chicago Press, 1996.

Friedlander, Eli. *J.J. Rousseau: An Afterlife of Words.* Cambridge, MA: Harvard University Press, 2004.

Fulda, Hans Friedrich, and Rolf-Peter Horstmann. *Rousseau, die Revolution und der Junge Hegel.* Stuttgart, Germany: Klett-Cotta, 1991.

Gans, Eric Lawrence. *The End of Culture: Toward a Generative Anthropology.* Berkeley: University of California Press, 1985.

———. *The Origin of Language: A Formal Theory of Representation.* Berkeley: University of California Press, 1981.

———. *Science and Faith: The Anthropology of Revelation.* Lanham, MD: Rowman and Littlefield, 1990.

———. *Signs of Paradox: Irony, Resentment, and Other Mimetic Structures.* Stanford, CA: Stanford University Press, 1997.

Gauthier, David. *Moral Dealing: Contract, Ethics, and Reason.* Ithaca, NY: Cornell University Press, 1990.

———. "*Le Promeneur Solitaire*: Rousseau and the Emergence of the Post-Social Self." *Social Philosophy & Policy* 8, no. 1:35–58.

Gearhart, Suzanne. "Philosophy *before* Literature: Deconstruction, Historicity, and the Work of Paul De Man." *Diacritics* (Winter 1983): 63–81.

Gildin, Hilail. *Rousseau's Social Contract: The Design of the Argument.* Chicago: University of Chicago Press, 1983.

Girard, René. *Deceit, Desire, and the Novel: Self and Other in Literary Structure.* Baltimore: Johns Hopkins University Press, 1965.

———. *I Saw Satan Fall Like Lightning.* Maryknoll, NY: Orbis, 2001.

———. *The Scapegoat.* Baltimore: Johns Hopkins University Press, 1986.

———. *A Theater of Envy: William Shakespeare.* New York: Oxford University Press, 1991.

———. *"To Double Business Bound": Essays on Literature, Mimesis, and Anthropology.* Baltimore: Johns Hopkins University Press, 1978.

———. *Violence and the Sacred.* Baltimore: Johns Hopkins University Press, 1977.

Girard, René, Jean-Michel Oughourlian, and Guy Lefort. *Des choses cachées depuis la fondation du monde.* Paris: Grasset, 1978.

———. *Resurrection from the Underground: Feodor Dostoevsky.* New York: Crossroad, 1997.

———. *Things Hidden since the Foundation of the World.* Stanford, CA: Stanford University Press, 1987.

Glum, Friedrich. *Jean Jacques Rousseau Religion und Staat: Grundlegung Einer Demokratischen Staatslehre.* Stuttgart, Germany: Kohlhammer, 1956.

Goldschmidt, Victor. *Anthropologie et politique: les principes du systèm de Rousseau.* Paris: J. Vrin, 1974.

Goodheart, Eugene. *The Cult of the Ego; the Self in Modern Literature.* Chicago: University of Chicago Press, 1968.

Gouhier, Henri Gaston. *Les méditations métaphysiques de Jean-Jacques Rousseau.* Paris: J. Vrin, 1970.

Gourevitch, Victor. "Rousseau on the Arts and Sciences." *Journal of Philosophy* 69 (1972): 737–54.

———. "Rousseau on Lying: A Provisional Reading of the Fourth Reverie." *Berkshire Review* 15 (1980): 93–107.

———. "Rousseau on Providence." *Review of Metaphysics* 53 (March 2000): 565–611.

———. "Rousseau's Pure State of Nature." *Interpretation* 16 no.1 (1988): 23–59.

Goyard-Fabre, Simone. *Politique et philosophie dans l'œuvre de Jean-Jacques Rousseau.* Paris: Presses universitaires de France, 2001.

Grange, Henri. *"L'essai sur l'origine des langues* dans son rapport avec le *Discours l'origine de l'inégalité."* *Annales historiques de la Révolution Française* 39 (1967): 291–307.

Grant, Ruth Weissbourd. *Hypocrisy and Integrity: Machiavelli, Rousseau, and the Ethics of Politics.* Chicago: University of Chicago Press, 1997.

Green, Frederick Charles. *Jean-Jacques Rousseau; a Critical Study of His Life and Writings.* Cambridge: Cambridge University Press, 1955.

Green, Joel B., and Mark D. Baker. *Recovering the Scandal of the Cross: Atonement in New Testament & Contemporary Contexts.* Downers Grove, IL: InterVarsity Press, 2000.

Grimsley, Ronald. *Jean-Jacques Rousseau: A Study in Self-Awareness.* 2nd ed. Cardiff: University of Wales Press, 1969.

———. *Rousseau and the Religious Quest.* Oxford: Clarendon Press, 1968.

Groethuysen, Bernhard. *J.-J. Rousseau.* Paris: Gallimard, 1983.

Groupe Jean-Jacques Rousseau. *Index des Confessions.* Geneva: Slatkine; Paris: Champion, 1978.

Guéhenno, Jean. *Jean-Jacques.* Nouv. éd. Paris: Gallimard, 1962.

———. *Jean-Jacques Rousseau.* London: Routledge and K. Paul; New York: Columbia University Press, 1966.

Guillemin, Henri. *La cause de Dieu.* Paris: Arléa, 1990.

Habib, Claude. *Le consentement amoureux: Rousseau, les Femmes et la cité.* Paris: Hachette Littérature, 1998.

Halbertal, Moshe, and Avishai Margalit. *Idolatry.* Cambridge, MA: Harvard University Press, 1992.

Halliwell, Stephen. *The Aesthetics of Mimesis: Ancient Texts and Modern Problems.* Princeton, NJ: Princeton University Press, 2002.

Hamerton-Kelly, Robert. "Popular Sovereignty and the Sacred: A Mimetic Reading of Rousseau's Doctrine of the General Will." *Paragrana* 4, no. 2 (1995): 215–44.

Hamilton, James F. *Rousseau's Theory of Literature: The Poetics of Art and Nature.* York, SC: French Literature Publications, 1979.

Hartle, Ann. *The Modern Self in Rousseau's Confessions: A Reply to St. Augustine.* Notre Dame, IN: University of Notre Dame Press, 1983.

Harvey, Irene E. *Labyrinths of Exemplarity: At the Limits of Deconstruction.* Albany: State University of New York Press, 2002.

Harvey, Simon, Marian Hobson, and David Kelley. *Reappraisals of Rousseau: Studies in Honour of R. A. Leigh.* Manchester: Manchester University, 1980.

Havens, George Remington. *Jean-Jacques Rousseau.* Boston: Twayne, 1978.

———. "La théorie de la bonté naturelle de l'homme chez J.-J. Rousseau." *Revue d'histoire littéraire de la France* (1924–25): 629–42.

———. *Voltaire's Marginalia on the Pages of Rousseau; a Comparative Study of Ideas.* New York: B. Franklin, 1971.

Haymann, Franz. *Jean Jacques Rousseau's Sozialphilosophie.* Leipzig, Germany: Verlag von Veit, 1898.

Hendel, Charles William. *Jean-Jacques Rousseau: Moralist.* 2nd ed. Indianapolis: Bobbs-Merrill, 1934.

Hobson, Marian. *Jacques Derrida: Opening Lines.* London: Routledge, 1998.

———. *The Object of Art: The Theory of Illusion in Eighteenth-Century.* Cambridge: Cambridge University Press, 1982.

Hobson, Marian, J. T. A. Leigh, Robert Wokler, and Voltaire Foundation. *Rousseau & the Eighteenth Century: Essays in Memory of R. A. Leigh.* Oxford: Voltaire Foundation at the Taylor Institution, 1992.

Hoffman, Paul. "L'âme et la liberté: quelques réflexions sur le dualisme dans la 'Profession de foi du vicaire savoyard.'" *Annales de la Société Jean-Jacques Rousseau* (1992): 29–64.

Hondrich, Karl Otto. *Enthüllung Und Entrüstung: Eine Phänomenologie Des Politischen Skandals.* Frankfurt: Suhrkamp, 2002.

Horowitz, Asher. *Rousseau, Nature, and History.* Toronto: University of Toronto Press, 1987.

Howells, R. J. "The Metaphysic of Nature: Basic Values and Their Application in the Social Philosophy of Rousseau." *Studies on Voltaire and the Eighteenth Century* 60 (1968).

Huizinga, Jakob Herman. *The Making of a Saint: The Tragi-Comedy of Jean-Jacques Rousseau.* London: H. Hamilton, 1976.

Hulliung, Mark. *The Autocritique of Enlightenment: Rousseau and the Philosophes.* Cambridge, MA: Harvard University Press, 1994.

Jackson, Susan K. *Rousseau's Occasional Autobiographies.* Columbus: Ohio State University Press, 1992.

Jacquet, Christian. *La pensée religieuse de Jean-Jacques Rousseau.* Louvain, Belgium: Bibliothèque de l'Université, 1975.

Janke, Wolfgang. *Entgegensetzungen: Studien Zu Fichte-Konfrontationen Von Rousseau Bis Kierkegaard*. Amsterdam: Rodopi, 1994.

Jenny, Laurent. *L'expérience de la chute: de Montaigne à Michaux*. Paris: Presses universitaires de France, 1997.

Jimack, Peter. *Rousseau, 'Emile.'* London: Grant and Cutler, 1983.

Johnston, Guillemette. *Lectures poétiques: la représentation poétique du discours théorique chez Jean-Jacques Rousseau*. Birmingham, AL: Summa Publications, 1996.

Johnston, Steven. *Encountering Tragedy: Rousseau and the Project of Democratic Order*. Ithaca, NY: Cornell University Press, 1999.

Jones, James F. "The *Dialogues* as Autobiographical Truth." *Studies in Eighteenth-Century Culture* 14 (1985): 317–28.

———. *Rousseau's Dialogues: An Interpretive Essay*. Geneva: Librairie Droz, 1991.

Kavanagh, Thomas M. "Rousseau's *Le Lévite D'ephraïm*: Dream, Text, and Synthesis." *Eighteenth-Century Studies* 16 (1982–83): 141–61.

———. *Writing the Truth: Authority and Desire in Rousseau*. Berkeley: University of California Press, 1987.

Kelly, Christopher. *Rousseau as Author: Consecrating One's Life to the Truth*. Chicago: University of Chicago Press, 2003.

———. "Rousseau and the Case against (and for) the Arts." In *The Legacy of Rousseau*, edited by Clifford Orwin and Nathan Tarcov, 20–42. Chicago: University of Chicago Press, 1997.

———. "Rousseau's *Confessions*." In *The Cambridge Companion to Rousseau*, edited by Patrick Riley, 302–28. Cambridge: Cambridge University Press, 2001.

———. *Rousseau's Exemplary Life: The Confessions as Political Philosophy*. Ithaca, NY: Cornell University Press, 1987.

———. "Rousseau's Philosophic Dream." *Interpretation* 23, no. 3 (1996): 417–44.

———. "Taking Readers as They Are: Rousseau's Turn from Discourses to Novels." *Eighteenth-Century Studies* 33, no. 1 (1999): 85–101.

Kelly, Christopher, and Roger D. Masters. "Rousseau on Reading 'Jean-Jacques': The Dialogues." *Interpretation* 17, no. 2 (1989): 239–53.

Kierkegaard, Søren, Howard Vincent Hong, and Edna Hatlestad Hong. *Philosophical Fragments, or, a Fragment of Philosophy; Johannes Climacus, or, De Omnibus Dubitandum Est*. Princeton, NJ: Princeton University Press, 1985.

———. *The Sickness unto Death: A Christian Psychological Exposition for Upbuilding and Awakening*. Princeton, NJ: Princeton University Press, 1980.

Kintzler, Catherine. *Jean-Philippe Rameau: splendeur et naufragé de l'esthétique du plaisir à l'âge classique*. Paris: Le Sycomore, 1983.

Kittel, Gerhard, and Otto Bauernfeind. *Theologisches Wörterbuch Zum Neuen Testament*. Stuttgart, Germany: W. Kohlhammer, 1932.

Kries, Douglas. "Rousseau and the Problem of Religious Toleration." In *Piety and Humanity: Essays on Religion and Early Modern Political Philosophy*, edited by Douglas Kries, 259–86. New York: Rowman and Littlefield, 1997.

Kryger, Edna. *La notion de liberté chez Rousseau et ses répercussions sur Kant*. Paris: A. G. Nizet, 1978.

Labio, Catherine. *Origins and the Enlightenment: Aesthetic Epistemology from Descartes to Kant*. Ithaca, NY: Cornell University Press, 2004.

Lacroix, Jean. *Le désir et les désirs*. Paris: Presses universitaires de France, 1975.

Lange, Lynda. *Feminist Interpretations of Jean-Jacques Rousseau, Re-Reading the Canon*. University Park: Pennsylvania State University Press, 2002.

Lanson, Gustave. "L'unité de la pensée de Jean-Jacques Rousseau." *Annales de la Société Jean-Jacques Rousseau* 8 (1912): 1–32.

Launay, Lâeo, and Michel Launay. *Index-Concordance du* Discours sur les sciences et les arts *et du* Discours sur les origines de l'inégalité: *avec les discours inédits des concurrents de Rousseau pour le prix de 1750.* Geneva: Slatkine, 1981.

Launay, Michel. *Jean-Jacques Rousseau: écrivain politique (1712–1762).* Cannes: C.E.L., 1972.

Lecointre, S. and Le Galliot, J. "Essai sur la structure d'un mythe personnel dans les *Rêveries du promeneur solitaire.*" *Semiotica* 4 (1971): 339–64.

Lefebvre, Philippe. *L'esthétique de Rousseau.* Paris: SEDES, 1997.

———. *Les pouvoirs de la parole: l'église et Rousseau, 1762–1848.* Paris: éditions du Cerf, 1992.

Lemaître, Jules. *Jean Jacques Rousseau.* Port Washington, NY: Kennikat Press, 1968.

Léon, Paul L. "Rousseau et les fondements de l'etat modern." *Archives de Philosophie du droit et de Sociologie juridique.* (1934): 197–238.

Levenson, J. Douglas. *The Death and Resurrection of the Beloved Son: The Transformation of Child Sacrifice in Judaism and Christianity.* New Haven, CT: Yale University Press, 1993.

Lévi-Strauss, Claude. *The Elementary Structures of Kinship [Les Structures élémentaires de la Parenté].* Revised ed. London: Eyre and Spottiswoode, 1969.

Livingston, Paisley. *Models of Desire: René Girard and the Psychology of Mimesis.* Baltimore: Johns Hopkins University Press, 1992.

Locke, John. *Some Thoughts Concerning Education.* Edited by Ruth Grant, and Nathan Tarcov. Indianapolis: Hackett, 1996.

Lorgnet, Michele. "*Rousseau juge de Jean-Jaques—Dialogues*: L'imaginaire de l'argumentation." *Francophonia* 4, no. 6 (1984): 29–41.

Lyons, John D. *The Tragedy of Origins: Pierre Corneille and Historical Perspective.* Stanford, CA: Stanford University Press, 1996.

MacCannell, Juliet Flower. "The Post-Fictional Self: Authorial Consciousness in Three Texts by Rousseau." *MLN* 89 (1974): 580–99.

Macdonald, Frederika. *Jean Jacques Rousseau, a New Criticism.* New York: G. P. Putnam's Sons; London: Chapman and Hall, 1906.

Macy, Jeffrey. "'God Helps Those Who Help Themselves': New Light on the Theological-Political Teaching in Rousseau's *Profession of Faith of the Savoyard Vicar.*" *Polity* 24, no. 4 (1992): 615–32.

Maistre, Joseph Marie. *Against Rousseau: "On the State of Nature" and "On the Sovereignty of the Peuple."* Translated by Richard Lebrun. Montreal: McGill Queen's University Press, 1996.

Malebranche, Nicolas. *Treatise on Nature and Grace.* Translated by Patrick Riley. Oxford: Clarendon Press, 1992.

Mall, Laurence. Emile, *ou les figures de la fiction, SVEC, 2002:04.* Oxford: Voltaire Foundation, 2002.

Maritain, Jacques. *Three Reformers: Luther—Descartes—Rousseau.* New ed. London: Sheed and Ward, 1944.

Marks, Jonathan. "The Savage Pattern: The Unity of Rousseau's Thought Revisited." *Polity* 31, no. 1 (1998): 75–105.

Marshall, David. *The Surprising Effects of Sympathy: Marivaux, Diderot, Rousseau, and Mary Shelley.* Chicago: University of Chicago Press, 1988.

Marso, Lori Jo. *(Un)Manly Citizens: Jean-Jacques Rousseau's and Germaine De Staël's Subversive Women.* Baltimore: Johns Hopkins University Press, 1999.

Mason, John Hope. "'Forced to Be Free.'" In *Rousseau and Liberty*, edited by Robert Wokler. Manchester: Manchester University Press, 1995.

———. "Reading Rousseau's First Discourse." *Studies on Voltaire and the Eighteenth Century* 22 (1987): 251–66.

Masson, Pierre Maurice. *La "Profession de foi du vicaire savoyard" de Jean-Jacques Rousseau.* Fribourg: (Suisse) Librairie de l'Université (O. Gschwend); Paris: Hachette, 1914.

———.*La religion de Jean-Jacques Rousseau.* Paris: Hachette, 1916.

Masters, Roger D. *The Political Philosophy of Rousseau.* Princeton, NJ: Princeton University Press, 1968.

Mattéi, Jean-François. *De l'indignation.* In *Contretemps,* edited by Chantal Delsol. Paris: La Table Ronde, 2005.

McCarthy, Vincent. "Christus as Chrestus in Rousseau and Kant." *Kant-Studien* 2 (1982): 191–207.

McCracken, David. *The Scandal of the Gospels: Jesus, Story, and Offense.* New York: Oxford University Press, 1994.

McDonald, Christie. "The Model of Reading in Rousseau's *Dialogues.*" *MLN* 93 (1978): 723–32.

McEachern, Jo-Ann E., and Voltaire Foundation. *Bibliography of the Writings of Jean Jacques Rousseau to 1800.* Oxford: Voltaire Foundation at the Taylor Institution, 1989.

McKenna, Andrew J. *Violence and Difference: Girard, Derrida, and Deconstruction.* Urbana: University of Illinois Press, 1992.

McManners, John. "The Religion of Rousseau." *The Journal of Religious History* 5 (1969): 348–53.

Meier, Heinrich. "The *Discourse on the Origin and the Foundations of Inequality among Men*: On the Intention of Rousseau's Most Philosophical Work." *Interpretation* 16, no. 2 (1988–89): 211–27.

Melzer, Arthur M. *The Natural Goodness of Man: On the System of Rousseau's Thought.* Chicago: University of Chicago Press, 1990.

———. "The Origin of the Counter-Enlightenment: Rousseau and the New Religion of Sincerity." *American Political Science Review* 90, no. 2 (1996): 344–60.

Mercken-Spaas, Godelieve. "The Social Anthropology of Rousseau's *Emile.*" *Studies on Voltaire and the Eighteenth Century* 132, no. 11 (1975): 137–81.

Miller, J. Hillis. "Tradition and Difference." *Diacritics* 2, no. 4 (1972): 6–13.

Miller, Jim. *Rousseau: Dreamer of Democracy.* New Haven, CT: Yale University Press, 1984.

Moreau-Rendu, S. *L'idée De Bonté Naturelle Chez J.-J. Rousseau.* Paris: Libraire Marcel Rivière, 1929.

Morgenstern, Mira. *Rousseau and the Politics of Ambiguity: Self, Culture, and Society.* University Park: Pennsylvania State University Press, 1996.

Mounier, Jacques. *La fortune de ecrits de J.-J. Rousseau dans pays de langue Allemande de 1782 à 1813.* Paris: Presses universitaires de France, 1980.

Mulhall, Stephen. *Philosophical Myths of the Fall.* Princeton, NJ: Princeton University Press, 2005.

Munteano, B. *Solitude Et Contradictions De Jean-Jacques Rousseau.* Paris: A. G. Nizet, 1975.

Murat, Michel. "Jean-Jacques Rousseau: Imitation Musicale Et Origine Des Langues." *Travaux de Linguistique et de Littérature* 18, no. 2 (1980): 145–68.

Neiman, Susan. *Evil in Modern Thought: An Alternative History of Philosophy.* Princeton, NJ: Princeton University Press, 2002.

Neuhouser, Frederick. "Freedom, Dependence, and the General Will." *The Philosophical Review* 102, no. 3 (1993): 363–95.

Nietzsche, Friedrich Wilhelm. *The Birth of Tragedy; and, the Genealogy of Morals.* 1st ed. New York: Anchor Books, 1990.

Nishikawa, Nagao. "Concept De Révolutionnaire Chez J.-J. Rousseau." In *Etudes Sur J.-J. Rousseau*, edited by Takeo Kuwabara, 195–296. Kyoto: Iwanami, 1970.

———. "A Reexamination of the 'Experience at Vincennes' (2)." *Journal of Ritsumeikan University* 10 (1967): 1180–99.

———. "Speaking of the Experience of Vincennes: A Research Note on Rousseau (1)." *Journal of Ritsumeikan University* 5 (1967): 367–85.

O'Dea, Michael. "Fiction and the Ideal in *Rousseau Juge De Jean-Jacques*." *French Studies* 40 (1985): 141–50.

———. *Jean-Jacques Rousseau: Music, Illusion, and Desire*. New York: St. Martin's Press, 1995.

Ogrodnick, Margaret. *Instinct and Intimacy: Political Philosophy and Autobiography in Rousseau*. Toronto: University of Toronto Press, 1999.

O'Hagan, Timothy. *Jean-Jacques Rousseau and the Sources of the Self*. Brookfield, VT: Avebury, 1997.

———. *Rousseau*. New York: Routledge, 1999.

Okin, Susan Moller. *Women in Western Political Thought*. Princeton, NJ: Princeton University Press, 1979.

O'Neal, John C. *Seeing and Observing: Rousseau's Rhetoric of Perception*. Saratoga, CA: ANMA LIBRI, 1985.

O'Neal, John C., and Ourida Mostefai. *Approaches to Teaching Rousseau's* Confessions *and* Reveries of the Solitary Walker, *Approaches to Teaching World Literature*. New York: The Modern Language Association of America, 2004.

Orwin, Clifford. "Rousseau's Socratism." *Journal of Politics* 60, no. 1 (1998): 174–87.

Orwin, Clifford, and Nathan Tarcov. *The Legacy of Rousseau*. Chicago: University of Chicago Press, 1997.

Oxford University Press. *The Holy Bible: Containing the Old and New Testaments: New Revised Standard Version*. Anglicized ed. Oxford: Oxford University Press, 1995.

Palaver, Wolfgang. "Mimesis and Scapegoating in the Works of Hobbes, Rousseau, and Kant." *Contagion* 10 (Spring 2003): 126–48.

Payne, Harry. "The Philosophes and Popular Ritual: Turgot, Voltaire, Rousseau." *Studies in Eighteenth-Century Culture* 14 (1985): 307–16.

Perkins, Merle L. *Jean-Jacques Rousseau on the Individual and Society*. Lexington: University Press of Kentucky, 1974.

Perrin, Jean-François. *Le chant de l'origine: la mémoire et le temps dans les Confessions de Jean-Jacques Rousseau*. Oxford: Voltaire Foundation, 1996.

Philonenko, Alexis. *Jean-Jacques Rousseau et la pensée du malheur*. 3 vols. *Bibliothéque D'histoire De La Philosophie*. Paris: J. Vrin, 1984.

Plan, Pierre Paul. *J.-J. Rousseau raconté par les gazettes de son temps*. Paris: Mercure de France, 1912.

Plato. *The Republic of Plato*. Translated by Allan Bloom. New York: Basic Books 1968.

Plattner, Marc F. *Rousseau's State of Nature: An Interpretation of the Discourse on Inequality*. Dekalb: Northern Illinois University Press, 1979.

Porset, Charles. "L'inquiétante étrangeté de l'*Essai Sur L'origine Des Langues*: Rousseau et ses exégètes." *Studies on Voltaire and the Eighteenth Century* 154 (1976): 1715–58.

Porter, Dennis. *Rousseau's Legacy: Emergence and Eclipse of the Writer in France*. New York: Oxford University Press, 1995.

Poulet, Georges. *Studies in Human Time*. Westport, CT: Greenwood, 1979.

Pufendorf, Samuel, and Michael Seidler. *Samuel Pufendorf's on the Natural State of Men: The 1678 Latin Edition and English Translation, Studies in the History of Philosophy (Lewiston, N.Y.); V.13*. Lewiston, NY: Mellen, 1990.

Pufendorf, Samuel, James Tully, and Michael Silverthorne. *On the Duty of Man and Citizen According to Natural Law, Cambridge Texts in the History of Political Thought.* Cambridge: Cambridge University Press, 1991.

Quint, David. *Montaigne and the Quality of Mercy: Ethical and Political Themes in the* Essais. Princeton, NJ: Princeton University Press, 1998.

Ravier, André. "Le Dieu de Rousseau et le Christianisme." *Archives de Philosophie* 41, no. 1 (1978): 353–434.

———. *L'education de l'homme nouveau: essai historique et critique sur le livre de l'*émile *de J.-J. Rousseau.* Issoudun, France: Spes, 1941.

———. "Emile Est-Il Chretien?" *La Table ronde* 176 (1962): 8–18.

———. "Jean-Jacques Rousseau et l'education d'une conscience d'homme." In *Jean-Jacques Rousseau et la crise contemporaine de la conscience.* Chantilly: B.A.P., 1978.

Raymond, Marcel. *Jean-Jacques Rousseau: la quête de soi et la rêverie.* Paris: Librairie J. Corti, 1962.

Reisert, Joseph R. "Authenticity, Justice, and Virtue in Taylor and Rousseau." *Polity* (2001): 305–30.

———. *Jean-Jacques Rousseau: A Friend of Virtue.* Ithaca, NY: Cornell University Press, 2003.

Rex, Walter. "On the Background of Rousseau's *First Discourse.*" *Studies in Eighteenth-Century Culture* 9 (1980): 131–50.

Ricatte, Robert. "Réflexions sur les *Rêveries.*" Paris: Librairie José Corti, 1965.

Ricoeur, Paul. *The Symbolism of Evil.* Boston: Beacon Press, 1969.

Riley, Patrick (1941–). *The Cambridge Companion to Rousseau, Cambridge Companions to Philosophy.* Cambridge: Cambridge University Press, 2001.

———. *The General Will before Rousseau: The Transformation of the Divine into the Civic, Studies in Moral, Political, and Legal Philosophy.* Princeton, NJ: Princeton University Press, 1986.

———. "Rousseau's General Will: Freedom of a Particular Kind." In *Rousseau and Liberty,* edited by Robert Wokler. Manchester: Manchester University Press, 1995.

Riley, Patrick (1966–). *Character and Conversion in Autobiography: Augustine, Montaigne, Descartes, Rousseau, and Sartre.* Charlottesville: University of Virginia Press, 2004.

———. "The Inversion of Conversion: Rousseau's Rewriting of Augustinian Autobiography." *Studies in Eighteenth-Century Culture* 28 (1999): 229–55.

Ritter, Eugene. "La famille et la jeunesse de J.-J. Rousseau." *Annales de la Société Jean-Jacques Rousseau* 16 (1924–25): 9–250.

Roosevelt, Grace G., and Jean-Jacques Rousseau. *Reading Rousseau in the Nuclear Age.* Philadelphia: Temple University Press, 1990.

Rosen, Stanley. *The Ancients and the Moderns: Rethinking Modernity.* New Haven, CT: Yale University Press, 1989.

———. *The Limits of Analysis.* New Haven, CT: Yale University Press, 1985.

———. *Nihilism: A Philosophical Essay.* New Haven, CT: Yale University Press, 1969.

———. *Plato's Sophist: The Drama of Original and Image.* New Haven, CT: Yale University Press, 1983.

———. *The Quarrel between Philosophy and Poetry: Studies in Ancient Thought.* New York: Routledge, 1988.

Rosenblatt, Helena. *Rousseau and Geneva: From the First Discourse to the Social Contract, 1749–1762.* Cambridge: Cambridge University Press, 1997.

Rousseau, Jean-Jacques. *The Confessions; and, Correspondence, Including the Letters to Malesherbes.* Edited by Chrâetien Guillaume de Lamoignon de Malesherbes, Christopher Kelly, Roger D. Masters, and Peter G. Stillman. Hanover, NH: Dartmouth College Press; Hanover, NH: University Press of New England, 1995.

———. *Du Contrat Social*. Edited by Edmond Dreyfus-Brisac Paris: F. Alcan, 1896.

———. *The Collected Writings of Rousseau*. Edited by Roger D. Masters and Christopher Kelly. Hanover, NH: Dartmouth College Press; Hanover, NH: University Press of New England, 1990–present.

———. *Discourse on the Origins of Inequality (Second Discourse); Polemics; and, Political Economy*. Edited by Roger D. Masters and Christopher Kelly. Hanover, NH: Dartmouth College Press; Hanover, NH: University Press of New England, 1992.

———. *Discourse on the Sciences and Arts: (First Discourse) and Polemics*. Edited by Roger D. Masters, Christopher Kelly, and Judith R. Bush. Hanover, NH: Dartmouth College Press; Hanover, NH: University Press of New England, 1992.

———. *The Discourses and Other Political Writings, Cambridge Texts in the History of Political Thought*. Edited by Victor Gourevitch. Cambridge: Cambridge University Press, 1997.

———. *Diskurs über die Ungleichheit = Discours sur l'inégalité*. Edited by Heinrich Meier. Paderborn, Germany: F. Schöningh, 1984.

———. *Emile: Or, on Education*. Edited by Allan Bloom. New York: Basic Books, 1979.

———. *The First and Second Discourses*. Edited by Roger D. Masters and Judith R. Masters. New York: St. Martin's Press, 1964.

———. *The First and Second Discourses Together with the Replies to Critics and Essay on the Origin of Languages*. 1st ed. Edited by Victor Gourevitch. New York: Harper and Row, 1986.

———. *Letter to Beaumont, Letters Written from the Mountain, and Related Writings*. Edited by Christopher Kelly and Eve Grace. Hanover, NH: Dartmouth College Press; Hanover, NH: University Press of New England, 2001.

———. *Œuvres complètes*. Edited by Bernard Gagnebin and Marcel Raymond. Paris: Gallimard, 1959.

———. *Œuvres complètes*. Edited by Michel Launay, and Jean Fabre. 2 vols. Paris: Editions du Seuil [Collection l'Intégrale], 1969.

———. *The Political Writings of Jean Jacques Rousseau*. 2 vols. Edited by Charles Edwyn Vaughan. Oxford: Basil Blackwell, 1962.

———. *Religious Writings*. Edited by Ronald Grimsley. Oxford: Clarendon Press, 1970.

———. *The Reveries of the Solitary Walker; Botanical Writings; and Letter to Franquières*. Edited by Christopher Kelly, Charles E. Butterworth, Alexandra Parma Cook, and Terence Marshall. Hanover, NH: University Press of New England, 2000.

———. *Rousseau, Juge De Jean Jaques; Dialogues*. Edited by Michel Foucault. Paris: A. Colin, 1962.

———. *Rousseau, Judge of Jean-Jacques: Dialogues*. Hanover, NH: Dartmouth College; Press Hanover, NH: University Press of New England, 1990.

———. *Rousseau's Political Writings: New Translations, Interpretive Notes, Backgrounds, Commentaries*. 1st ed. Edited by Alan Ritter and Julia Conaway Bondanella. New York: W. W. Norton, 1988.

———. *Social Contract; Discourse on the Virtue Most Necessary for a Hero; Political Fragments; and, Geneva Manuscript*. Edited by Roger D. Masters and Christopher Kelly. Hanover, NH: Dartmouth College Press; Hanover, NH: University Press of New England, 1994.

———. *The Social Contract and the First and Second Discourses*. Edited by Susan Dunn. New Haven, CT: Yale University Press, 2002.

———. *The Social Contract and Other Later Political Writings, Cambridge Texts in the History of Political Thought*. Edited by Victor Gourevitch. Cambridge: Cambridge University Press, 1997.

Roussel, Jean. "Le phénomène de l'identification dans la lecture de Rousseau." *Annales de la Société Jean-Jacques Rousseau* 39 (1972–77): 65–77.

Salkever, Stephen G. "Interpreting Rousseau's Paradoxes." *Eighteenth-Century Studies* 132 (1975): 137–81.

Scanlon, Timothy. "Aspects of Figurative Language in Rousseau's 'Dialogues.'" *Essays in French Literature* 13 (1976): 13–27.

Schenk, Richard. *Zur Theorie Des Opfers: Ein Interdisziplinäres Gespräch, Collegium Philosophicum.* Stuttgart, Germany: frommann-holzboog, 1995.

Schinz, Albert. *État present des travaux sur J.-J. Rousseau.* Paris: Société d'édition Les Belles lettres; New York: Modern Language Association of America, 1941.

———. *La pensée religieuse de Rousseau et ses récents interprétes.* Paris: F. Alcan, 1927.

———. *La pensée de Jean-Jacques Rousseau.* Paris: Librairie Félix Alcan, 1929.

Schwager, Raymund. *Brauchen Wir Einen Sündenbock? Gewalt Und Erlösung in Den Biblischen Schriften.* Munich: Kösel, 1978.

———. *Jesus Im Heilsdrama: Entwurf Biblischen Erlösungslehre.* Innsbruck: Tyrolia, 1990.

Schwartz, Joel. *The Sexual Politics of Jean-Jacques Rousseau.* Chicago: University of Chicago Press, 1984.

Scott, Joan W. "Fantasy Echo: History and the Construction of Identity." *Critical Inquiry* 27 (2001): 284–304.

Scott, John T. "The Harmony Between Rousseau's Musical Theory and His Philosophy." *Journal of the History of Ideas* 59, no. 2 (1998): 287–308.

———. "Politics as the Imitation of the Divine in Rousseau's *Social Contract.*" *Polity* 26, no. 3 (1994): 473–501.

———. "The Theodicy of the *Second Discourse*: The 'Pure State of Nature' and Rousseau's Political Thought." *American Political Science Review* 86, no. 3 (1992): 696–711.

Shell, Susan Meld. "Emile: Nature and the Education of Sophie." In *The Cambridge Companion to Rousseau*, edited by Patrick Riley, 272–301. Cambridge: Cambridge University Press, 2001.

Shklar, Judith N. *Men and Citizens: A Study of Rousseau's Social Theory, Cambridge Studies in the History and Theory of Politics.* London: Cambridge University Press, 1969.

Shklar, Judith N., and Stanley Hoffmann. *Political Thought and Political Thinkers.* Chicago: Chicago University Press, 1998.

Silverthorne, Michael. "Rousseau's Plato." *Studies on Voltaire and the Eighteenth Century* 116, no. 16 (1973): 235–49.

Skillen, Anthony. "Rousseau and the Fall of Social Man." *Philosophy* 60 (1985): 105–21.

Spaemann, Robert. *Glück Und Wohlwollen: Versuch über Ethik.* Stuttgart, Germany: Klett-Cotta, 1989.

———. *Happiness and Benevolence.* Notre Dame, IN: University of Notre Dame Press, 2000.

———. *Rousseau—Bürger ohne Vaterland: Von der Polis zur Natur.* Munich: Piper, 1980.

Stählin, Gustav. *Skandalon: Untersuchungen zur Geschichte eines Biblischen Begriffs.* Gütersloh, Germany: C. Bertelsmann, 1930.

Starobinski, Jean. "The Accuser and the Accused." In *Jean-Jacques Rousseau*, edited by Harold Bloom, 173–93. New York: Chelsea House, 1988.

———. *Jean-Jacques Rousseau: La Transparence Et L'obstacle; Suivi De, Sept Essais Sur Rousseau, Bibliotháeque Des Idées.* Paris: Gallimard, 1971.

———. *Jean-Jacques Rousseau: Transparency and Obstruction.* Chicago: University of Chicago Press, 1988.

———. *The Living Eye, Harvard Studies in Comparative Literature; 40.* Cambridge, MA: Harvard University Press, 1989.

———. "Musik Und Gesellschaft Bei Rousseau." In *Rousseau Und Die Folgen*, edited by Rüdiger Bubner, Konrad Cramer, and Reiner Wiehl, 39–59. Göttingen, Germany: Vandenhoeck and Ruprecht, 1989.

———. "La Prosopopée De Fabricius." *Revue de Sciences Humaines* 41, no. 161 (1976): 83–96.

Stelzig, Eugene L. "Autobiography as Resurrection: Rousseau's *Dialogues*." *Auto/biography Studies* 10, no. 2 (1995): 39–51.

———. "Autobiography as Revision: Rousseau's *Reveries*." *Auto/biography Studies* 4 (1988): 97–106.

Still, Judith. *Justice and Difference in the Works of Rousseau: Bienfaisance and Pudeur*. Cambridge: Cambridge University Press, 1993.

Strauss, Leo. *Natural Right and History*. Chicago: University of Chicago Press, 1971.

———. "On the Intention of Rousseau." *Social Research* 14 (1947): 455–87.

Strong, Tracy B. *Jean-Jacques Rousseau: The Politics of the Ordinary*. Thousand Oaks, CA: Sage, 1994.

Swenson, James. *On Jean-Jacques Rousseau: Considered as One of the First Authors of the Revolution*. Stanford, CA: Stanford University Press, 2000.

Terrasse, Jean. "Les manipulations du lecteur dans *Emile*." *Studies on Voltaire and the Eighteenth Century* 264 (1989): 735–37.

Thomas, Downing A. *Music and the Origins of Language: Theories from the French Enlightenment*. Cambridge: Cambridge University Press, 1995.

Thomas, Jacques Francois. *Le Pélagianisme de J.-J. Rousseau*. Paris: Librairie Nizet, 1956.

Tisserand, Roger. *Les concurrents de J.-J. Rousseau à l'academie de Dijon pour le prix de 1754*. Paris: Ancienne Librairie Furne, 1936.

Todorov, Tzvetan. *Frêle bonheur: essai sur Rousseau*. Paris: Hachette, 1985.

———. *Imperfect Garden: The Legacy of Humanism*. Princeton, NJ: Princeton University Press, 2002.

———. *Life in Common: An Essay in General Anthropology*. Lincoln: University of Nebraska Press, 2001.

Touchefeu, Yves. *L'antiquité et le Christianisme dans la pensée de Jean-Jacques Rousseau*. Oxford: Voltaire Foundation, 1999.

Trachtenberg, Zev M. *Making Citizens: Rousseau's Political Theory of Culture*. London: Routledge, 1993.

Tripet, Arnaud. *La Rêverie Littéraire: Essai Sur Rousseau*. Geneva: Droz, 1979.

Trousson, Raymond "Le Christ dans le pensée de J.-J. Rousseau." *Problemes D'histoire Du Christianisme* 7 (1977): 31–56.

Ulmer, Gregory L. "Jacques Derrida and Paul De Man on/in Rousseau's Faults." *The Eighteenth Century* 20, no. 2 (1979): 164–81.

Valdés, Mario J., and Owen J. Miller, eds. *Interpretation of Narrative*. Toronto: University of Toronto Press, 1979.

Vanpée, Janie. "Rousseau's *Emile Ou De L'éducation*: A Resistance to Reading." *Yale French Studies* 77 (1990): 156–76.

Vargas, Yves. *Introduction à l'émile de Jean-Jacques Rousseau*. Paris: Presses universitaires de France, 1995.

Velguth, Madeleine. "Le texte comme prétexte: Jacques Derrida lit *Les Confessions* De Rousseau." *French Review* 58, no. 6 (1985): 811–19.

Velkley, Richard L. *Being after Rousseau: Philosophy and Culture in Question*. Chicago: University of Chicago Press, 2002.

———. *Freedom and the End of Reason: On the Moral Foundation of Kant's Critical Philosophy*. Chicago: University of Chicago Press, 1989.

Viroli, Maurizio. *Jean-Jacques Rousseau and the "Well-Ordered Society."* Cambridge: Cambridge University Press, 1988.

Voltaire, and Simon Harvey. *Treatise on Tolerance, Cambridge Texts in the History of Philosophy.* Cambridge: Cambridge University Press, 2000.

Weaver, J. Denny. *The Nonviolent Atonement.* Grand Rapids, MI: W. B. Eerdmans, 2001.

Webb, Eugene. *The Self Between: From Freud to the New Social Psychology of France.* Seattle: University of Washington Press, 1993.

Williams, Huntington. *Rousseau and Romantic Autobiography.* Oxford: Oxford University Press, 1983.

Wingrove, Elizabeth Rose. *Rousseau's Republican Romance.* Princeton, NJ: Princeton University Press, 2000.

Winwar, Frances. *Jean-Jacques Rousseau: Conscience of an Era.* New York: Random House, 1961.

Wokler, Robert, ed. *Rousseau and Liberty.* Manchester: Manchester University Press, 1995

———. *Rousseau on Society, Politics, Music and Language: An Historical Interpretation of His Early Writings, Political Theory and Political Philosophy.* New York: Garland, 1987.

Wright, Ernest Hunter. *The Meaning of Rousseau.* New York: Russell and Russell, 1963.

Yoshioka, Yomoya. *Jan-Jakku Rusoh Ron [Jean-Jacques Rousseau-ology].* Tokyo: Tokyo University Press, 1988.

Zweig, Paul. *The Heresy of Self-Love: A Study of Subversive Individualism.* New York: Basic Books, 1968.

INDEX